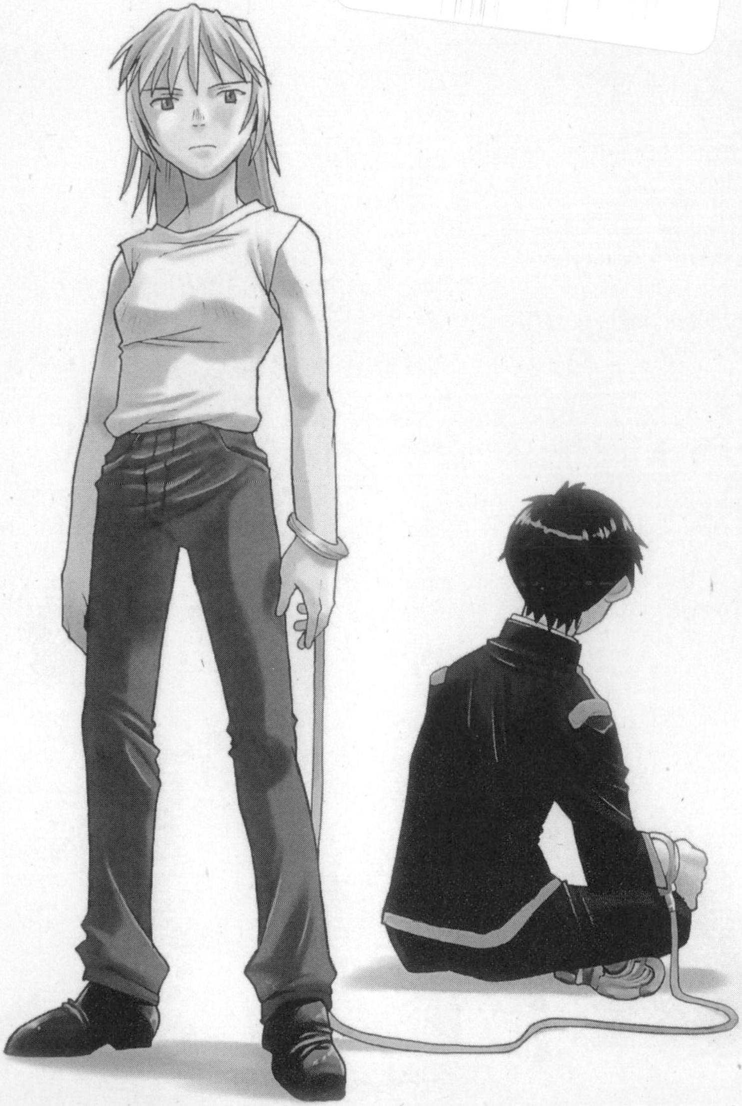

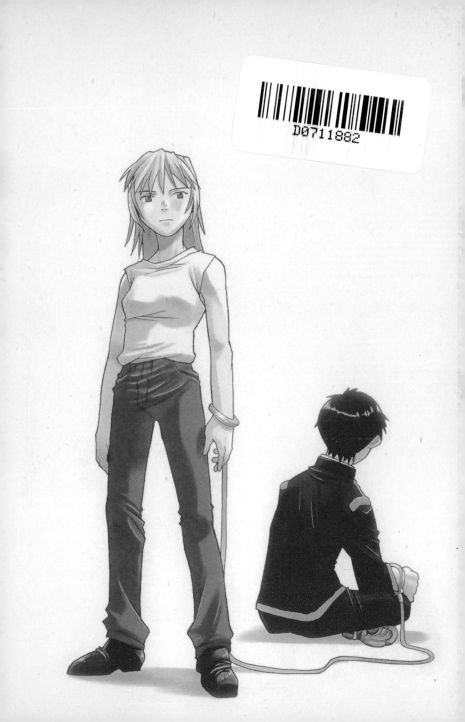

Translation and Adaptation – Christine Schilling
Production Assistant – Mallory Reaves
Lettering – TeamPokopen
Production Manager – James Dashiell
Editor – Brynne Chandler

A Go! Comi manga

Published by Go! Media Entertainment, LLC

Train + Train Volume 1
© HIDEYUKI KURATA - TOMOMASA TAKUMA 2000
First published in 2000 by Media Works Inc., Tokyo, Japan.
English translation rights arranged with Media Works Inc.

English Text © 2007 Go! Media Entertainment, LLC. All rights reserved.

Visit us online at www.gocomi.com
e-mail: info@gocomi.com

ISBN 978-1-933617-18-3

First printed in January 2007

1   2   3   4   5   6   7   8   9

Manufactured in the United States of America

TRAIN + TRAIN

Volume 1

Original Story by

HIDEYUKI KURATA

Art by

TOMOMASA TAKUMA

go!comi

Concerning Honorifics

At Go! Comi, we do our best to ensure that our translations read seamlessly in English while respecting the original Japanese language and culture. To this end, the original honorifics (the suffixes found at the end of characters' names) remain intact. In Japan, where politeness and formality are more integrated into every aspect of the language, honorifics give a better understanding of character relationships. They can be used to indicate both respect and affection. Whether a person addresses someone by first name or last name also indicates how close their relationship is.

Here are some of the honorifics you might encounter in reading this book:

-san: This is the most common and neutral of honorifics. The polite way to address someone you're not on close terms with is to use "-san." It's kind of like Mr. or Ms., except you can use "-san" with first names as easily as family names.

-chan: Used for friendly familiarity, mostly applied towards young girls. "-chan" also carries a connotation of cuteness with it, so it is frequently used with nicknames towards both boys and girls (such as "Na-chan" for "Natsu").

-kun: Like "-chan," it's an informal suffix for friends and classmates, only "-kun" is usually associated with boys. It can also be used in a professional environment by someone addressing a subordinate.

-sama: Indicates a great deal of respect or admiration.

Sempai: In school, "sempai" is used to refer to an upperclassman or club leader. It can also be used in the workplace by a new employee to address a mentor or staff member with seniority.

Sensei: Teachers, doctors, writers or any master of a trade are referred to as "sensei." When addressing a manga creator, the polite thing to do is attach "-sensei" to the manga-ka's name (as in Takuma-sensei).

Onii: This is the more casual term for an older brother. Usually you'll see it with an honorific attached, such as "onii-chan."

Onee: The casual term for older sister, it's used like "onii" with honorifics.

[blank]: Not using an honorific when addressing someone indicates that the speaker has permission to speak intimately with the other person. This relationship is usually reserved for close friends and family.

TRAIN

TRAIN + TRAIN
VOLUME 1

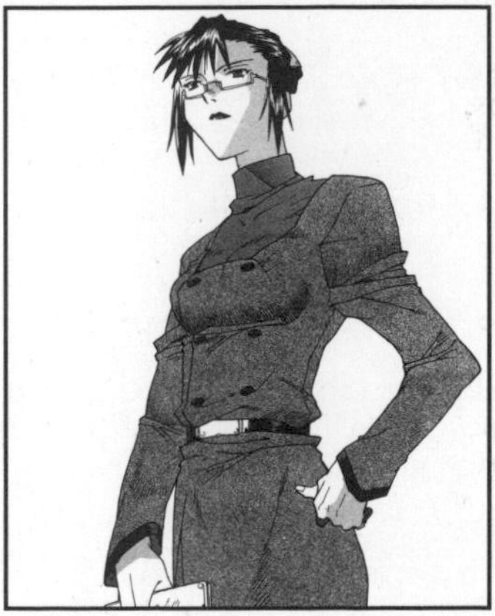

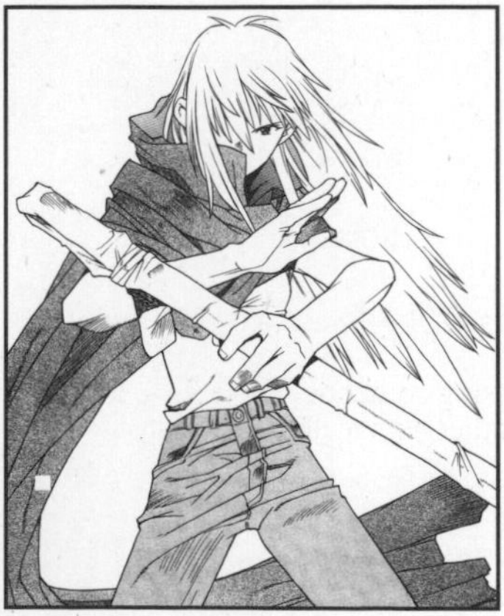

TRAIN

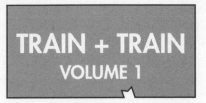

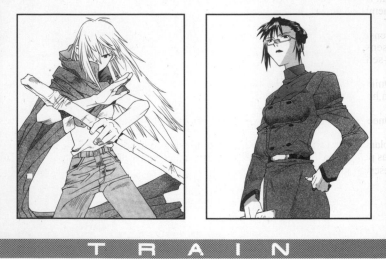

TRAIN
+
TRAIN

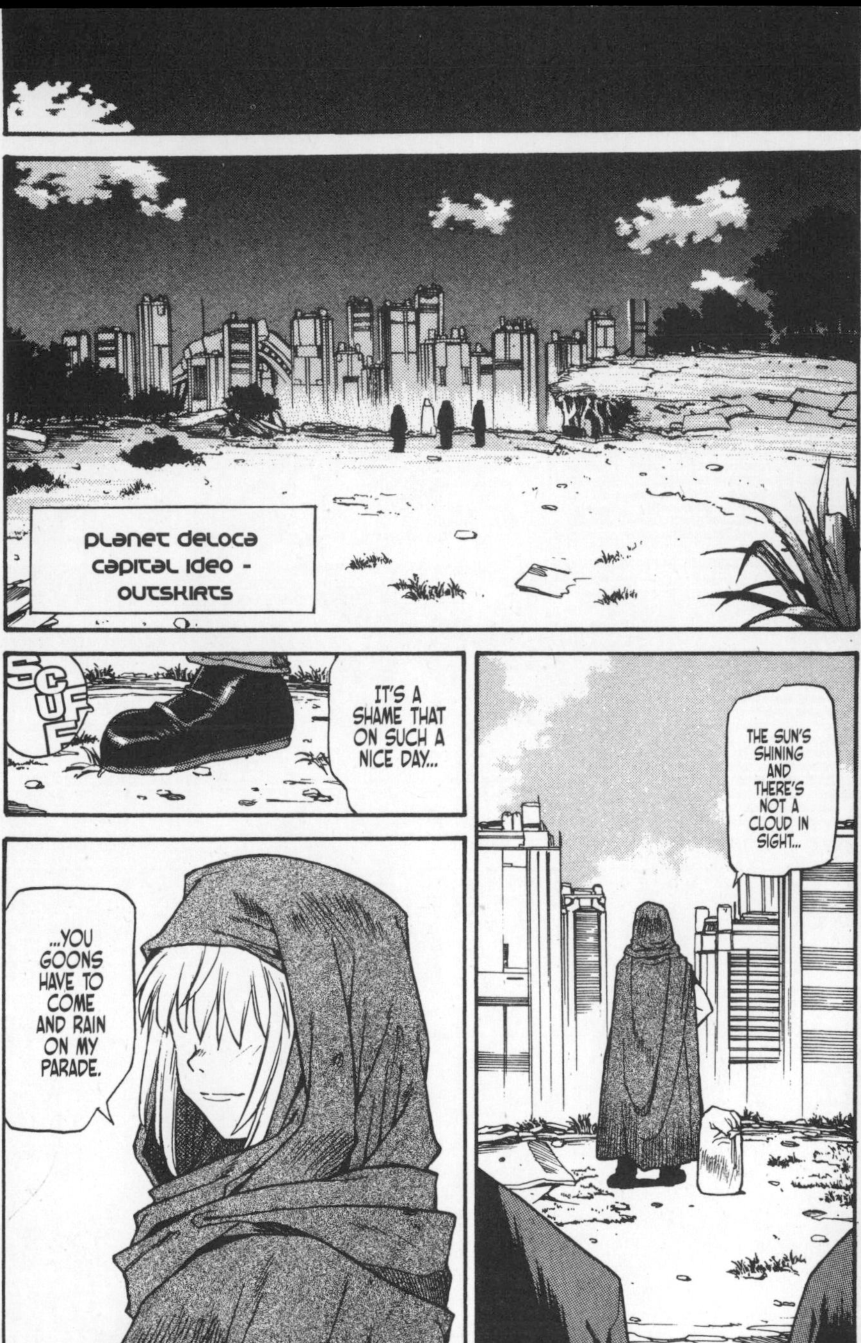
PLANET DELOCA
CAPITAL IDEO -
OUTSKIRTS
THE SUN'S SHINING AND THERE'S NOT A CLOUD IN SIGHT...
SCUFF
IT'S A SHAME THAT ON SUCH A NICE DAY...
...YOU GOONS HAVE TO COME AND RAIN ON MY PARADE.

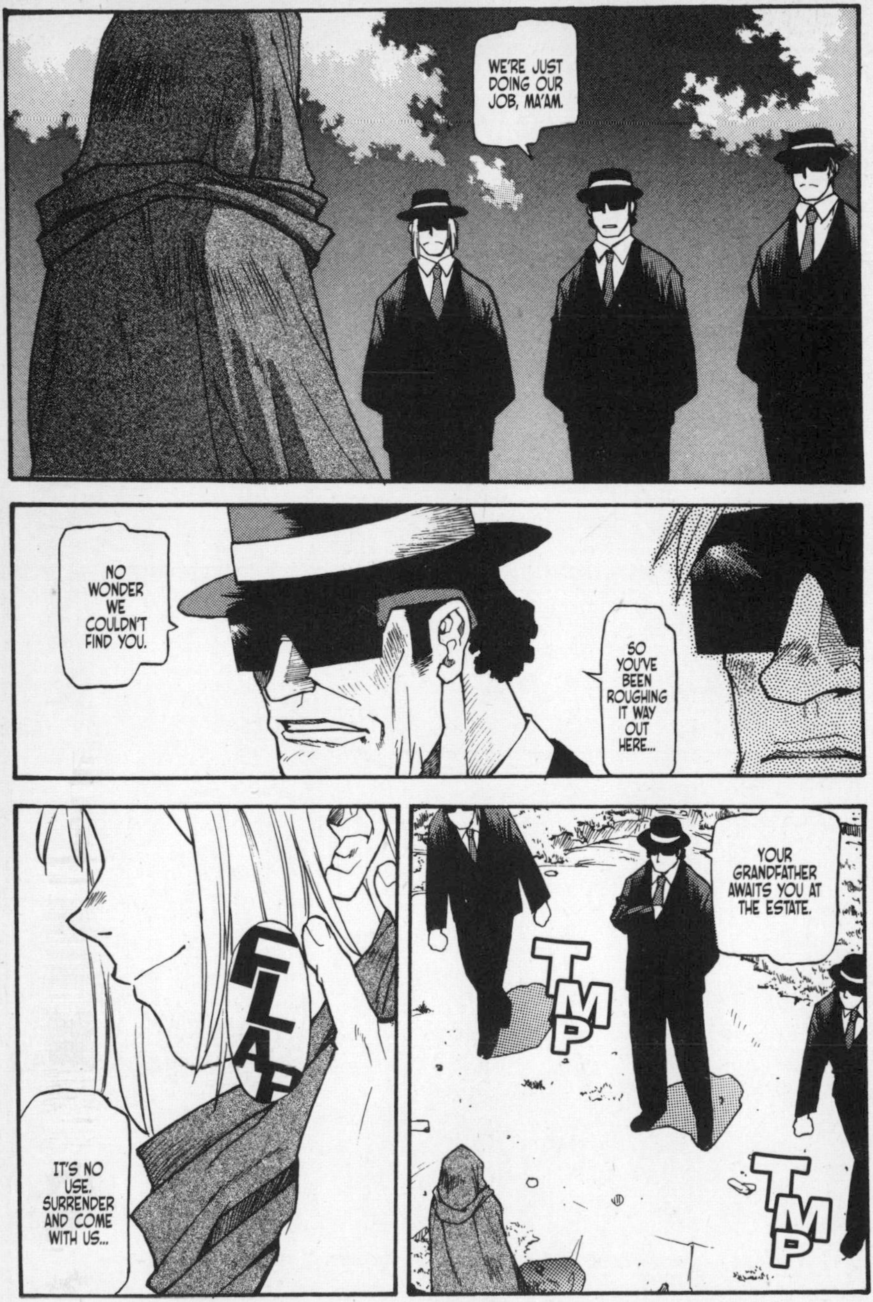
WE'RE JUST DOING OUR JOB, MA'AM.
SO YOU'VE BEEN ROUGHING IT WAY OUT HERE...
NO WONDER WE COULDN'T FIND YOU.
YOUR GRANDFATHER AWAITS YOU AT THE ESTATE.
TMP
TMP
FLAP
IT'S NO USE. SURRENDER AND COME WITH US...

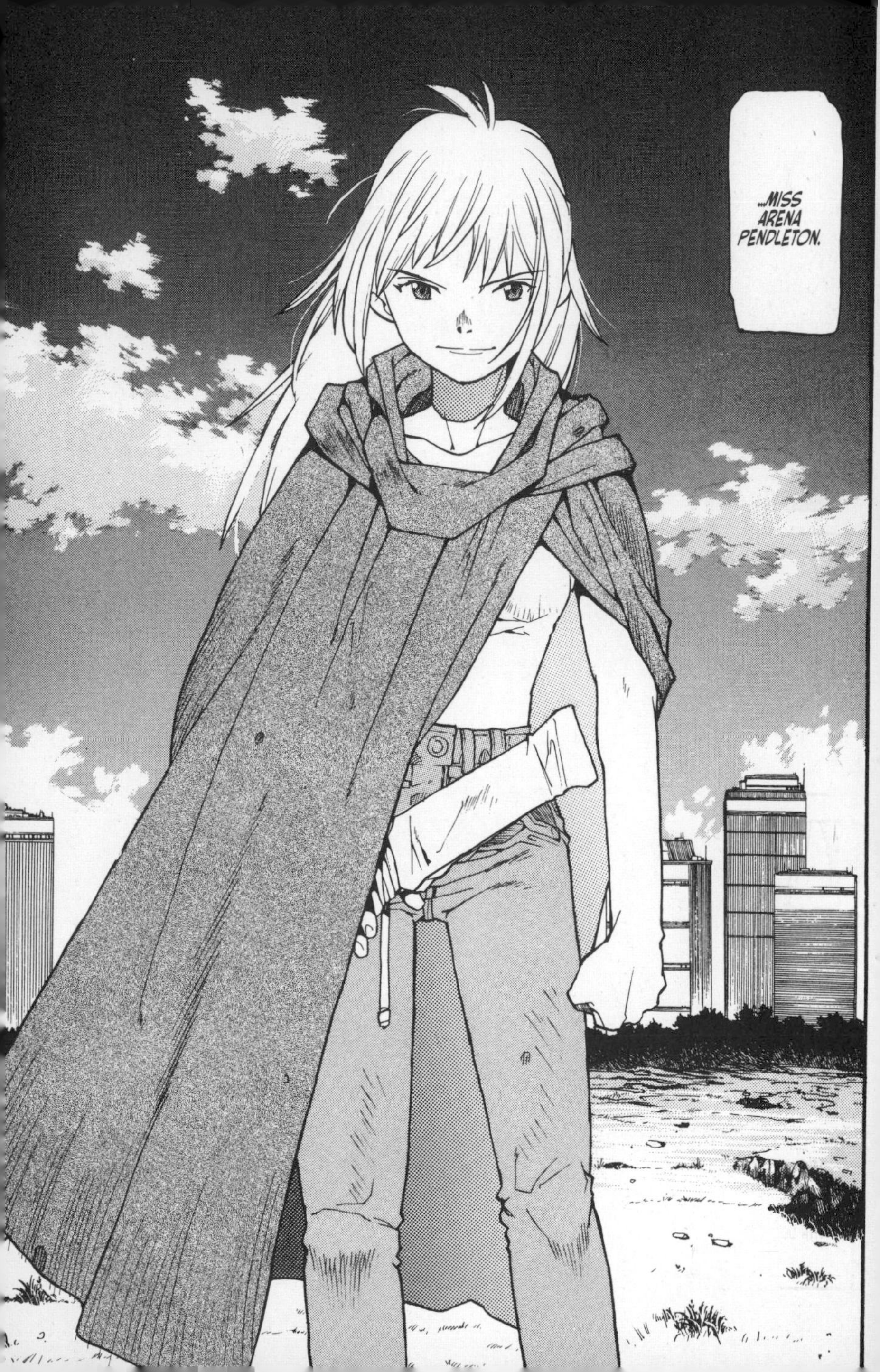
...MISS ARENA PENDLETON.

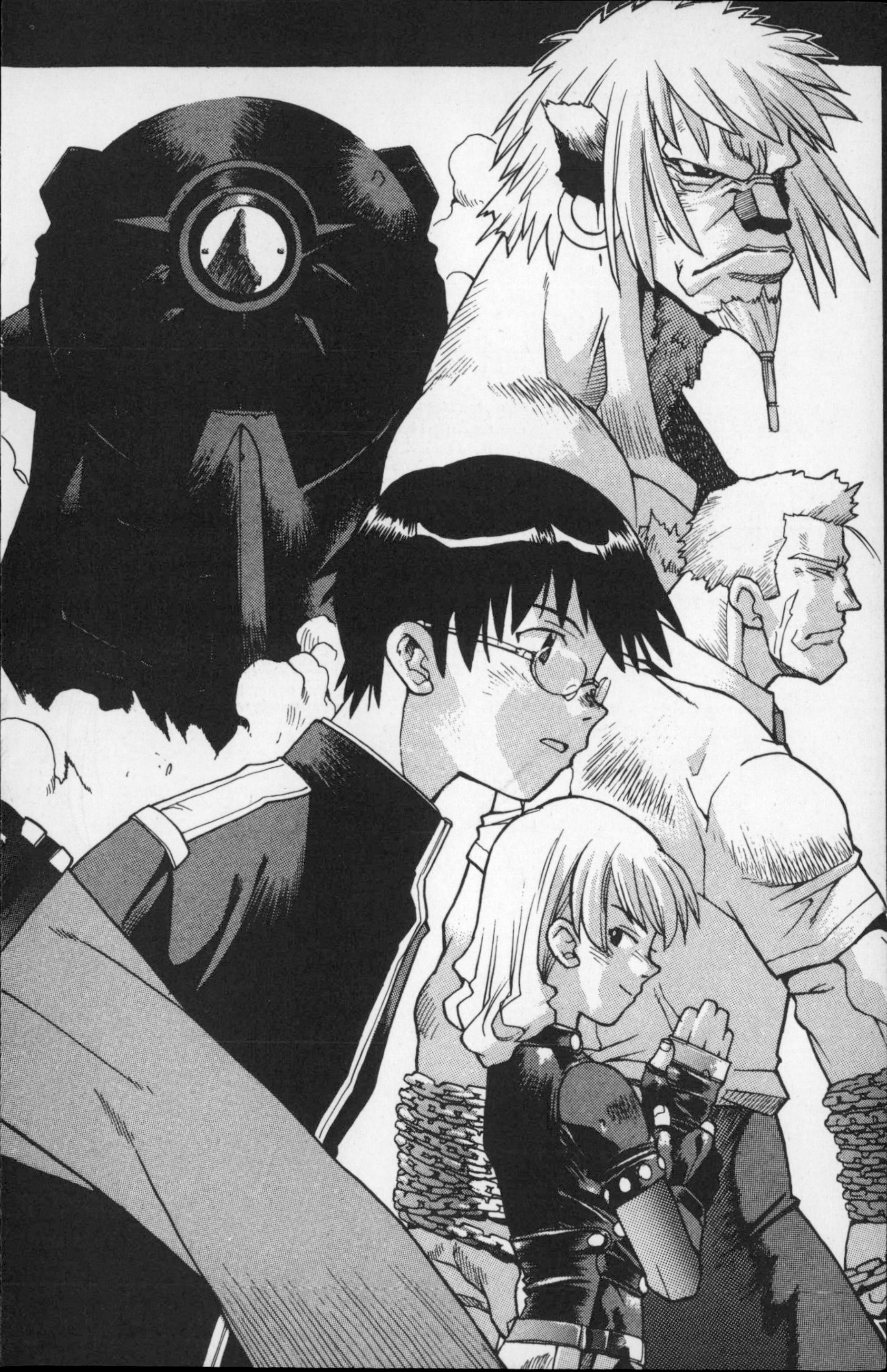

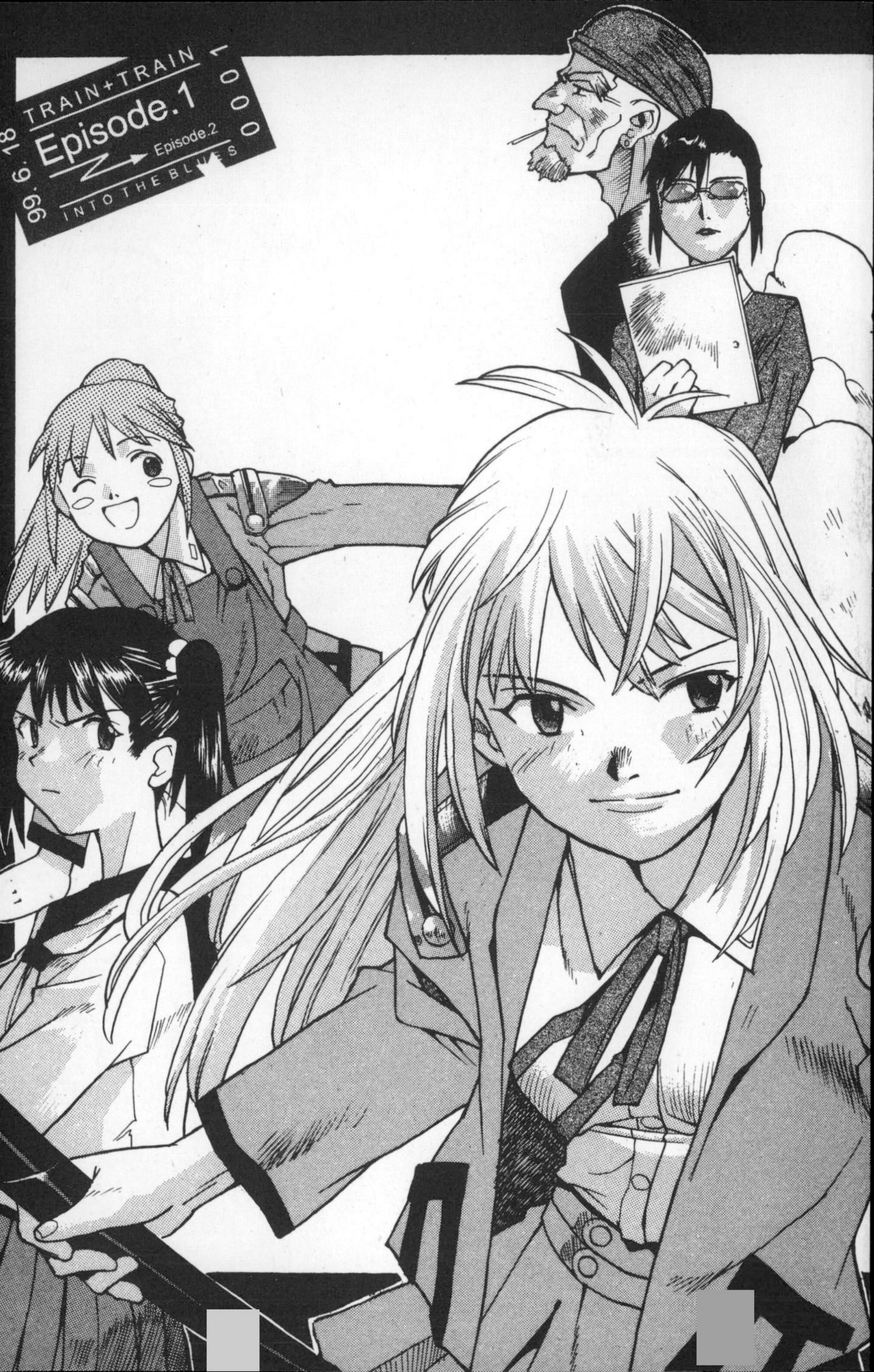
TRAIN+TRAIN
Episode.1
Episode.2
INTO THE BLUES
99. 6. 18

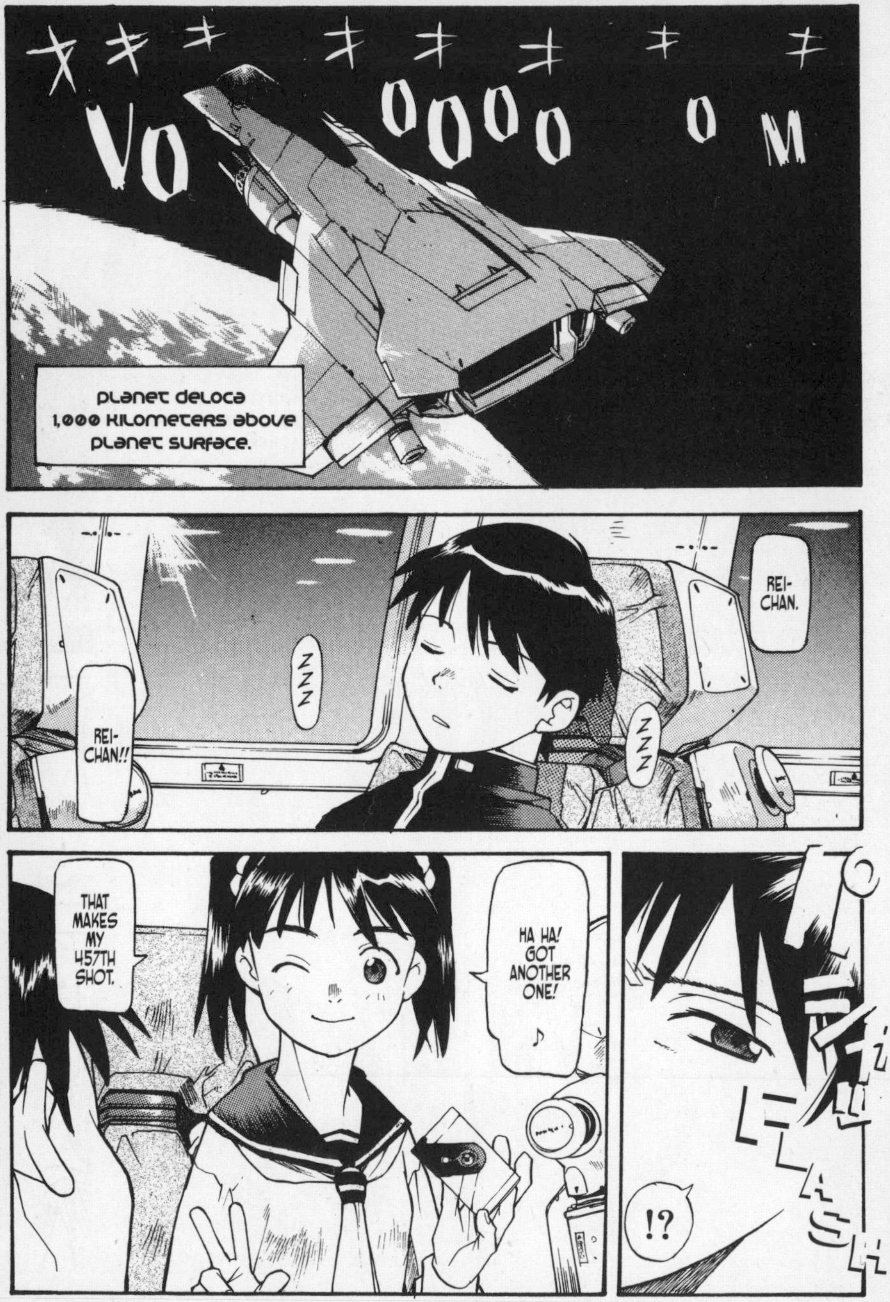
VOOOOOOOM
PLANET DELOCA
1,000 KILOMETERS ABOVE
PLANET SURFACE.
REI-CHAN.
ZZZ
ZZZ
REI-CHAN!!
FLASH
!?
HA HA! GOT ANOTHER ONE! ♪
THAT MAKES MY 457TH SHOT.

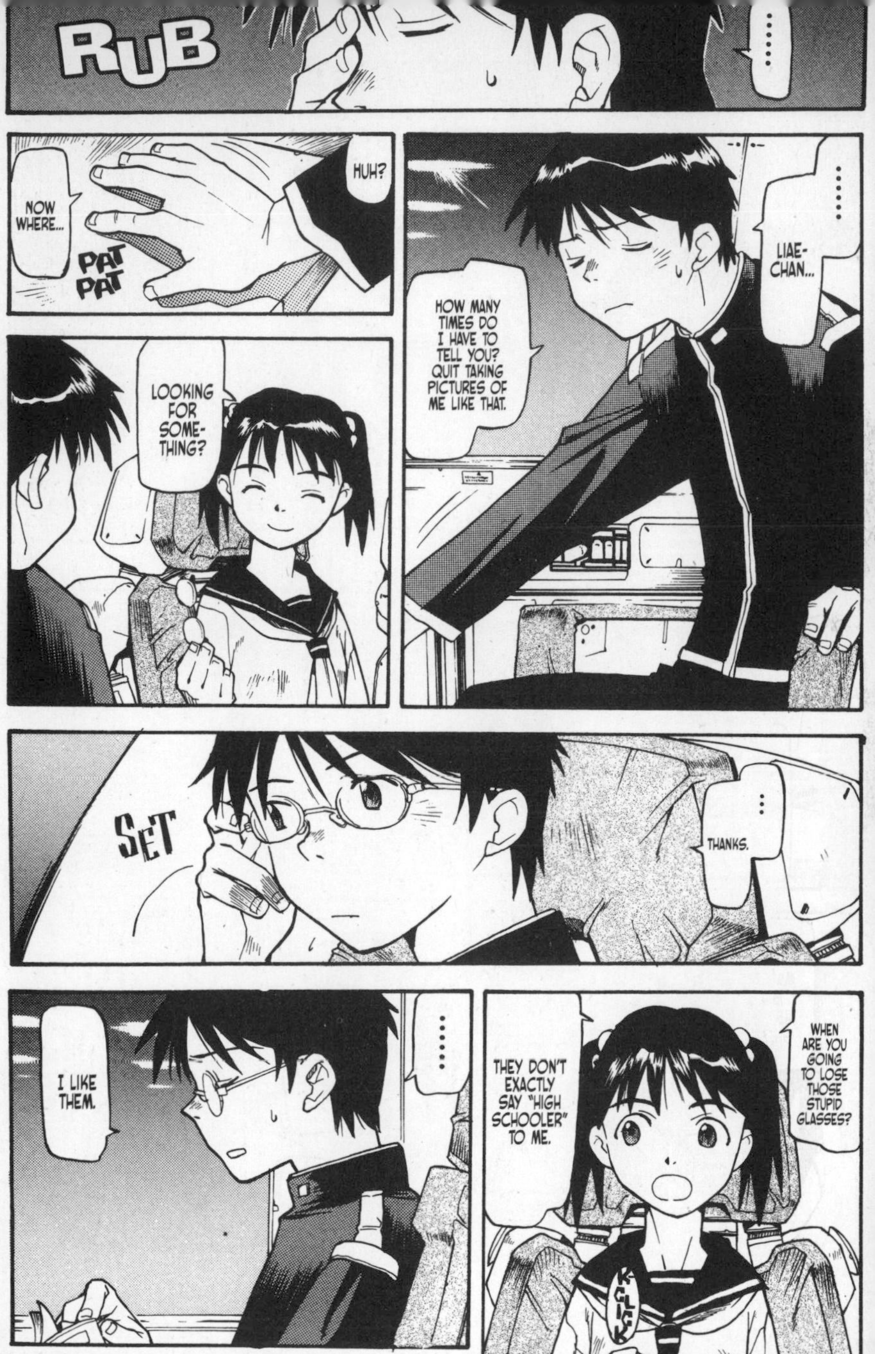
……
RUB
……
LIAE-CHAN...
HOW MANY TIMES DO I HAVE TO TELL YOU? QUIT TAKING PICTURES OF ME LIKE THAT.
HUH?
NOW WHERE...
PAT PAT
LOOKING FOR SOME-THING?
……
THANKS.
SET
WHEN ARE YOU GOING TO LOSE THOSE STUPID GLASSES?
THEY DON'T EXACTLY SAY "HIGH SCHOOLER" TO ME.
K-CLICK
……
I LIKE THEM.

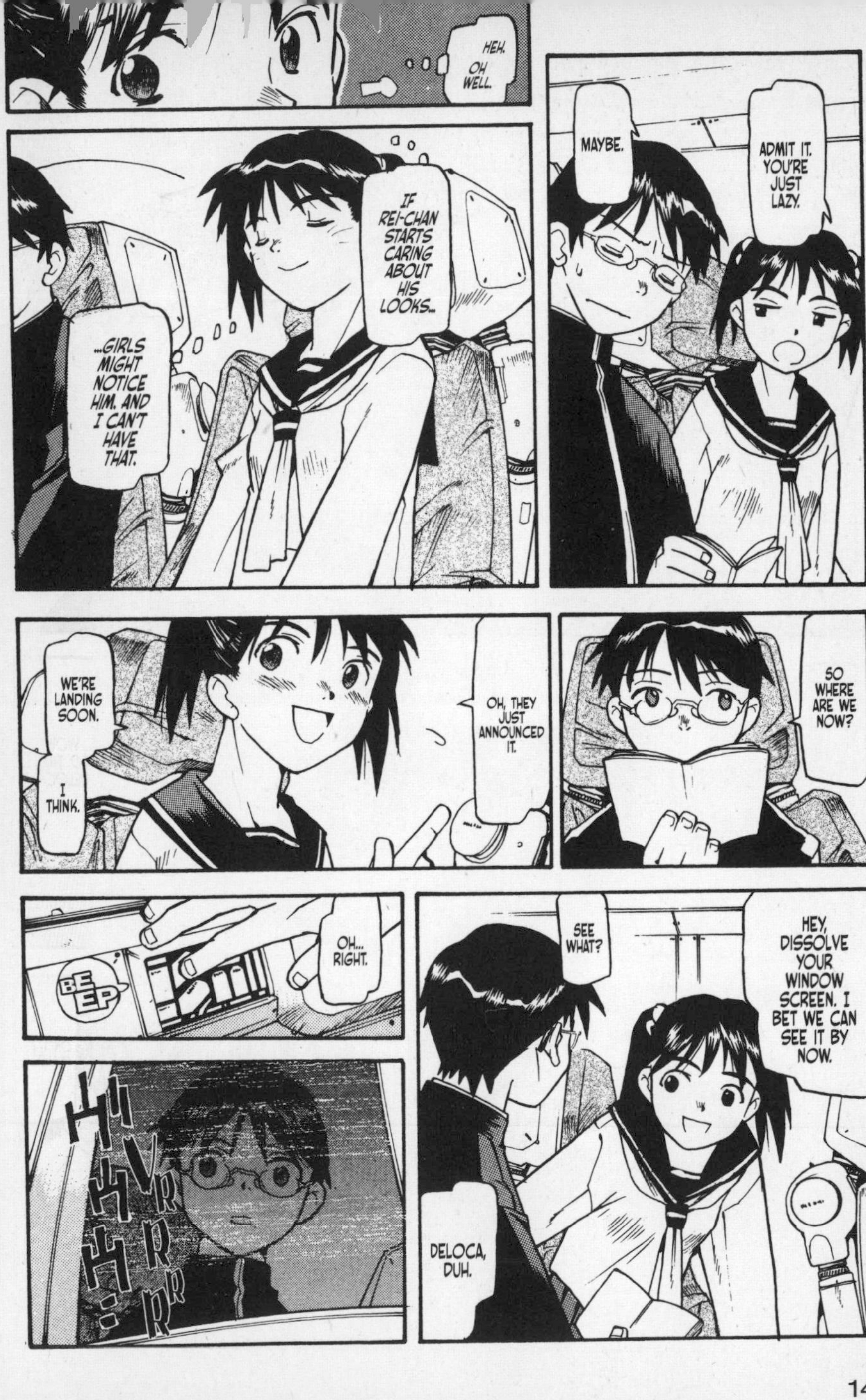
ADMIT IT. YOU'RE JUST LAZY.
MAYBE.
HEH. OH WELL.
IF REI-CHAN STARTS CARING ABOUT HIS LOOKS...
...GIRLS MIGHT NOTICE HIM. AND I CAN'T HAVE THAT.
SO WHERE ARE WE NOW?
OH, THEY JUST ANNOUNCED IT.
WE'RE LANDING SOON.
I THINK.
HEY, DISSOLVE YOUR WINDOW SCREEN. I BET WE CAN SEE IT BY NOW.
SEE WHAT?
DELOCA, DUH.
OH... RIGHT.
BEEP
VRRRRR

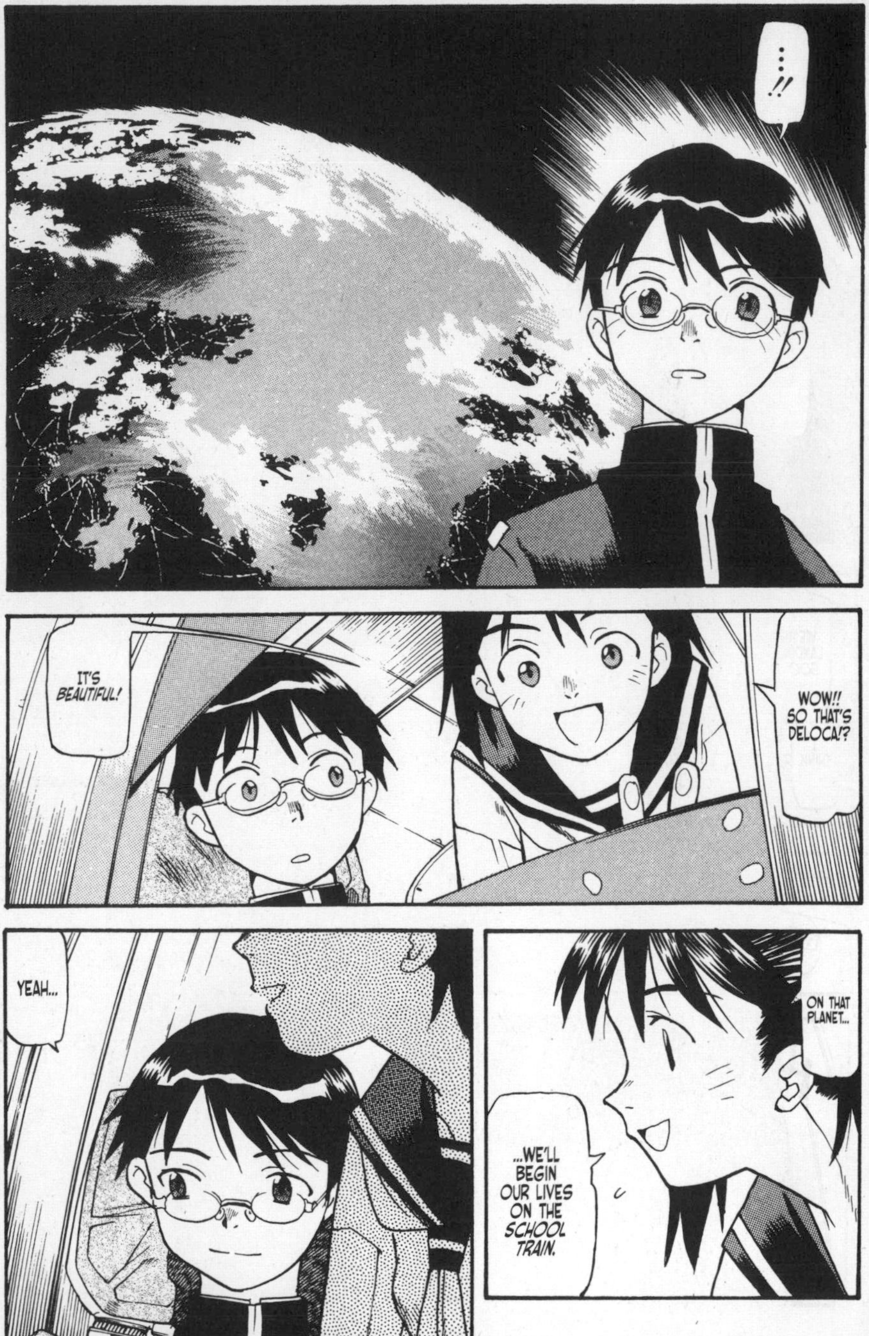
...!!
WOW!! SO THAT'S DELOCA!?
IT'S *BEAUTIFUL!*
ON THAT PLANET...
...WE'LL BEGIN OUR LIVES ON THE *SCHOOL TRAIN.*
YEAH...

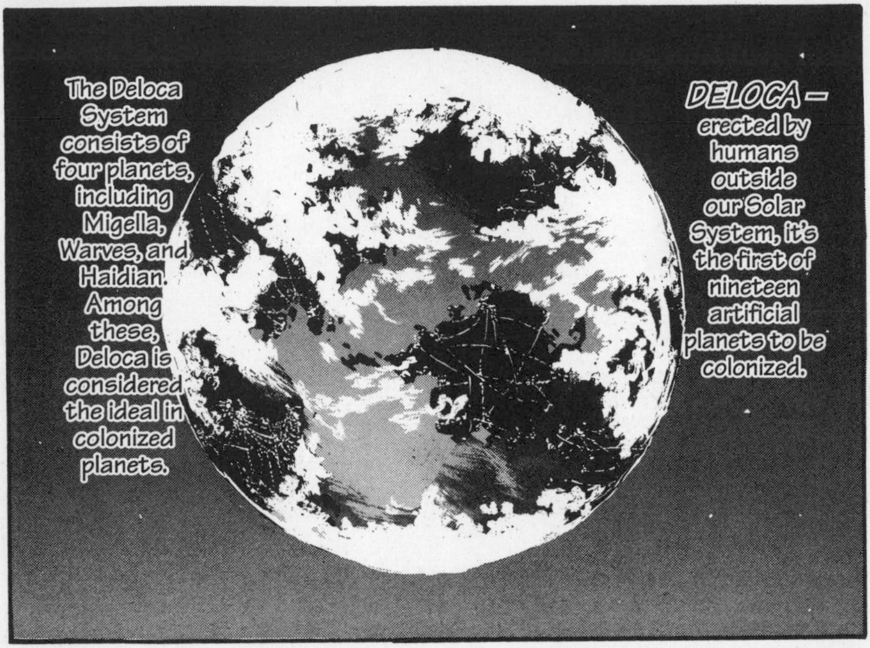
DELOCA — erected by humans outside our Solar System, it's the first of nineteen artificial planets to be colonized.
The Deloca System consists of four planets, including Migella, Warves, and Haidian. Among these, Deloca is considered the ideal in colonized planets.

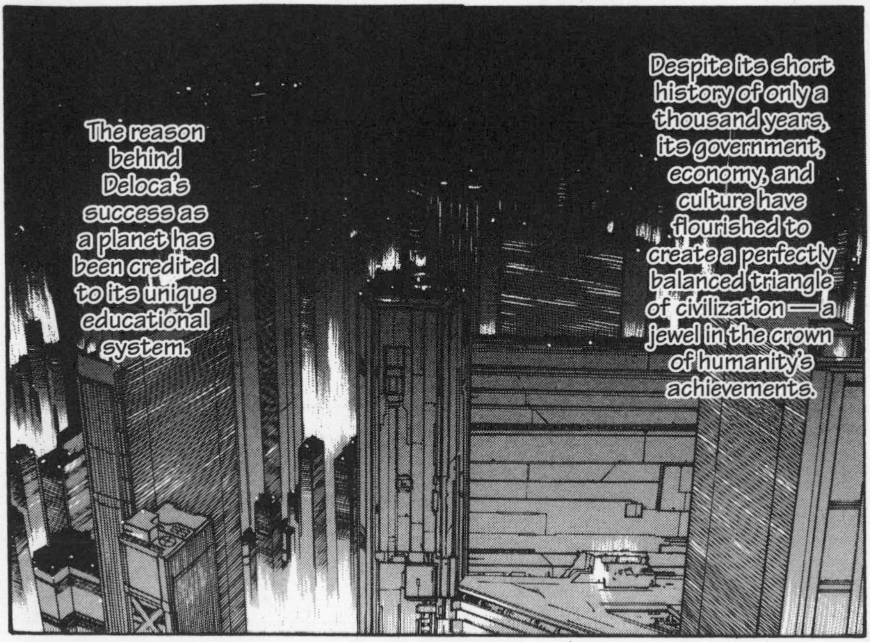
Despite its short history of only a thousand years, its government, economy, and culture have flourished to create a perfectly balanced triangle of civilization — a jewel in the crown of humanity's achievements.
The reason behind Deloca's success as a planet has been credited to its unique educational system.

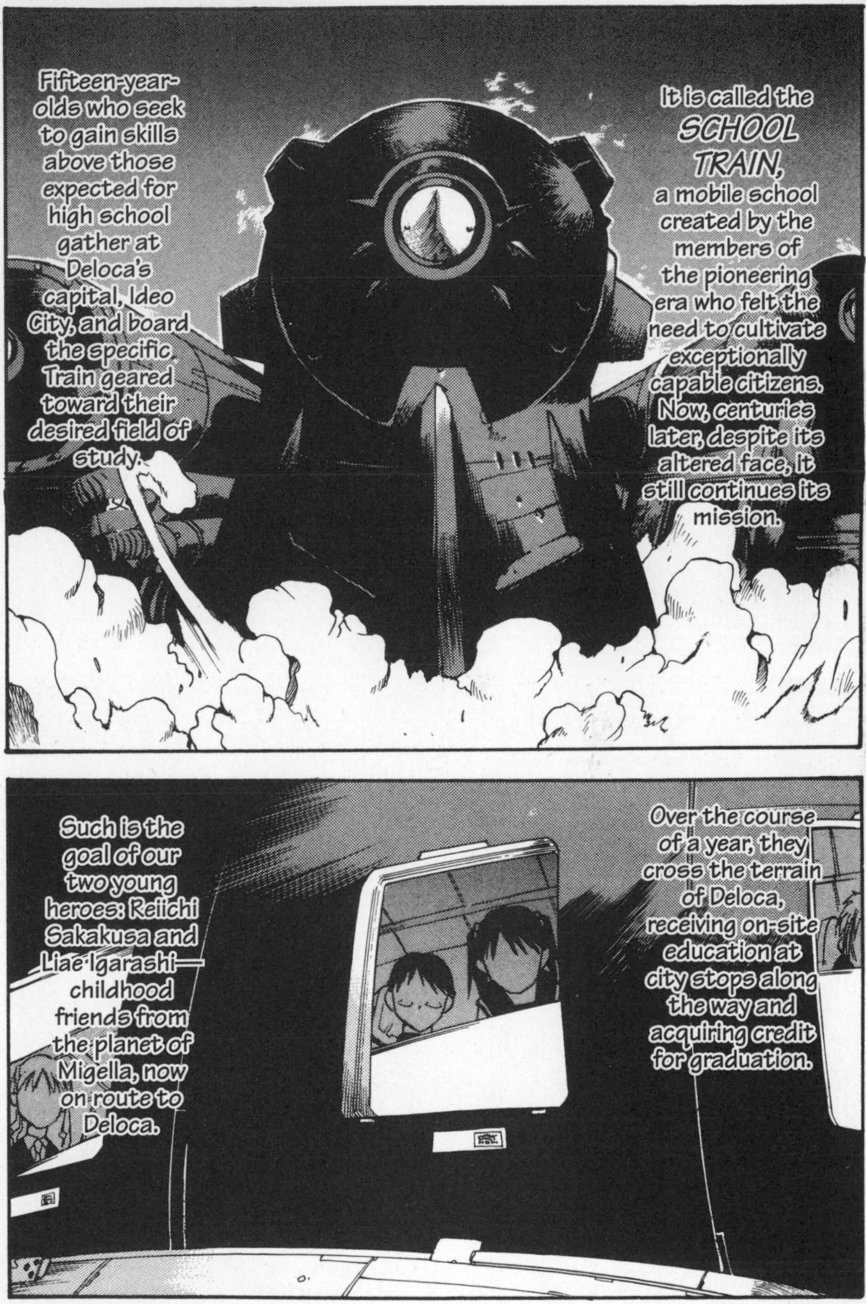
It is called the SCHOOL TRAIN, a mobile school created by the members of the pioneering era who felt the need to cultivate exceptionally capable citizens. Now, centuries later, despite its altered face, it still continues its mission.
Fifteen-year-olds who seek to gain skills above those expected for high school gather at Deloca's capital, Ideo City, and board the specific Train geared toward their desired field of study.
Over the course of a year, they cross the terrain of Deloca, receiving on-site education at city stops along the way and acquiring credit for graduation.
Such is the goal of our two young heroes: Reiichi Sakakusa and Liae Igarashi—childhood friends from the planet of Migella, now on route to Deloca.

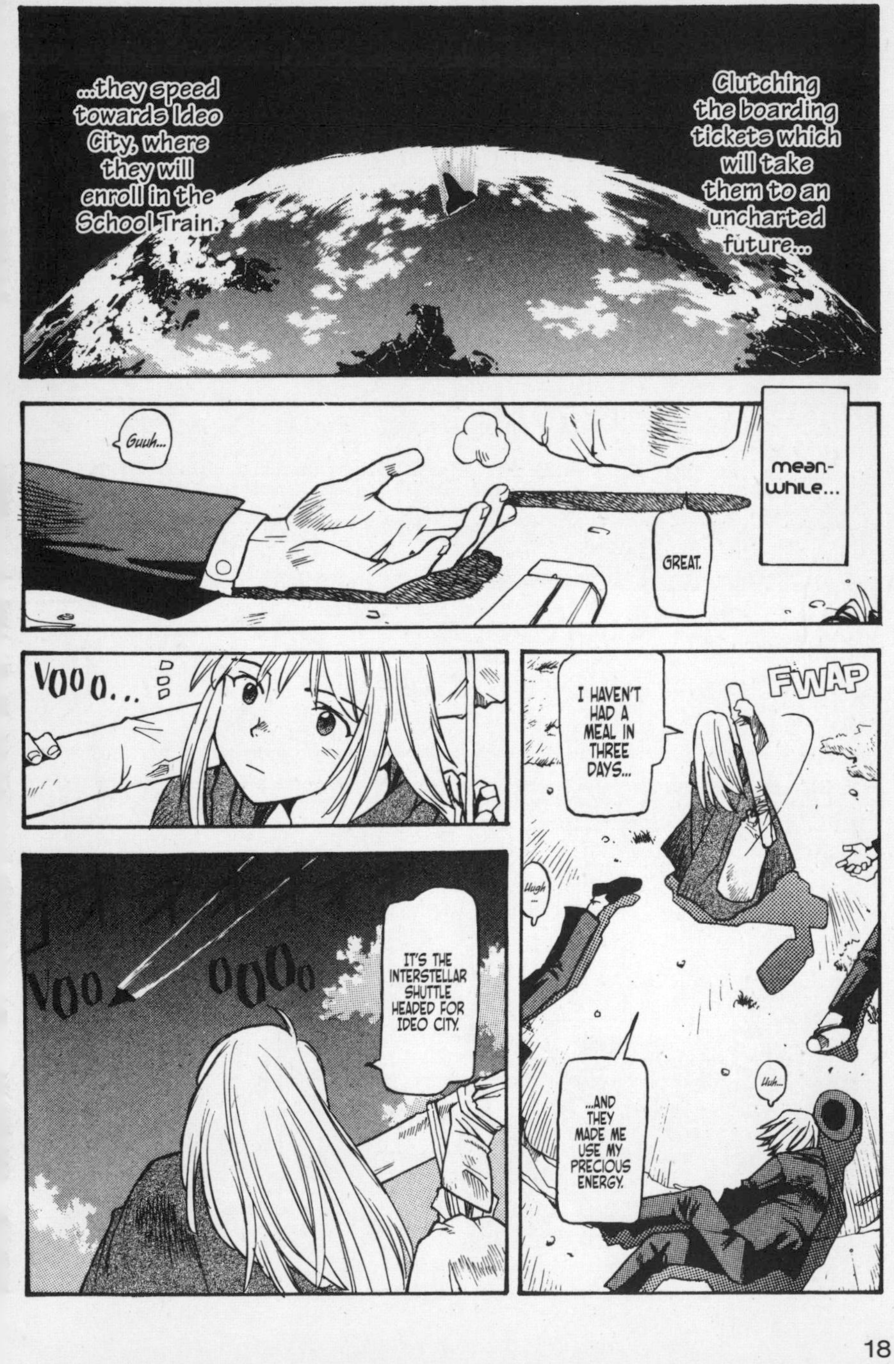

Clutching the boarding tickets which will take them to an uncharted future...
...they speed towards Ideo City, where they will enroll in the School Train.
mean-while...
Guuh...
GREAT.
FWAP
I HAVEN'T HAD A MEAL IN THREE DAYS...
Uugh...
Uuh...
...AND THEY MADE ME USE MY PRECIOUS ENERGY.
VOOO...
VOOOOOOO
IT'S THE INTERSTELLAR SHUTTLE HEADED FOR IDEO CITY.

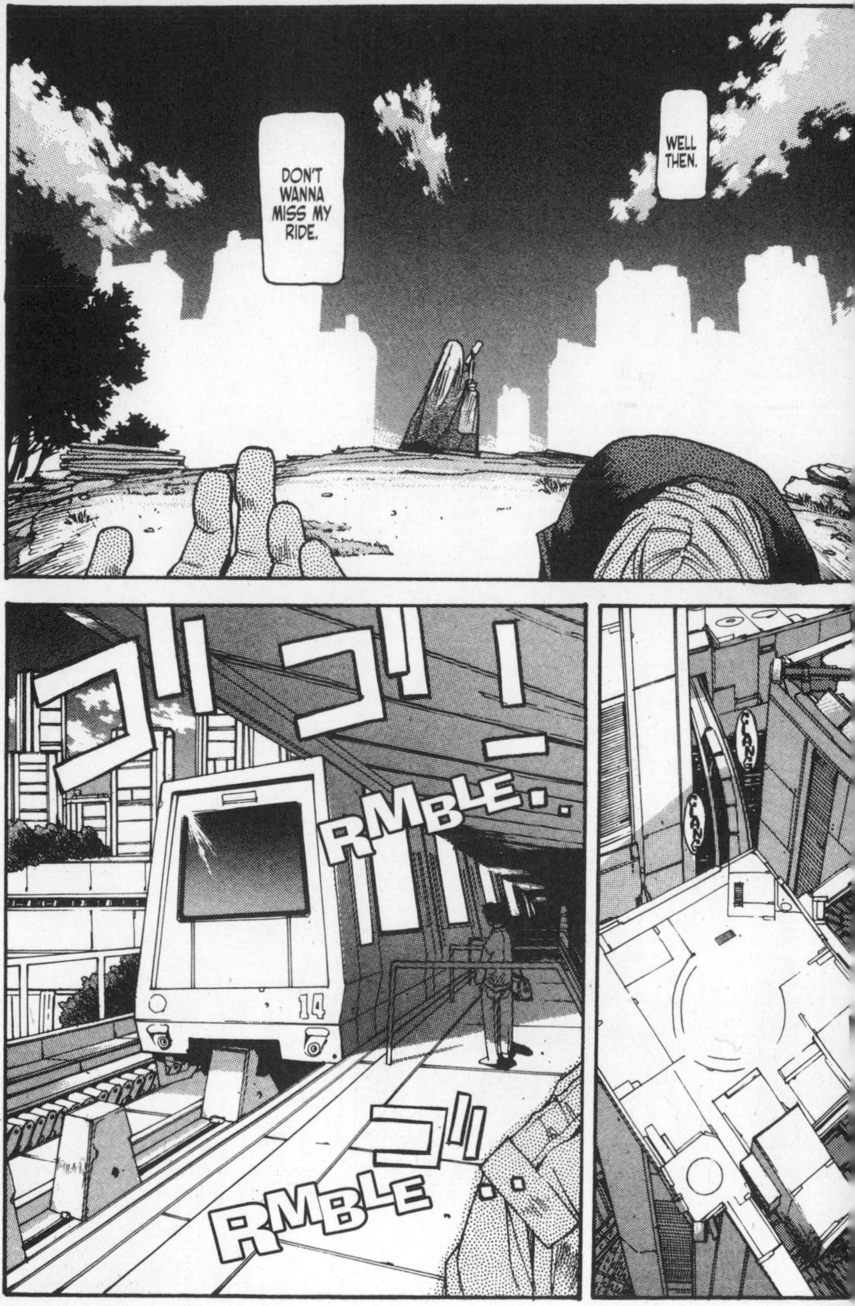
WELL THEN.
DON'T WANNA MISS MY RIDE.
CLANG
CLANG
RMBLE..
RMBLE..

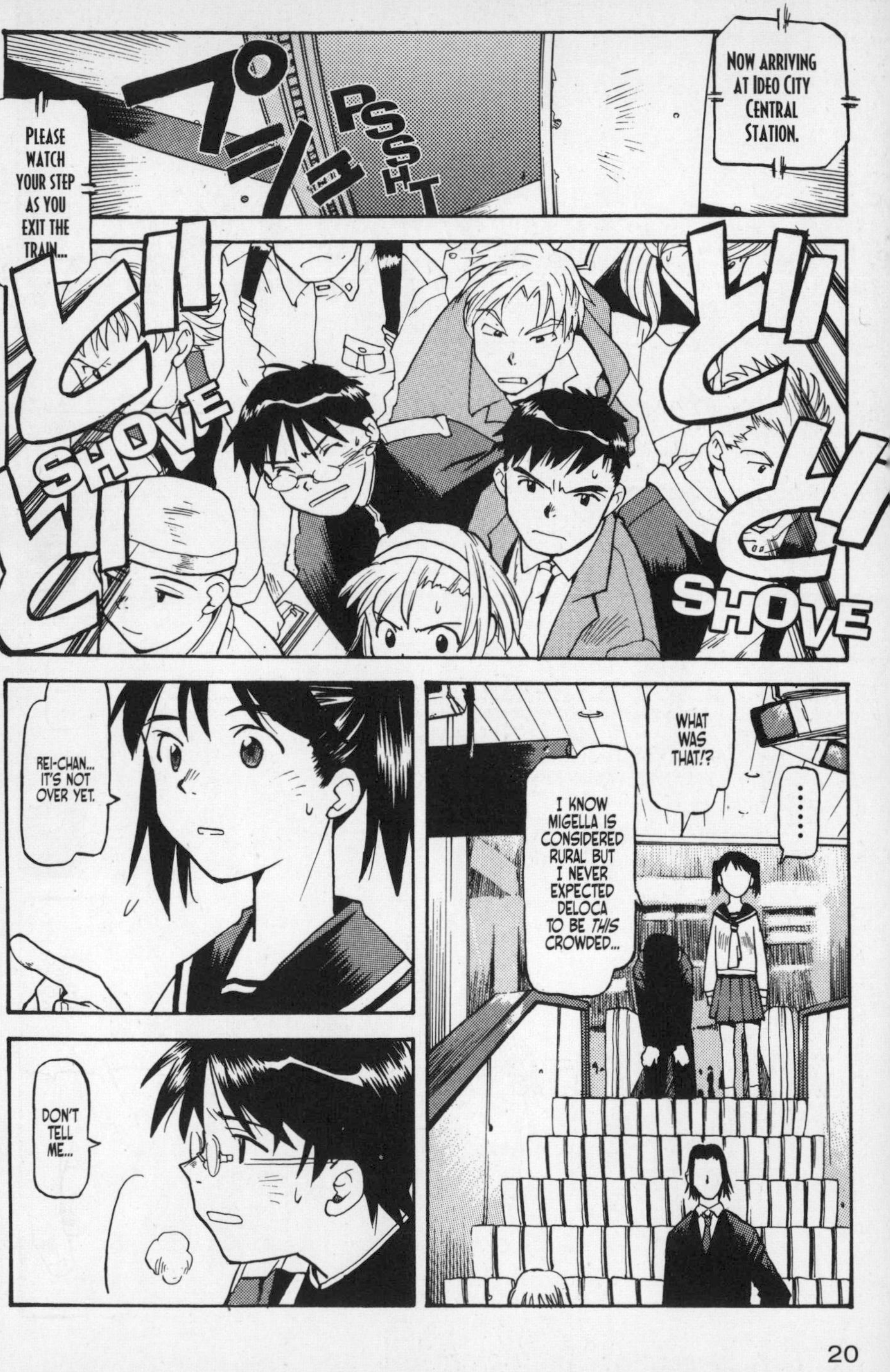
NOW ARRIVING AT IDEO CITY CENTRAL STATION.
PSSHT
PLEASE WATCH YOUR STEP AS YOU EXIT THE TRAIN...
SHOVE
SHOVE
WHAT WAS THAT!?
......
I KNOW MIGELLA IS CONSIDERED RURAL BUT I NEVER EXPECTED DELOCA TO BE *THIS* CROWDED...
REI-CHAN... IT'S NOT OVER YET.
DON'T TELL ME...

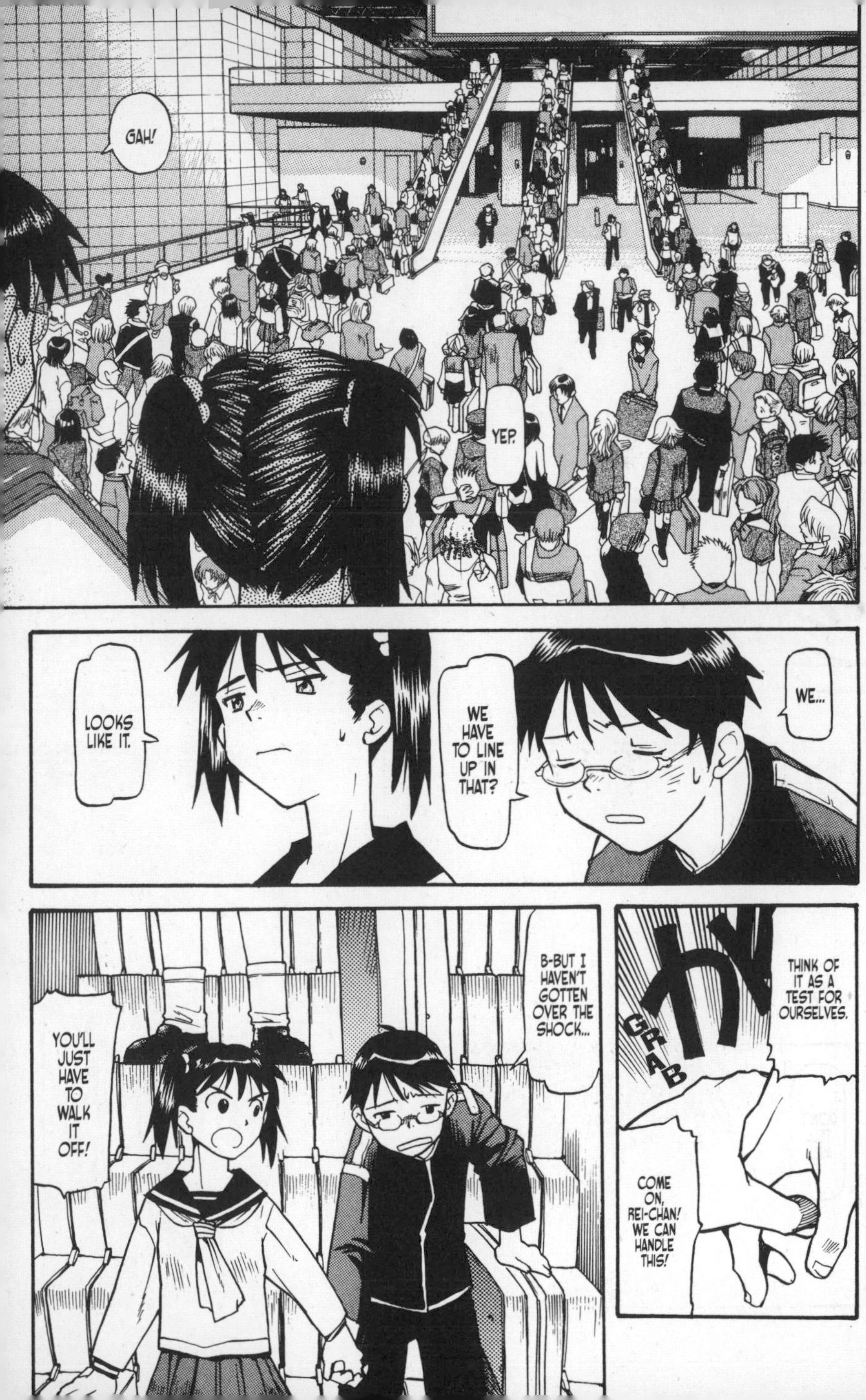
GAH!
YEP.
WE...
WE HAVE TO LINE UP IN THAT?
LOOKS LIKE IT.
THINK OF IT AS A TEST FOR OURSELVES.
GRAB
COME ON, REI-CHAN! WE CAN HANDLE THIS!
B-BUT I HAVEN'T GOTTEN OVER THE SHOCK...
YOU'LL JUST HAVE TO WALK IT OFF!

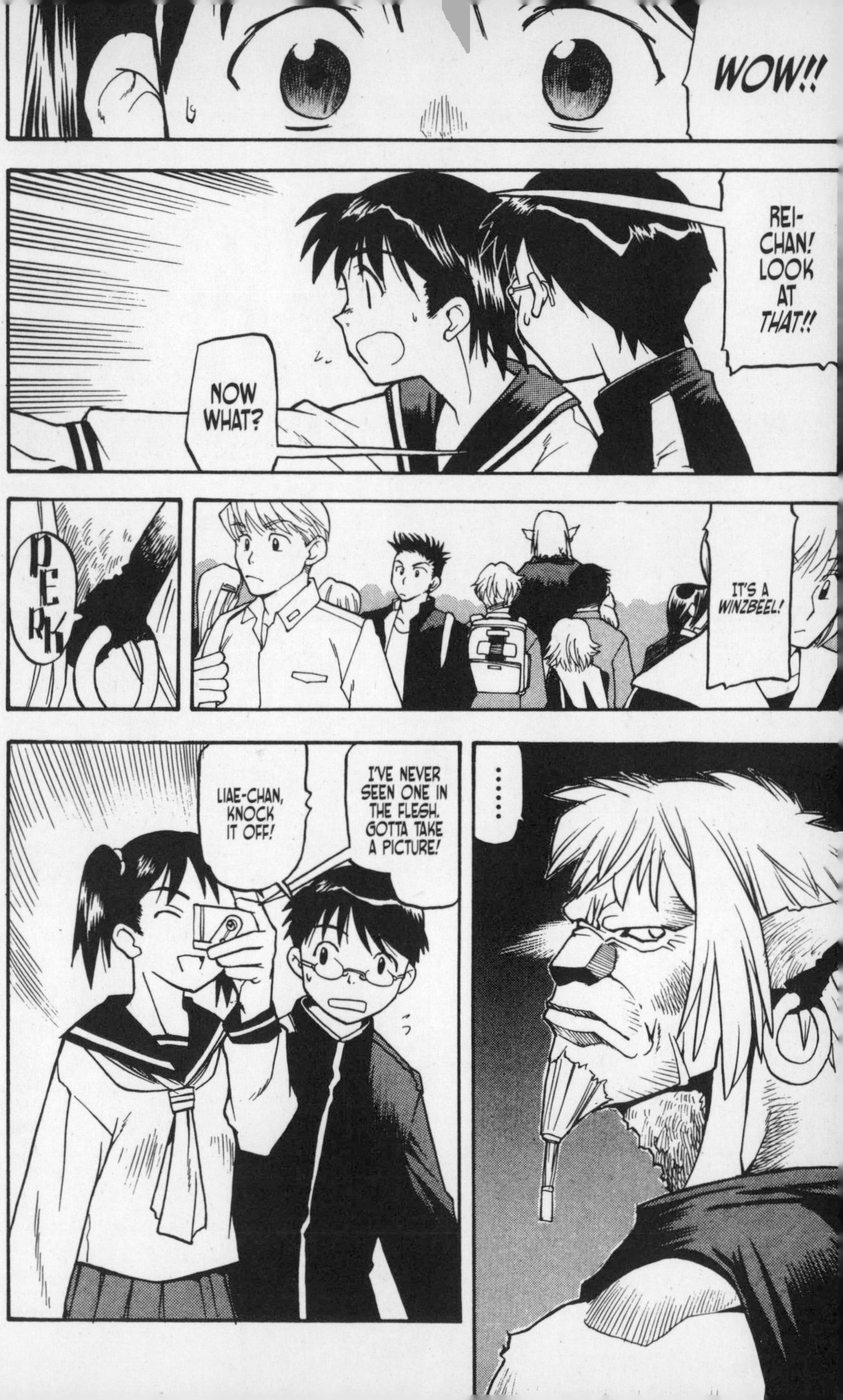
WOW!!
REI-CHAN! LOOK AT THAT!!
NOW WHAT?
IT'S A WINZBEEL!
PERK
......
I'VE NEVER SEEN ONE IN THE FLESH. GOTTA TAKE A PICTURE!
LIAE-CHAN, KNOCK IT OFF!

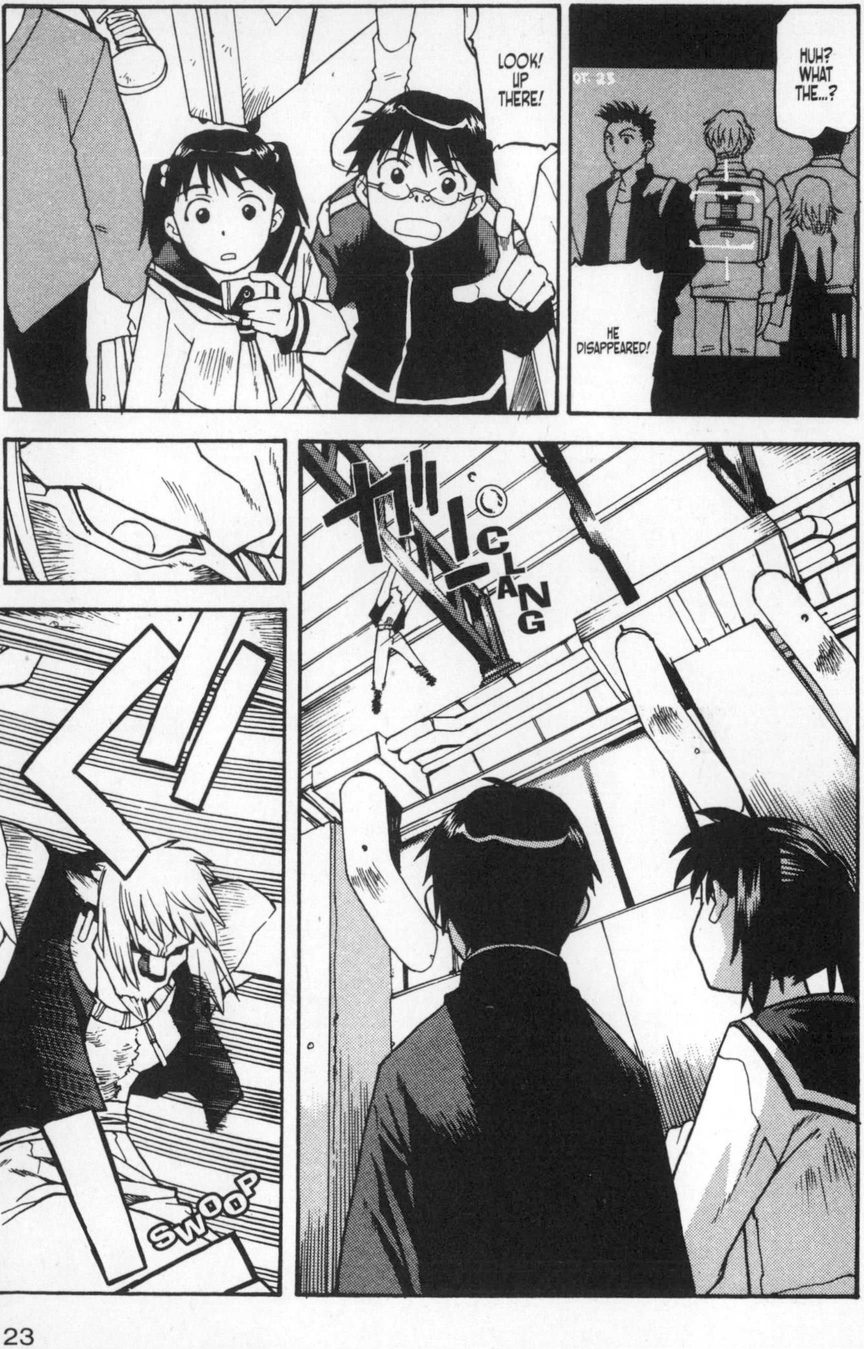
HUH? WHAT THE...?
HE DISAPPEARED!
LOOK! UP THERE!
CLANG
SWOOP

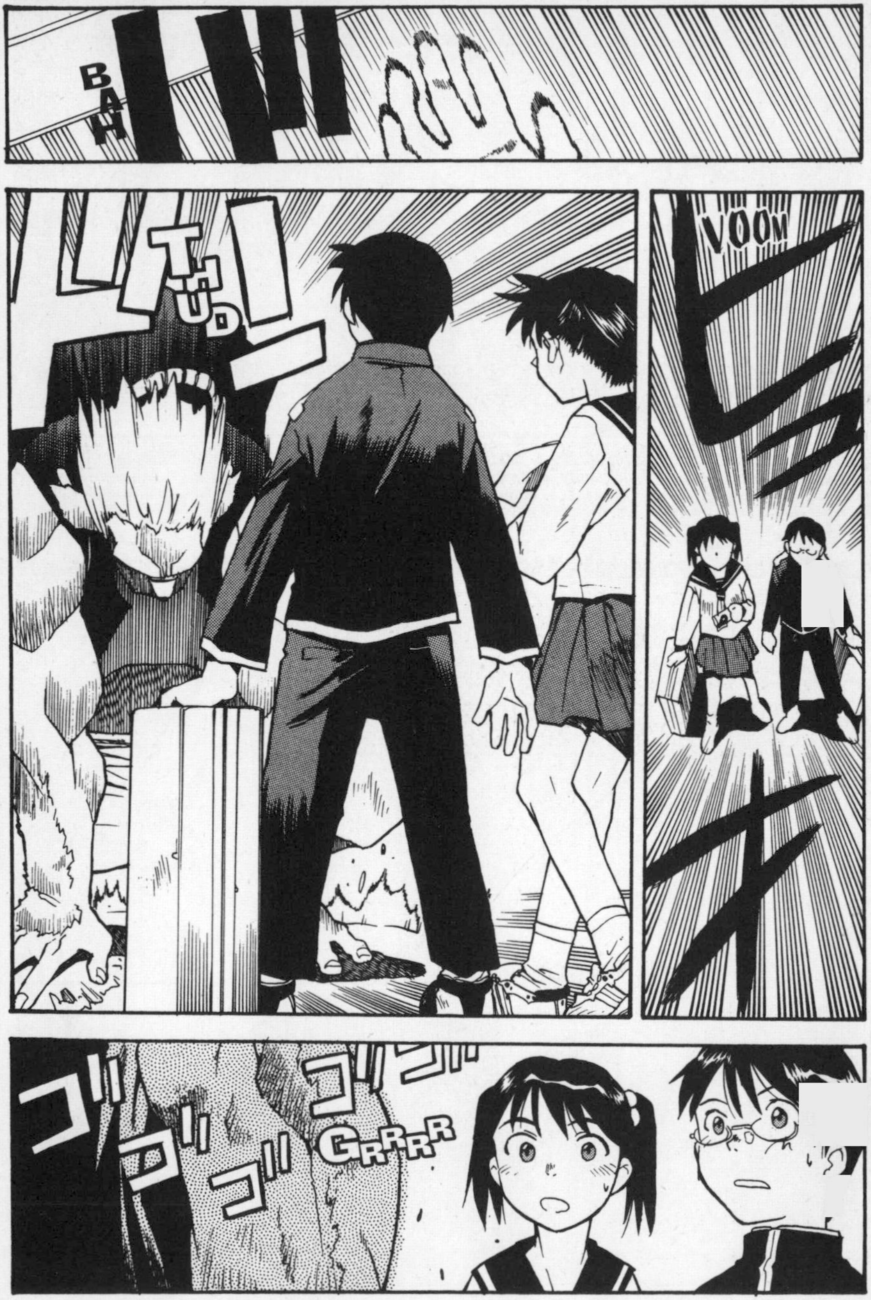
BAH
VOOM
THUD
GRRRR

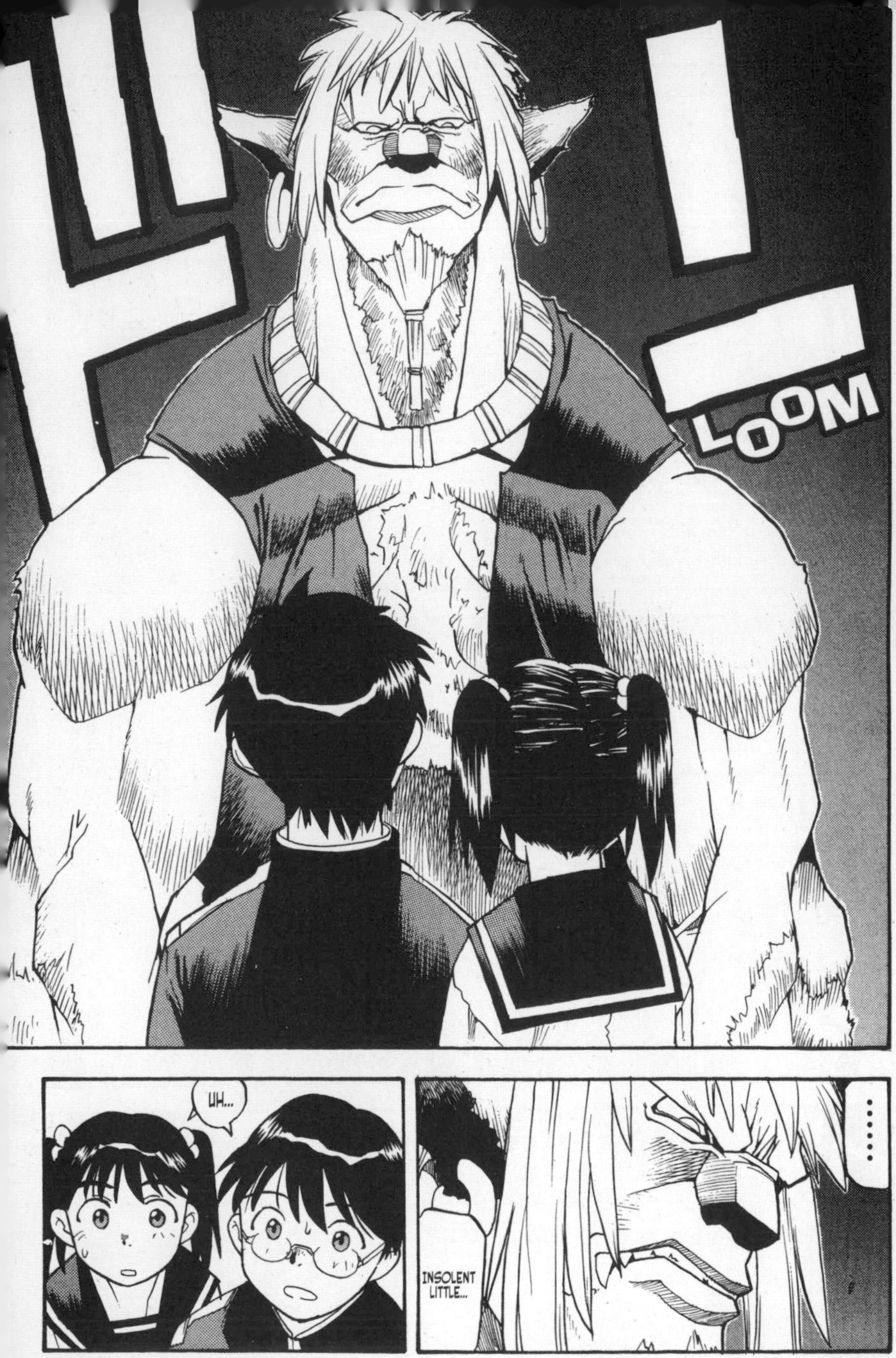
LOOM
......
INSOLENT LITTLE...
UH...

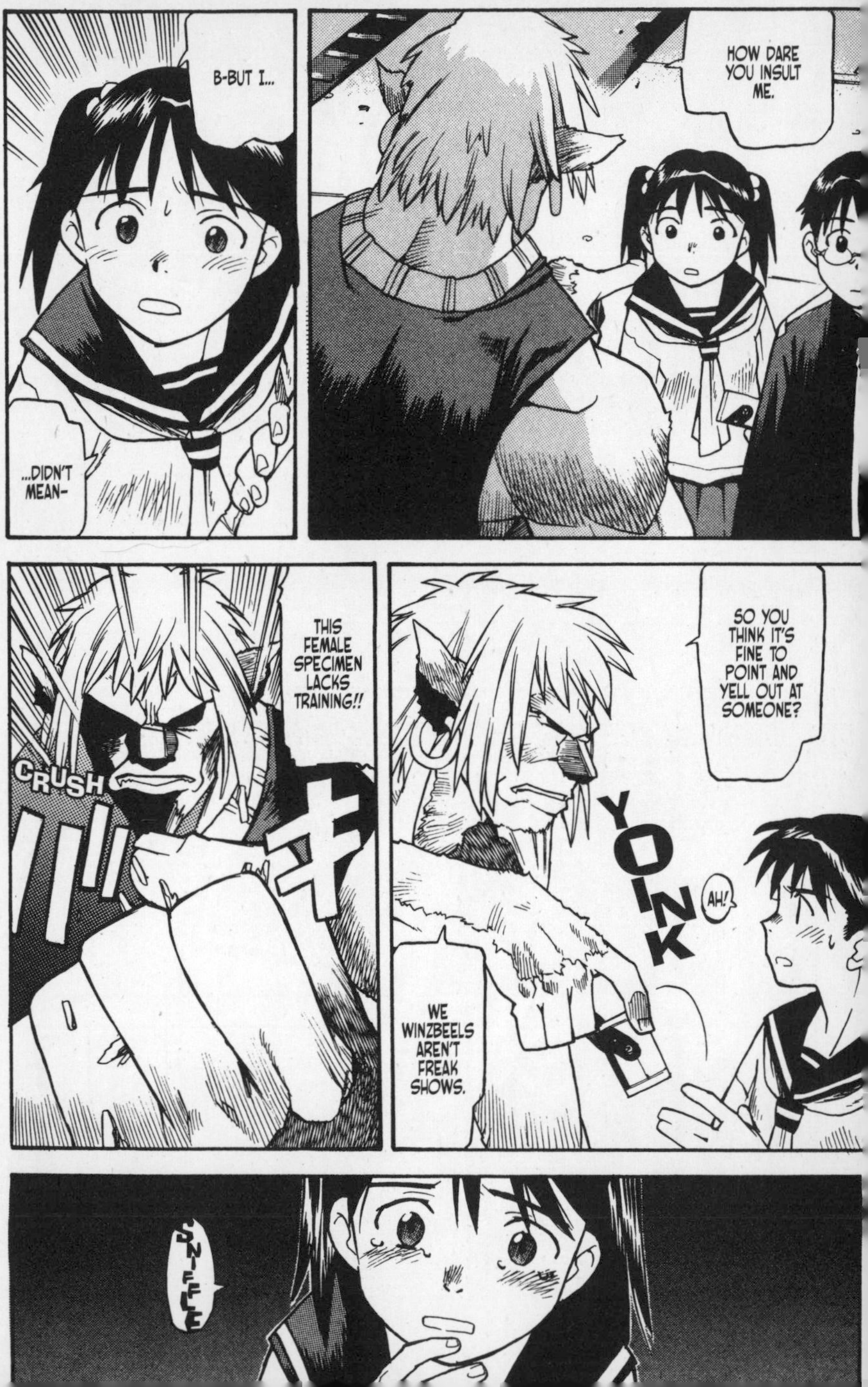
HOW DARE YOU INSULT ME.
B-BUT I...
...DIDN'T MEAN-
SO YOU THINK IT'S FINE TO POINT AND YELL OUT AT SOMEONE?
YOINK
AH!
WE WINZBEELS AREN'T FREAK SHOWS.
THIS FEMALE SPECIMEN LACKS TRAINING!!
CRUSH
SNIFFLE

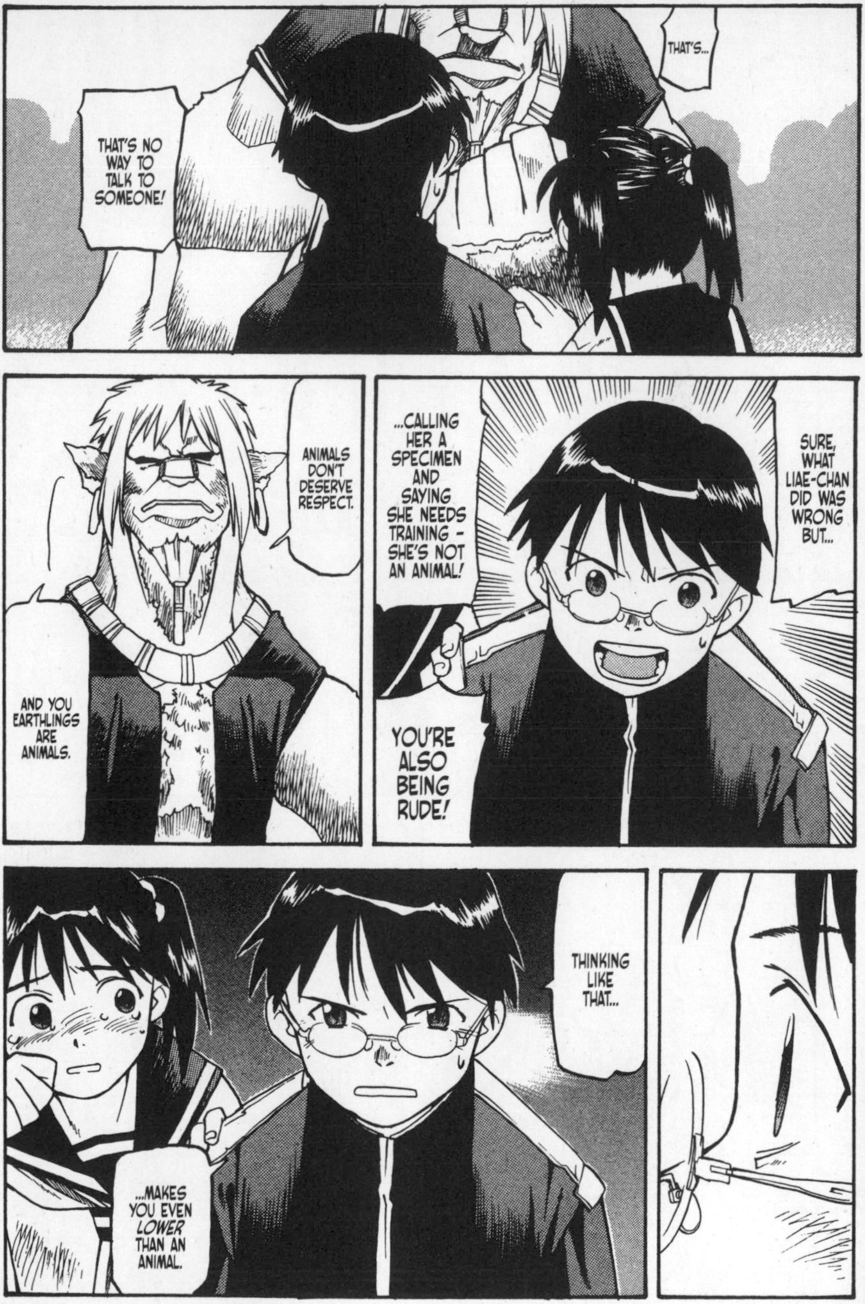
THAT'S...
THAT'S NO WAY TO TALK TO SOMEONE!
SURE, WHAT LIAE-CHAN DID WAS WRONG BUT...
...CALLING HER A SPECIMEN AND SAYING SHE NEEDS TRAINING - SHE'S NOT AN ANIMAL!
YOU'RE ALSO BEING RUDE!
ANIMALS DON'T DESERVE RESPECT.
AND YOU EARTHLINGS ARE ANIMALS.
THINKING LIKE THAT...
...MAKES YOU EVEN *LOWER* THAN AN ANIMAL.

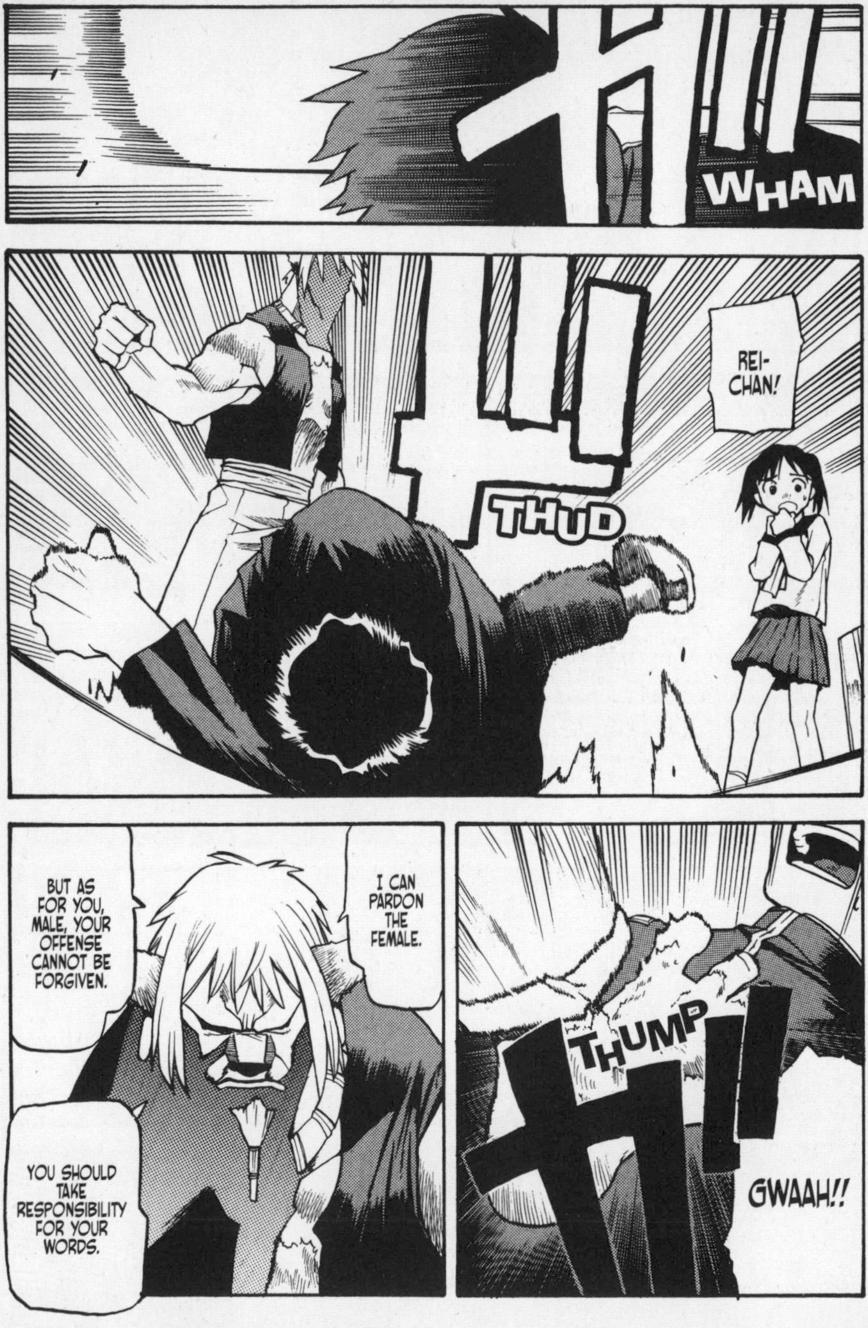
WHAM
REI-CHAN!
THUD
THUMP
GWAAH!!
I CAN PARDON THE FEMALE.
BUT AS FOR YOU, MALE, YOUR OFFENSE CANNOT BE FORGIVEN.
YOU SHOULD TAKE RESPONSIBILITY FOR YOUR WORDS.

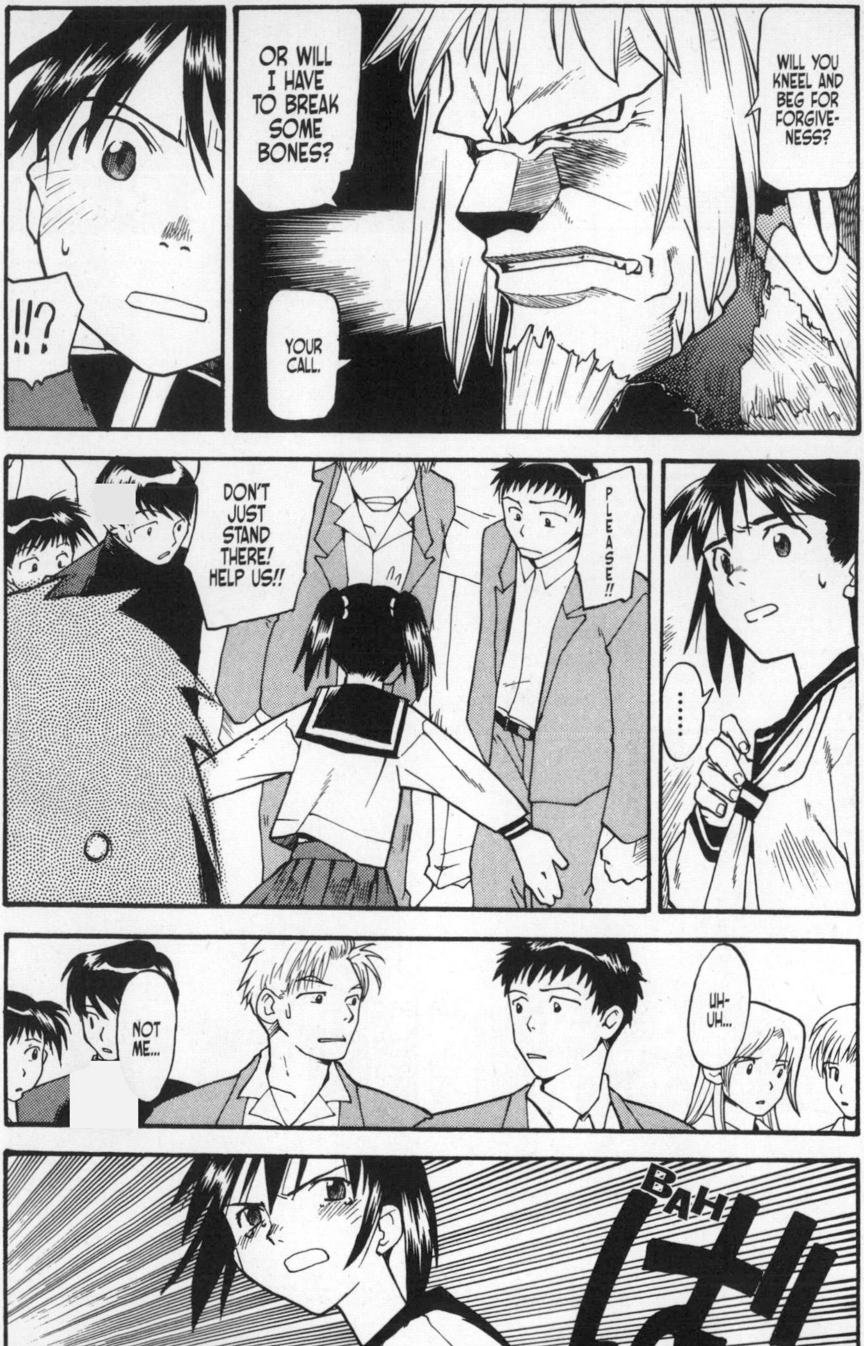
WILL YOU KNEEL AND BEG FOR FORGIVE-NESS?
OR WILL I HAVE TO BREAK SOME BONES?
YOUR CALL.
!!?
......
PLEASE!!
DON'T JUST STAND THERE! HELP US!!
UH-UH...
NOT ME...
BAH

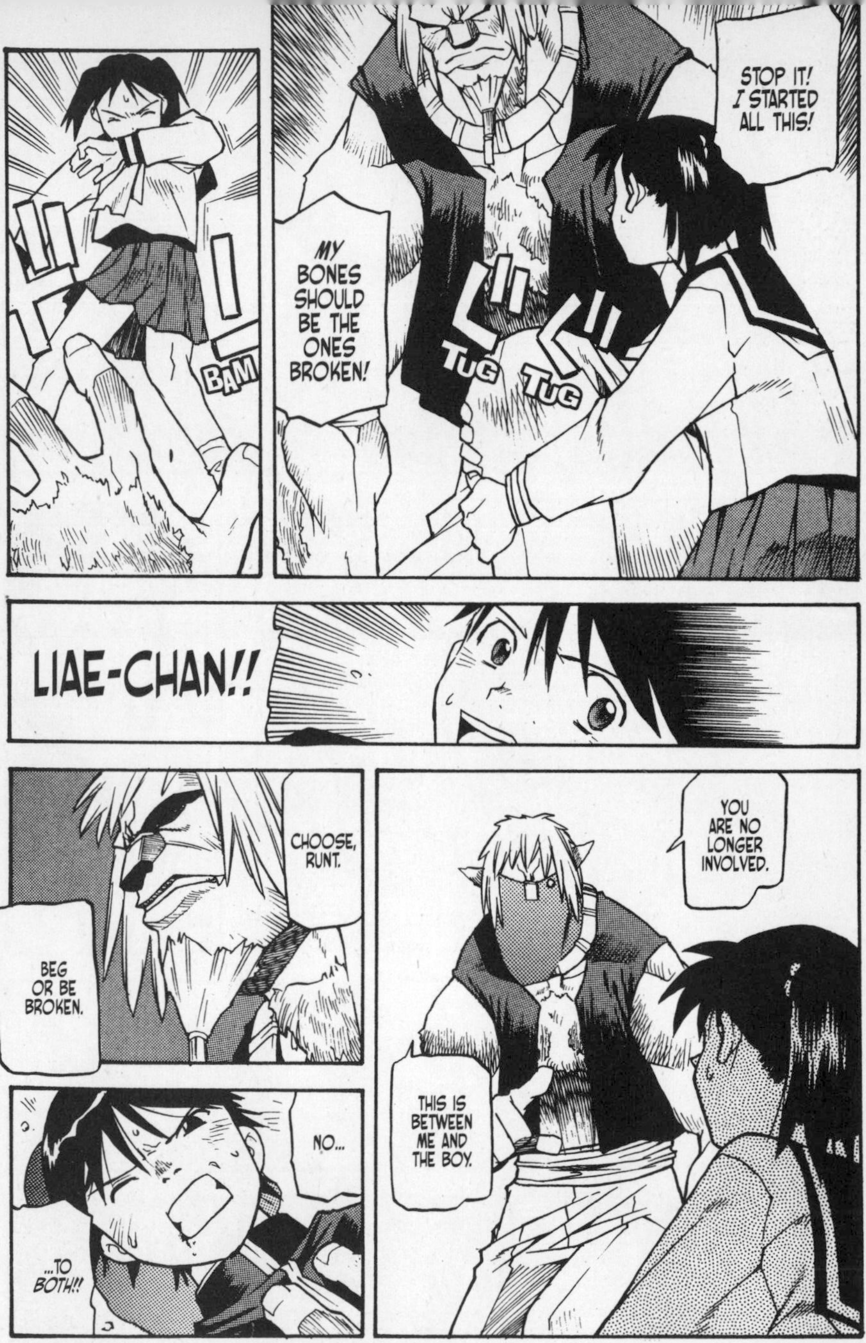
STOP IT! I STARTED ALL THIS!
MY BONES SHOULD BE THE ONES BROKEN!
TUG
TUG
BAM
LIAE-CHAN!!
YOU ARE NO LONGER INVOLVED.
THIS IS BETWEEN ME AND THE BOY.
CHOOSE, RUNT.
BEG OR BE BROKEN.
NO...
...TO BOTH!!

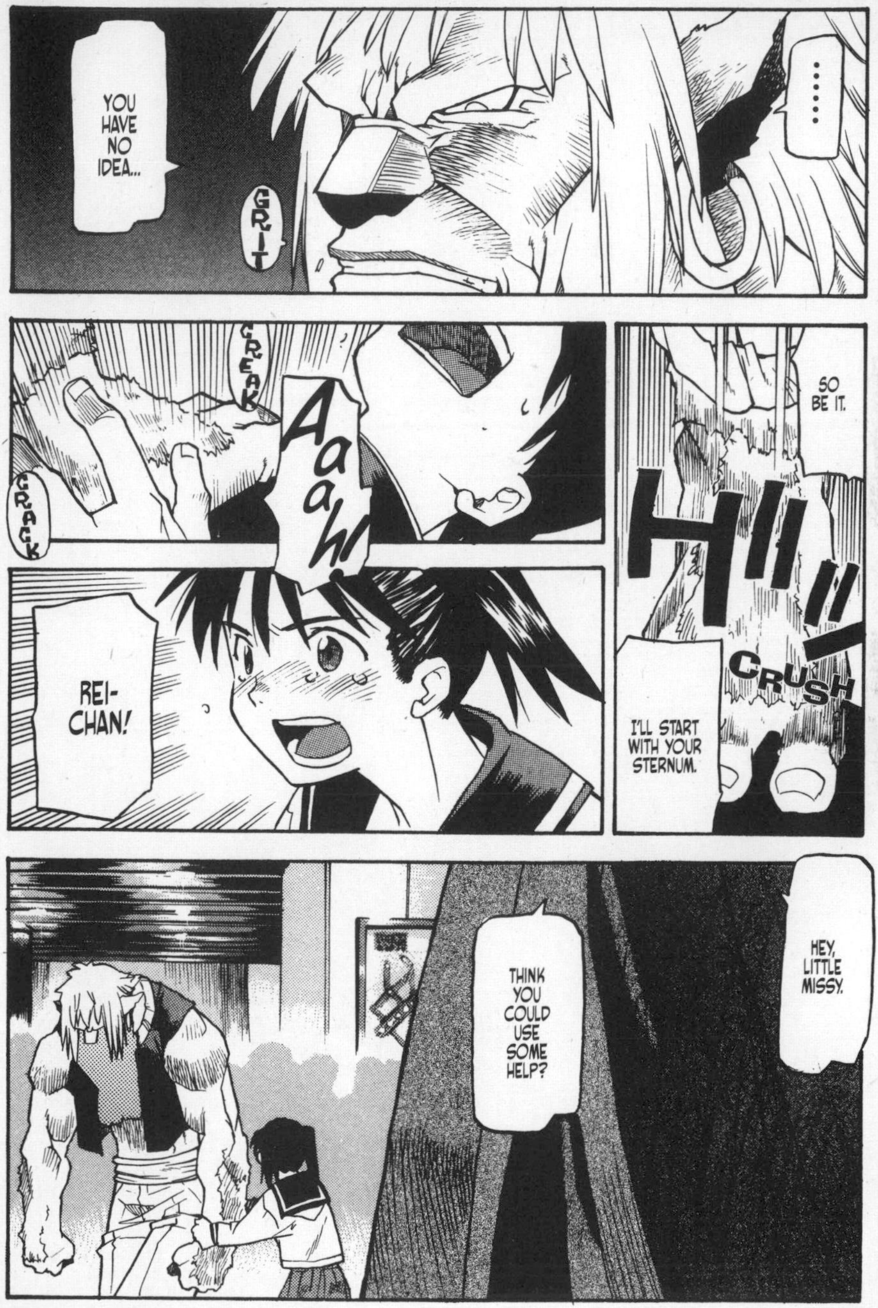
......
YOU HAVE NO IDEA...
GRIT
SO BE IT.
HIII!!
CRUSH
I'LL START WITH YOUR STERNUM.
CREAK
Aaah!
CRACK
REI-CHAN!
HEY, LITTLE MISSY.
THINK YOU COULD USE SOME HELP?

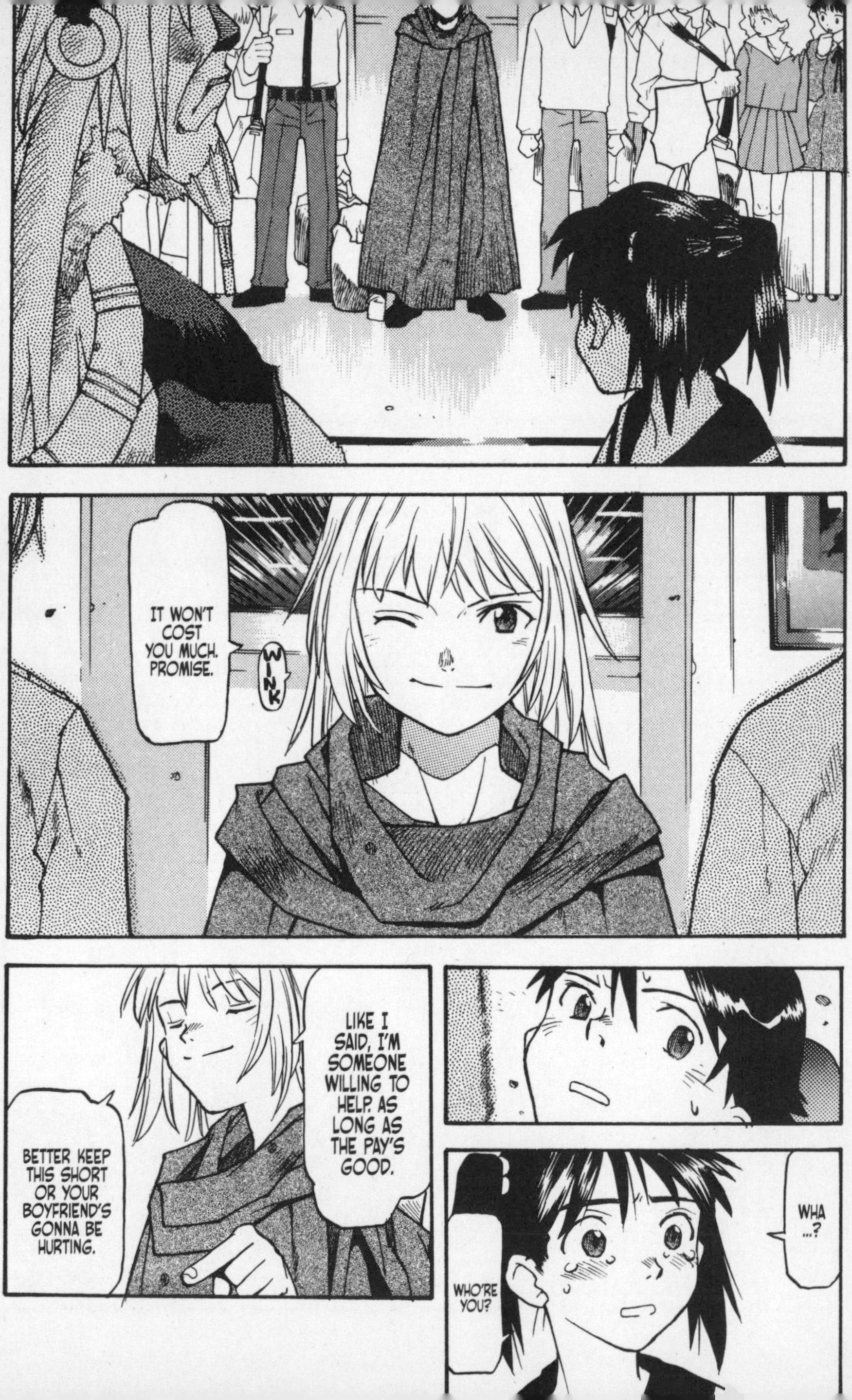
IT WON'T COST YOU MUCH. PROMISE.
WINK
WHA ...?
WHO'RE YOU?
LIKE I SAID, I'M SOMEONE WILLING TO HELP. AS LONG AS THE PAY'S GOOD.
BETTER KEEP THIS SHORT OR YOUR BOYFRIEND'S GONNA BE HURTING.

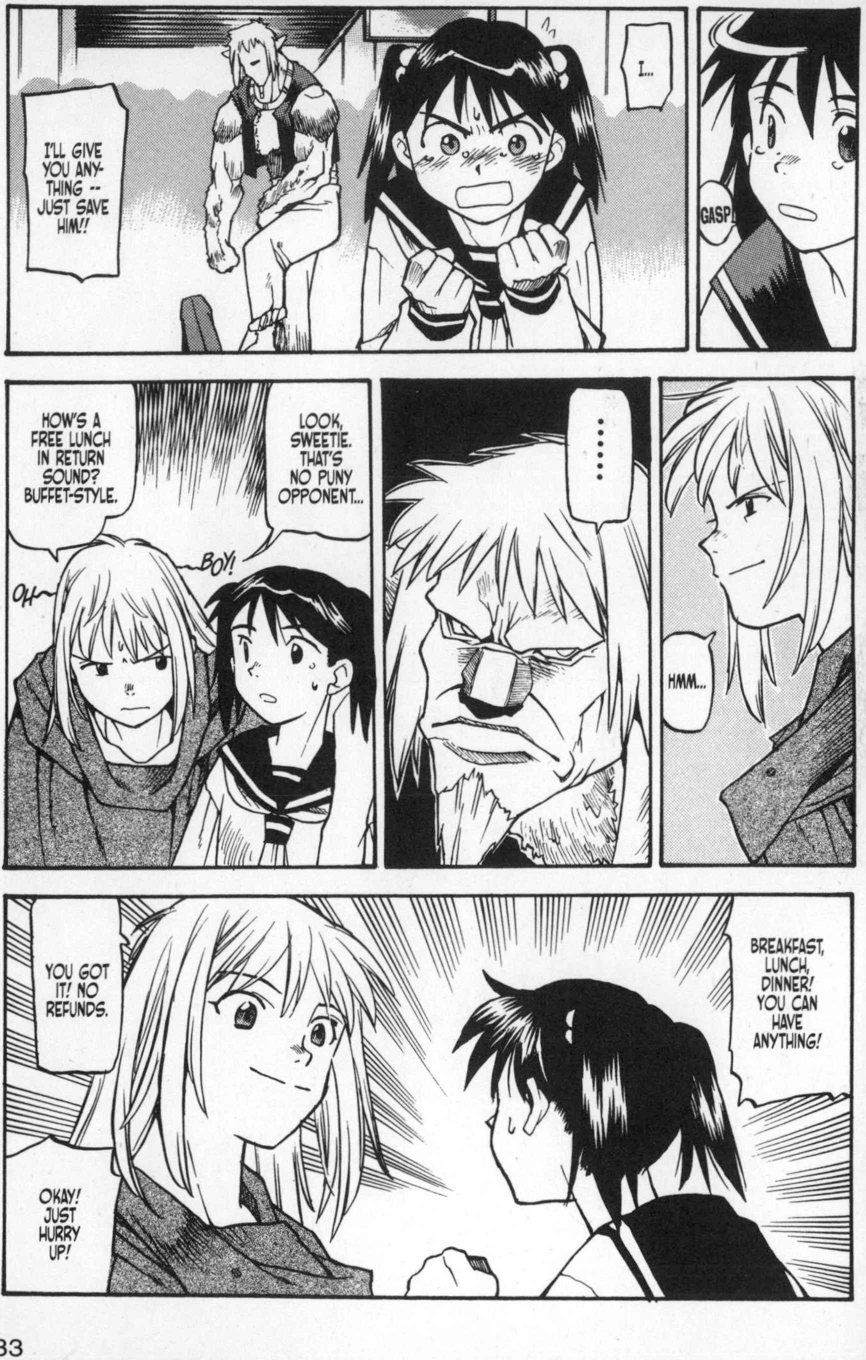
GASP!
I...
I'LL GIVE YOU ANYTHING -- JUST SAVE HIM!!
HMM...
......
LOOK, SWEETIE. THAT'S NO PUNY OPPONENT...
HOW'S A FREE LUNCH IN RETURN SOUND? BUFFET-STYLE.
OH~
BOY!
BREAKFAST, LUNCH, DINNER! YOU CAN HAVE ANYTHING!
YOU GOT IT! NO REFUNDS.
OKAY! JUST HURRY UP!

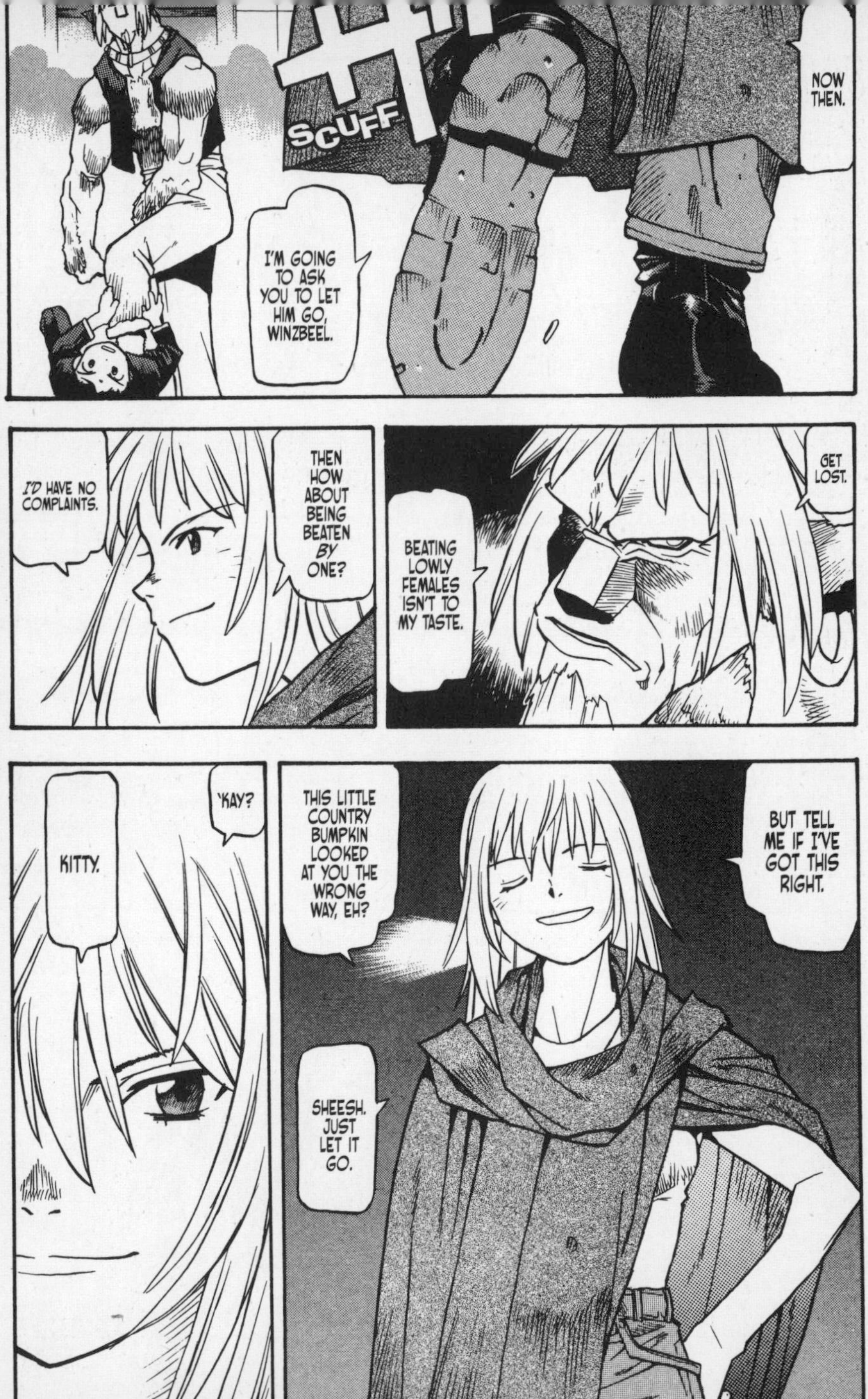
NOW THEN.
SCUFF
I'M GOING TO ASK YOU TO LET HIM GO, WINZBEEL.
GET LOST.
BEATING LOWLY FEMALES ISN'T TO MY TASTE.
THEN HOW ABOUT BEING BEATEN *BY* ONE?
I'D HAVE NO COMPLAINTS.
BUT TELL ME IF I'VE GOT THIS RIGHT.
THIS LITTLE COUNTRY BUMPKIN LOOKED AT YOU THE WRONG WAY, EH?
SHEESH. JUST LET IT GO.
'KAY?
KITTY.

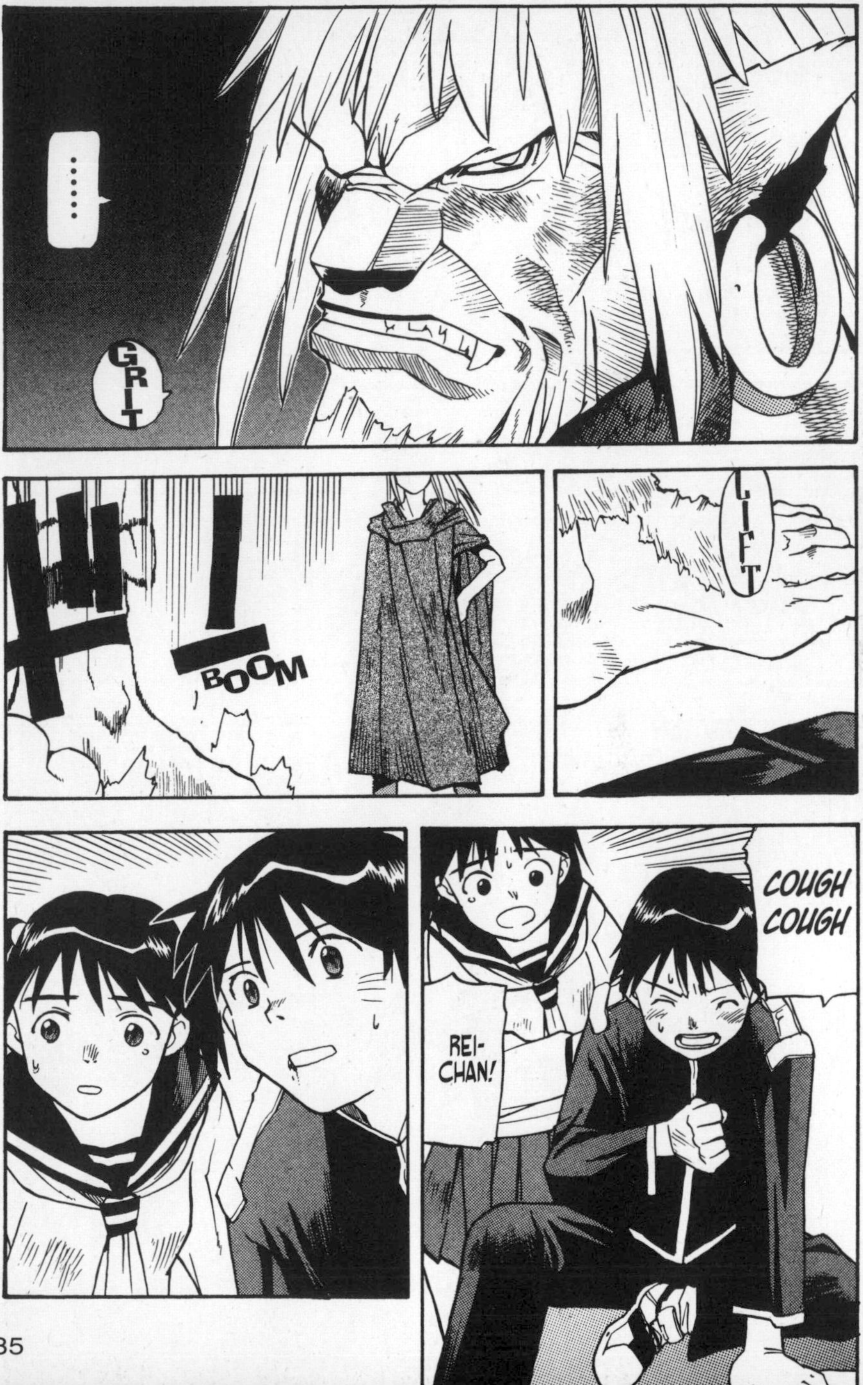
......
GRIT
LIFT
BOOM
COUGH COUGH
REI-CHAN!

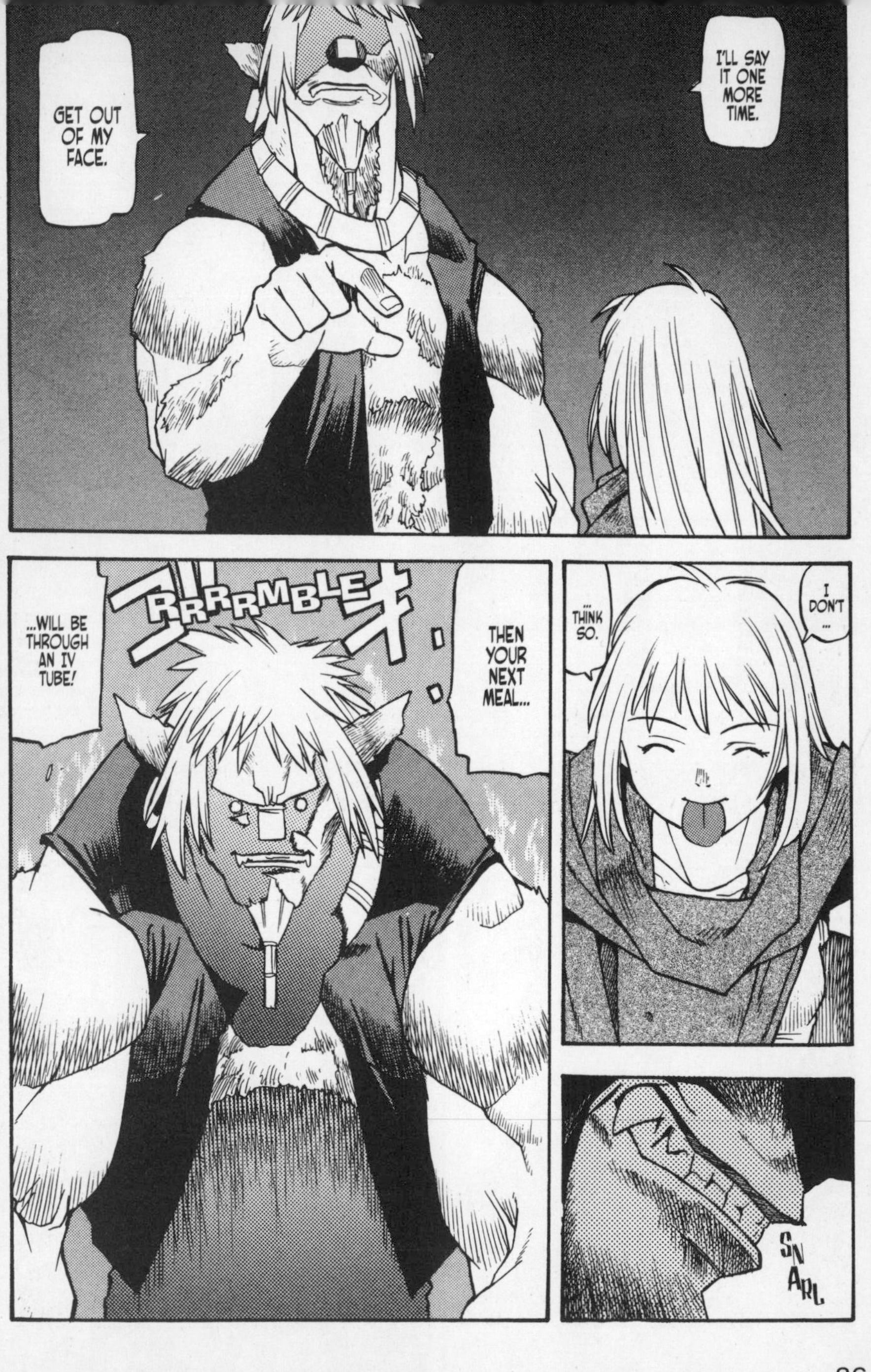
I'LL SAY IT ONE MORE TIME.
GET OUT OF MY FACE.
I DON'T ...
... THINK SO.
SNARL
THEN YOUR NEXT MEAL...
RRRRMBLE
...WILL BE THROUGH AN IV TUBE!

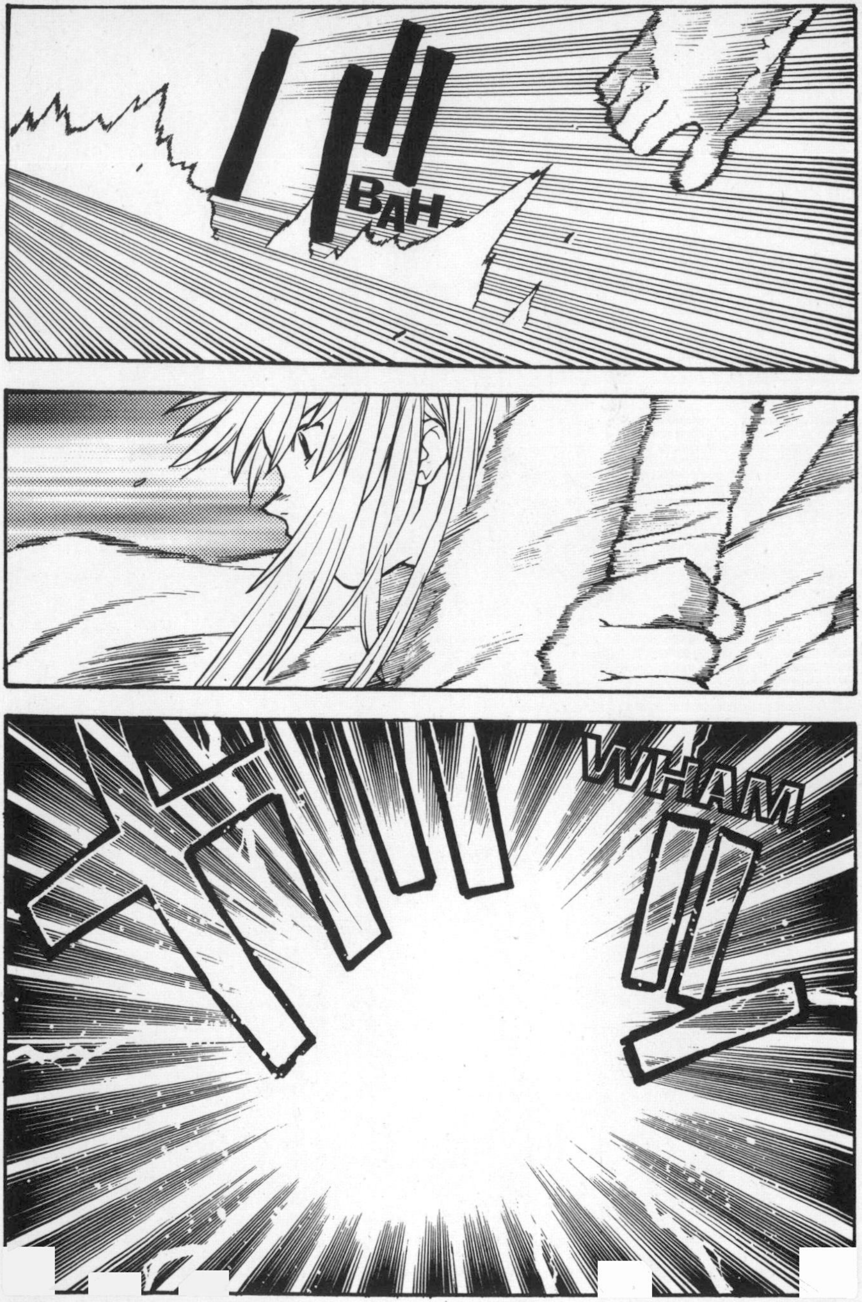
BAH
WHAM

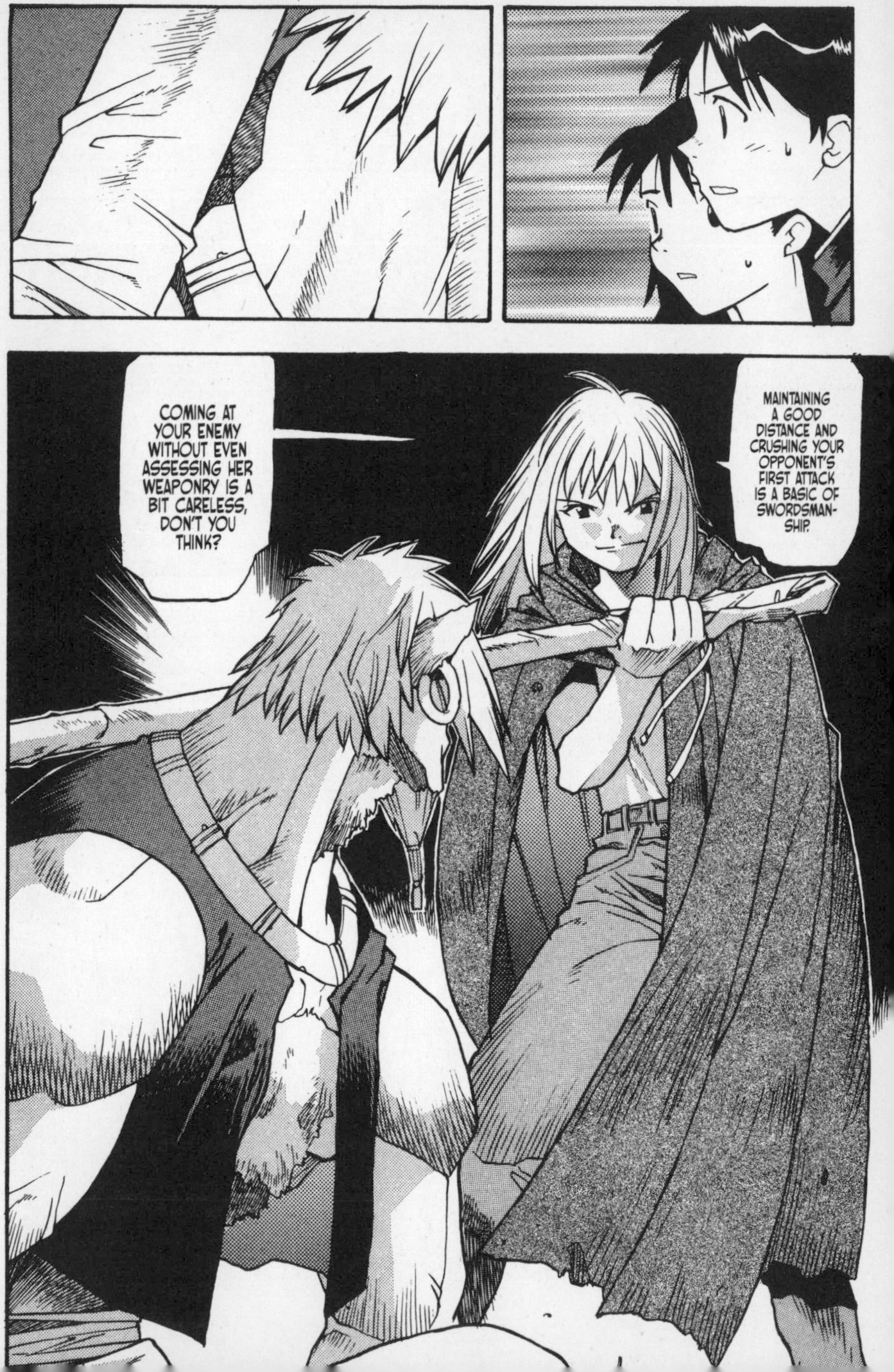
MAINTAINING A GOOD DISTANCE AND CRUSHING YOUR OPPONENT'S FIRST ATTACK IS A BASIC OF SWORDSMAN-SHIP.
COMING AT YOUR ENEMY WITHOUT EVEN ASSESSING HER WEAPONRY IS A BIT CARELESS, DON'T YOU THINK?

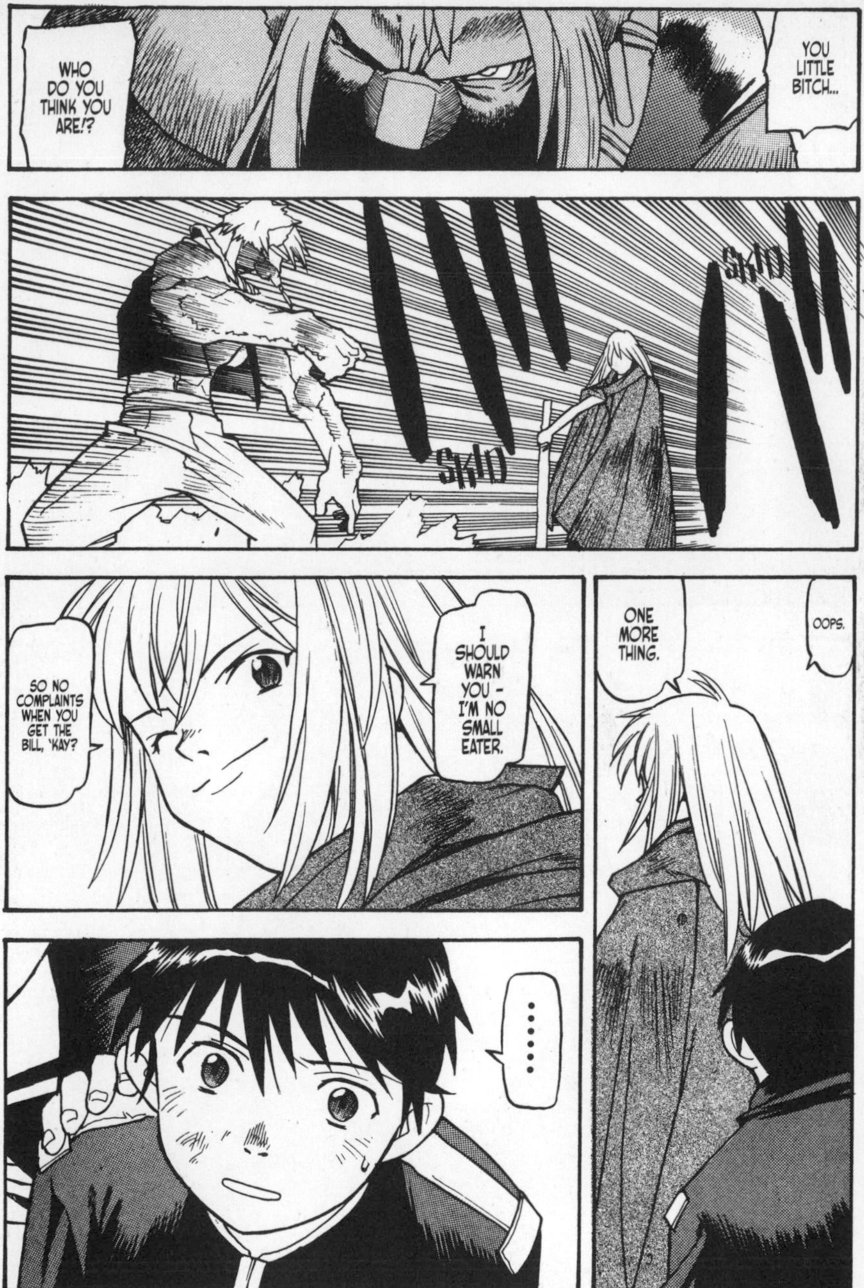
YOU LITTLE BITCH...
WHO DO YOU THINK YOU ARE!?
SKID
SKID
OOPS.
ONE MORE THING.
I SHOULD WARN YOU - I'M NO SMALL EATER.
SO NO COMPLAINTS WHEN YOU GET THE BILL, 'KAY?
......

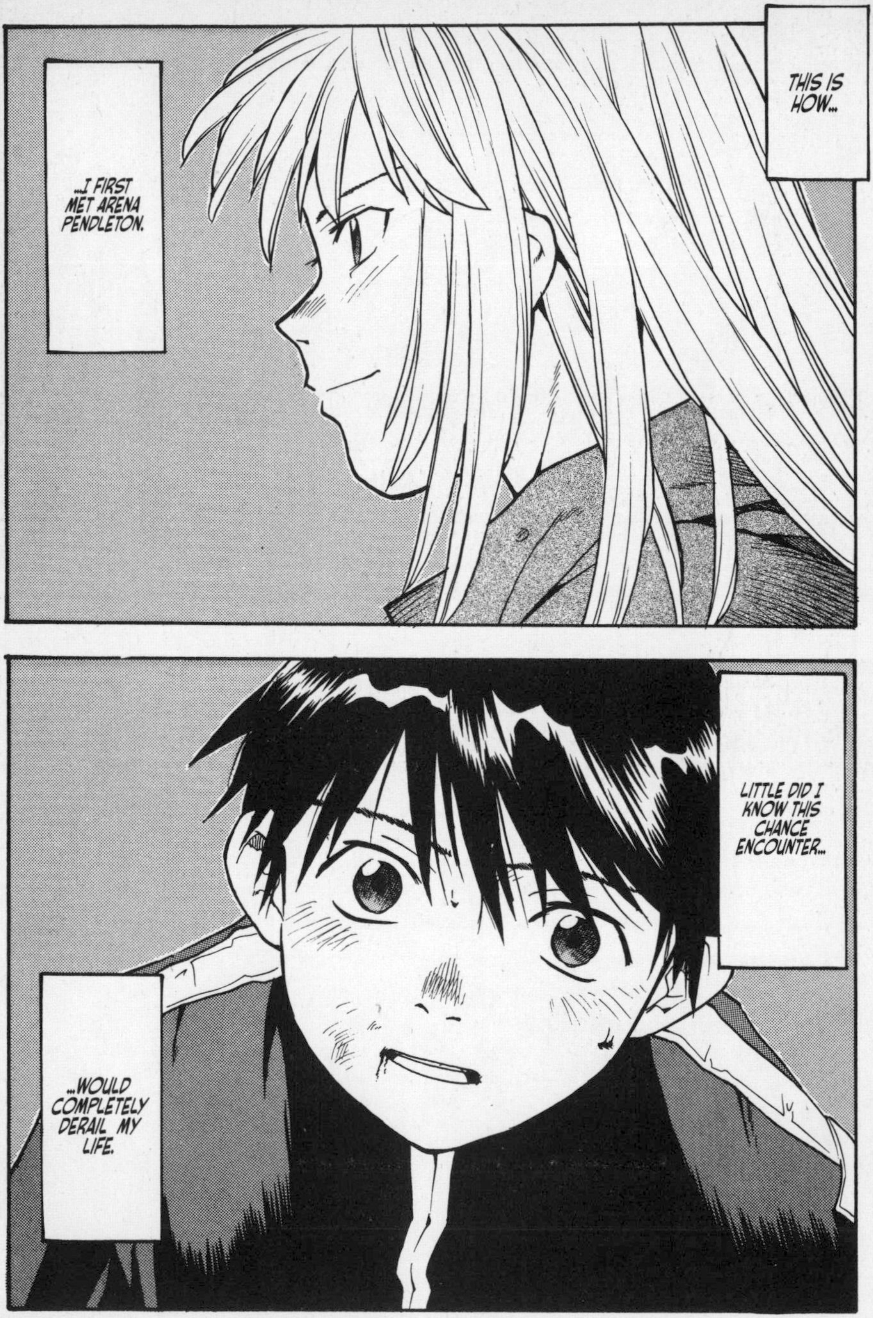
THIS IS HOW...
...I FIRST MET ARENA PENDLETON.
LITTLE DID I KNOW THIS CHANCE ENCOUNTER...
...WOULD COMPLETELY DERAIL MY LIFE.

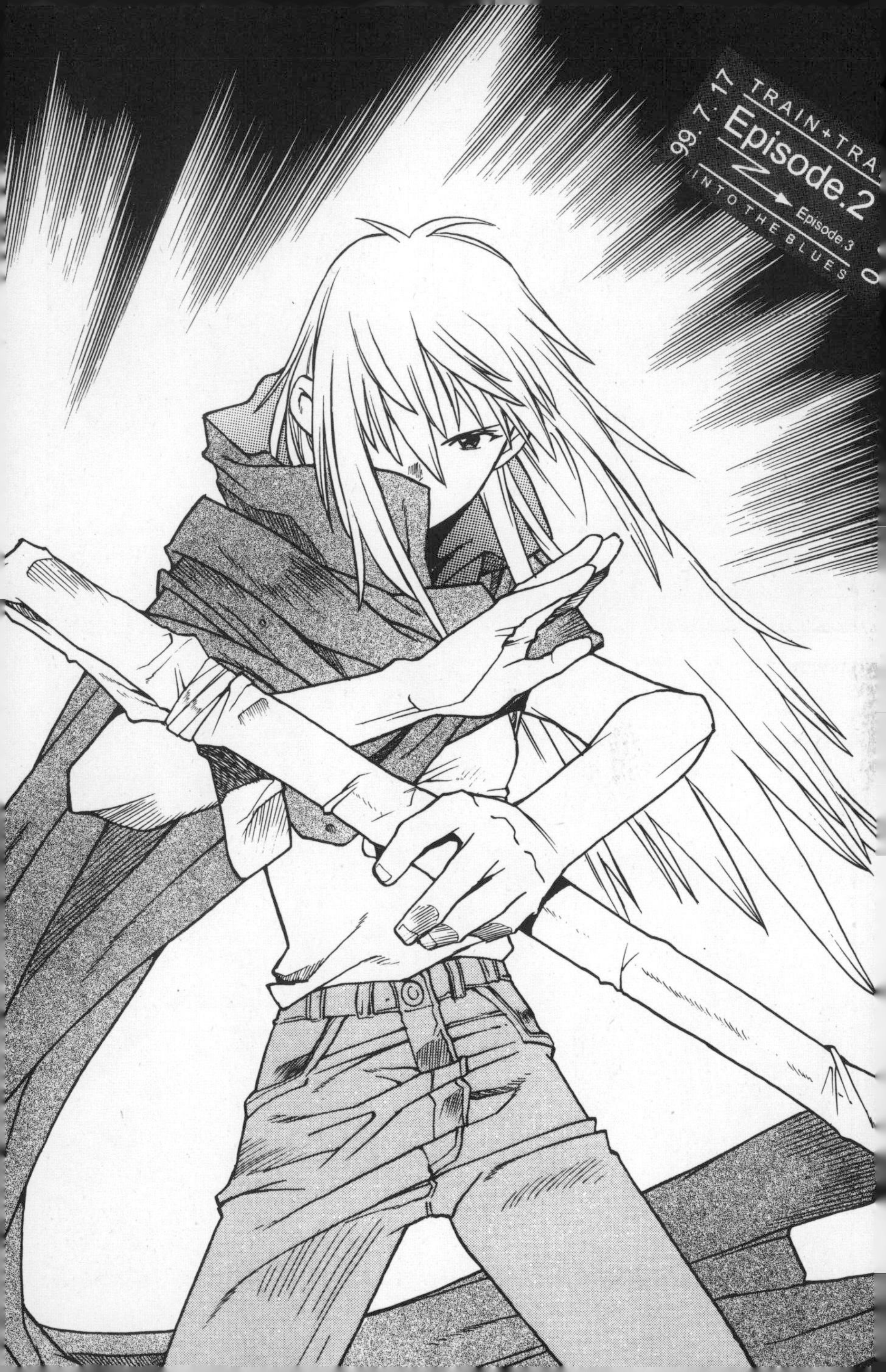
TRAIN+TRA
99. 7. 17
Episode.2
Episode.3
INTO THE BLUES
0

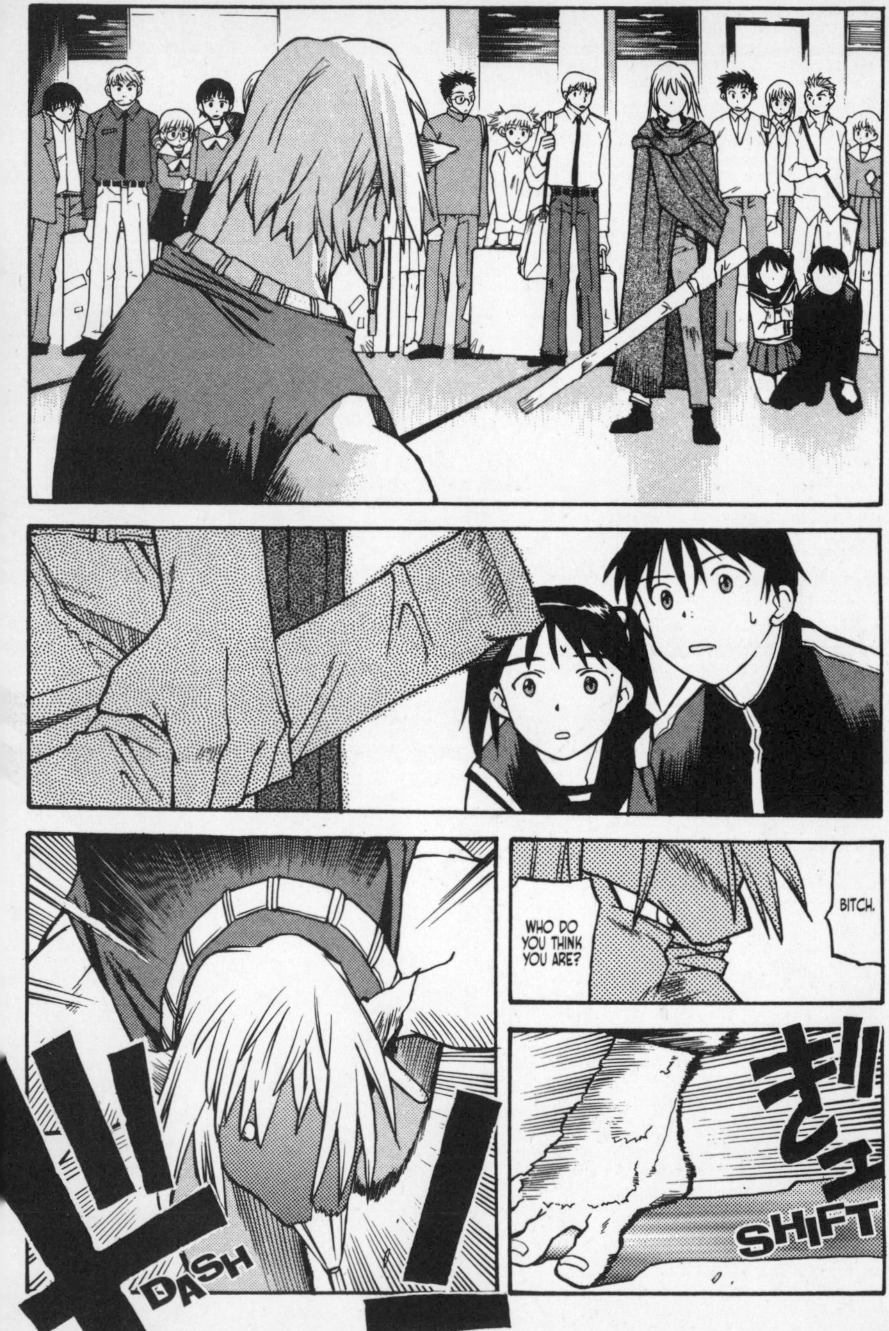
BITCH.
WHO DO YOU THINK YOU ARE?
SHIFT
DASH

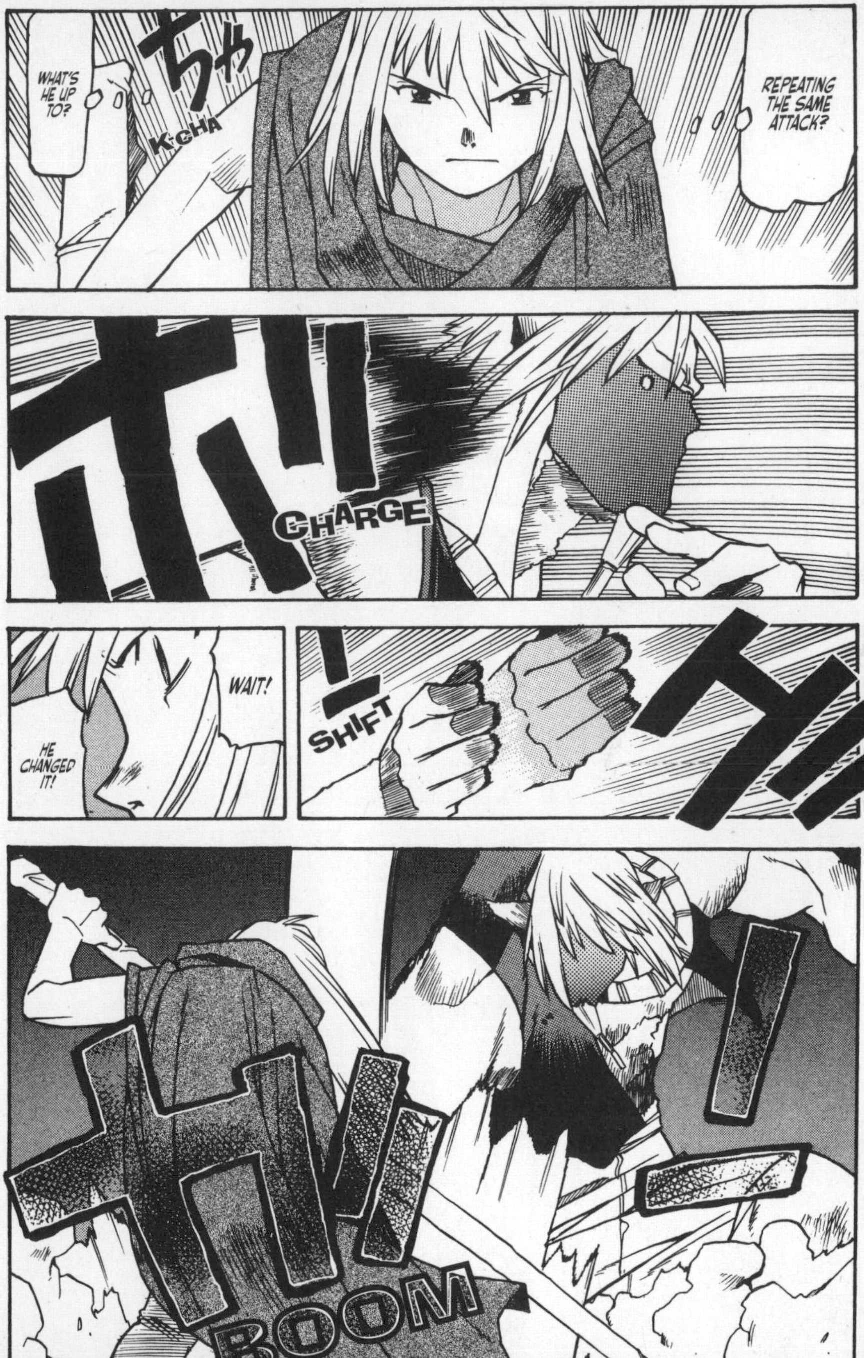
REPEATING THE SAME ATTACK?
ちゃ
K-CHA
WHAT'S HE UP TO?
CHARGE
SHIFT
WAIT!
HE CHANGED IT!
BOOM

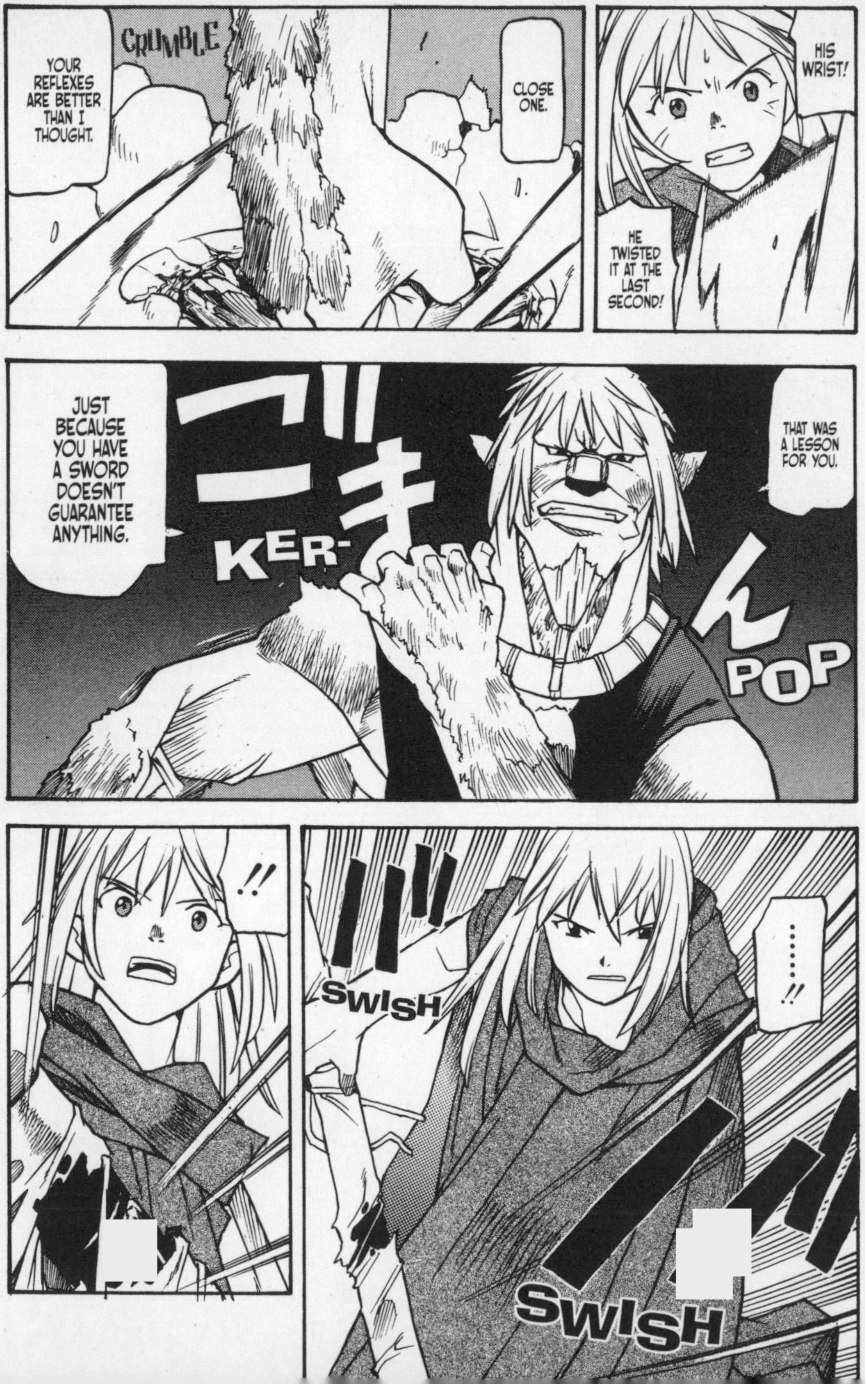
HIS WRIST!
HE TWISTED IT AT THE LAST SECOND!
CLOSE ONE.
CRUMBLE
YOUR REFLEXES ARE BETTER THAN I THOUGHT.
THAT WAS A LESSON FOR YOU.
ごきん
KER-
POP
JUST BECAUSE YOU HAVE A SWORD DOESN'T GUARANTEE ANYTHING.
……!!
SWISH
SWISH
!!

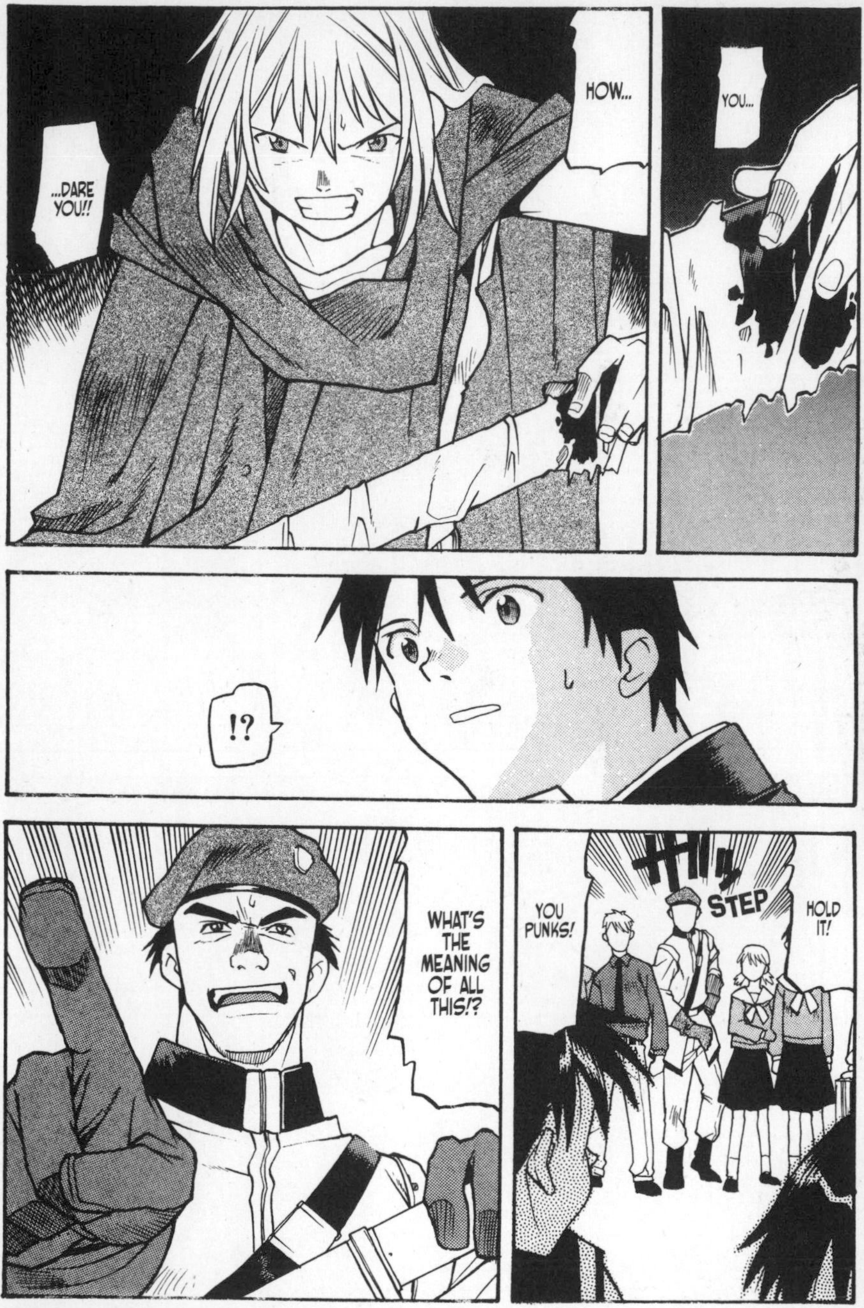
YOU...
HOW...
...DARE YOU!!
!?
HOLD IT!
STEP
YOU PUNKS!
WHAT'S THE MEANING OF ALL THIS!?

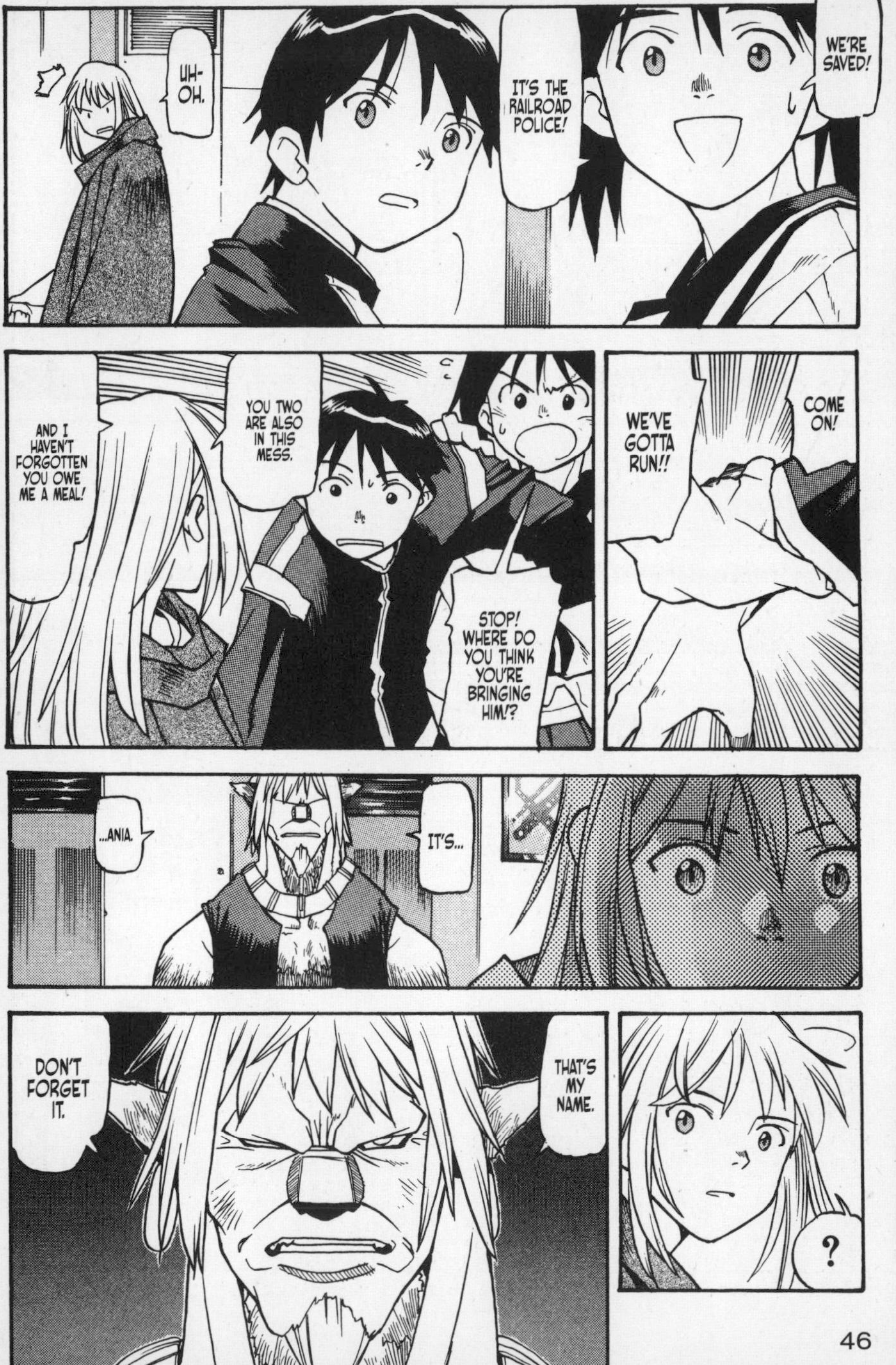
WE'RE SAVED!
IT'S THE RAILROAD POLICE!
UH-OH.
COME ON!
WE'VE GOTTA RUN!!
STOP! WHERE DO YOU THINK YOU'RE BRINGING HIM!?
YOU TWO ARE ALSO IN THIS MESS.
AND I HAVEN'T FORGOTTEN YOU OWE ME A MEAL!
IT'S...
...ANIA.
?
THAT'S MY NAME.
DON'T FORGET IT.

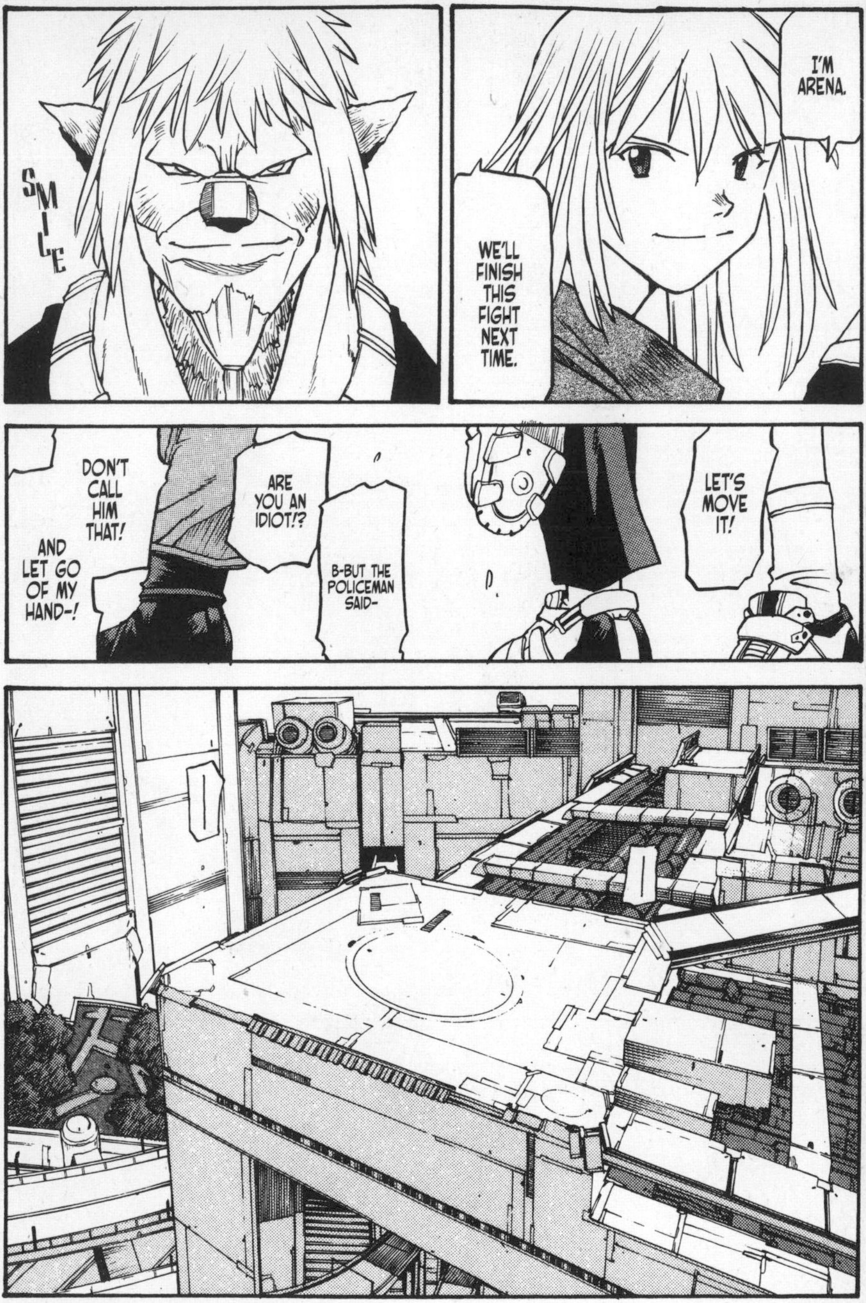
I'M ARENA.
WE'LL FINISH THIS FIGHT NEXT TIME.
SMILE
LET'S MOVE IT!
ARE YOU AN IDIOT!?
B-BUT THE POLICEMAN SAID-
DON'T CALL HIM THAT!
AND LET GO OF MY HAND-!

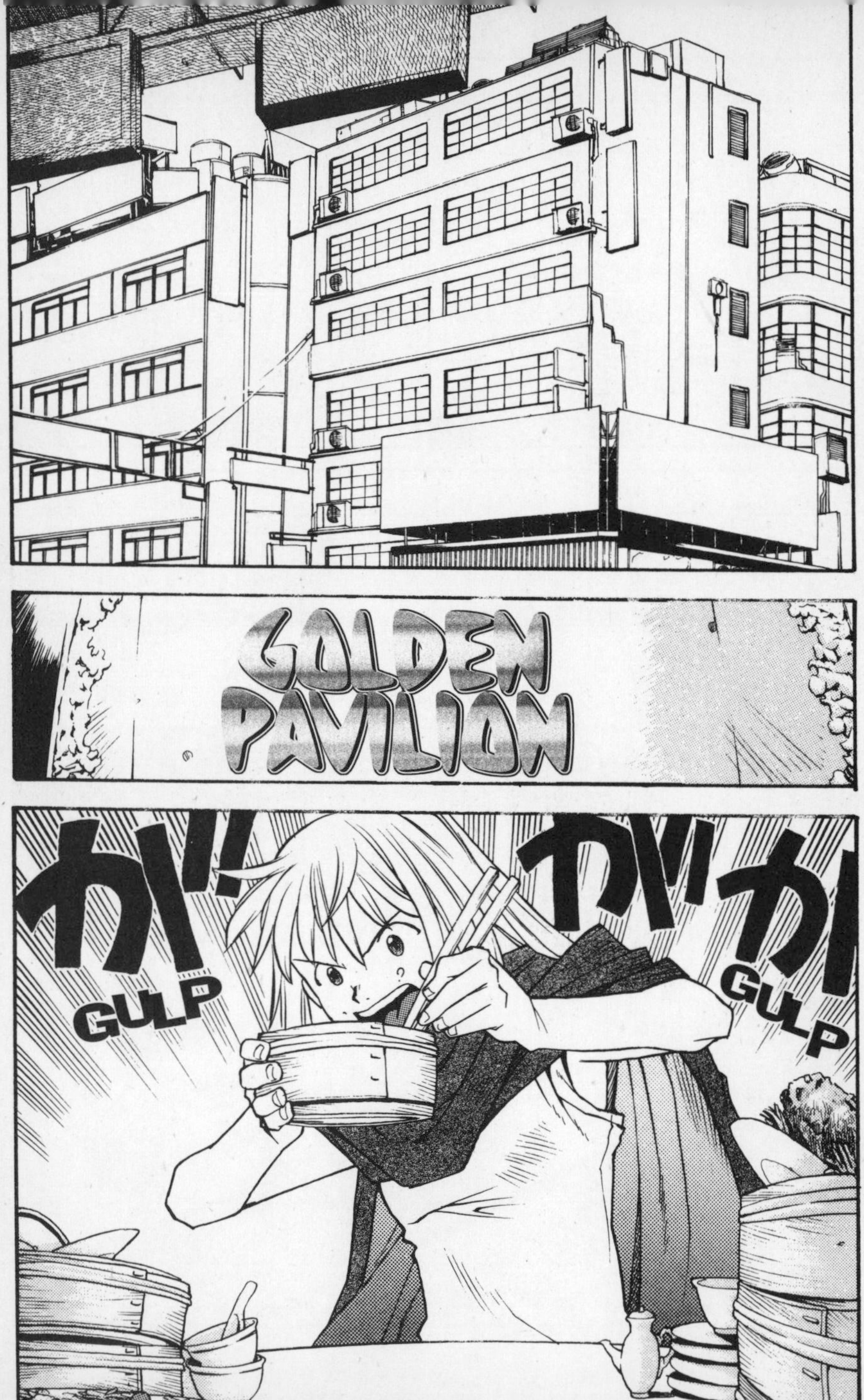
GOLDEN PAVILION
GULP
GULP

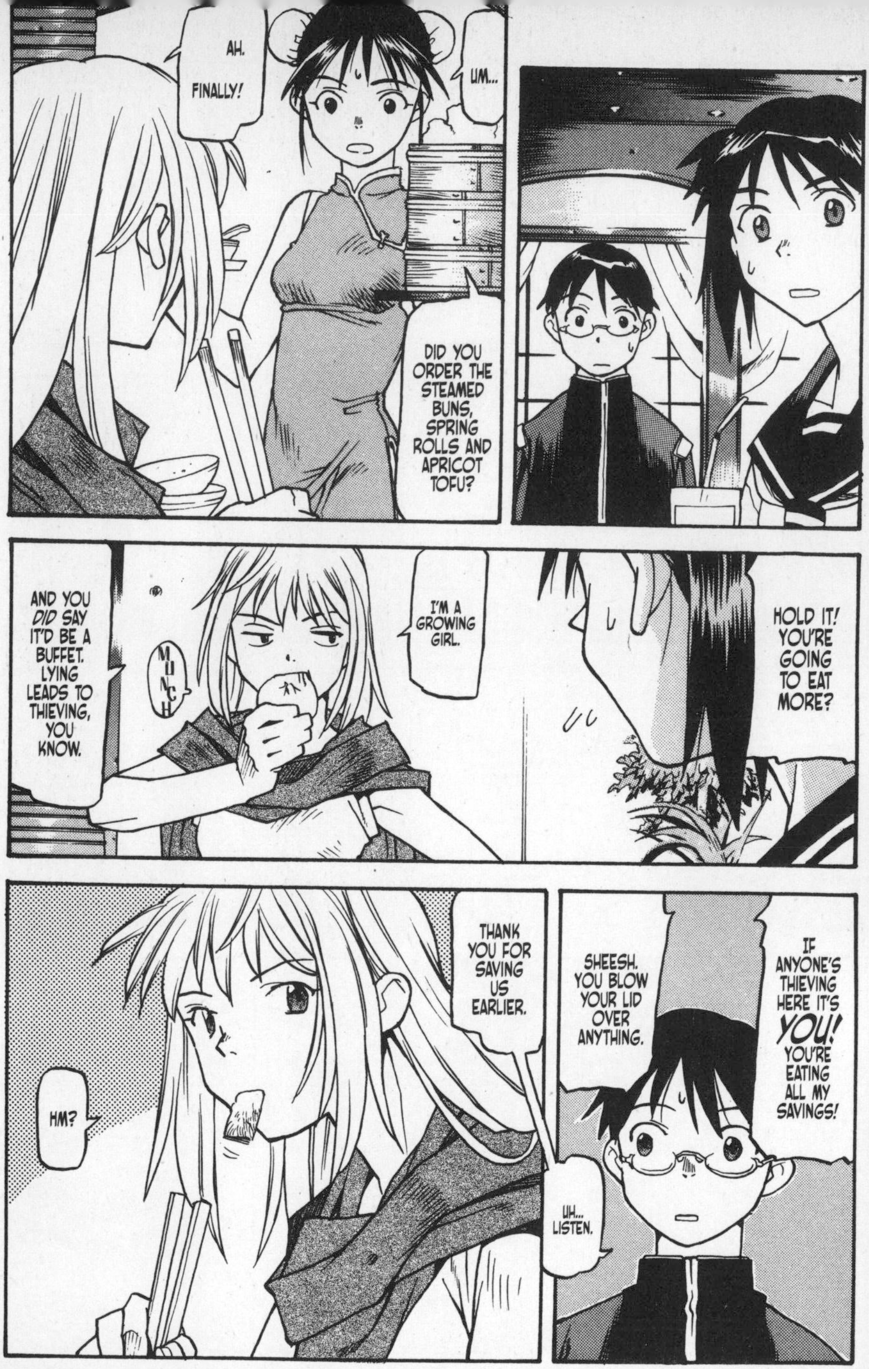
UM...
AH. FINALLY!
DID YOU ORDER THE STEAMED BUNS, SPRING ROLLS AND APRICOT TOFU?
HOLD IT! YOU'RE GOING TO EAT MORE?
I'M A GROWING GIRL.
MUNCH
AND YOU *DID* SAY IT'D BE A BUFFET. LYING LEADS TO THIEVING, YOU KNOW.
IF ANYONE'S THIEVING HERE IT'S *YOU!* YOU'RE EATING ALL MY SAVINGS!
SHEESH. YOU BLOW YOUR LID OVER ANYTHING.
UH... LISTEN.
THANK YOU FOR SAVING US EARLIER.
HM?

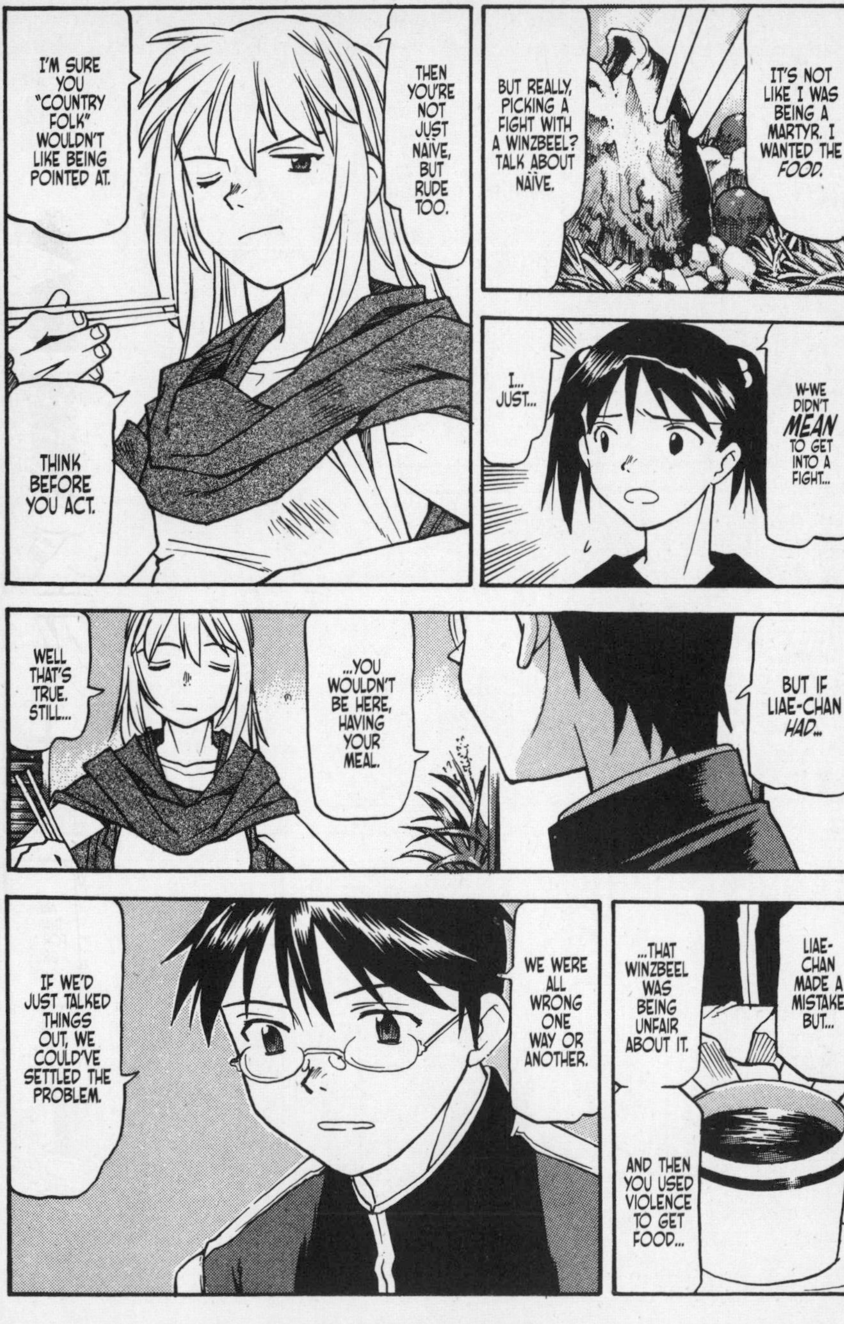
IT'S NOT LIKE I WAS BEING A MARTYR. I WANTED THE *FOOD.*
BUT REALLY, PICKING A FIGHT WITH A WINZBEEL? TALK ABOUT NAÏVE.
W-WE DIDN'T **MEAN** TO GET INTO A FIGHT...
I... JUST...
THEN YOU'RE NOT JUST NAÏVE, BUT RUDE TOO.
I'M SURE YOU "COUNTRY FOLK" WOULDN'T LIKE BEING POINTED AT.
THINK BEFORE YOU ACT.
BUT IF LIAE-CHAN *HAD*...
...YOU WOULDN'T BE HERE, HAVING YOUR MEAL.
WELL THAT'S TRUE. STILL...
LIAE-CHAN MADE A MISTAKE BUT...
...THAT WINZBEEL WAS BEING UNFAIR ABOUT IT.
AND THEN YOU USED VIOLENCE TO GET FOOD...
WE WERE ALL WRONG ONE WAY OR ANOTHER.
IF WE'D JUST TALKED THINGS OUT, WE COULD'VE SETTLED THE PROBLEM.

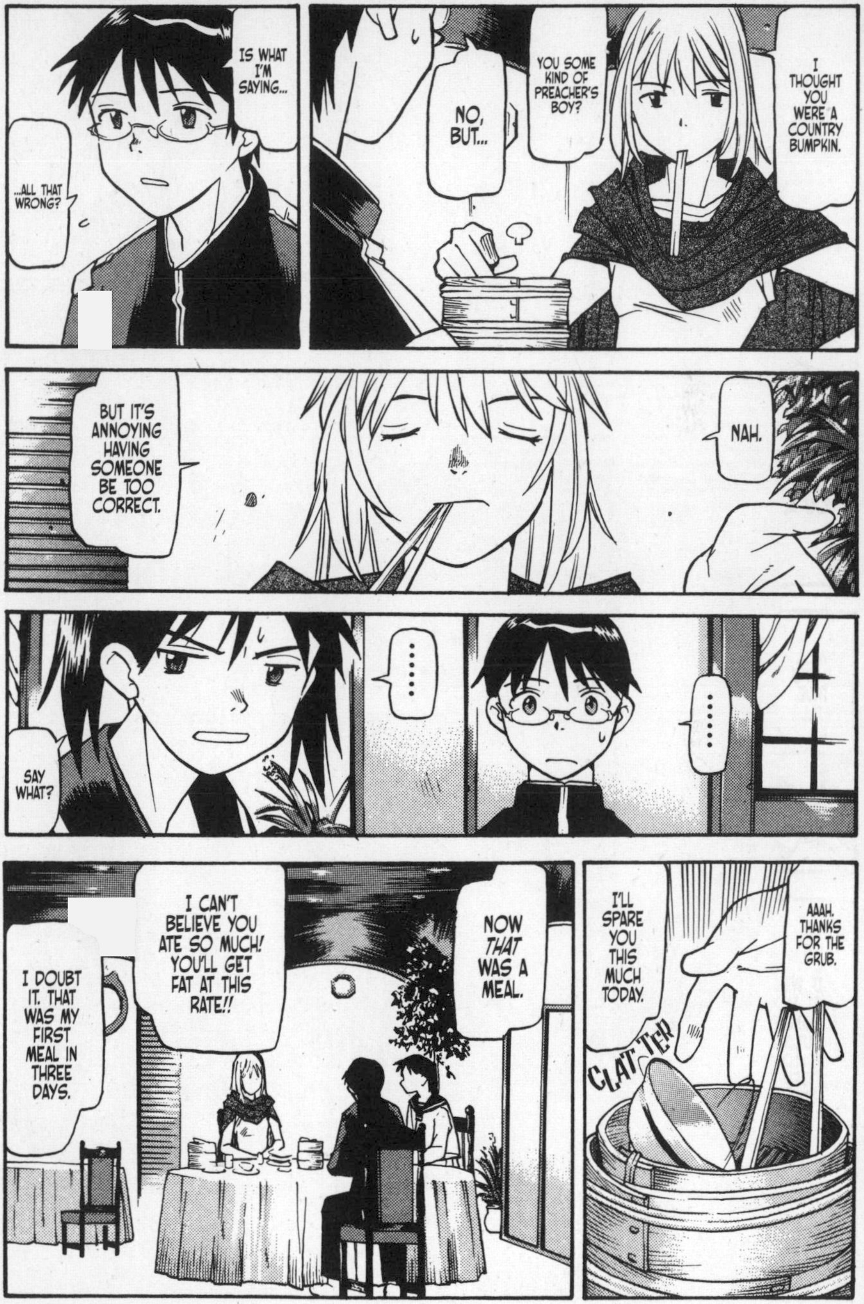
I THOUGHT YOU WERE A COUNTRY BUMPKIN.
YOU SOME KIND OF PREACHER'S BOY?
NO, BUT...
IS WHAT I'M SAYING...
...ALL THAT WRONG?
NAH.
BUT IT'S ANNOYING HAVING SOMEONE BE TOO CORRECT.
......
......
SAY WHAT?
AAAH. THANKS FOR THE GRUB.
I'LL SPARE YOU THIS MUCH TODAY.
CLATTER
NOW *THAT* WAS A MEAL.
I CAN'T BELIEVE YOU ATE SO MUCH! YOU'LL GET FAT AT THIS RATE!!
I DOUBT IT. THAT WAS MY FIRST MEAL IN THREE DAYS.

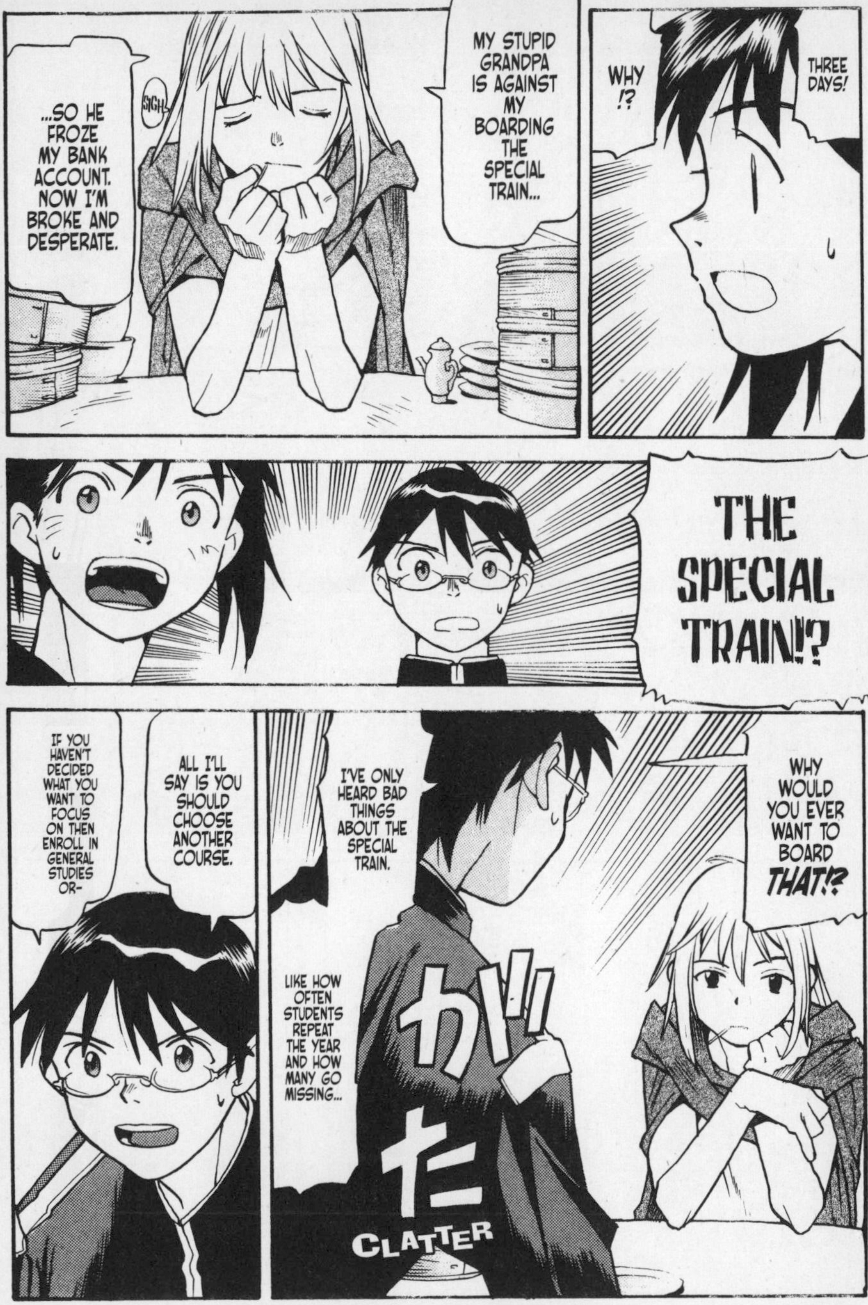
THREE DAYS!
WHY!?
MY STUPID GRANDPA IS AGAINST MY BOARDING THE SPECIAL TRAIN...
SIGH
...SO HE FROZE MY BANK ACCOUNT. NOW I'M BROKE AND DESPERATE.
THE SPECIAL TRAIN!?
WHY WOULD YOU EVER WANT TO BOARD THAT!?
I'VE ONLY HEARD BAD THINGS ABOUT THE SPECIAL TRAIN.
LIKE HOW OFTEN STUDENTS REPEAT THE YEAR AND HOW MANY GO MISSING...
CLATTER
ALL I'LL SAY IS YOU SHOULD CHOOSE ANOTHER COURSE.
IF YOU HAVEN'T DECIDED WHAT YOU WANT TO FOCUS ON THEN ENROLL IN GENERAL STUDIES OR-

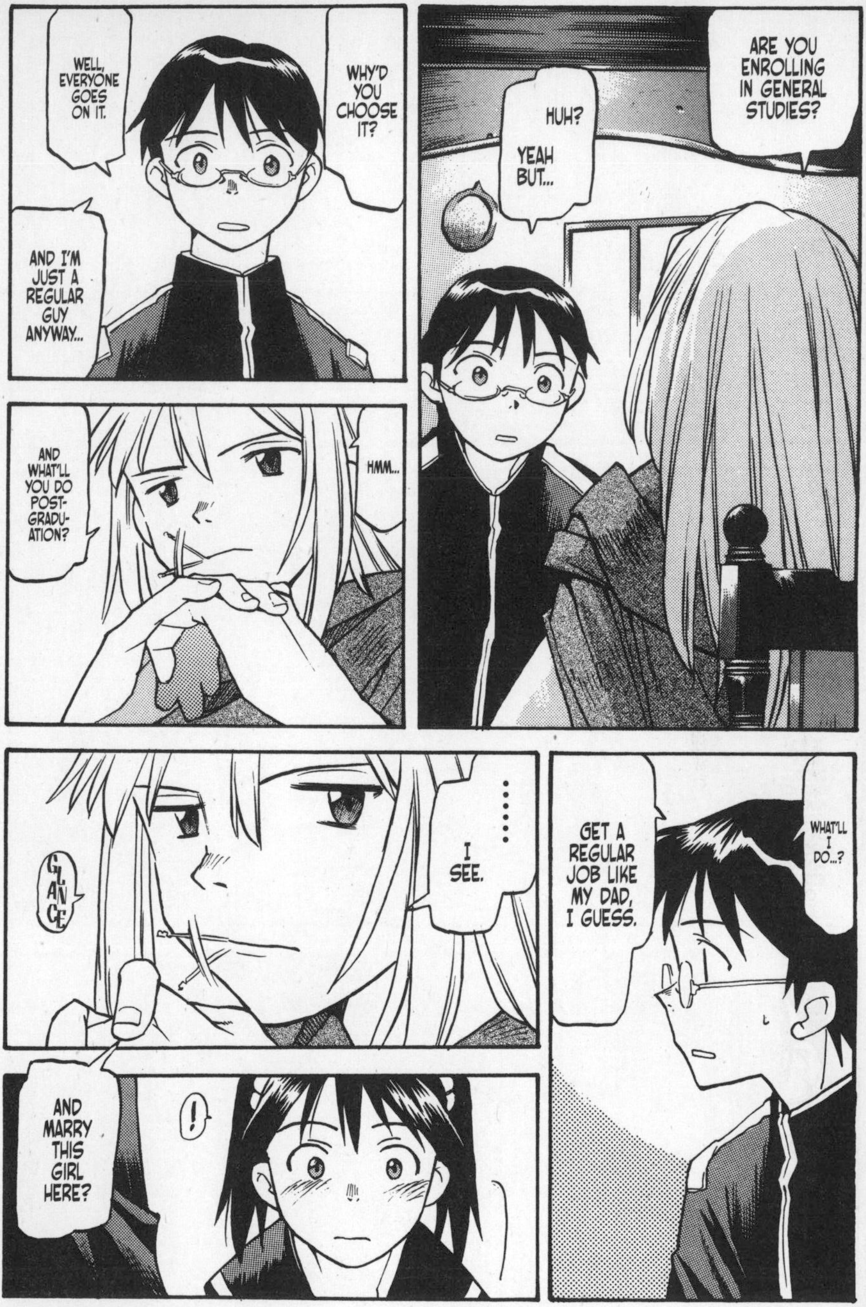
ARE YOU ENROLLING IN GENERAL STUDIES?
HUH?
YEAH BUT...
WHY'D YOU CHOOSE IT?
WELL, EVERYONE GOES ON IT.
AND I'M JUST A REGULAR GUY ANYWAY...
HMM...
AND WHAT'LL YOU DO POST-GRADUATION?
WHAT'LL I DO...?
GET A REGULAR JOB LIKE MY DAD, I GUESS.
......
I SEE.
GLANCE
AND MARRY THIS GIRL HERE?
!

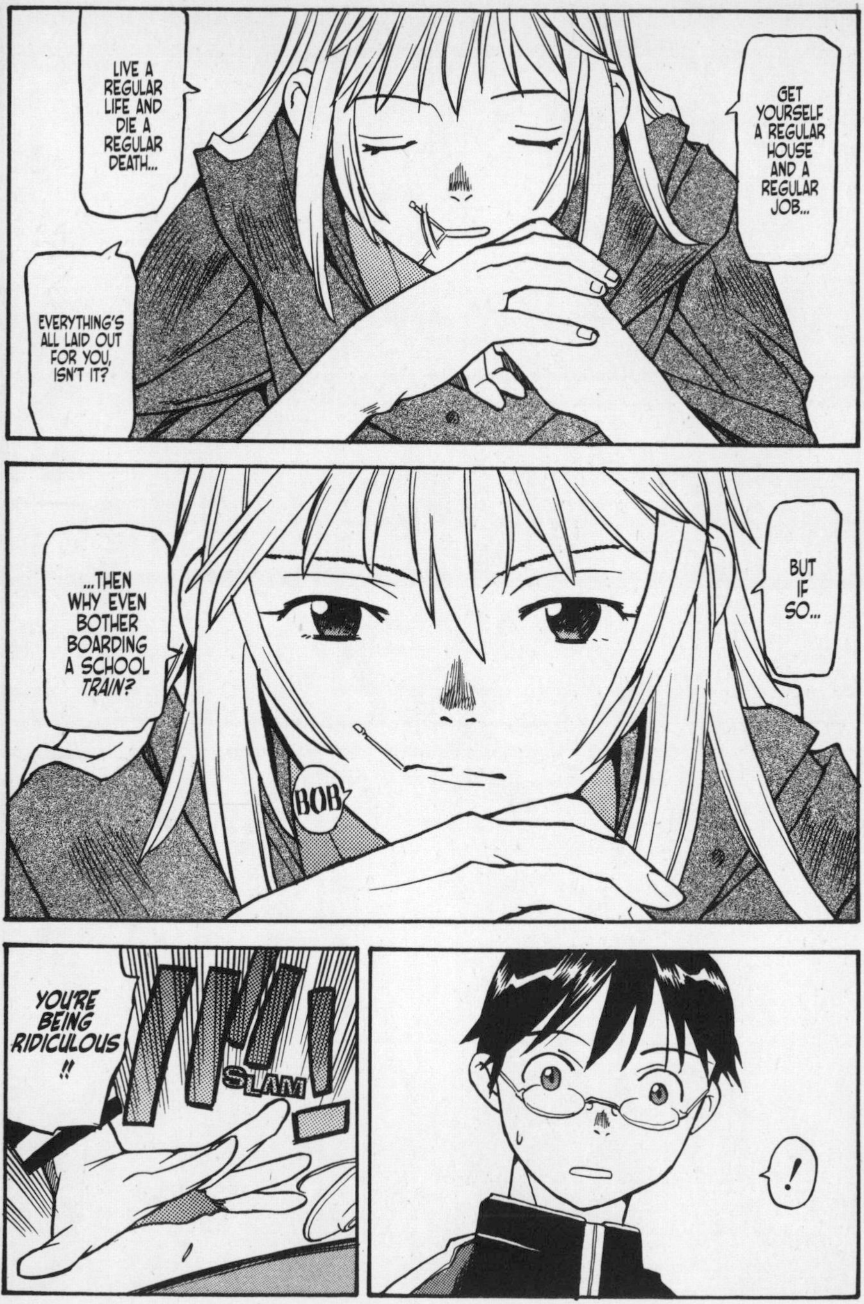
GET YOURSELF A REGULAR HOUSE AND A REGULAR JOB...
LIVE A REGULAR LIFE AND DIE A REGULAR DEATH...
EVERYTHING'S ALL LAID OUT FOR YOU, ISN'T IT?
BUT IF SO...
...THEN WHY EVEN BOTHER BOARDING A SCHOOL *TRAIN?*
BOB
!
YOU'RE BEING RIDICULOUS!!
SLAM

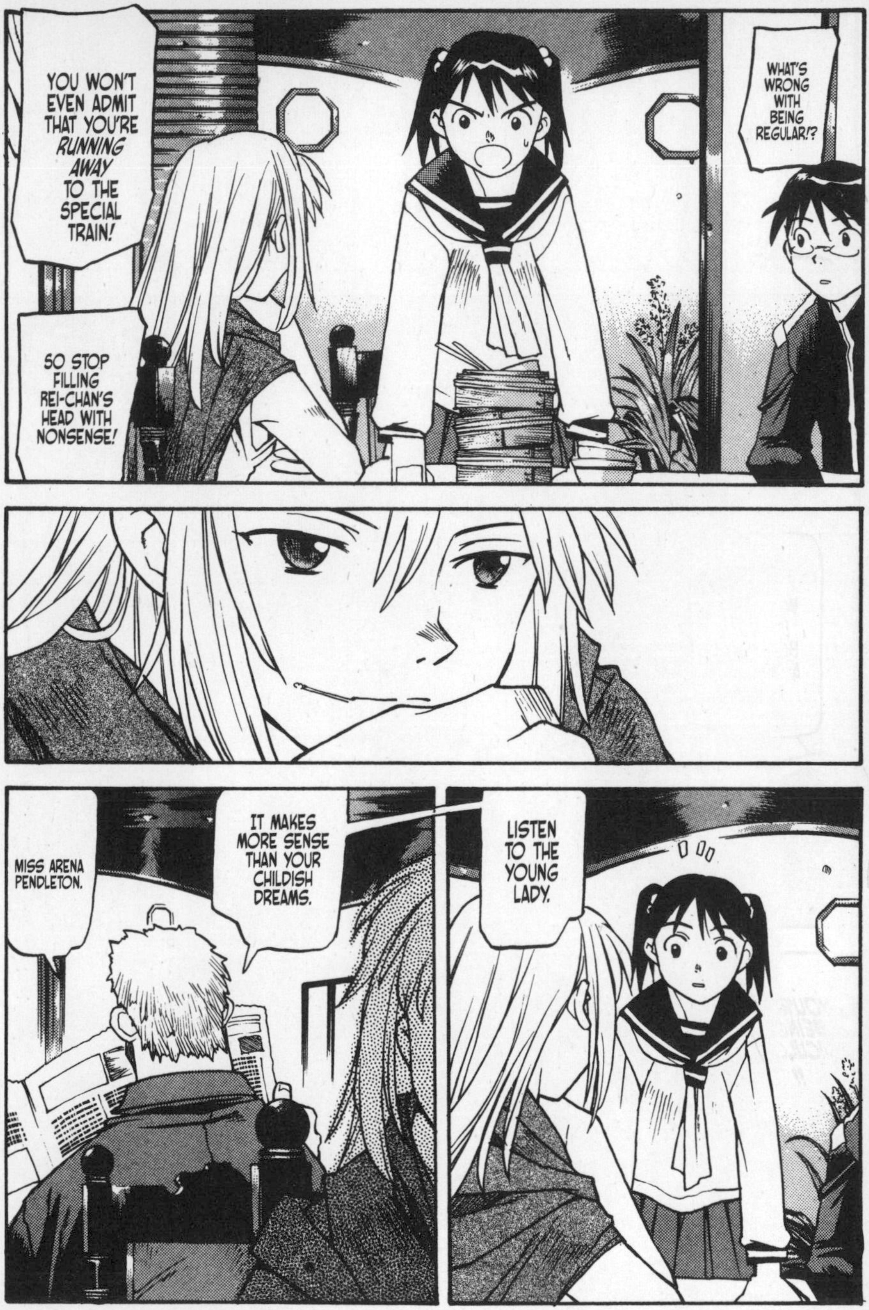
WHAT'S WRONG WITH BEING REGULAR!?
YOU WON'T EVEN ADMIT THAT YOU'RE *RUNNING AWAY* TO THE SPECIAL TRAIN!
SO STOP FILLING REI-CHAN'S HEAD WITH NONSENSE!
LISTEN TO THE YOUNG LADY.
IT MAKES MORE SENSE THAN YOUR CHILDISH DREAMS.
MISS ARENA PENDLETON.

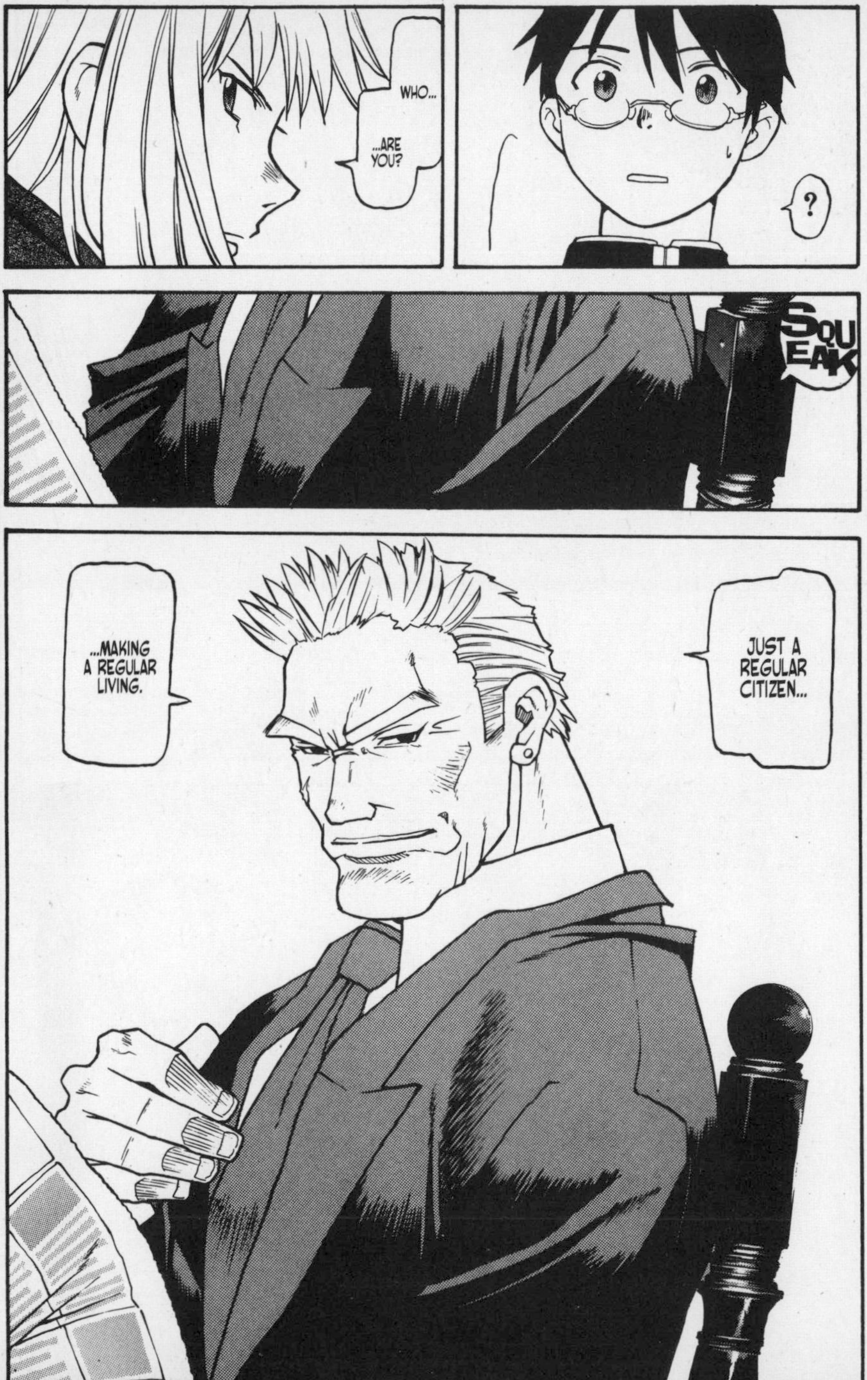
?
WHO...
...ARE YOU?
SQUEAK
JUST A REGULAR CITIZEN...
...MAKING A REGULAR LIVING.

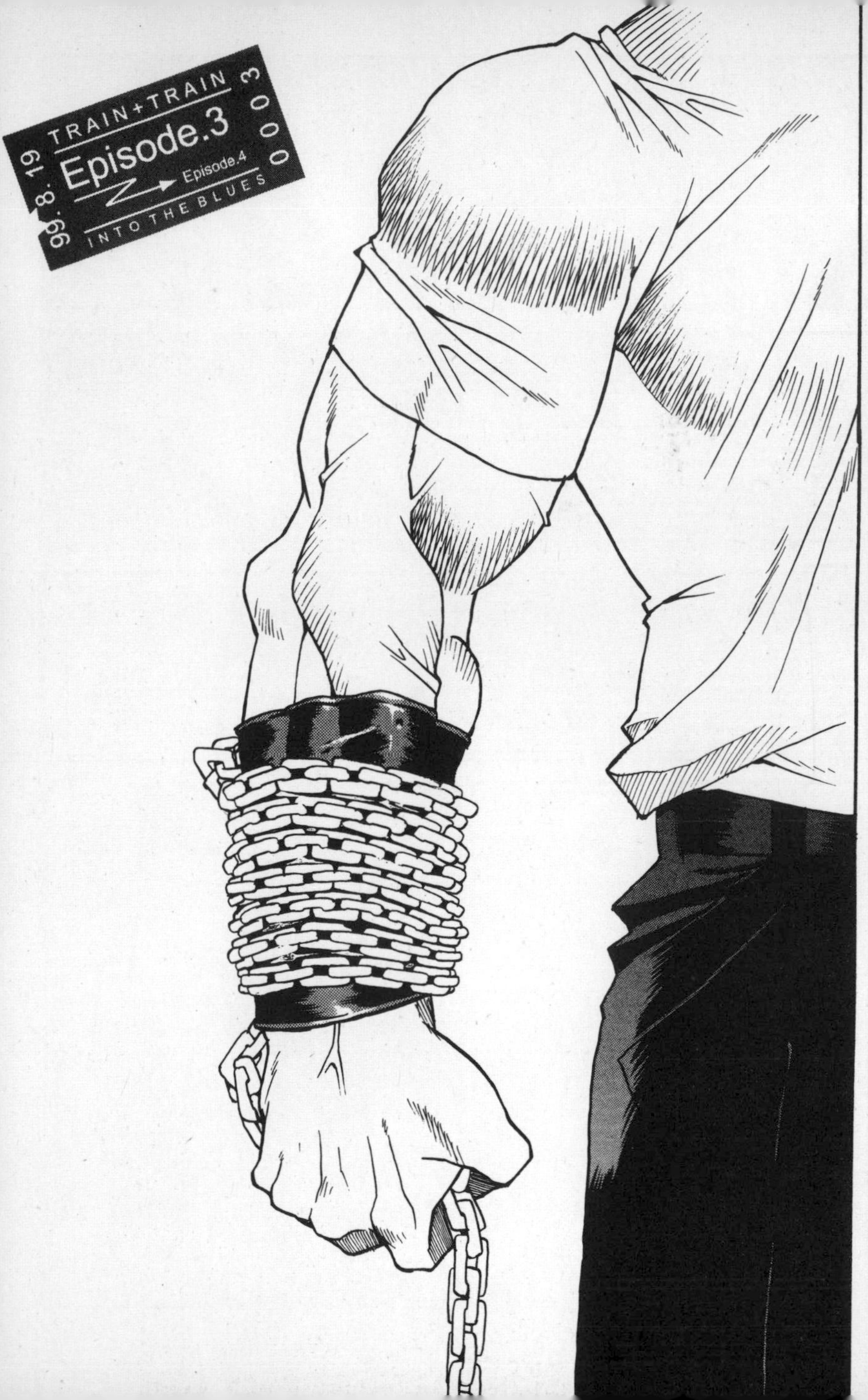
99. 8. 19
TRAIN+TRAIN
Episode.3
Episode.4
INTO THE BLUES
0003

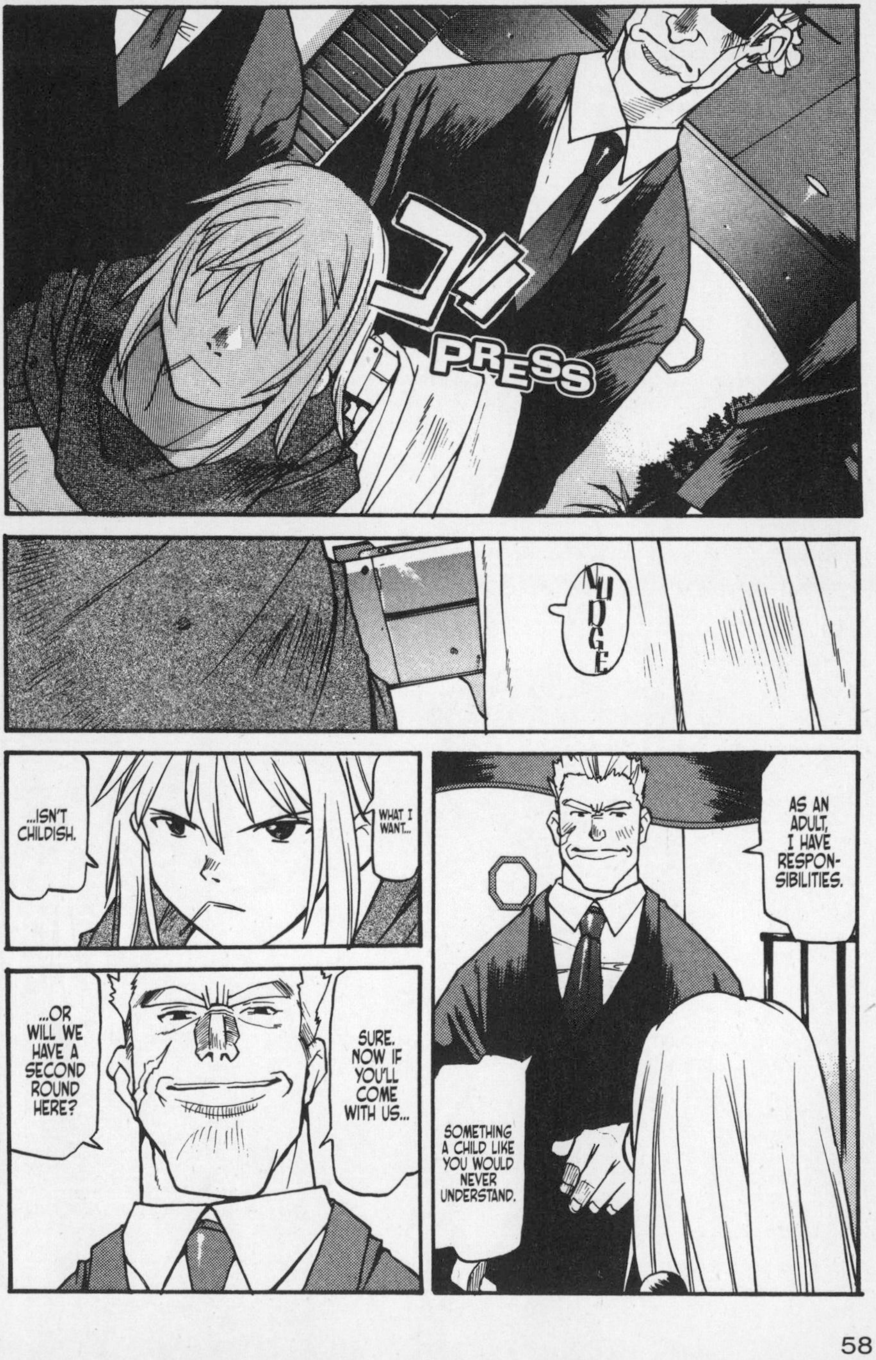
PRESS
NUDGE
AS AN ADULT, I HAVE RESPONSIBILITIES.
SOMETHING A CHILD LIKE YOU WOULD NEVER UNDERSTAND.
WHAT I WANT...
...ISN'T CHILDISH.
SURE. NOW IF YOU'LL COME WITH US...
...OR WILL WE HAVE A SECOND ROUND HERE?

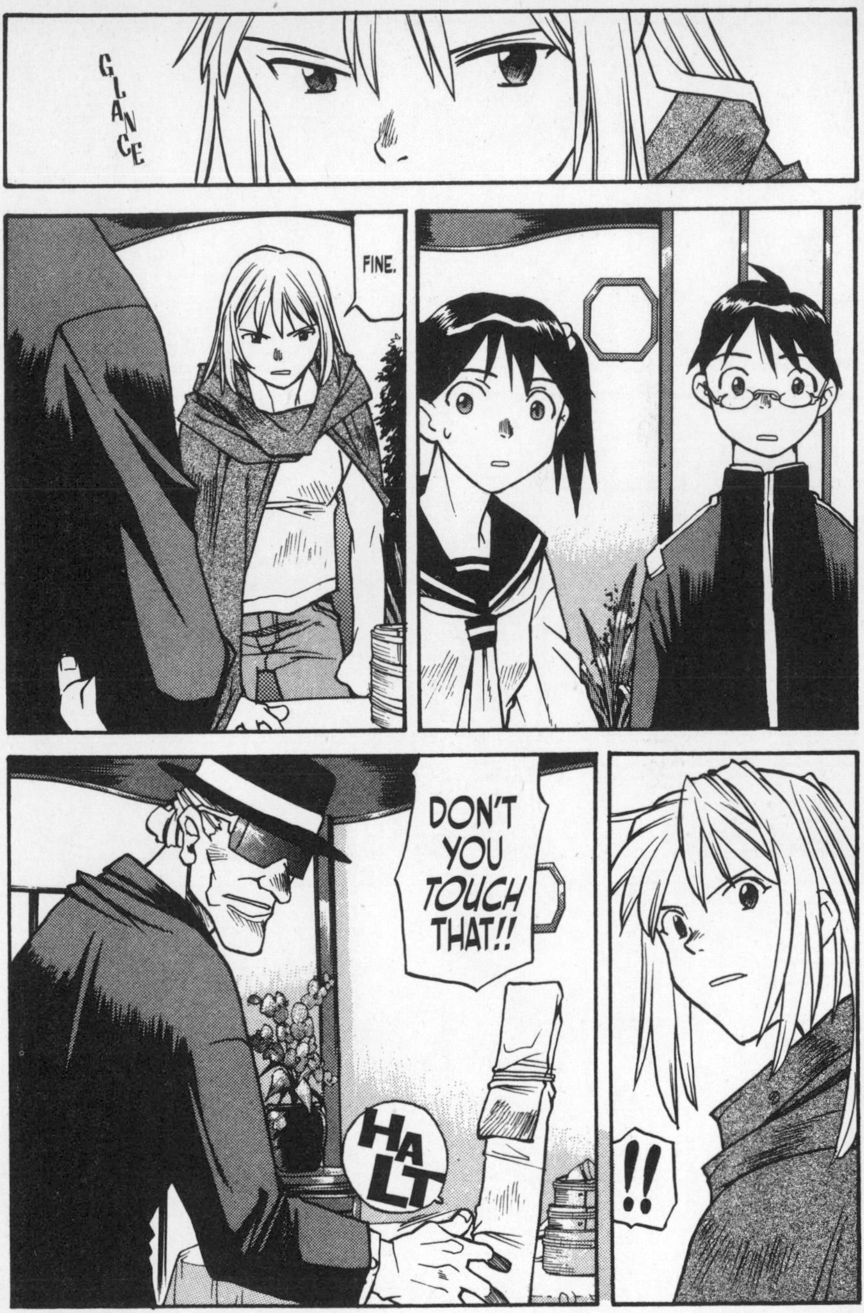
GLANCE
FINE.
!!
DON'T YOU *TOUCH* THAT!!
HALT

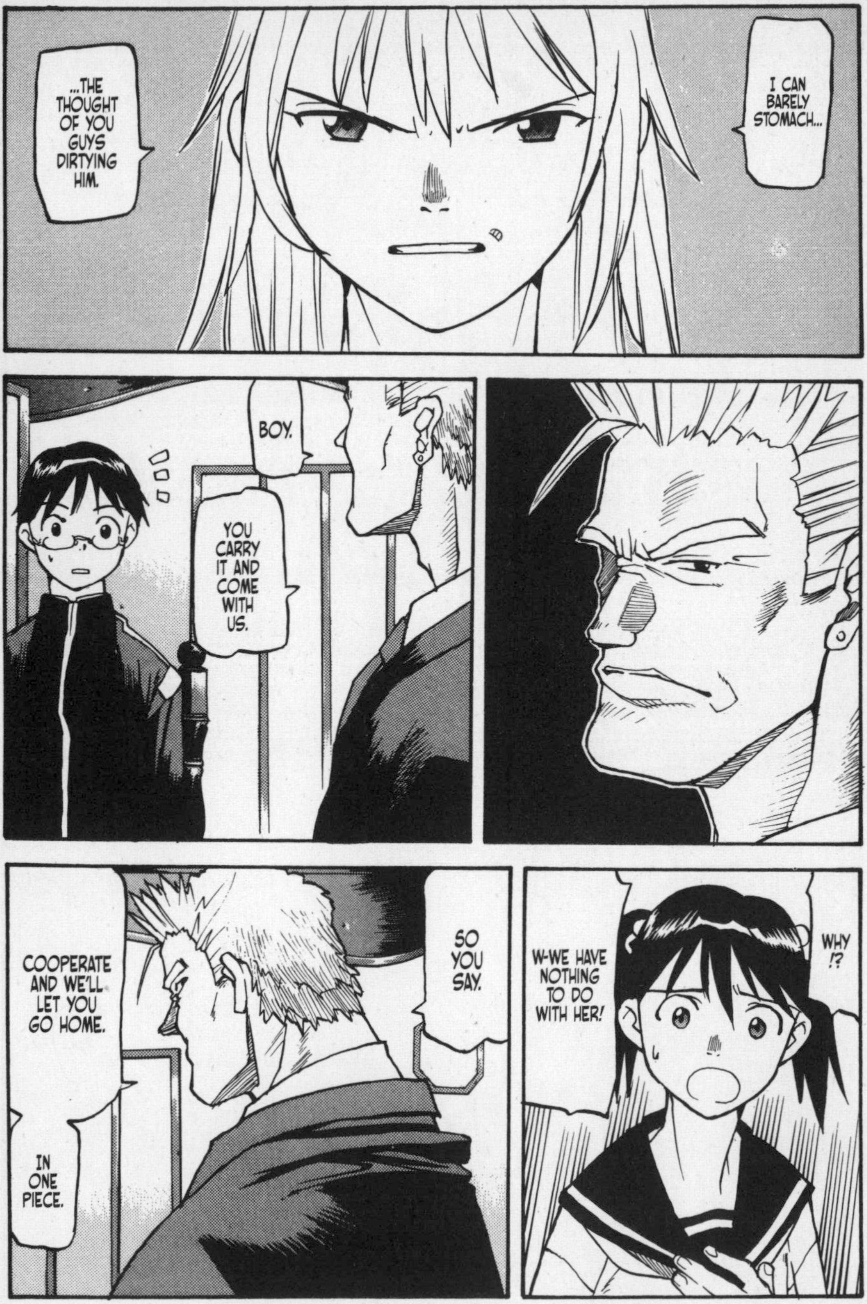
I CAN BARELY STOMACH...
...THE THOUGHT OF YOU GUYS DIRTYING HIM.
BOY.
YOU CARRY IT AND COME WITH US.
WHY!?
W-WE HAVE NOTHING TO DO WITH HER!
SO YOU SAY.
COOPERATE AND WE'LL LET YOU GO HOME.
IN ONE PIECE.

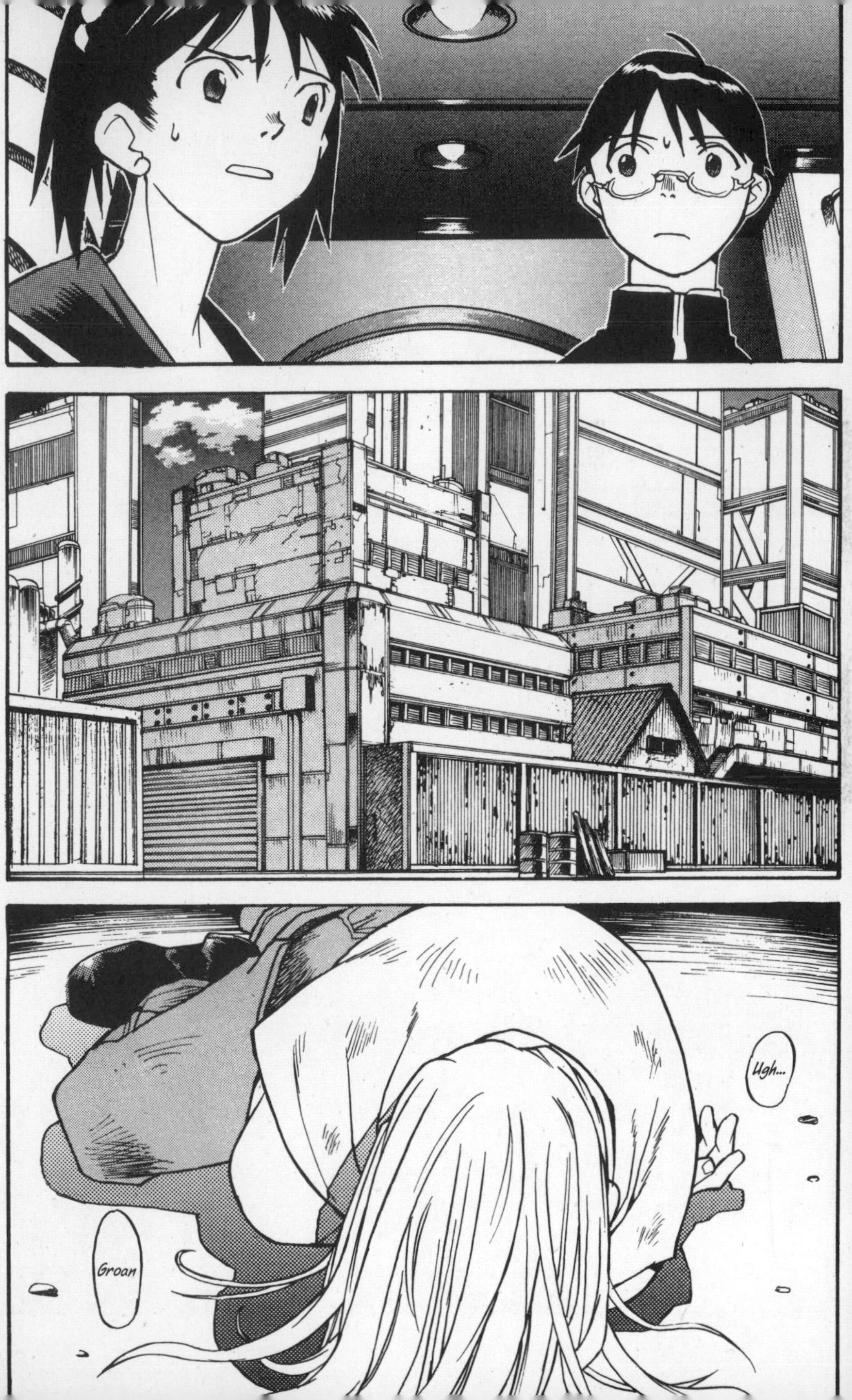
Ugh...
Groan

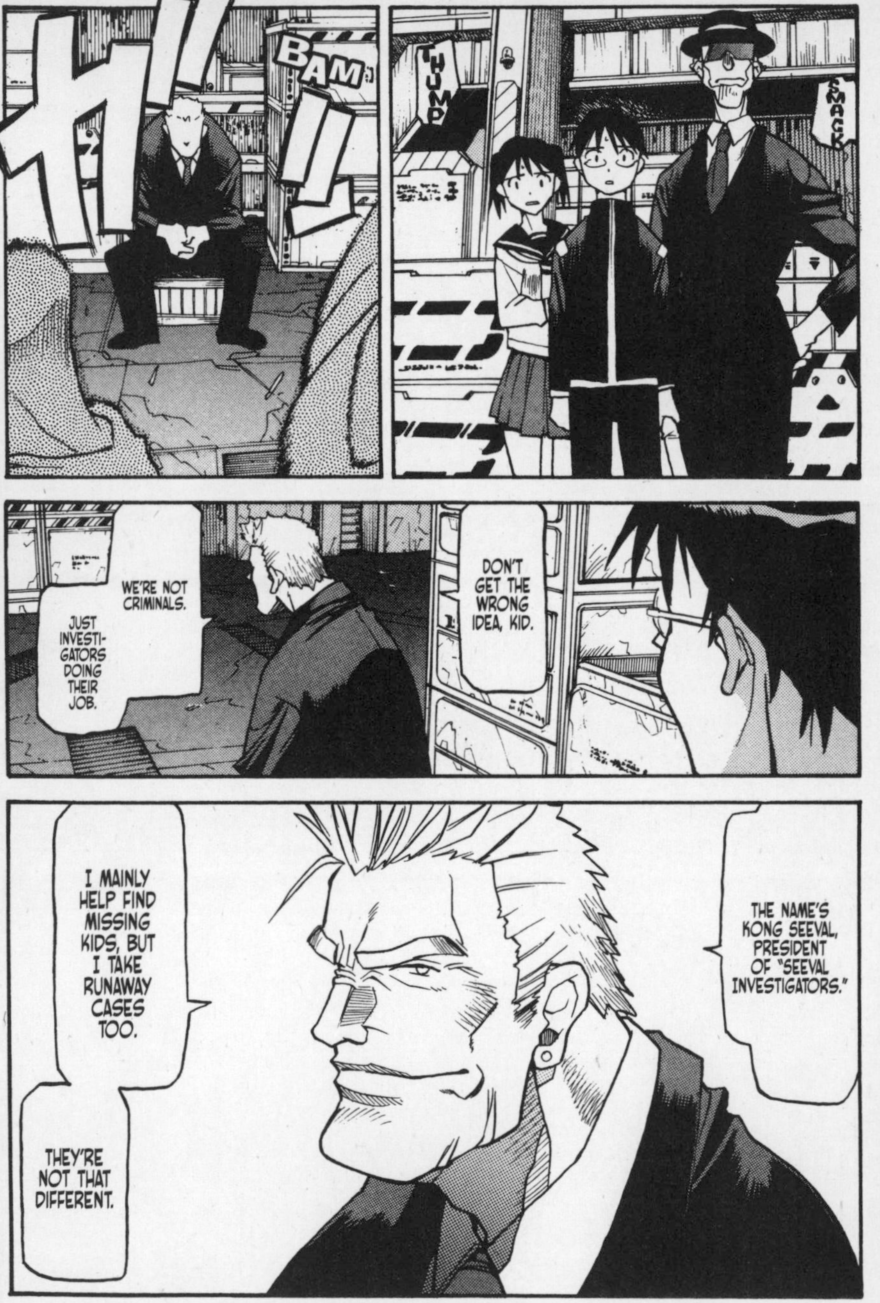
SMACK
THUMP
BAM
DON'T GET THE WRONG IDEA, KID.
WE'RE NOT CRIMINALS.
JUST INVESTIGATORS DOING THEIR JOB.
THE NAME'S KONG SEEVAL, PRESIDENT OF "SEEVAL INVESTIGATORS."
I MAINLY HELP FIND MISSING KIDS, BUT I TAKE RUNAWAY CASES TOO.
THEY'RE NOT THAT DIFFERENT.

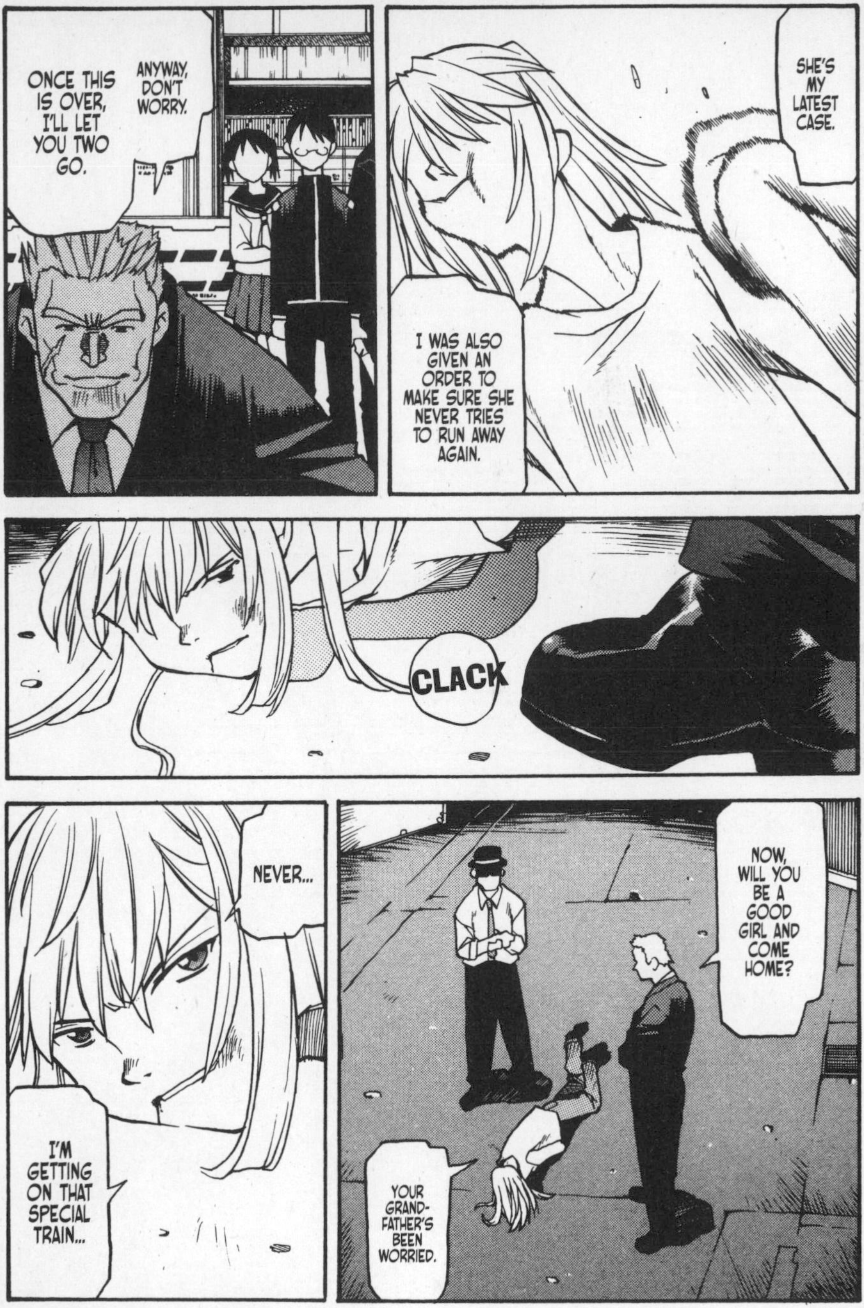
SHE'S MY LATEST CASE.
I WAS ALSO GIVEN AN ORDER TO MAKE SURE SHE NEVER TRIES TO RUN AWAY AGAIN.
ANYWAY, DON'T WORRY.
ONCE THIS IS OVER, I'LL LET YOU TWO GO.
CLACK
NOW, WILL YOU BE A GOOD GIRL AND COME HOME?
YOUR GRAND-FATHER'S BEEN WORRIED.
NEVER...
I'M GETTING ON THAT SPECIAL TRAIN...

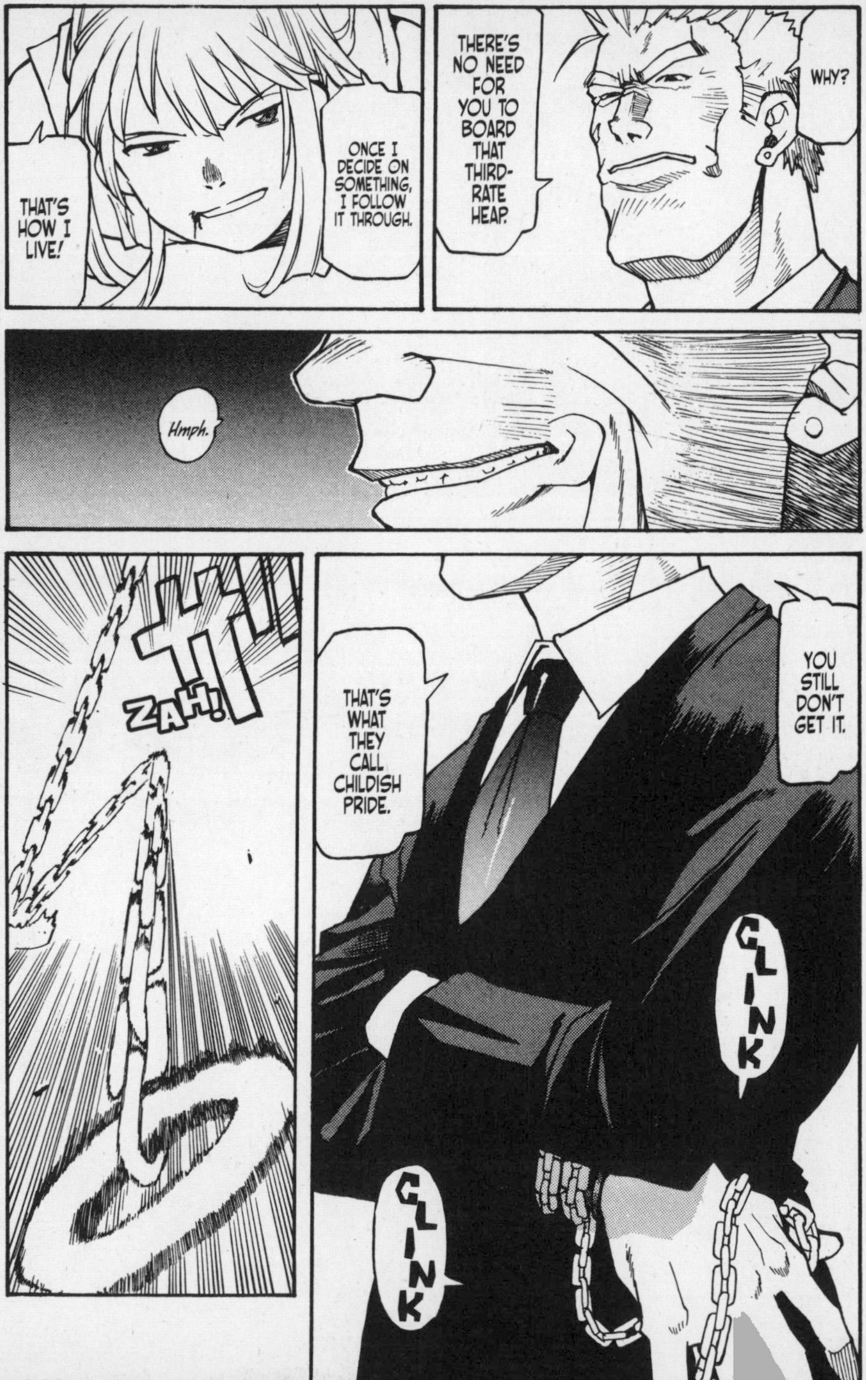
WHY?
THERE'S NO NEED FOR YOU TO BOARD THAT THIRD-RATE HEAP.
ONCE I DECIDE ON SOMETHING, I FOLLOW IT THROUGH.
THAT'S HOW I LIVE!
Hmph.
YOU STILL DON'T GET IT.
THAT'S WHAT THEY CALL CHILDISH PRIDE.
CLINK
CLINK
ZAH!

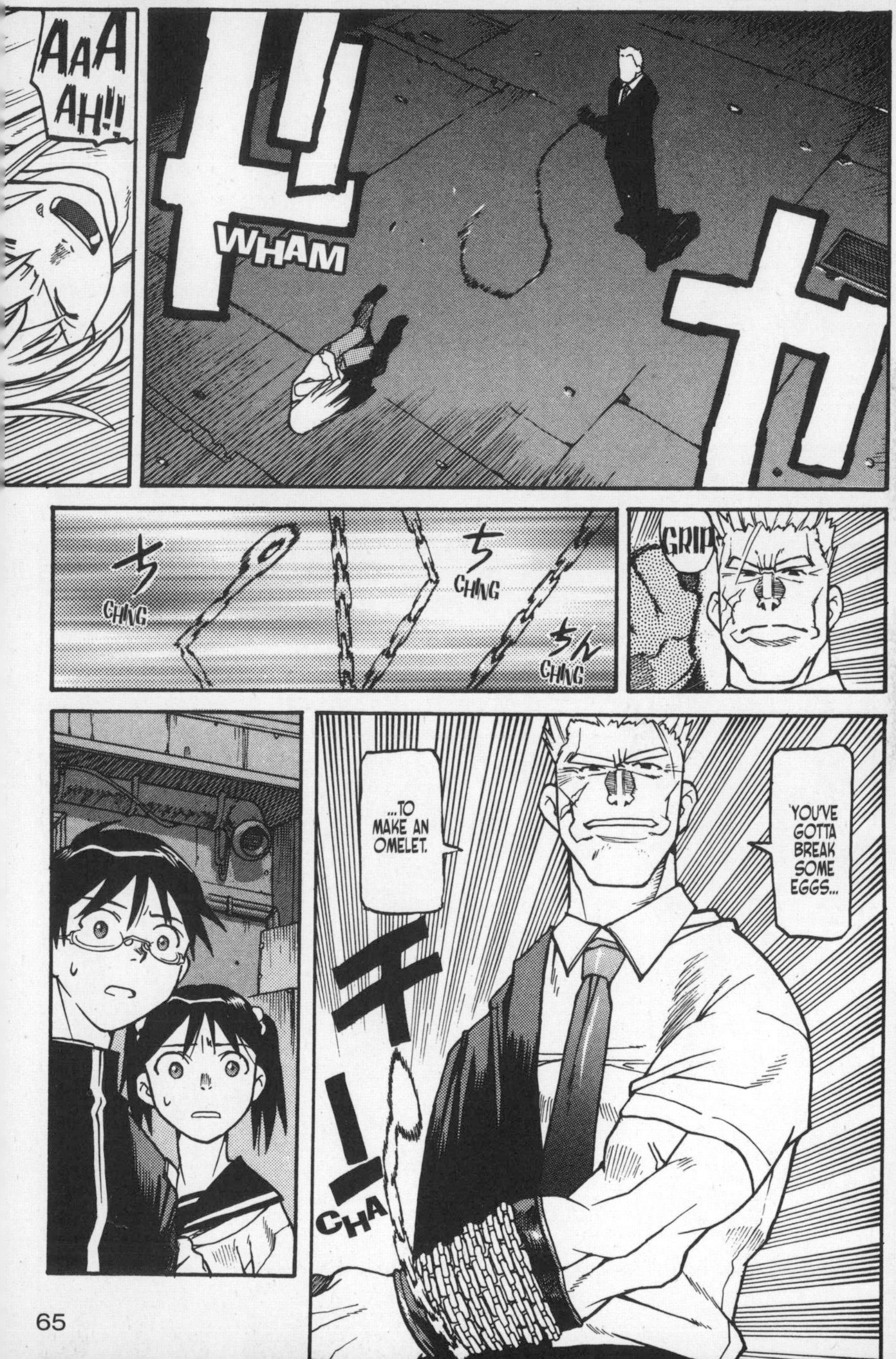
WHAM
AAA AH!!
GRIP
ち
CHING
ちん
CHING
ち
CHING
YOU'VE GOTTA BREAK SOME EGGS...
...TO MAKE AN OMELET.
CHA

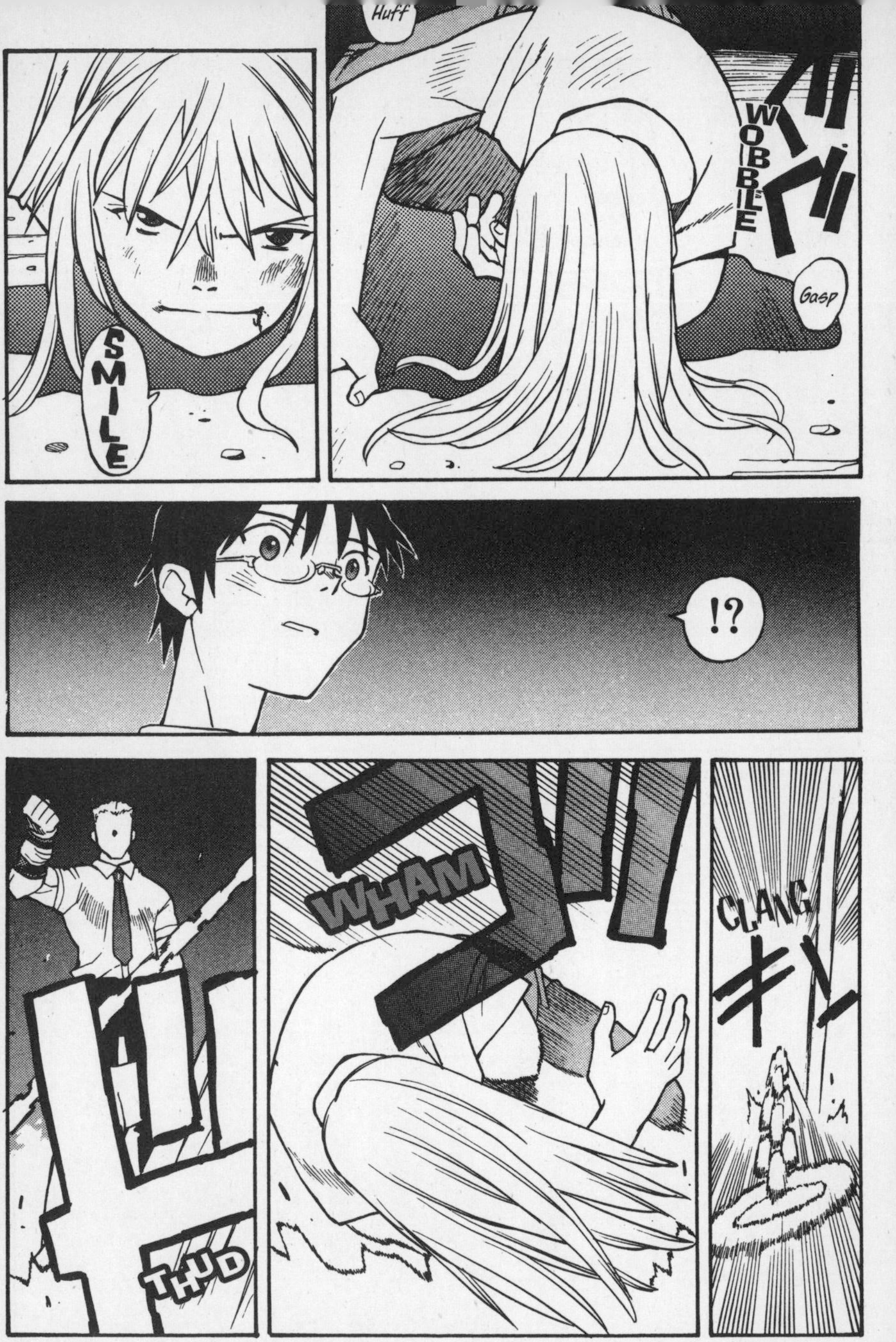
Huff
WOBBLE
Gasp
SMILE
!?
CLANG
WHAM
THUD

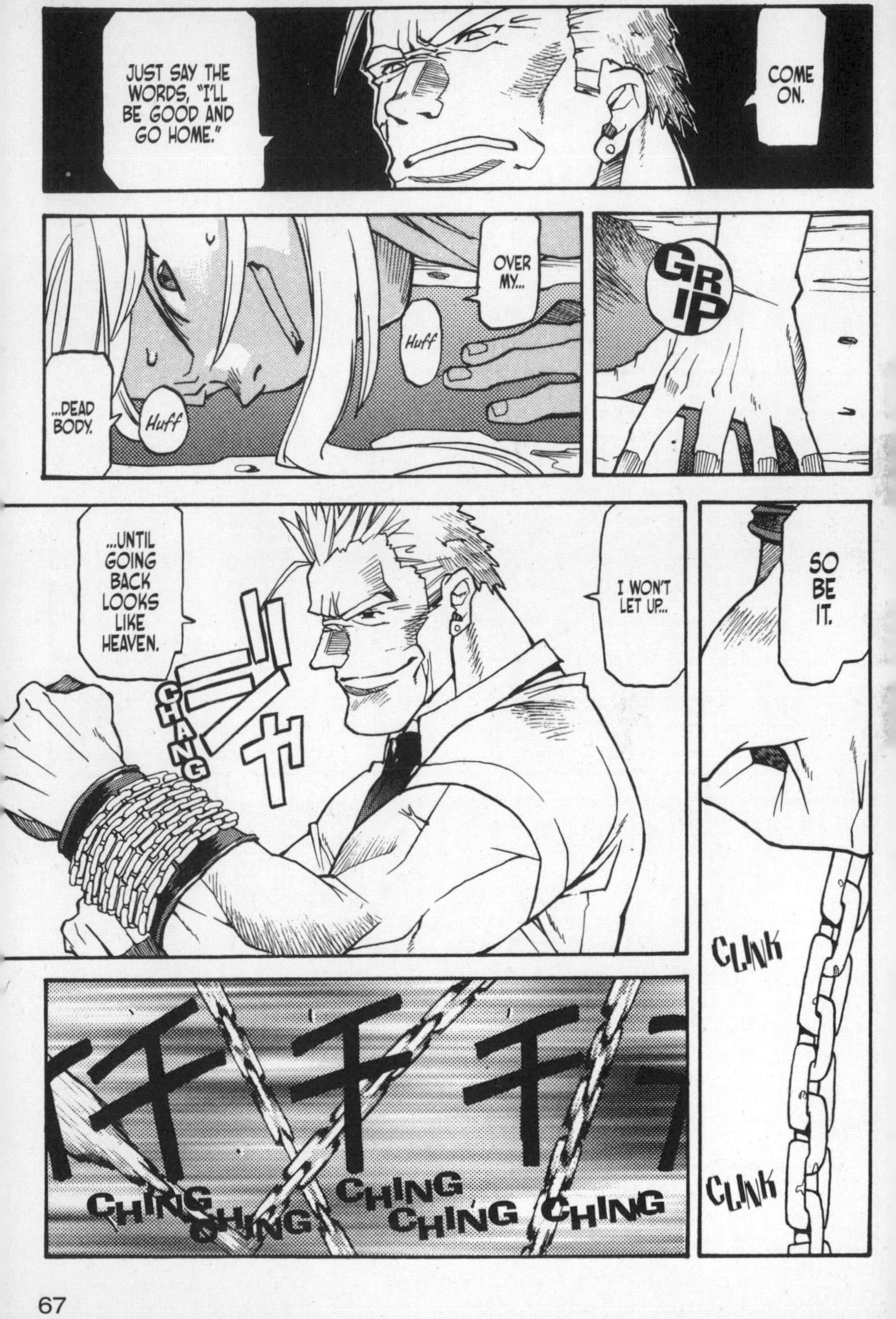
COME ON.
JUST SAY THE WORDS, "I'LL BE GOOD AND GO HOME."
GRIP
OVER MY...
Huff
Huff
...DEAD BODY.
SO BE IT.
CLINK
CLINK
I WON'T LET UP...
...UNTIL GOING BACK LOOKS LIKE HEAVEN.
CHANG
CHING CHING CHING CHING CHING CHING

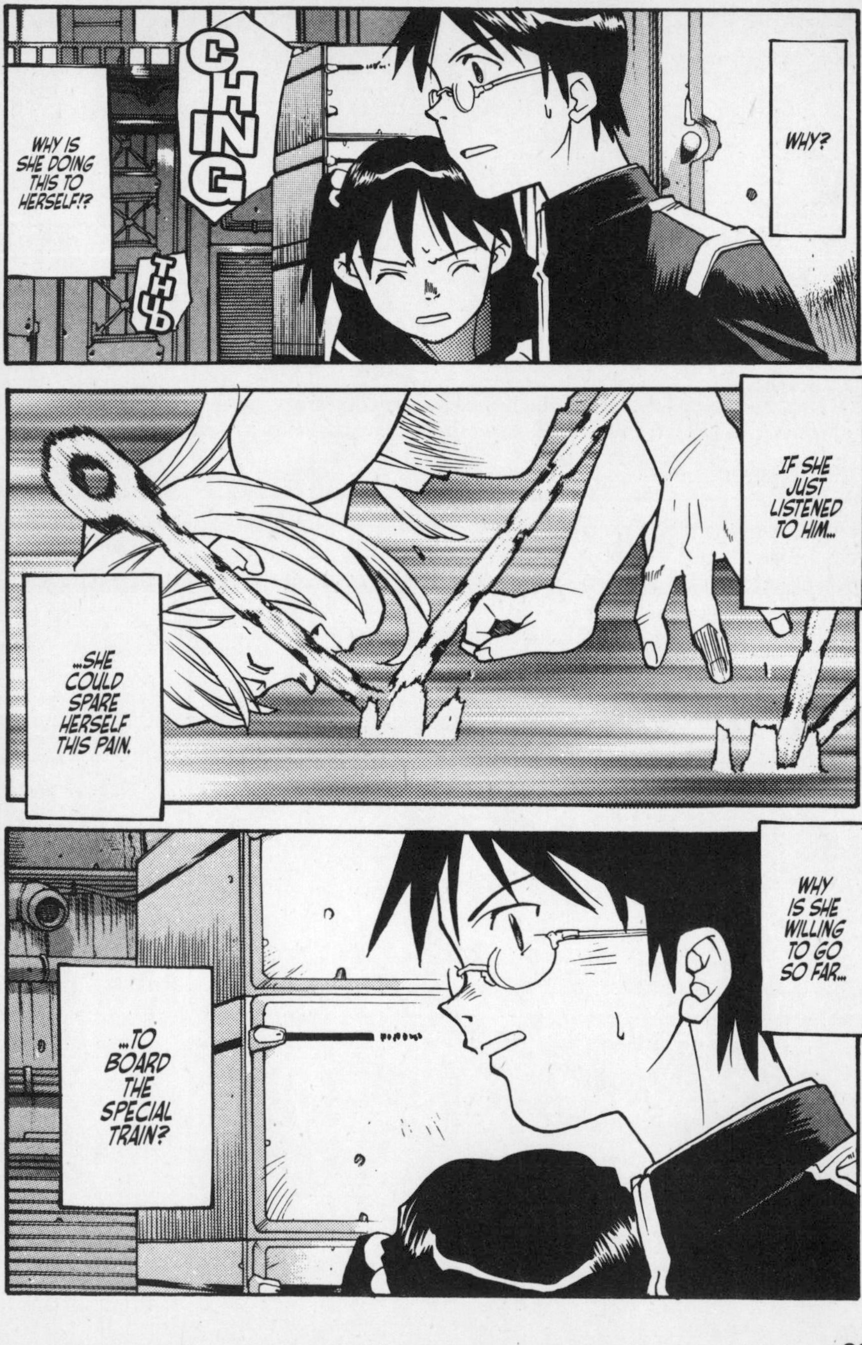
WHY?
CHING
THUD
WHY IS SHE DOING THIS TO HERSELF!?
IF SHE JUST LISTENED TO HIM...
...SHE COULD SPARE HERSELF THIS PAIN.
WHY IS SHE WILLING TO GO SO FAR...
...TO BOARD THE SPECIAL TRAIN?

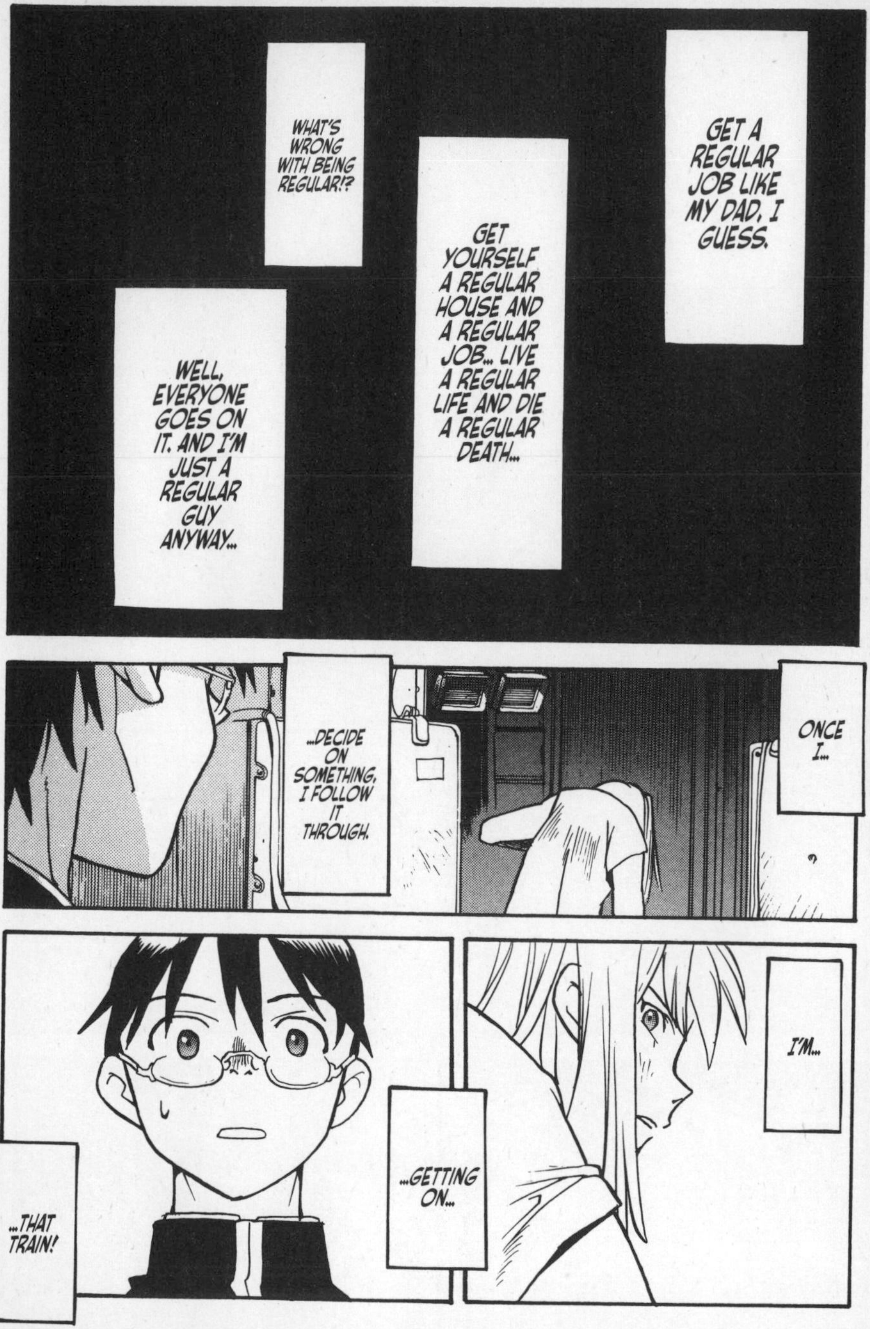
GET A REGULAR JOB LIKE MY DAD, I GUESS.
GET YOURSELF A REGULAR HOUSE AND A REGULAR JOB... LIVE A REGULAR LIFE AND DIE A REGULAR DEATH...
WHAT'S WRONG WITH BEING REGULAR!?
WELL, EVERYONE GOES ON IT. AND I'M JUST A REGULAR GUY ANYWAY...
ONCE I...
...DECIDE ON SOMETHING, I FOLLOW IT THROUGH.
I'M...
...GETTING ON...
...THAT TRAIN!

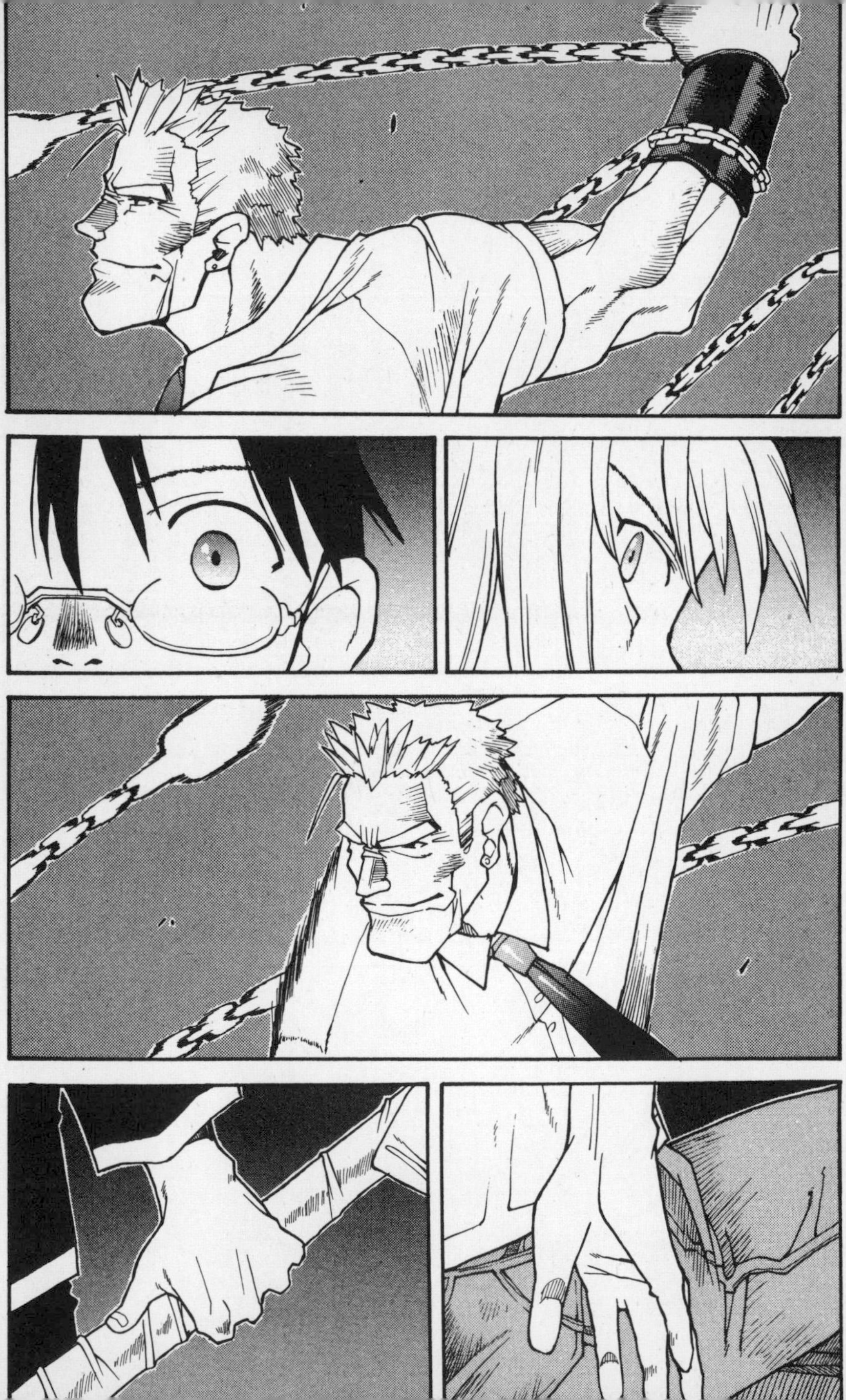

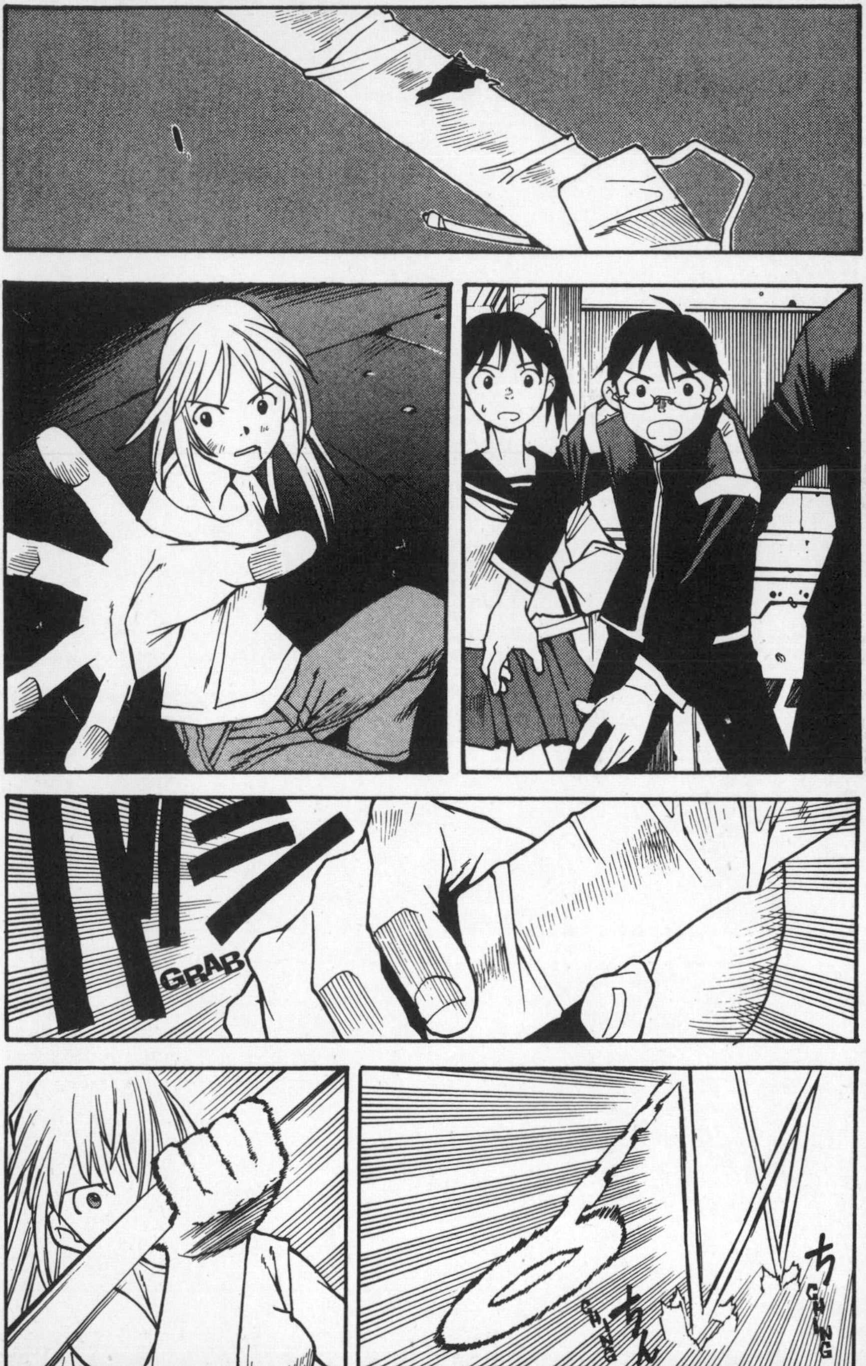
GRAB
ち
CHING
ちん
CHING

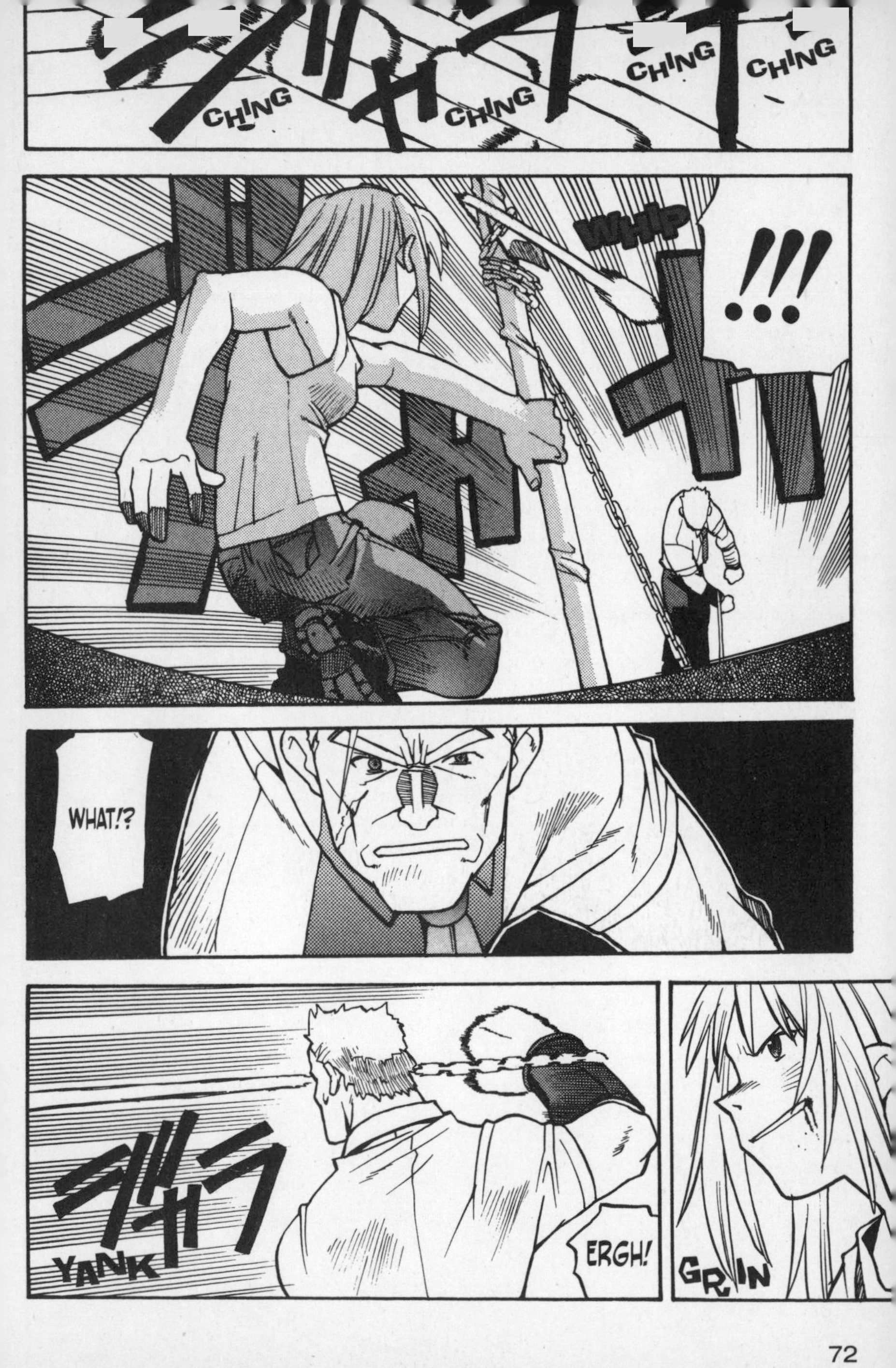
CHING
CHING
CHING
CHING
WHIP
!!!
WHAT!?
GRIN
ERGH!
YANK

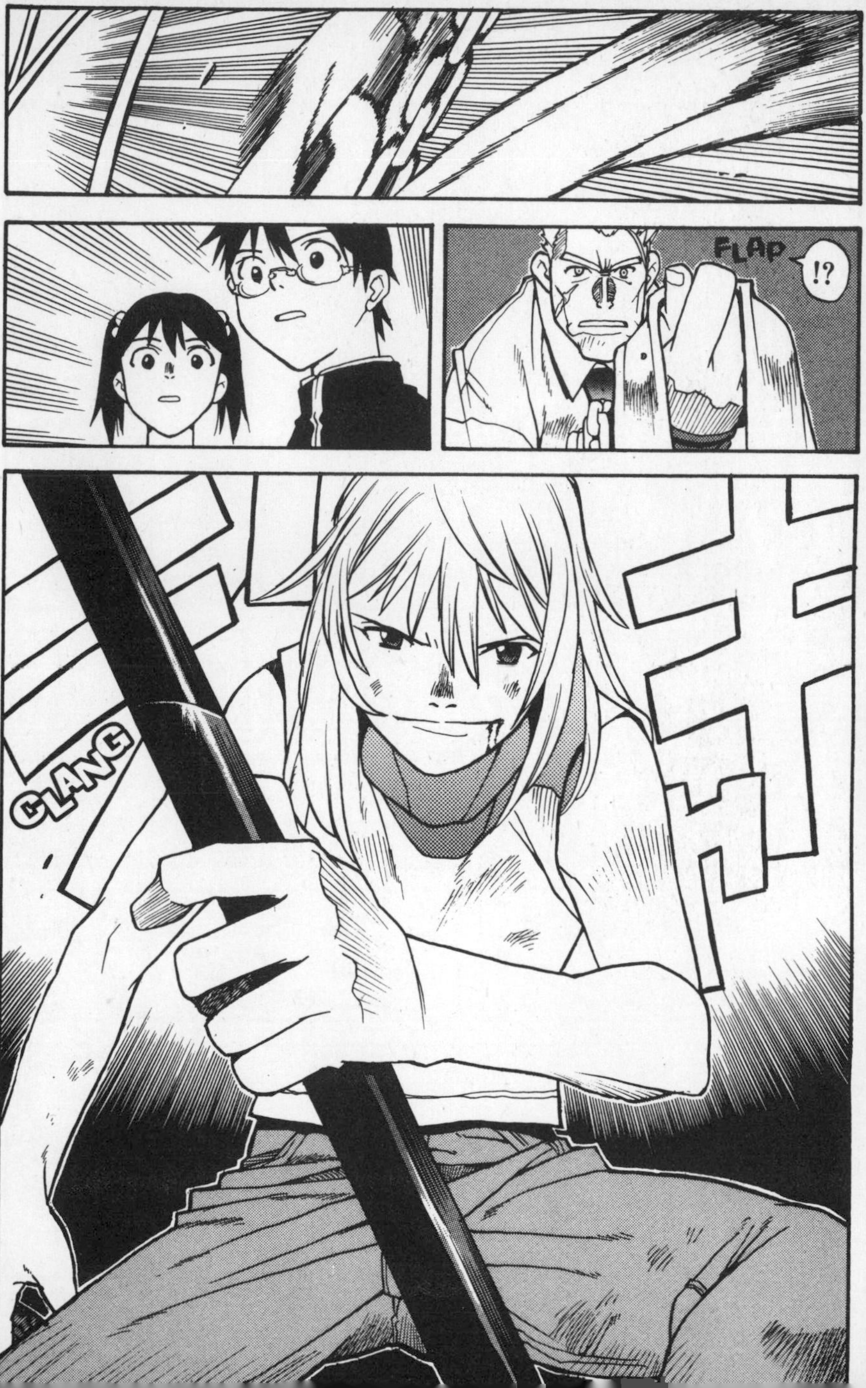
FLAP
!?
CLANG

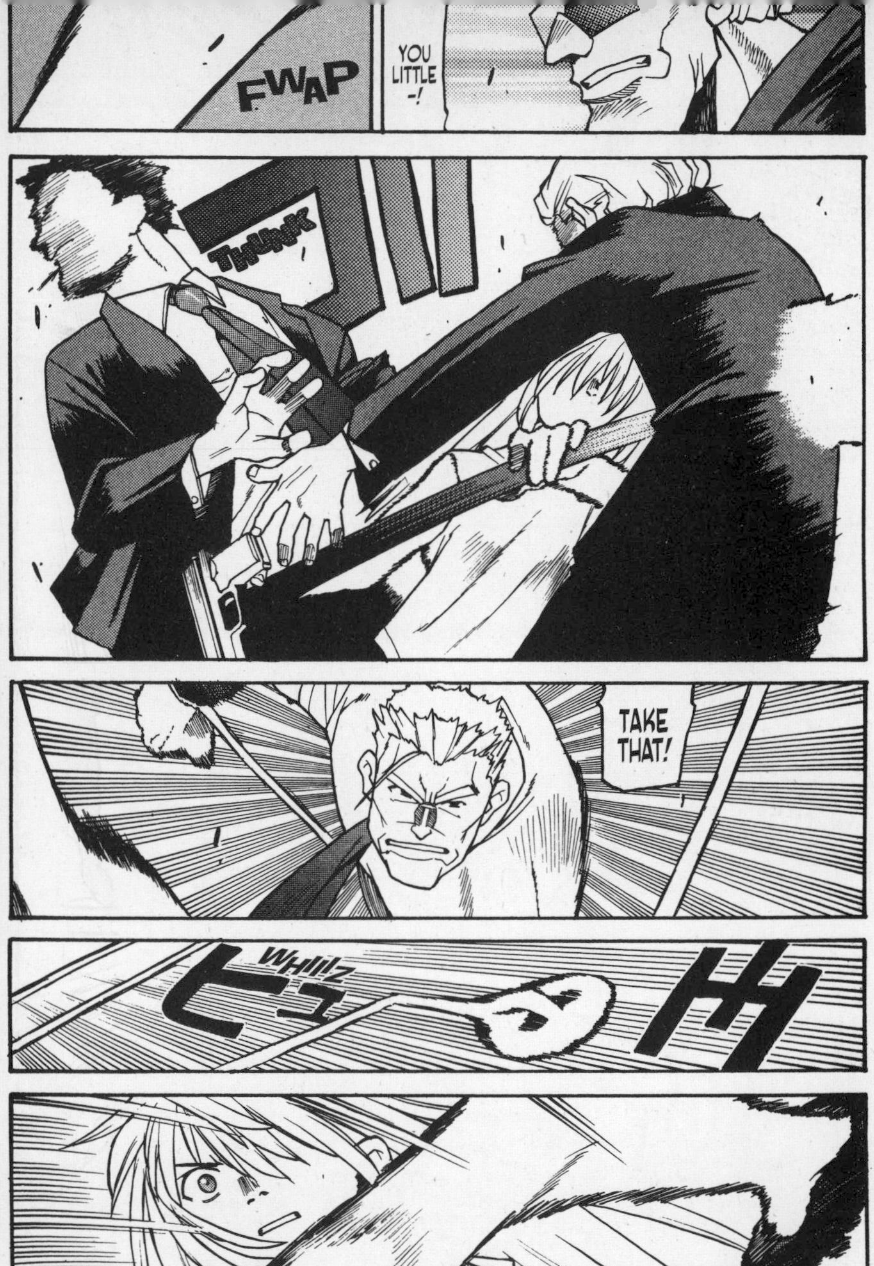
YOU LITTLE -!
FWAP
THUNK
TAKE THAT!
WHIIIZ

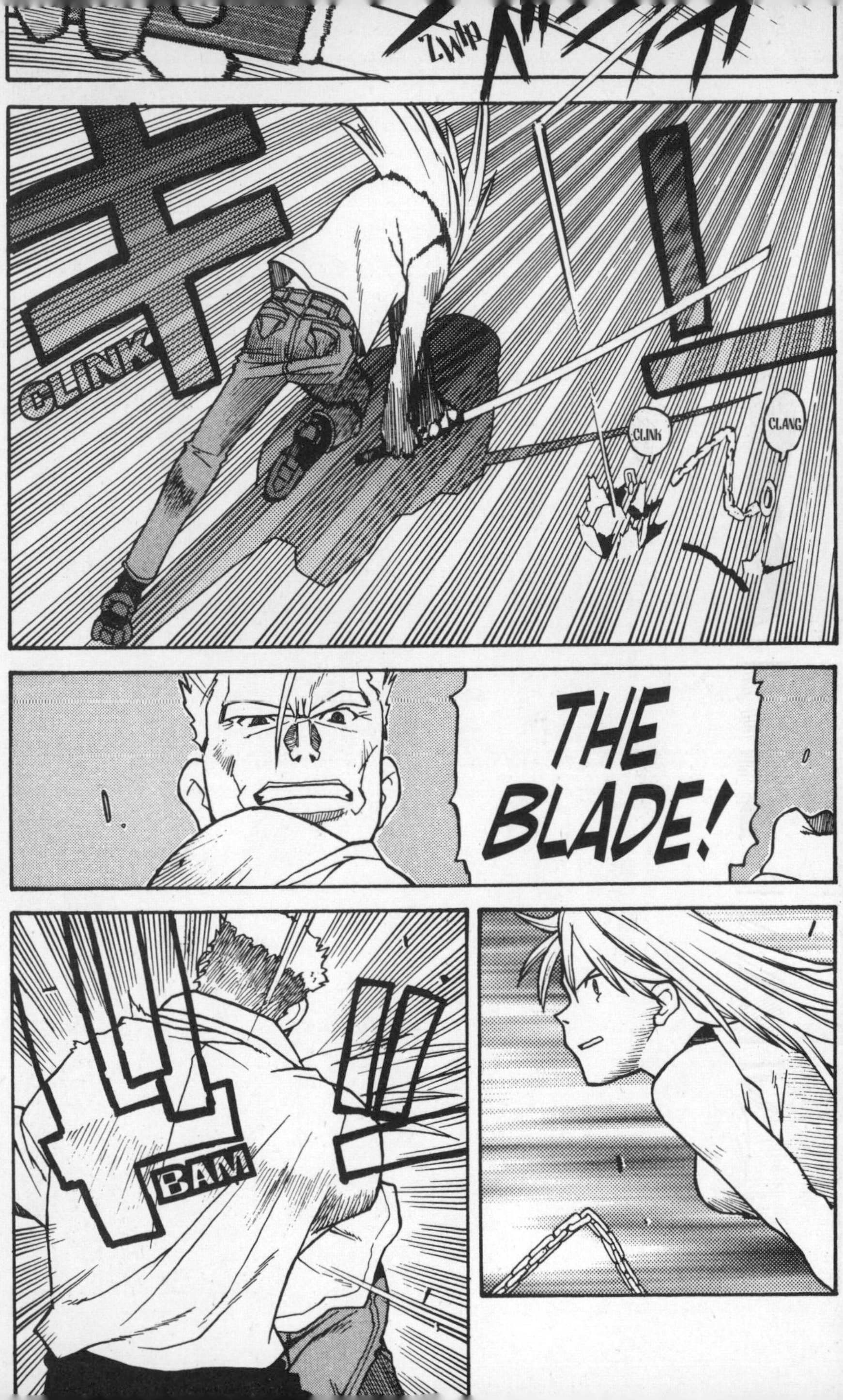
ZWIP
CLINK
CLANG
CLINK
THE BLADE!
BAM

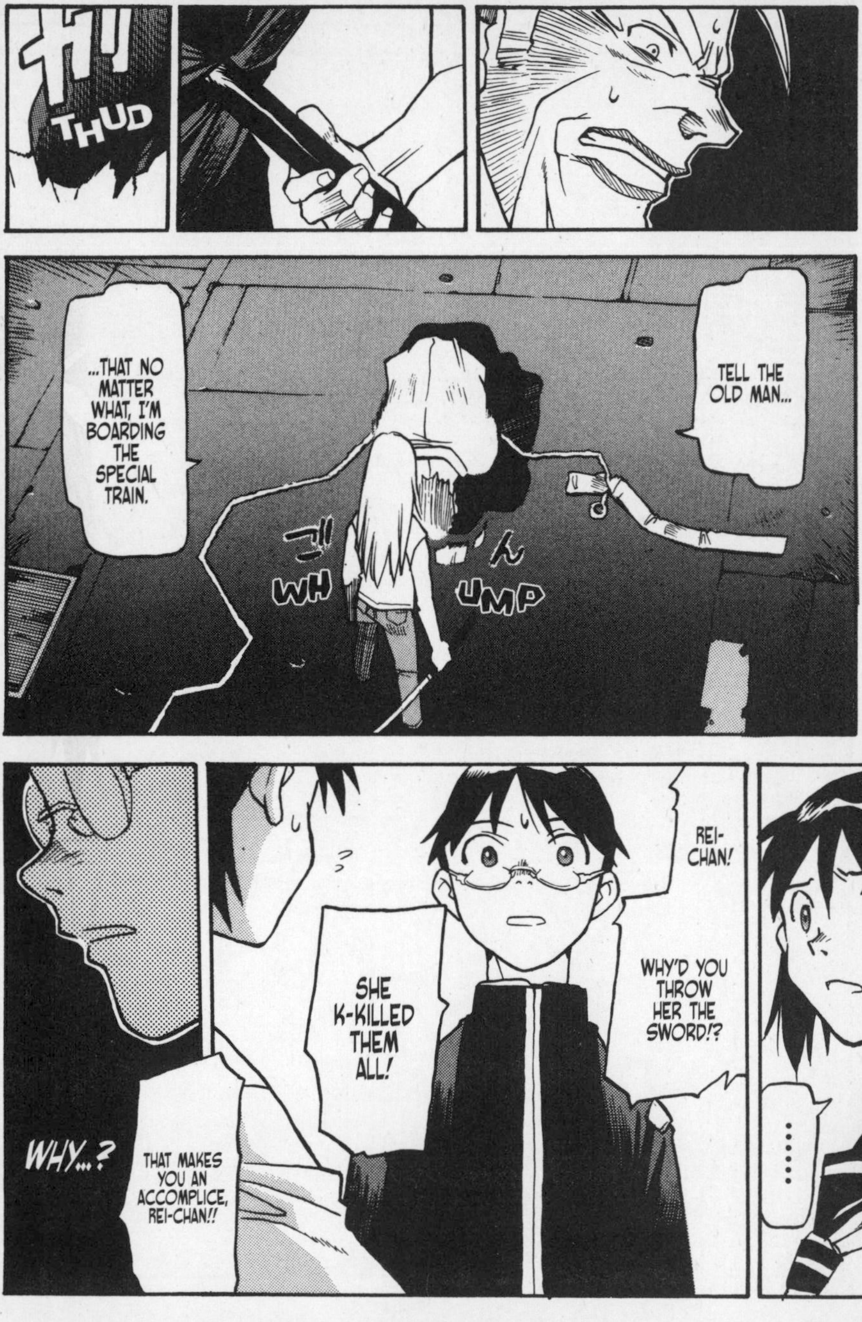
ガ!!
THUD
TELL THE OLD MAN...
...THAT NO MATTER WHAT, I'M BOARDING THE SPECIAL TRAIN.
ごん
WHUMP
......
REI-CHAN!
WHY'D YOU THROW HER THE SWORD!?
SHE K-KILLED THEM ALL!
THAT MAKES YOU AN ACCOMPLICE, REI-CHAN!!
WHY...?

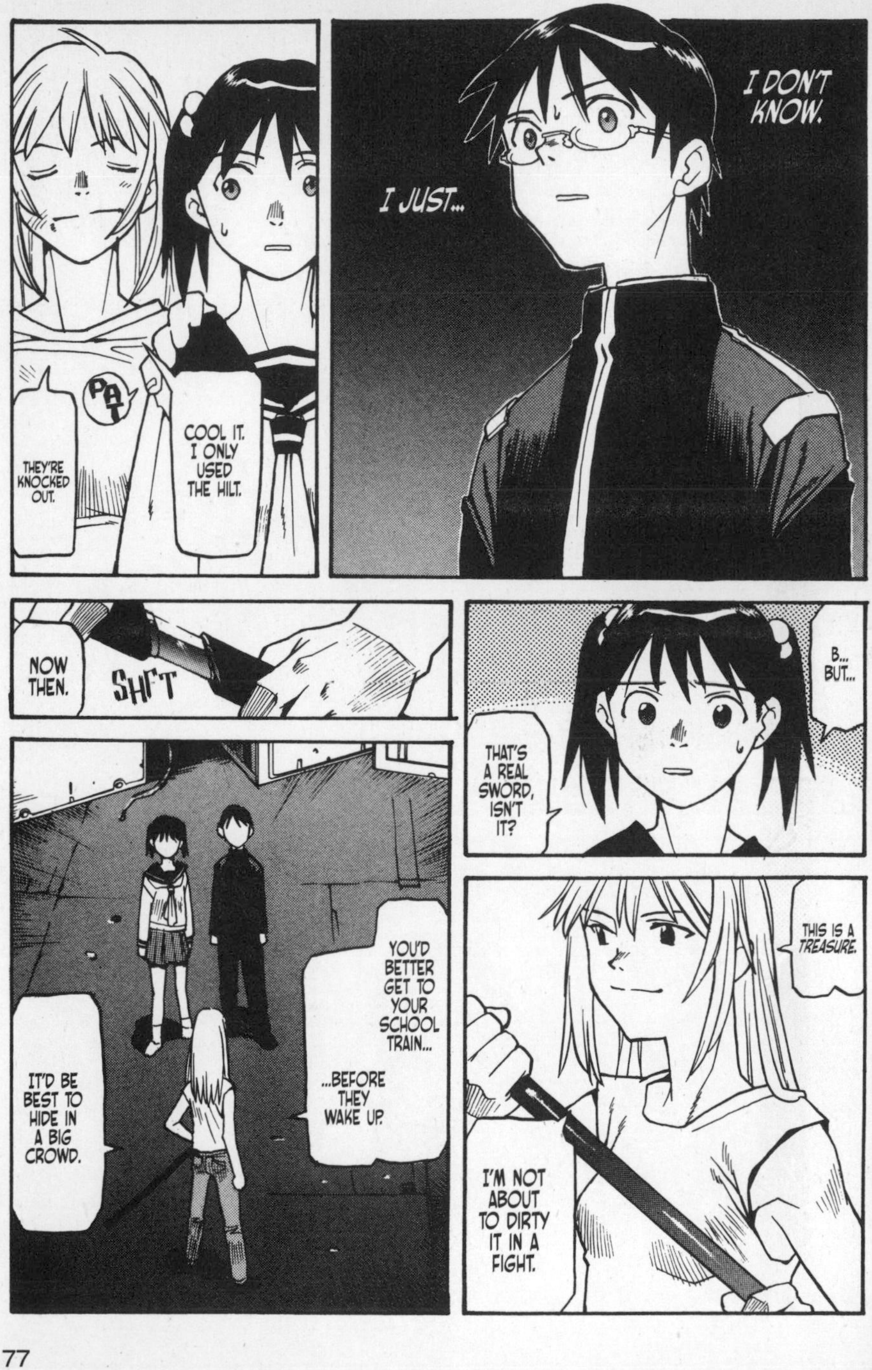
I DON'T KNOW.
I JUST...
COOL IT. I ONLY USED THE HILT.
PAT
THEY'RE KNOCKED OUT.
B... BUT...
THAT'S A REAL SWORD, ISN'T IT?
THIS IS A *TREASURE.*
I'M NOT ABOUT TO DIRTY IT IN A FIGHT.
NOW THEN.
SHFT
YOU'D BETTER GET TO YOUR SCHOOL TRAIN...
...BEFORE THEY WAKE UP.
IT'D BE BEST TO HIDE IN A BIG CROWD.

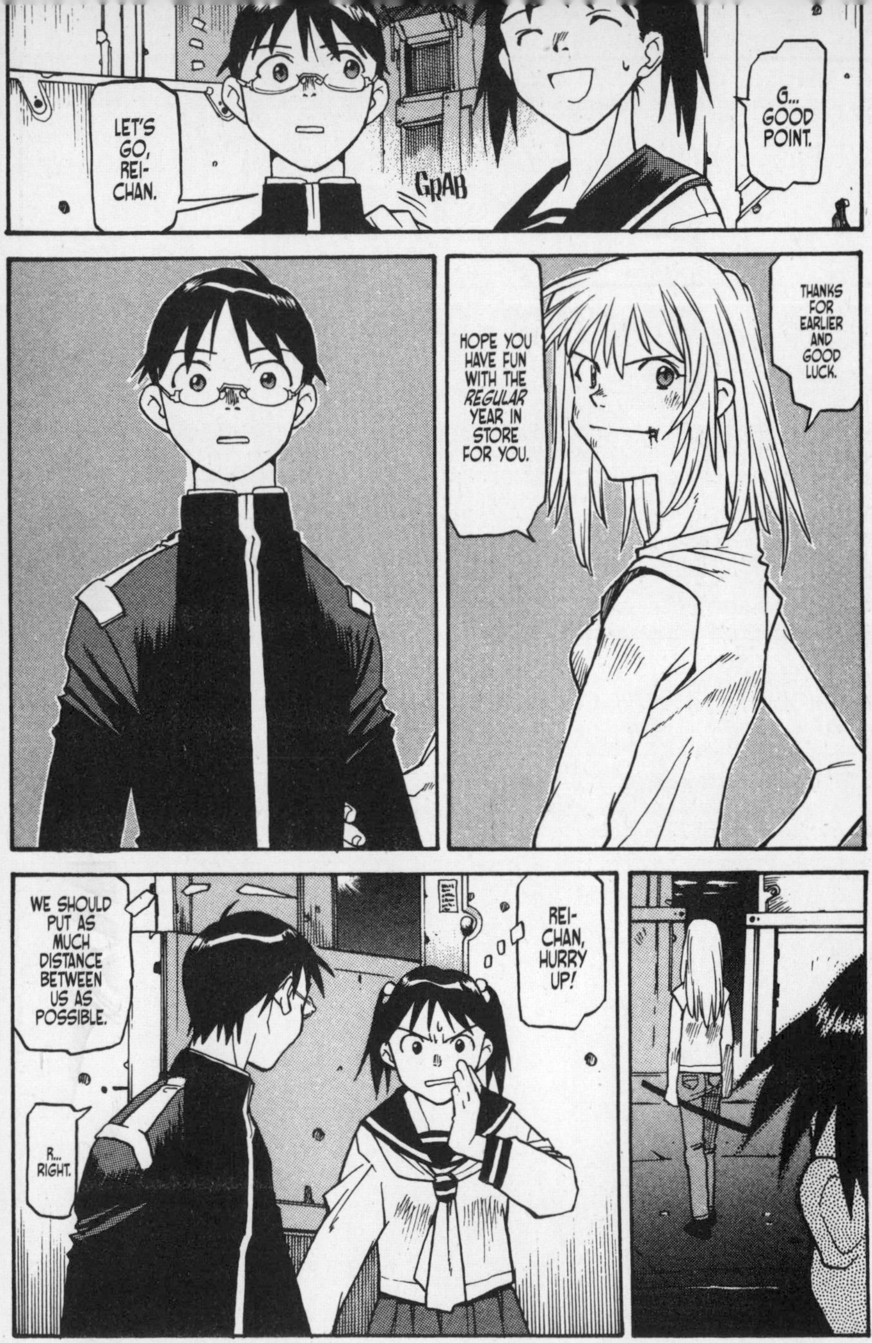
G... GOOD POINT.
LET'S GO, REI-CHAN.
GRAB
THANKS FOR EARLIER AND GOOD LUCK.
HOPE YOU HAVE FUN WITH THE *REGULAR* YEAR IN STORE FOR YOU.
REI-CHAN, HURRY UP!
WE SHOULD PUT AS MUCH DISTANCE BETWEEN US AS POSSIBLE.
R... RIGHT.

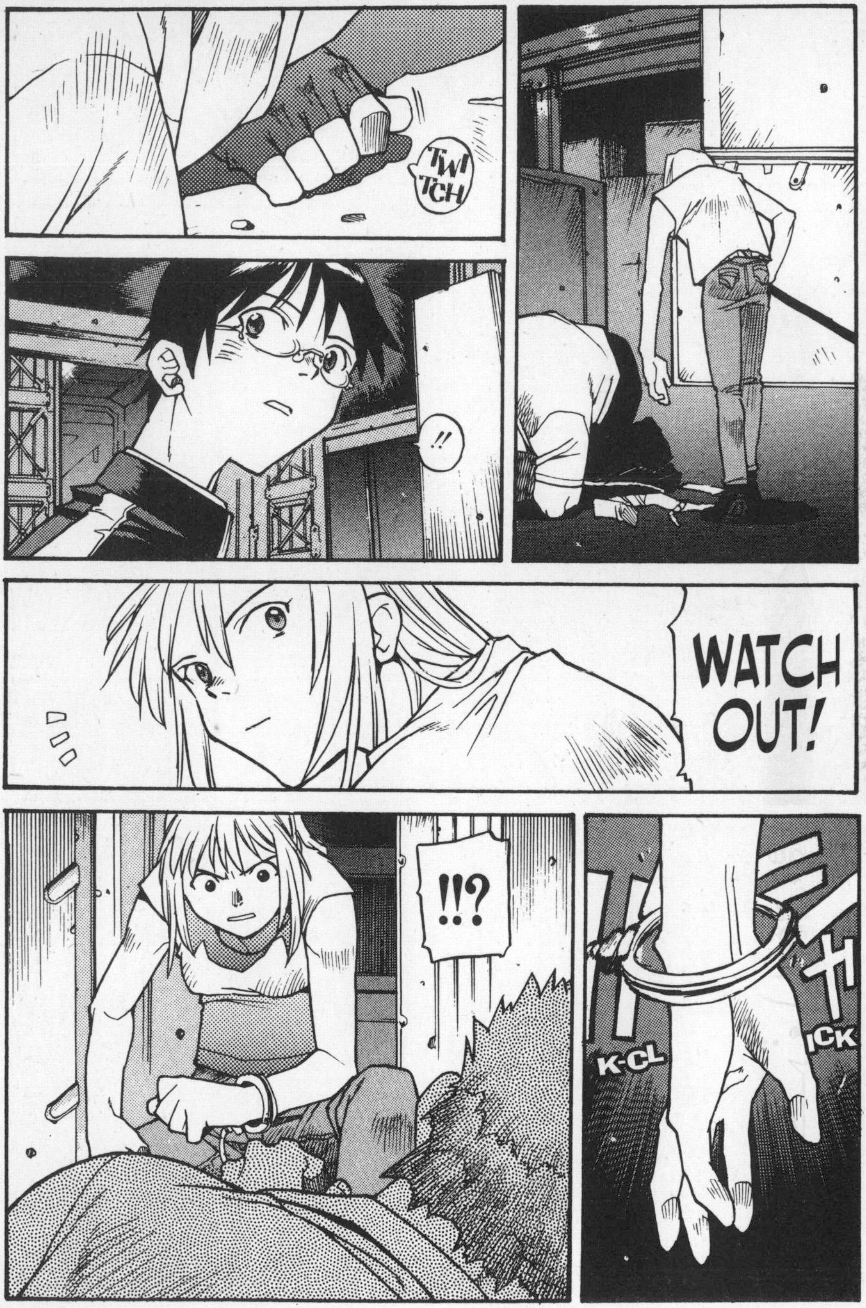
TWI TCH
!!
WATCH OUT!
K-CL
ICK
!!?

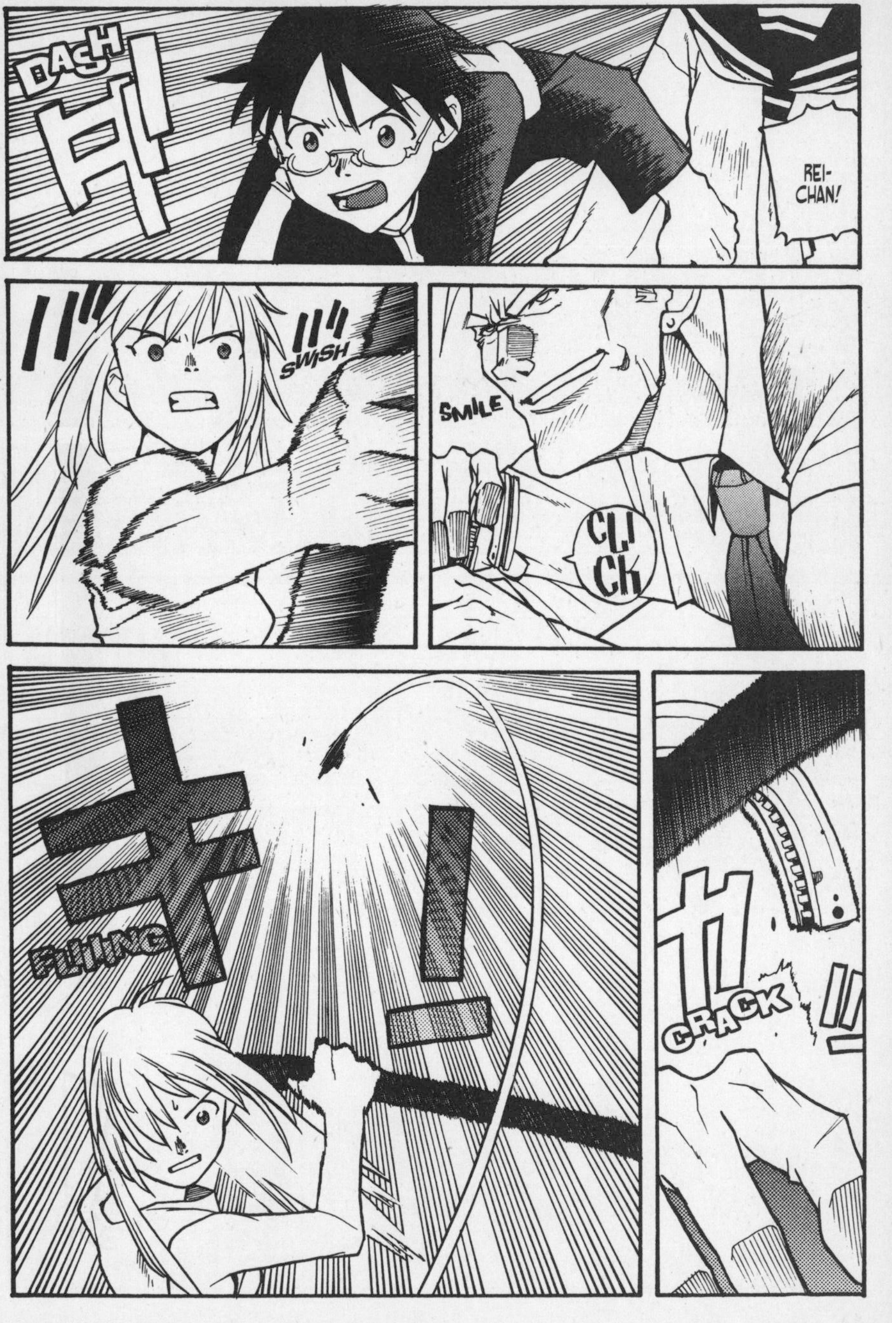
REI-CHAN!
DASH
SMILE
CLICK
SWISH
CRACK
FLIING

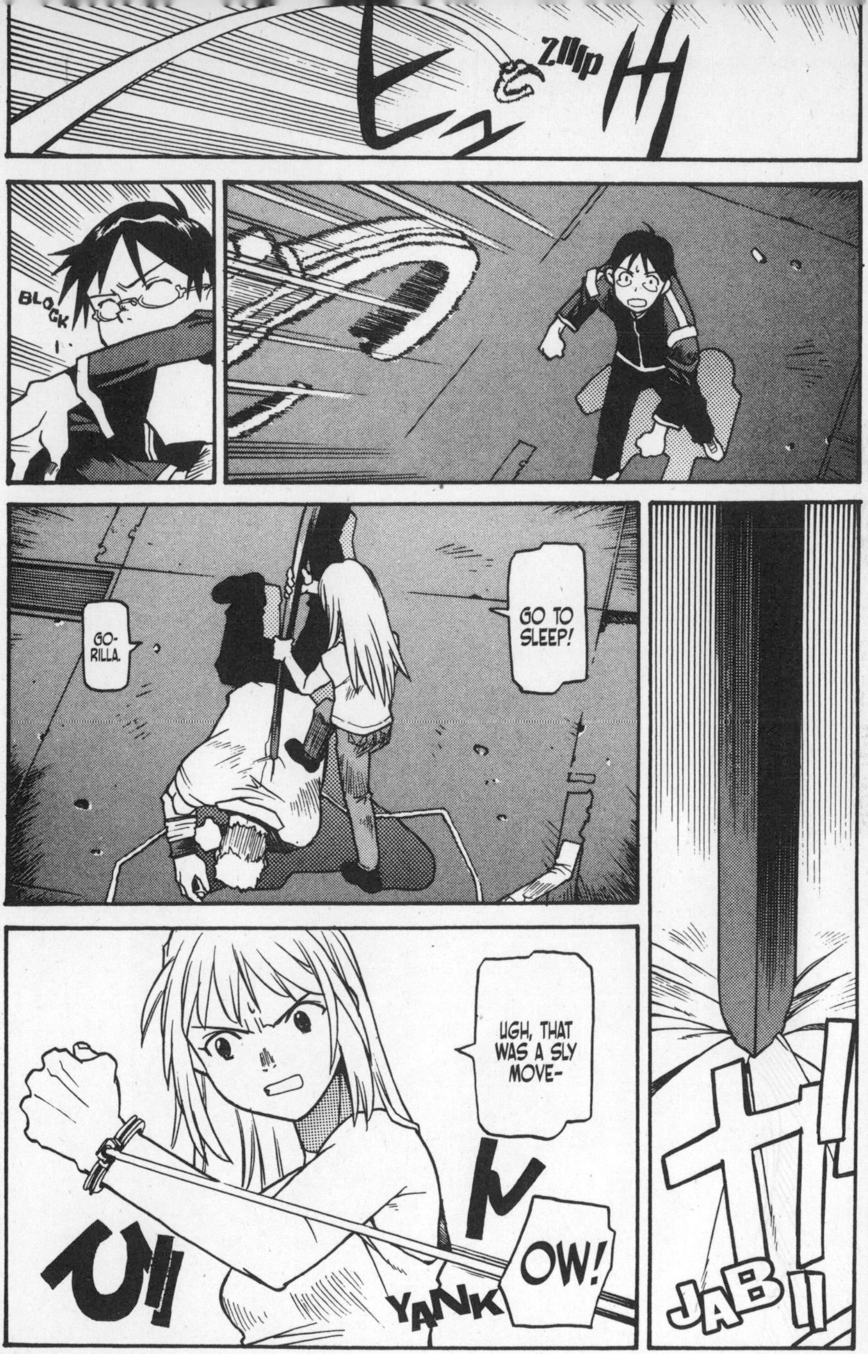
ZIIIP
BLOCK
JAB
GO TO SLEEP!
GO-RILLA.
UGH, THAT WAS A SLY MOVE-
OW!
YANK

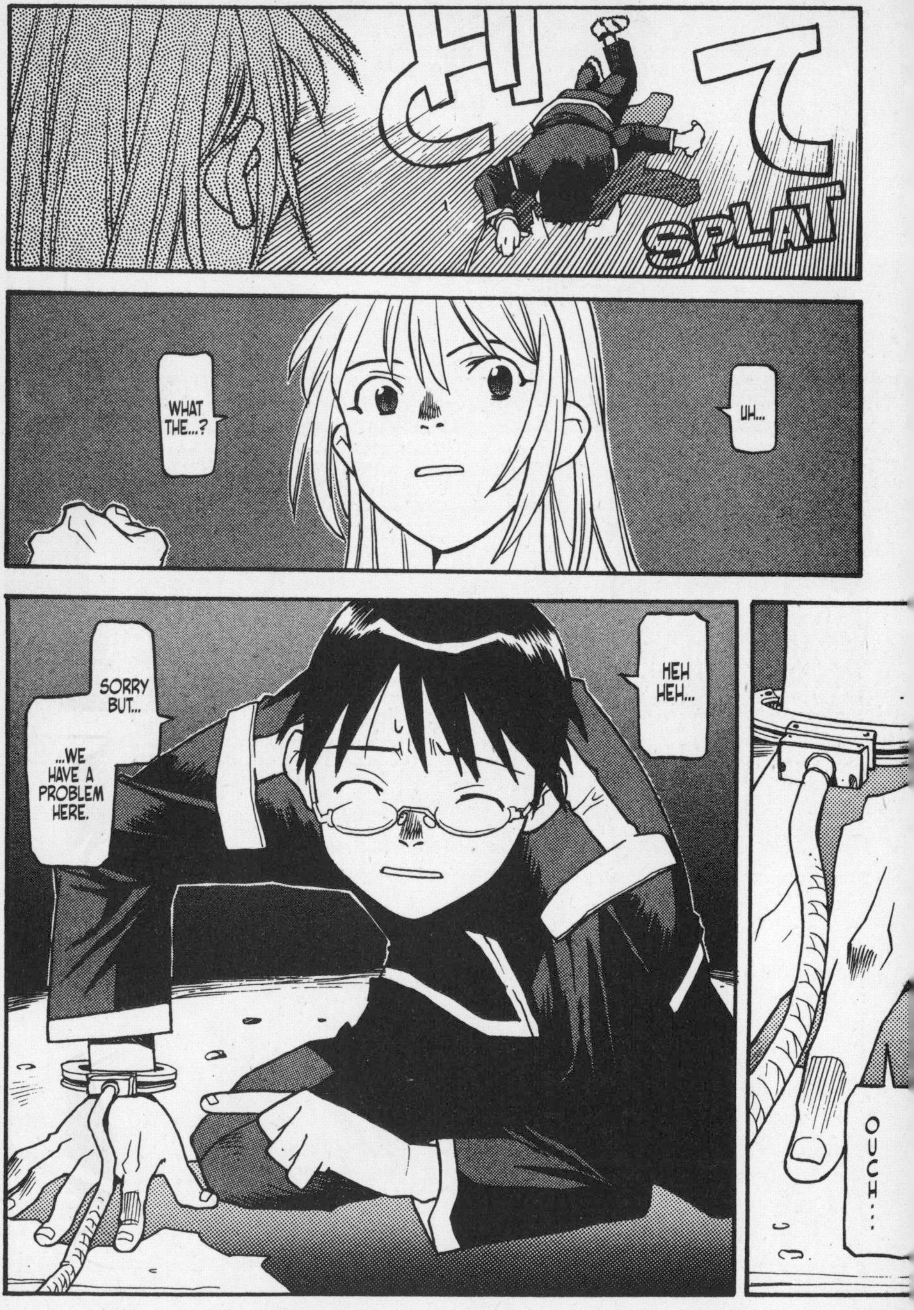
どて
SPLAT
UH...
WHAT THE...?
OUCH...
HEH HEH...
SORRY BUT...
...WE HAVE A PROBLEM HERE.

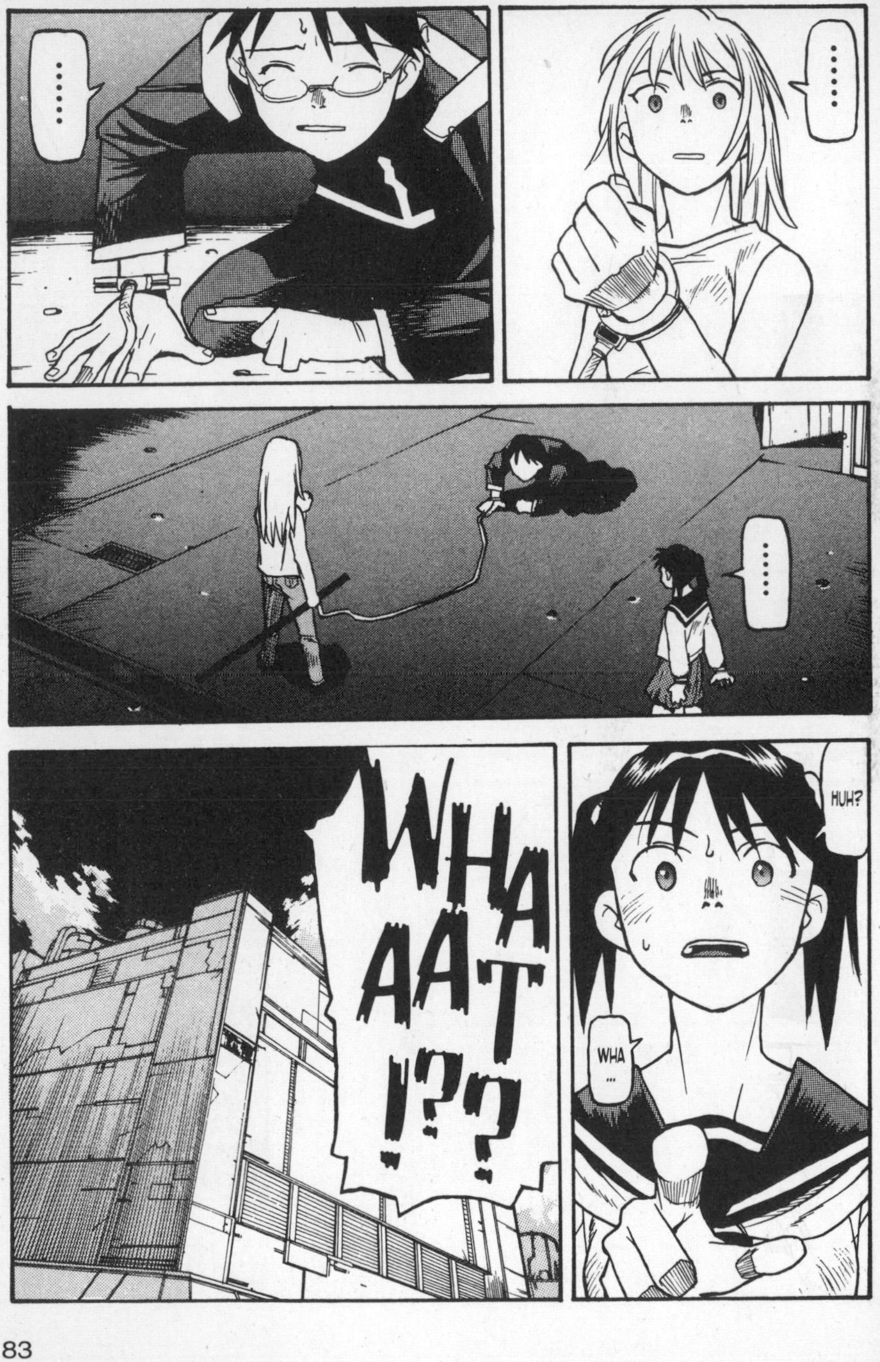
……
……
……
HUH?
WHA …
WHAAAT!??

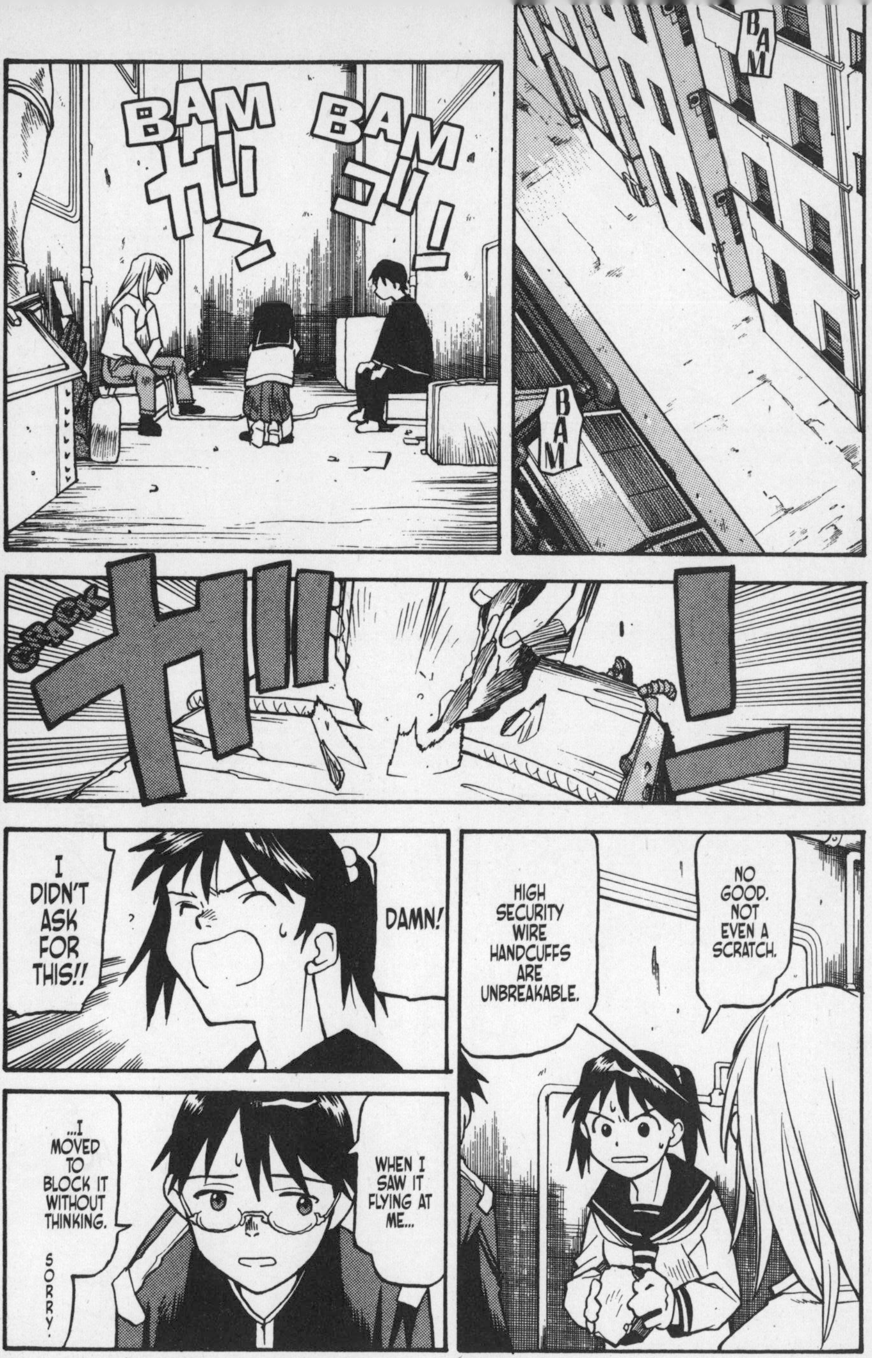
BAM
BAM
BAM
BAM
CRACK
NO GOOD. NOT EVEN A SCRATCH.
HIGH SECURITY WIRE HANDCUFFS ARE UNBREAKABLE.
DAMN!
I DIDN'T ASK FOR THIS!!
WHEN I SAW IT FLYING AT ME...
...I MOVED TO BLOCK IT WITHOUT THINKING.
SORRY.

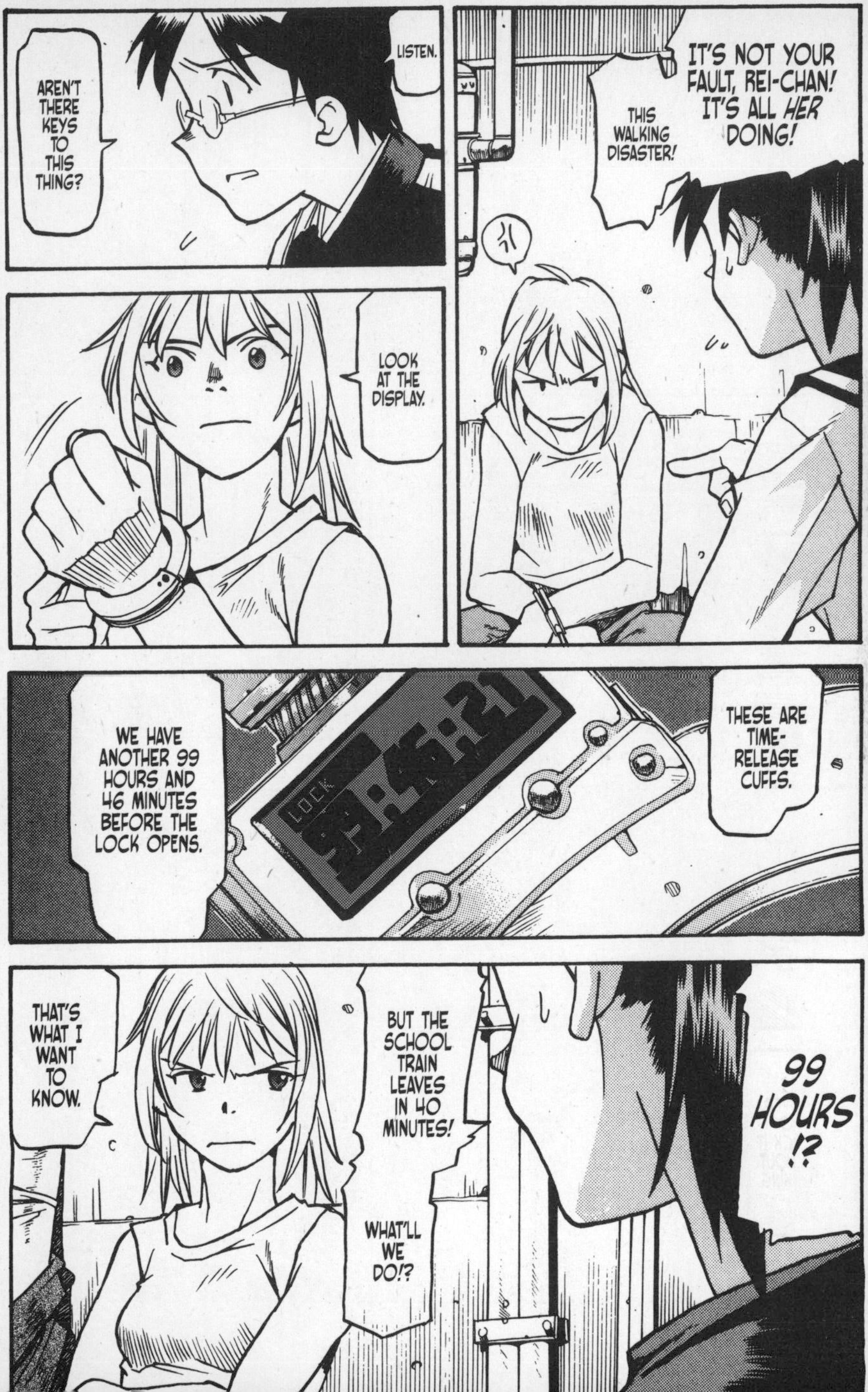
IT'S NOT YOUR FAULT, REI-CHAN! IT'S ALL HER DOING!
THIS WALKING DISASTER!
LISTEN.
AREN'T THERE KEYS TO THIS THING?
LOOK AT THE DISPLAY.
THESE ARE TIME-RELEASE CUFFS.
LOCK
WE HAVE ANOTHER 99 HOURS AND 46 MINUTES BEFORE THE LOCK OPENS.
99 HOURS !?
BUT THE SCHOOL TRAIN LEAVES IN 40 MINUTES!
WHAT'LL WE DO!?
THAT'S WHAT I WANT TO KNOW.

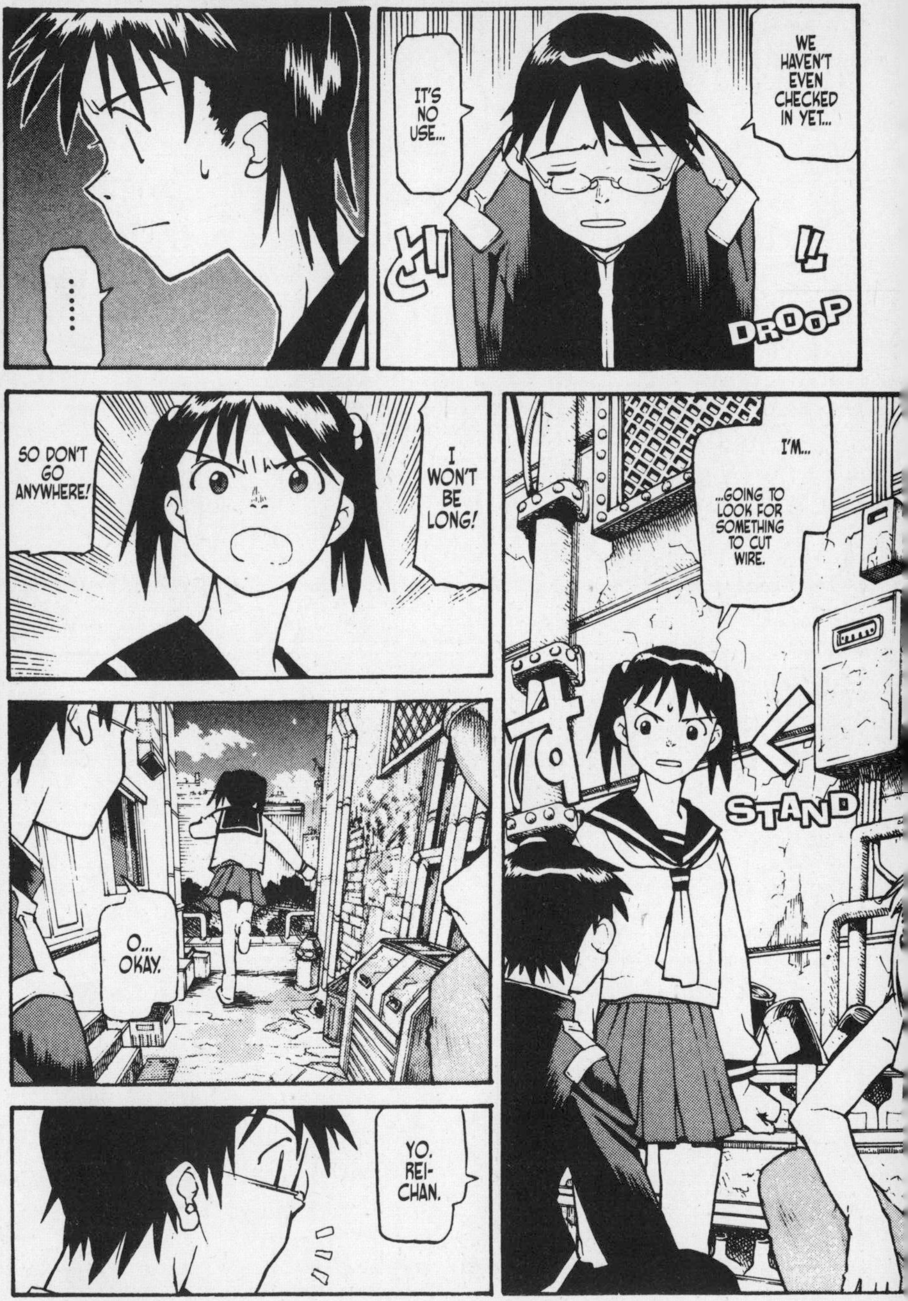
WE HAVEN'T EVEN CHECKED IN YET...
IT'S NO USE...
DROOP
......
I'M...
...GOING TO LOOK FOR SOMETHING TO CUT WIRE.
STAND
I WON'T BE LONG!
SO DON'T GO ANYWHERE!
O... OKAY.
YO. REI-CHAN.

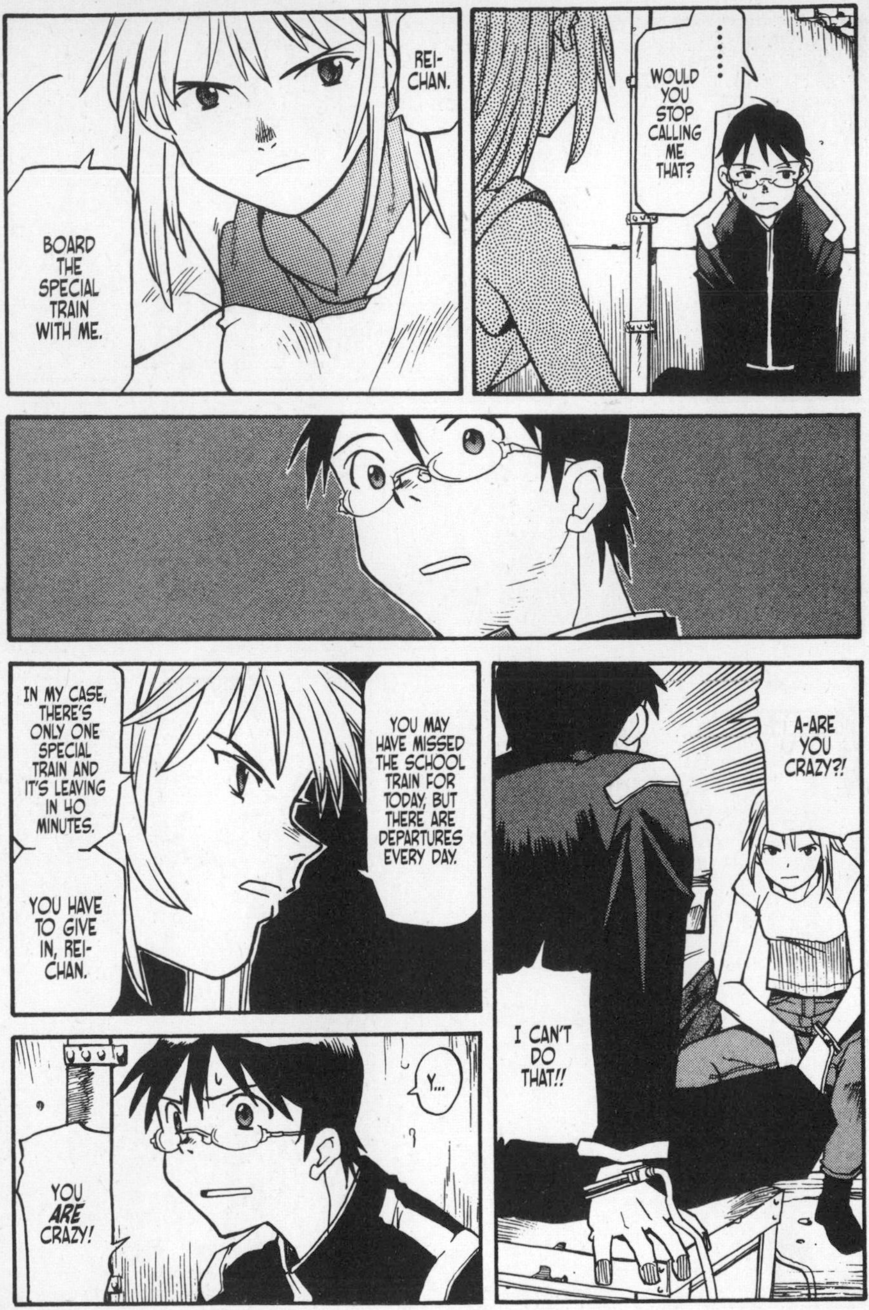
......
WOULD YOU STOP CALLING ME THAT?
REI-CHAN.
BOARD THE SPECIAL TRAIN WITH ME.
A-ARE YOU CRAZY?!
I CAN'T DO THAT!!
YOU MAY HAVE MISSED THE SCHOOL TRAIN FOR TODAY, BUT THERE ARE DEPARTURES EVERY DAY.
IN MY CASE, THERE'S ONLY ONE SPECIAL TRAIN AND IT'S LEAVING IN 40 MINUTES.
YOU HAVE TO GIVE IN, REI-CHAN.
Y...
YOU ***ARE*** CRAZY!

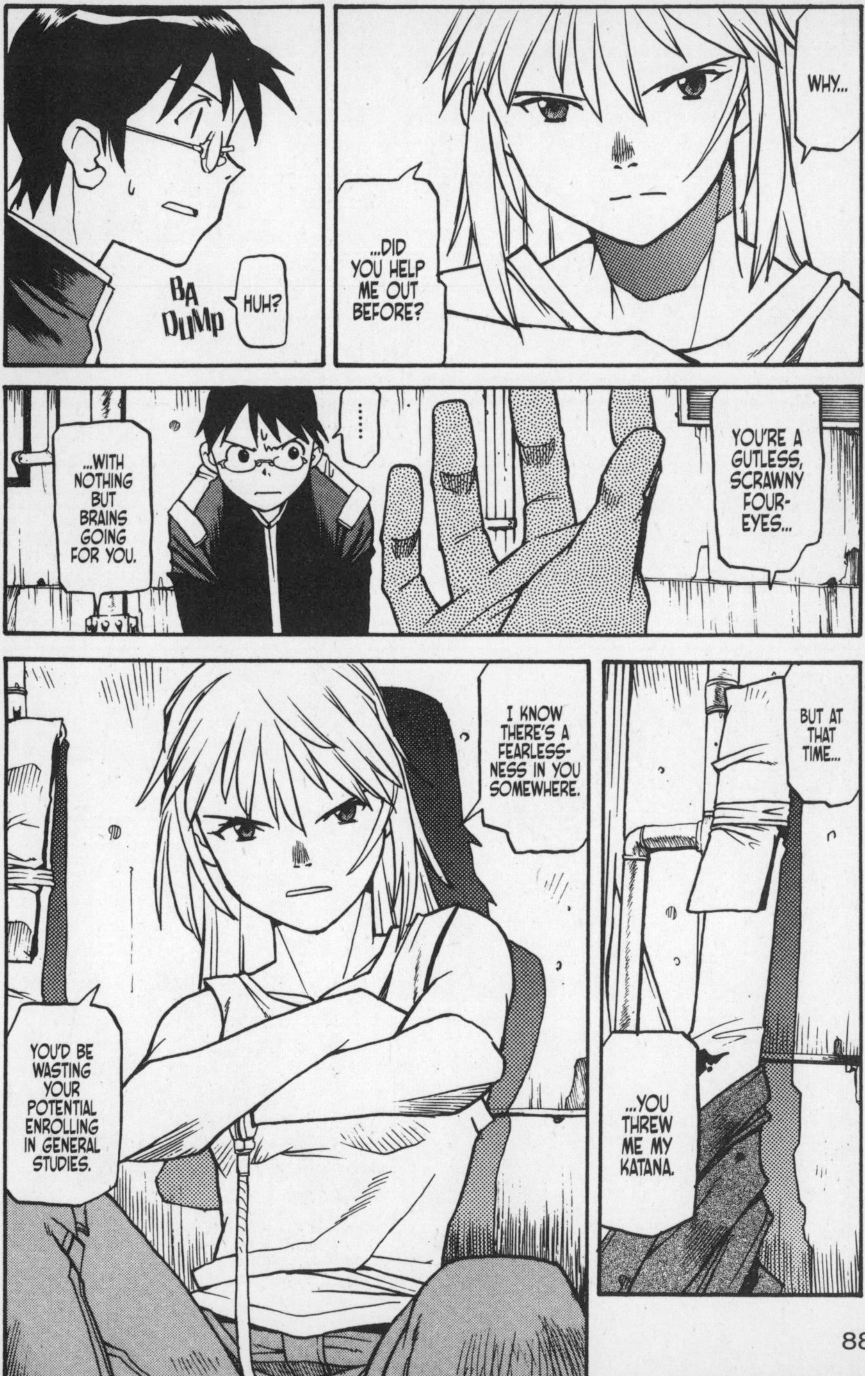
WHY...
...DID YOU HELP ME OUT BEFORE?
BA DUMP
HUH?
YOU'RE A GUTLESS, SCRAWNY FOUR-EYES...
......
...WITH NOTHING BUT BRAINS GOING FOR YOU.
BUT AT THAT TIME...
...YOU THREW ME MY KATANA.
I KNOW THERE'S A FEARLESSNESS IN YOU SOMEWHERE.
YOU'D BE WASTING YOUR POTENTIAL ENROLLING IN GENERAL STUDIES.

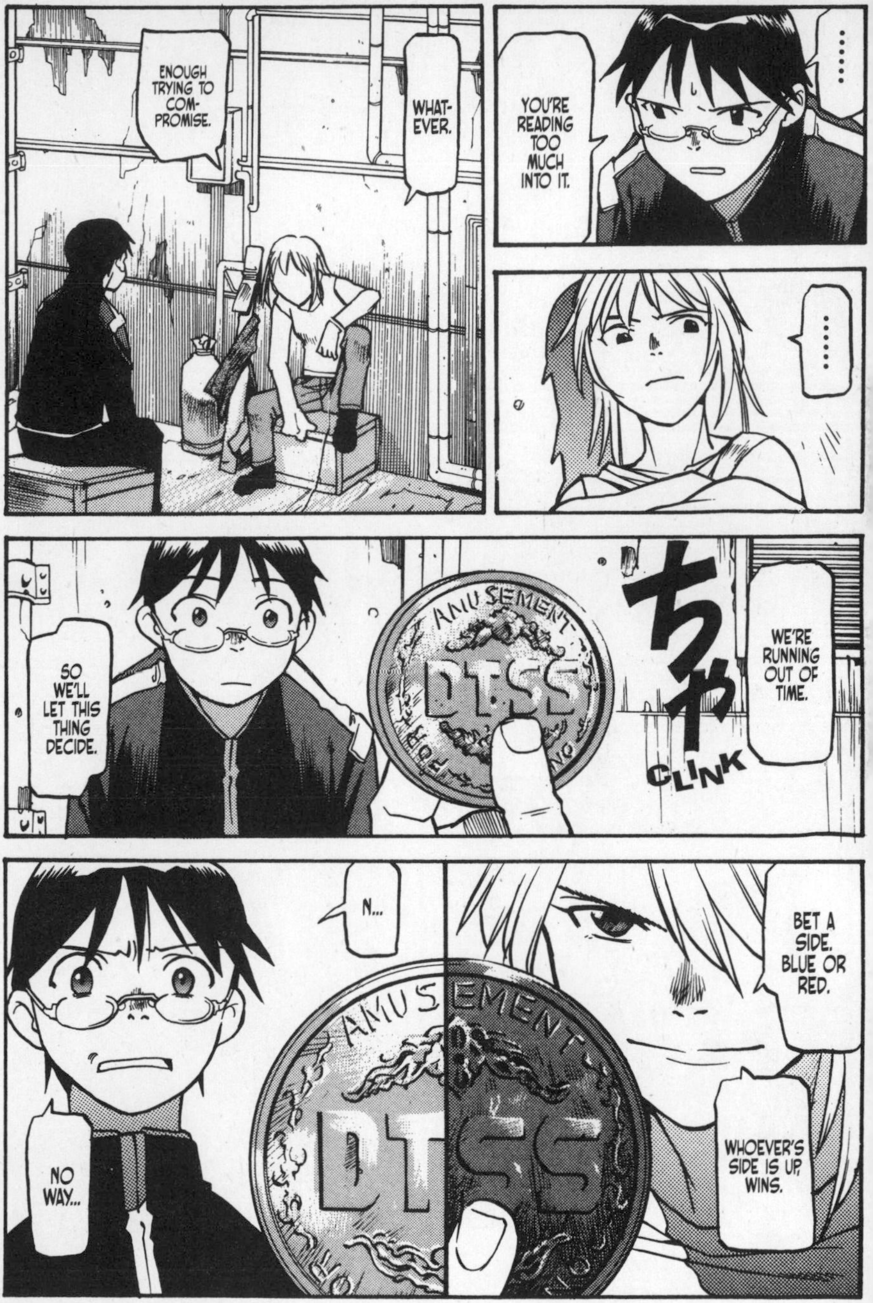
......
YOU'RE READING TOO MUCH INTO IT.
......
WHAT-EVER.
ENOUGH TRYING TO COM-PROMISE.
WE'RE RUNNING OUT OF TIME.
ちゃ
CLINK
AMUSEMENT
DT.S.S
SO WE'LL LET THIS THING DECIDE.
BET A SIDE. BLUE OR RED.
WHOEVER'S SIDE IS UP, WINS.
AMUSEMENT
DTSS
N...
NO WAY...

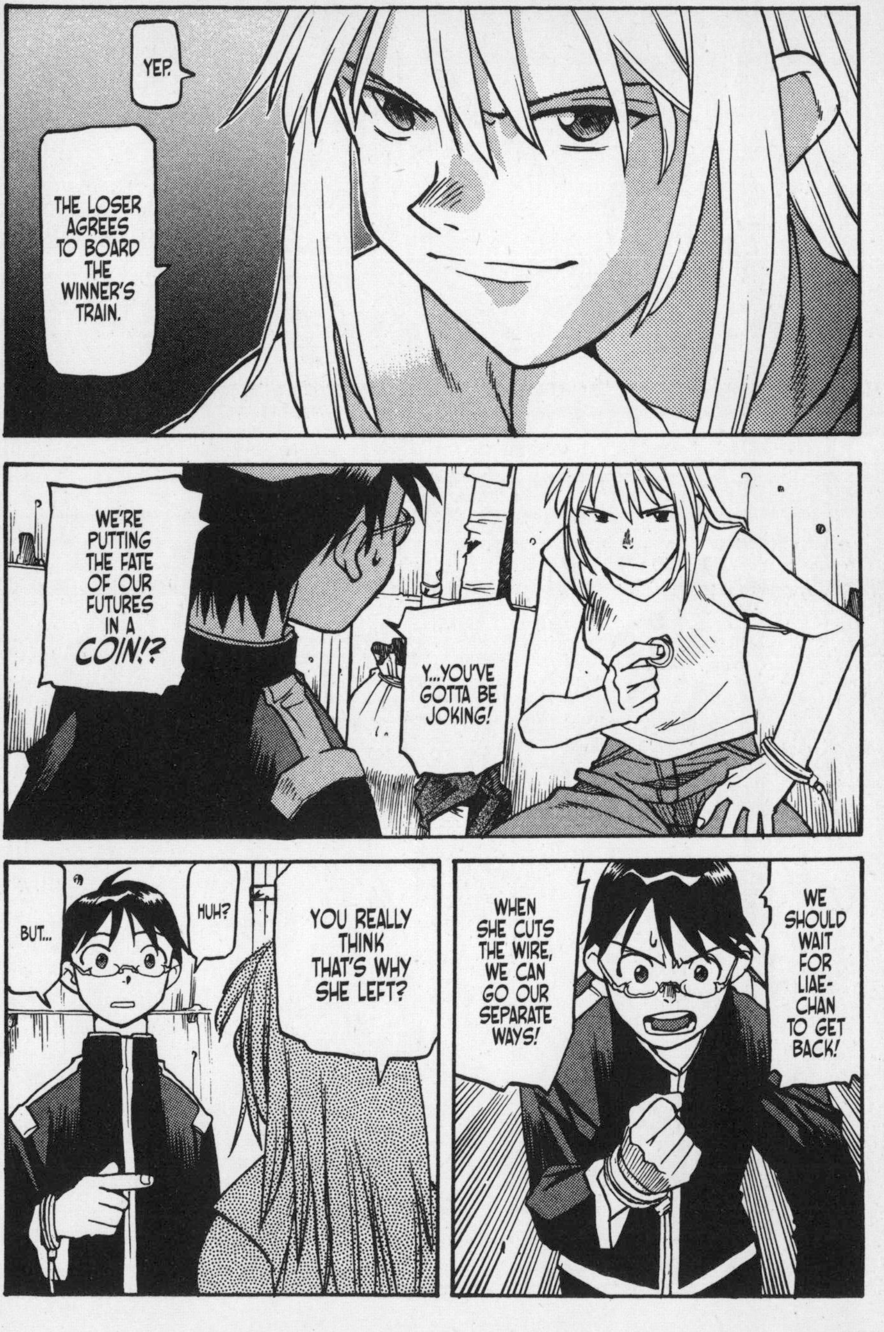
YEP.
THE LOSER AGREES TO BOARD THE WINNER'S TRAIN.
Y...YOU'VE GOTTA BE JOKING!
WE'RE PUTTING THE FATE OF OUR FUTURES IN A COIN!?
WE SHOULD WAIT FOR LIAE-CHAN TO GET BACK!
WHEN SHE CUTS THE WIRE, WE CAN GO OUR SEPARATE WAYS!
YOU REALLY THINK THAT'S WHY SHE LEFT?
HUH?
BUT...

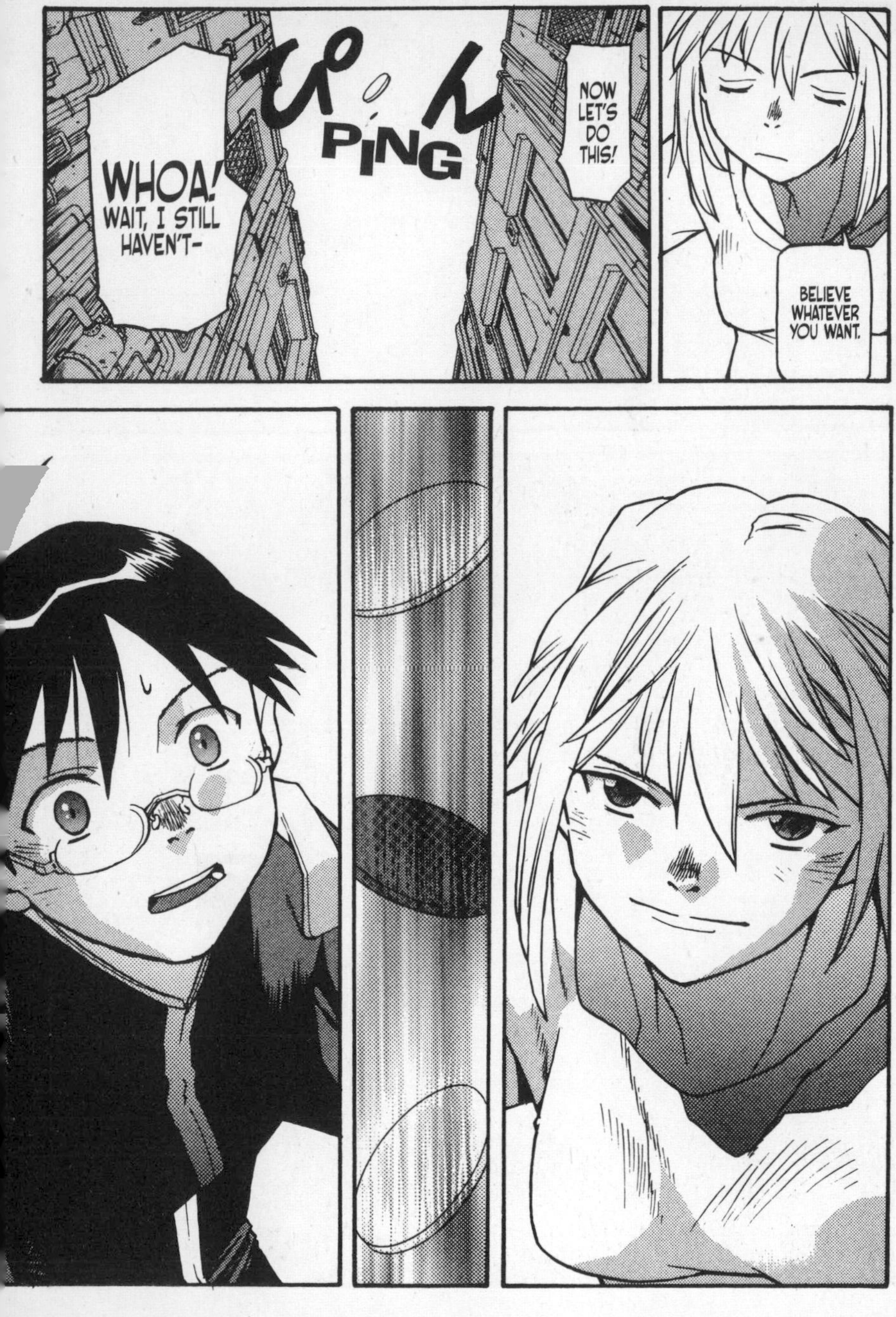
BELIEVE WHATEVER YOU WANT.
NOW LET'S DO THIS!
ぴん
PING
WHOA! WAIT, I STILL HAVEN'T-

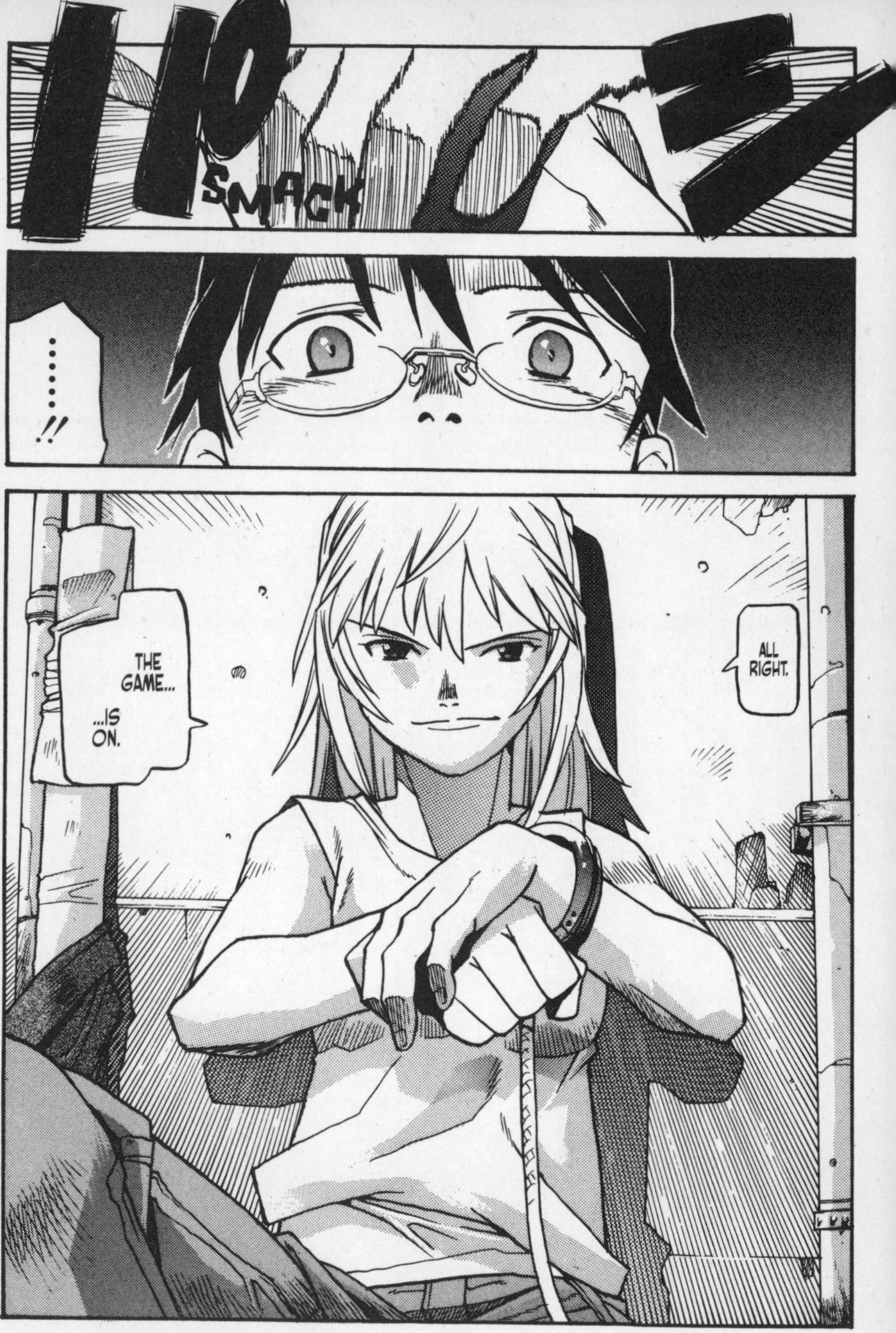
SMACK
......!!
ALL RIGHT.
THE GAME...
...IS ON.

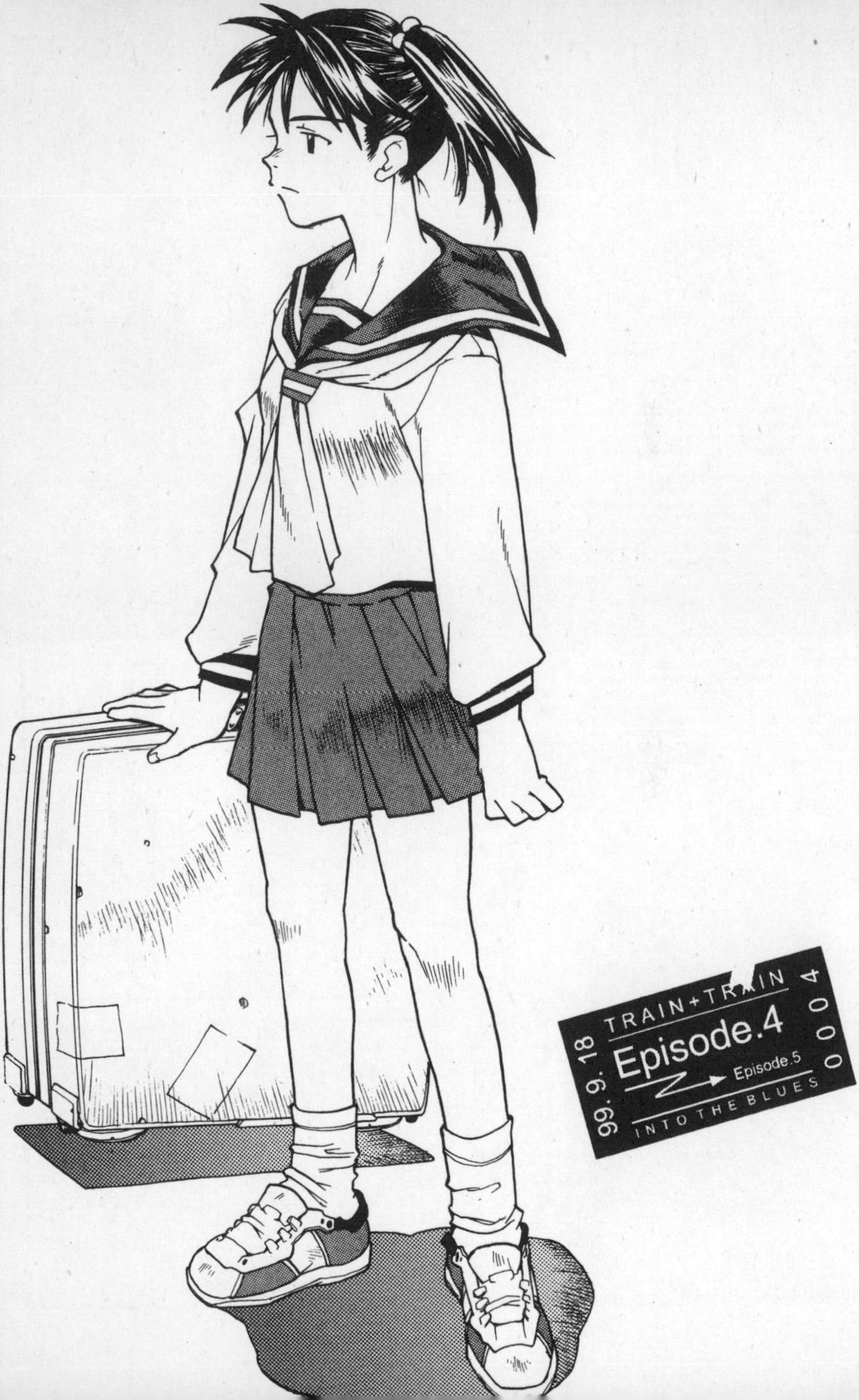
TRAIN+TRAIN
99. 9. 18
Episode.4
Episode.5
INTO THE BLUES
0004

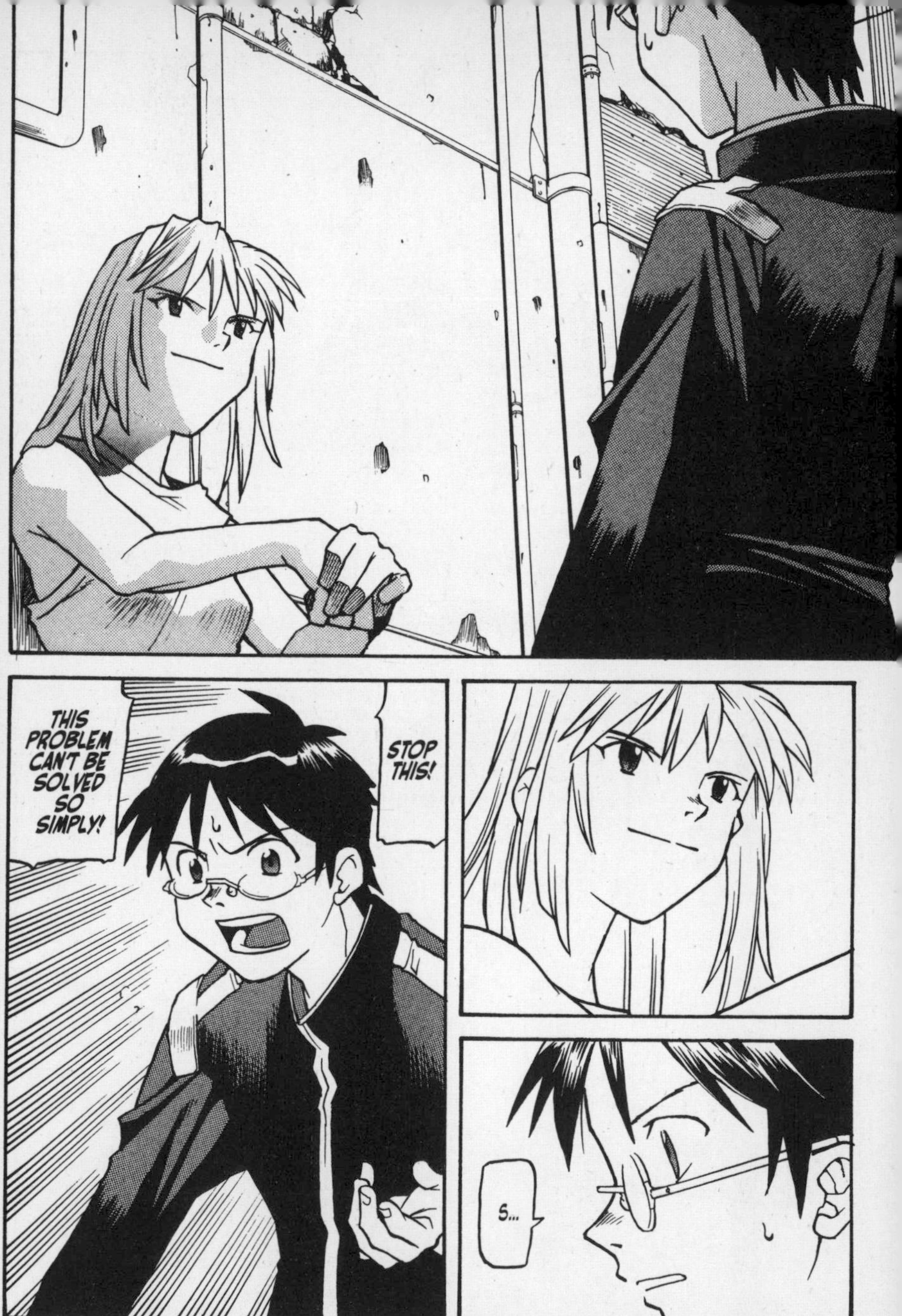
S...
STOP THIS!
THIS PROBLEM CAN'T BE SOLVED SO SIMPLY!

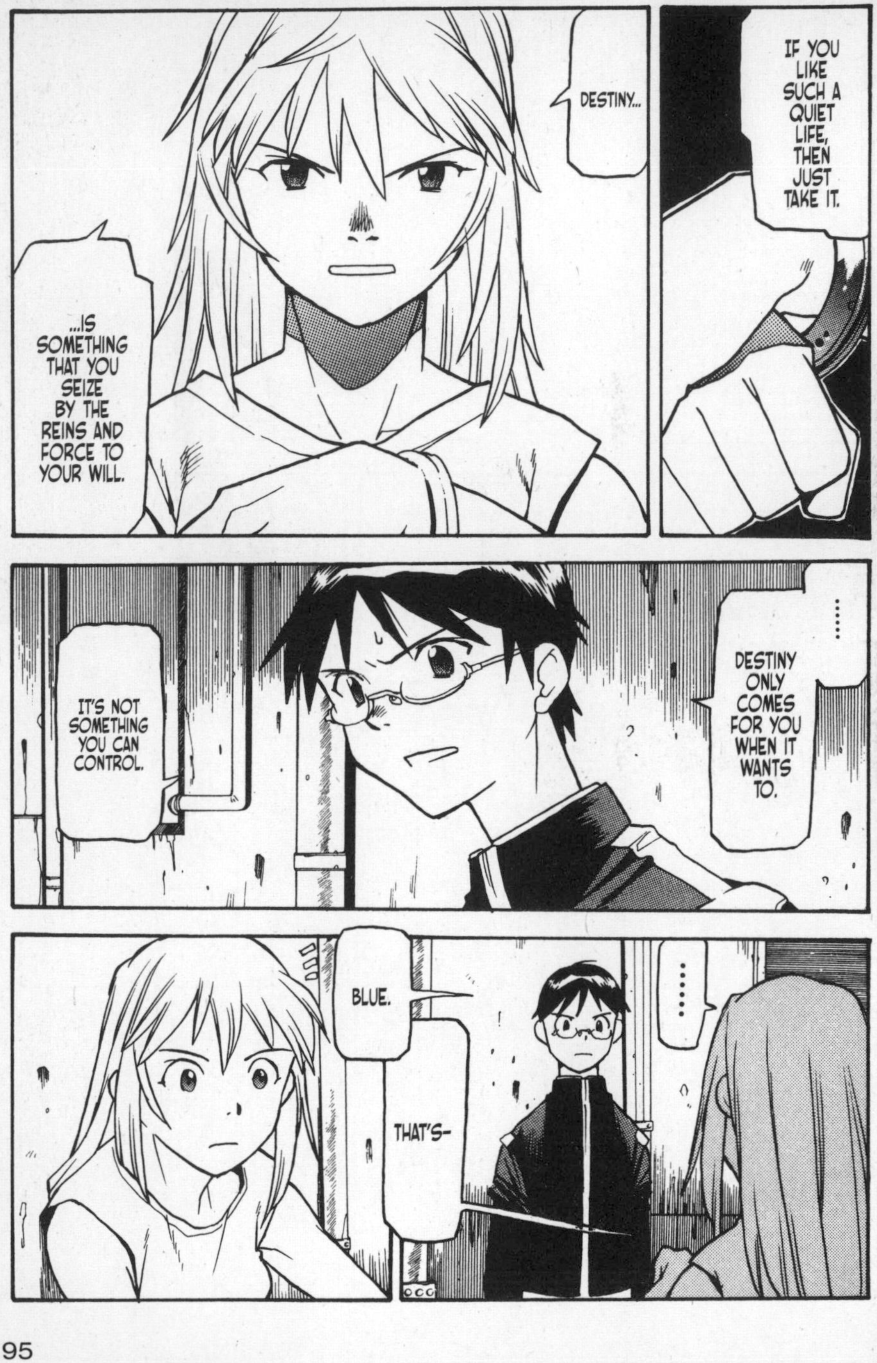
IF YOU LIKE SUCH A QUIET LIFE, THEN JUST TAKE IT.
DESTINY...
...IS SOMETHING THAT YOU SEIZE BY THE REINS AND FORCE TO YOUR WILL.
......
DESTINY ONLY COMES FOR YOU WHEN IT WANTS TO.
IT'S NOT SOMETHING YOU CAN CONTROL.
......
BLUE.
THAT'S-

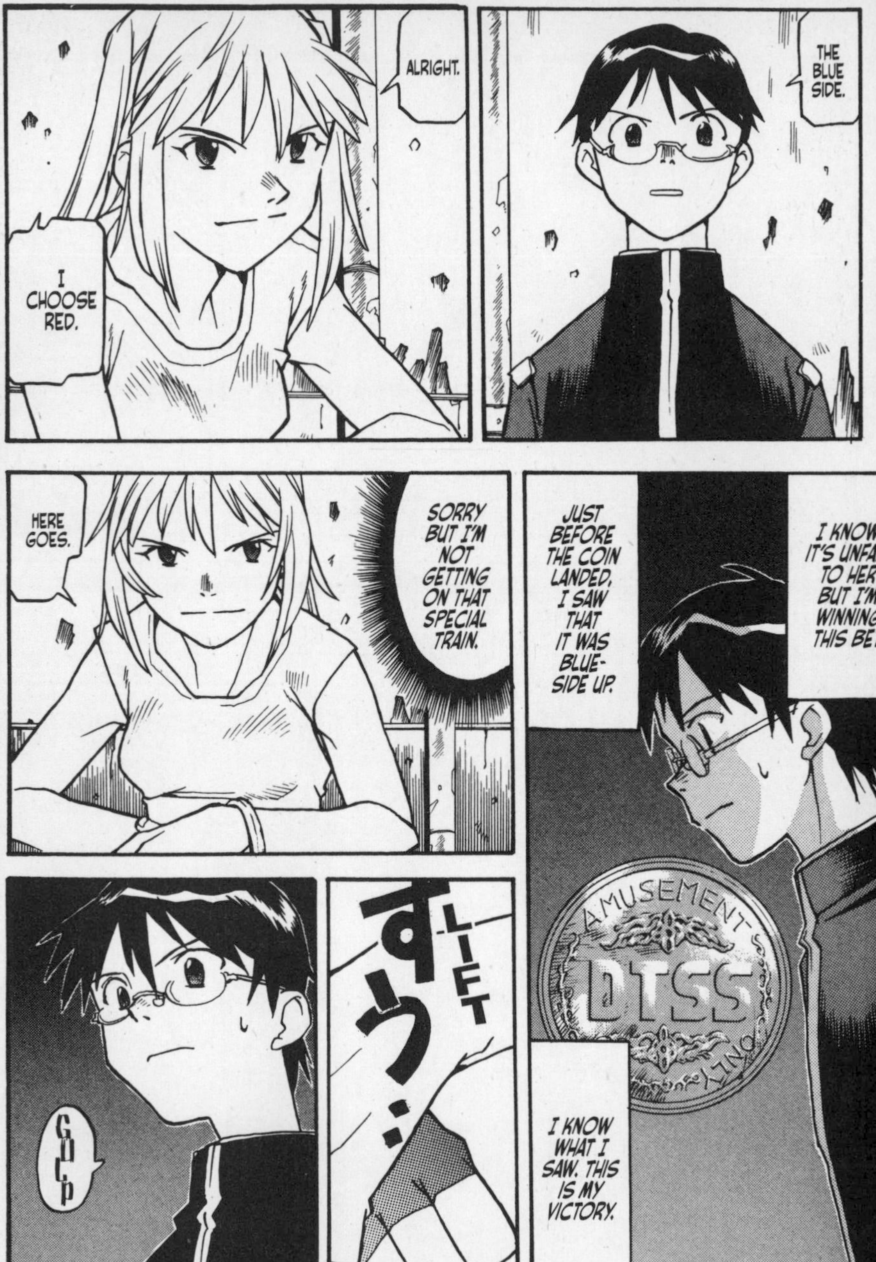
THE BLUE SIDE.
ALRIGHT.
I CHOOSE RED.
I KNOW IT'S UNFAIR TO HER BUT I'M WINNING THIS BET.
JUST BEFORE THE COIN LANDED, I SAW THAT IT WAS BLUE-SIDE UP.
AMUSEMENT
DTSS
ONLY
I KNOW WHAT I SAW. THIS IS MY VICTORY.
SORRY BUT I'M NOT GETTING ON THAT SPECIAL TRAIN.
HERE GOES.
すぅ…
LIFT
GULP

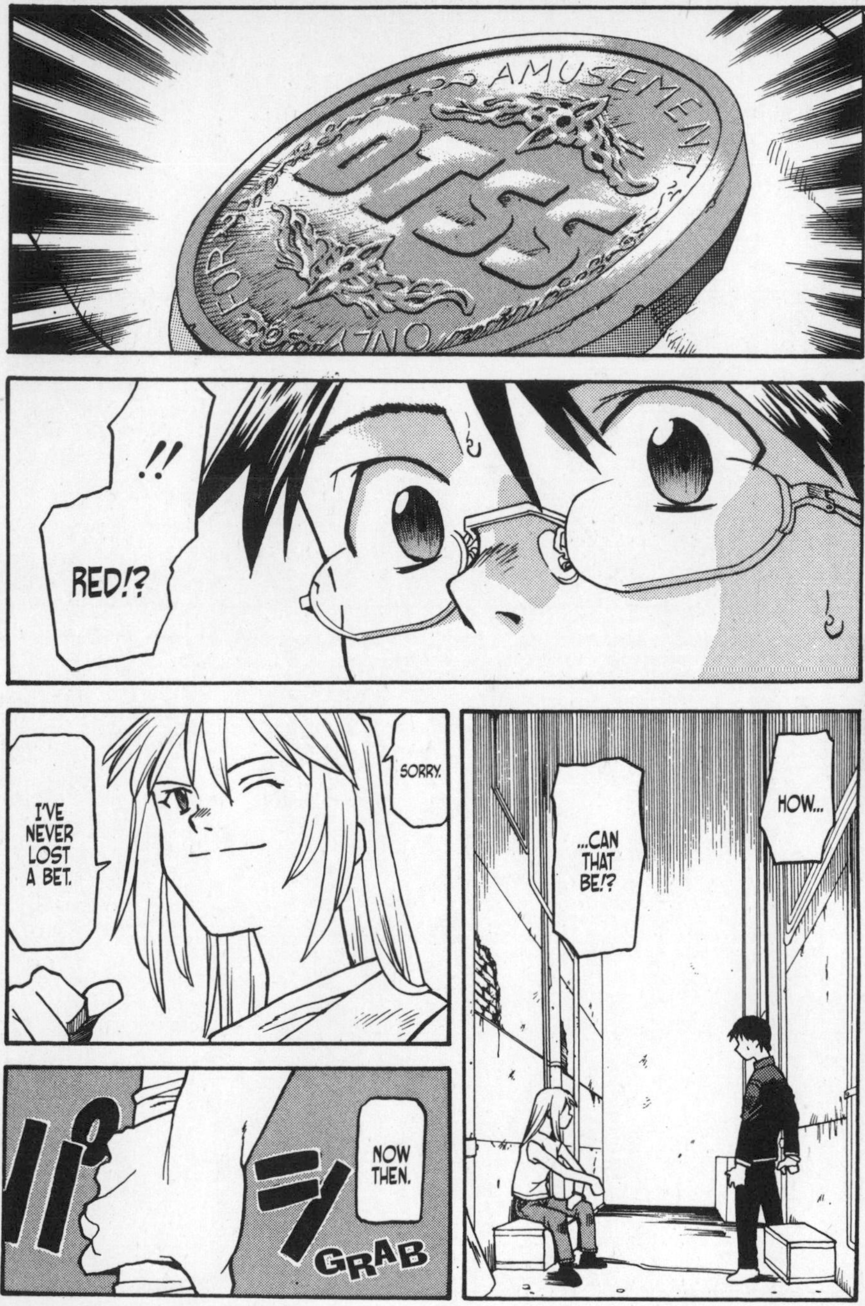
AMUSEMENT
!!
RED!?
HOW...
...CAN THAT BE!?
SORRY.
I'VE NEVER LOST A BET.
NOW THEN.
GRAB

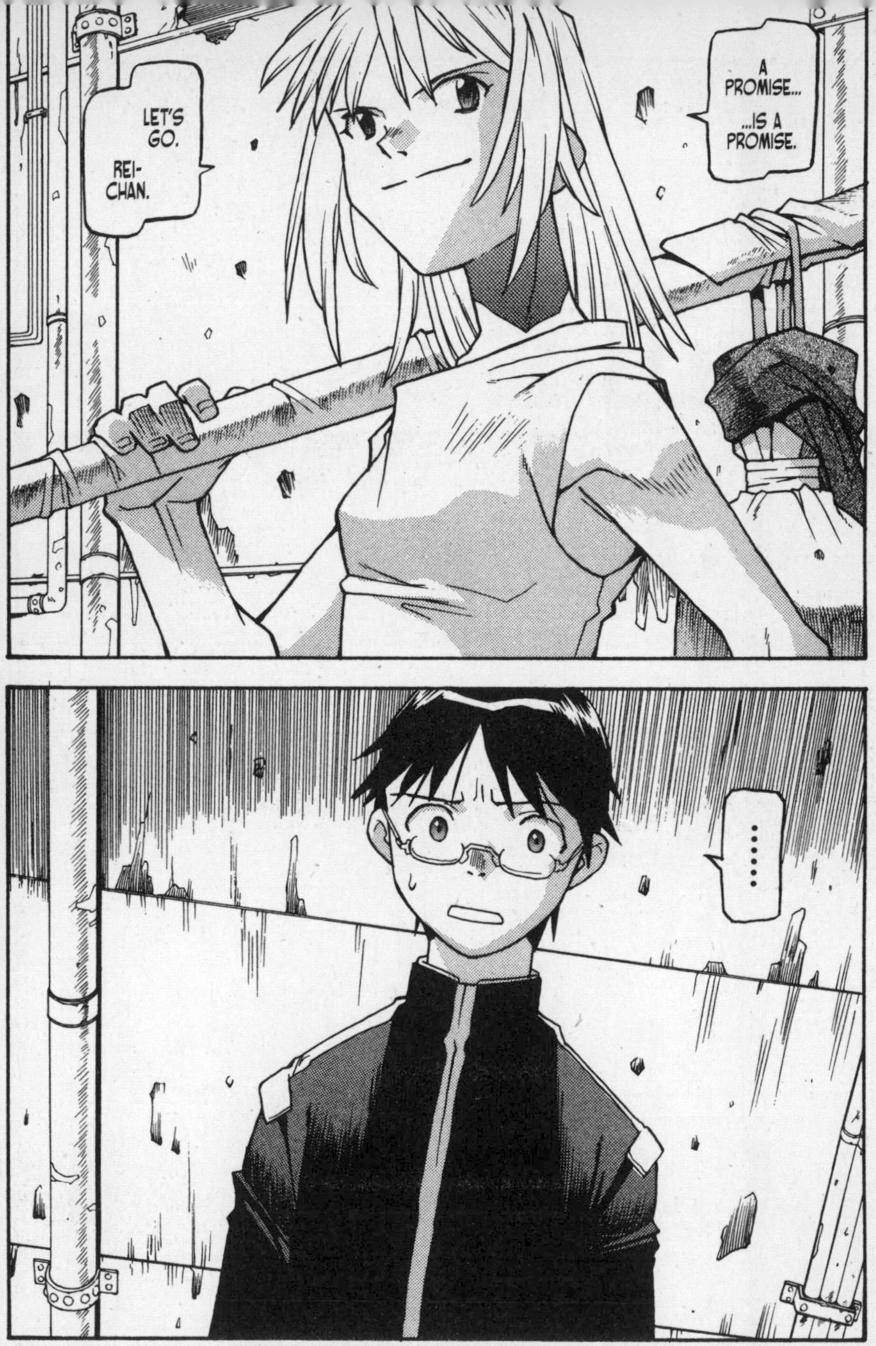
A PROMISE... ...IS A PROMISE.
LET'S GO. REI-CHAN.
......

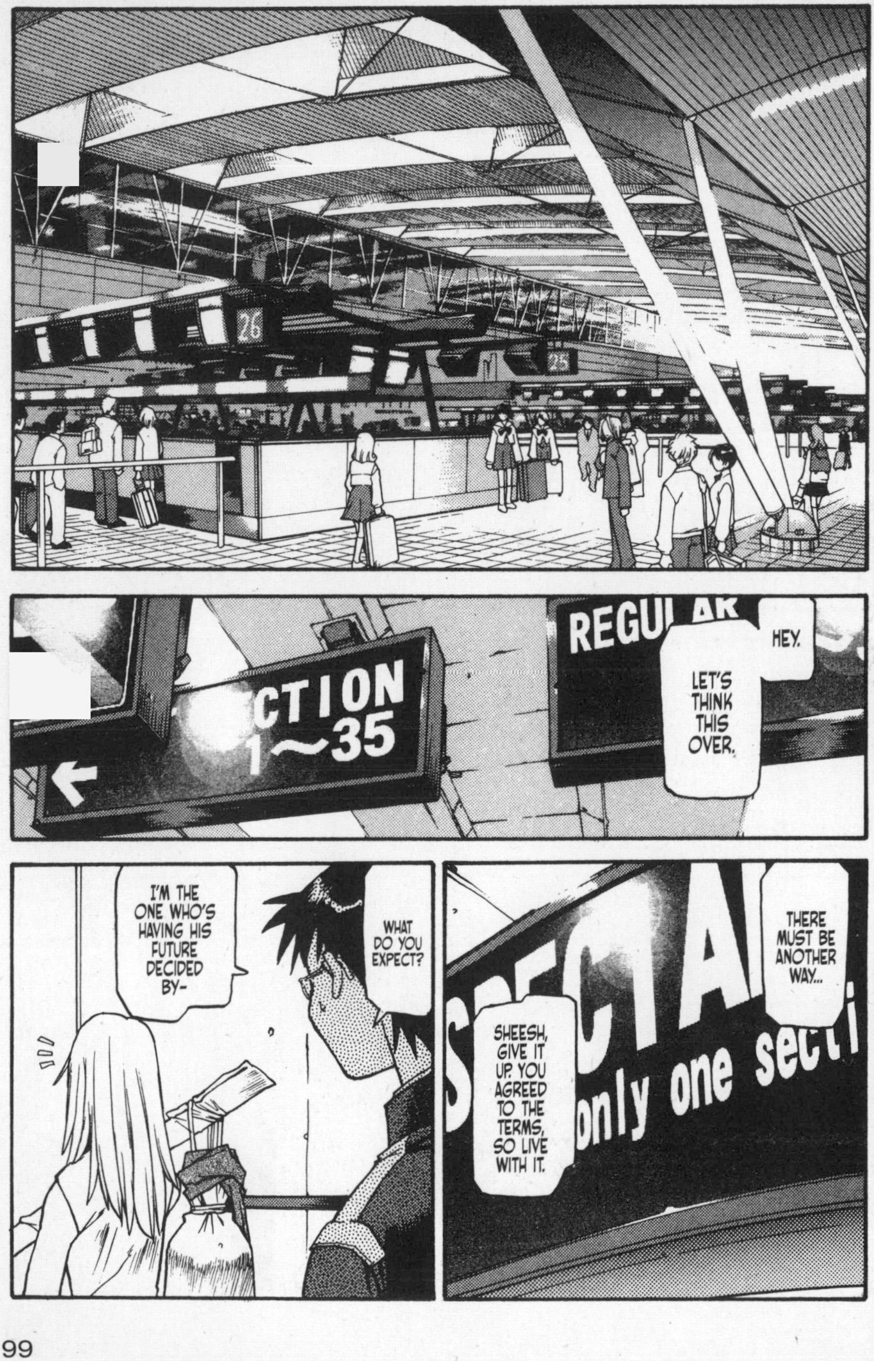
HEY.
LET'S THINK THIS OVER.
THERE MUST BE ANOTHER WAY...
SHEESH, GIVE IT UP. YOU AGREED TO THE TERMS, SO LIVE WITH IT.
WHAT DO YOU EXPECT?
I'M THE ONE WHO'S HAVING HIS FUTURE DECIDED BY-

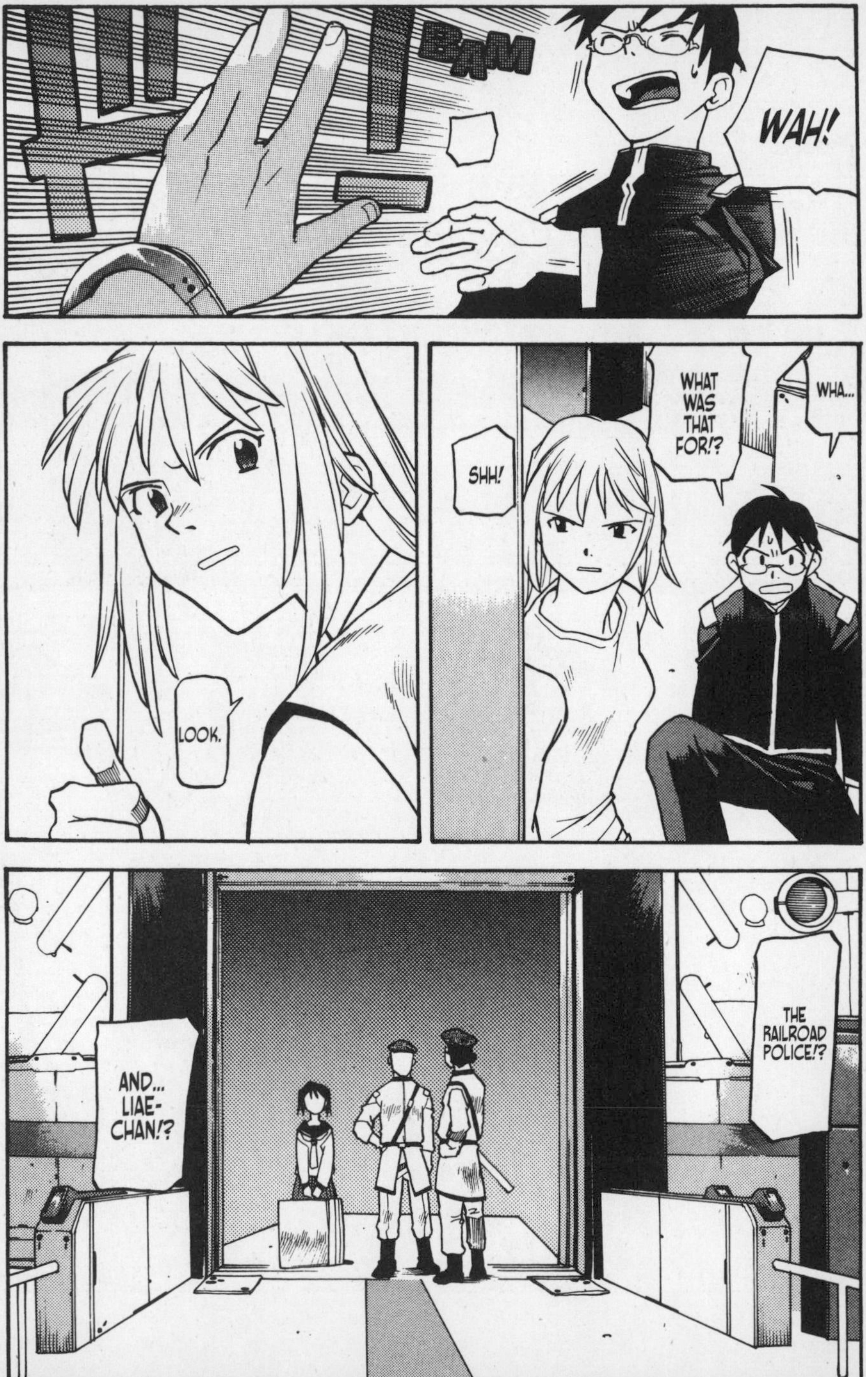
BAM
WAH!
WHA...
WHAT WAS THAT FOR!?
SHH!
LOOK.
THE RAILROAD POLICE!?
AND... LIAE-CHAN!?

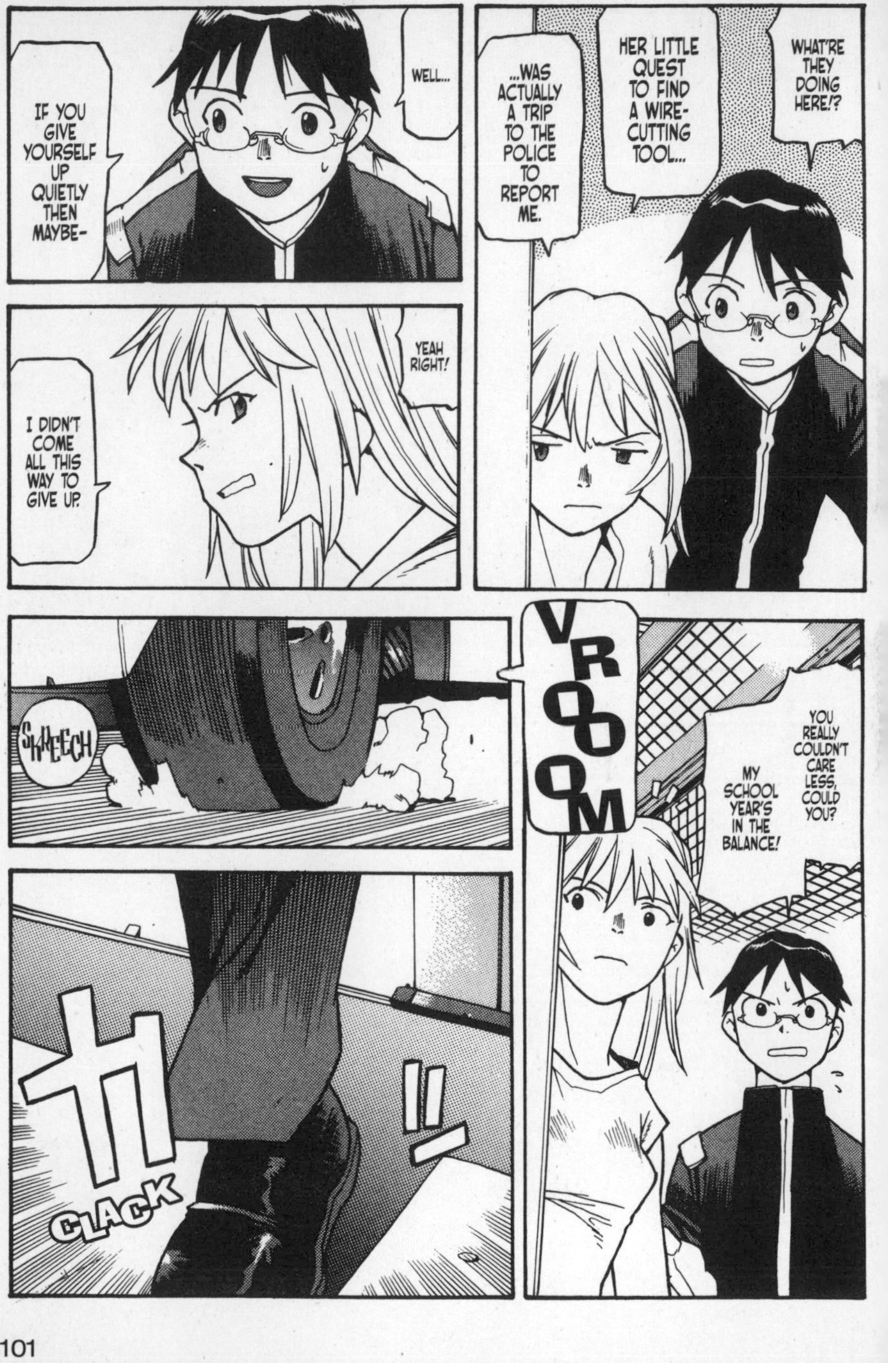
WHAT'RE THEY DOING HERE!?
HER LITTLE QUEST TO FIND A WIRE-CUTTING TOOL...
...WAS ACTUALLY A TRIP TO THE POLICE TO REPORT ME.
WELL...
IF YOU GIVE YOURSELF UP QUIETLY THEN MAYBE-
YEAH RIGHT!
I DIDN'T COME ALL THIS WAY TO GIVE UP.
VROOOOM
YOU REALLY COULDN'T CARE LESS, COULD YOU?
MY SCHOOL YEAR'S IN THE BALANCE!
SKREECH
CLACK

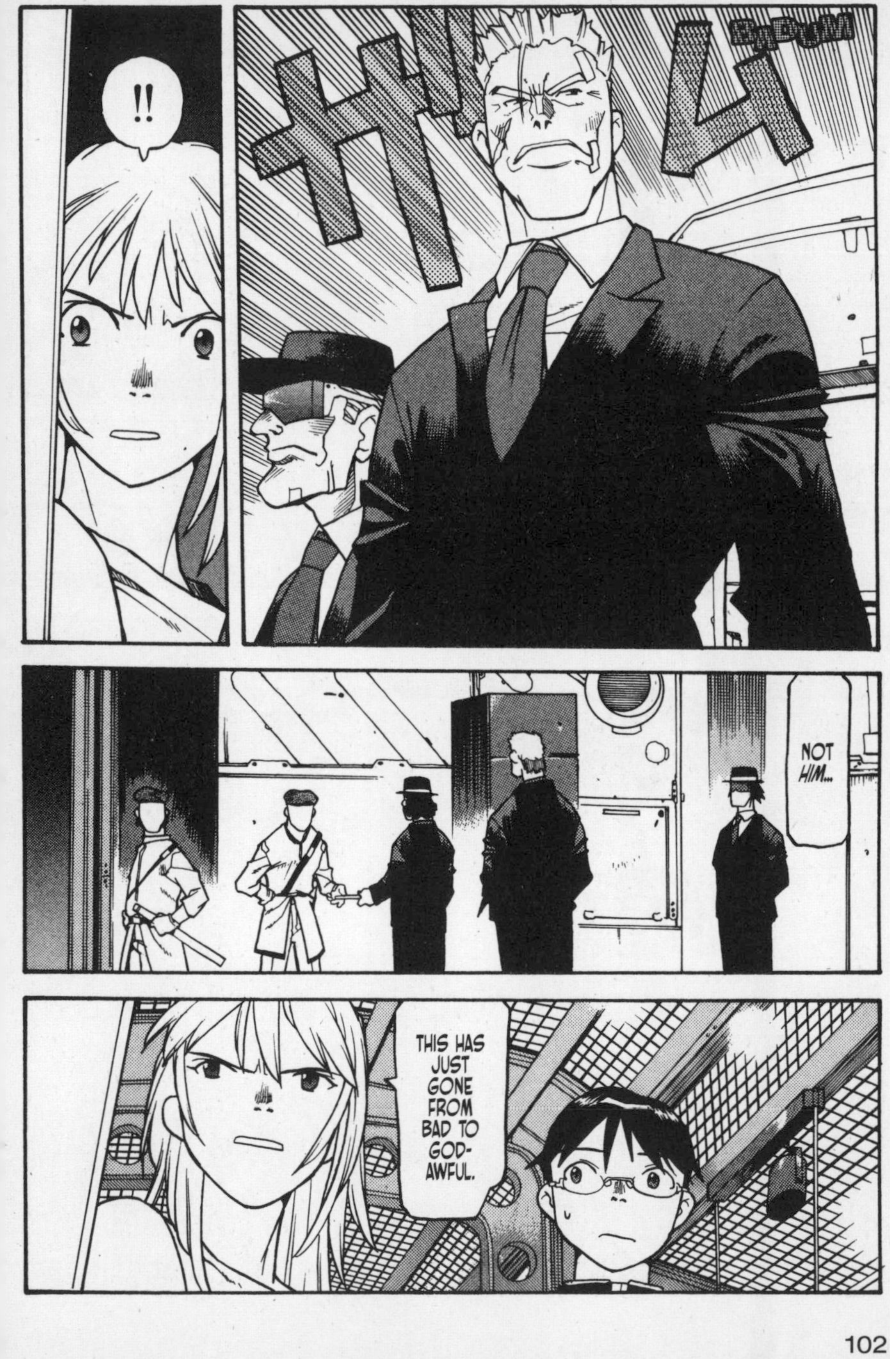
BaDuM
!!
NOT HIM...
THIS HAS JUST GONE FROM BAD TO GOD-AWFUL.

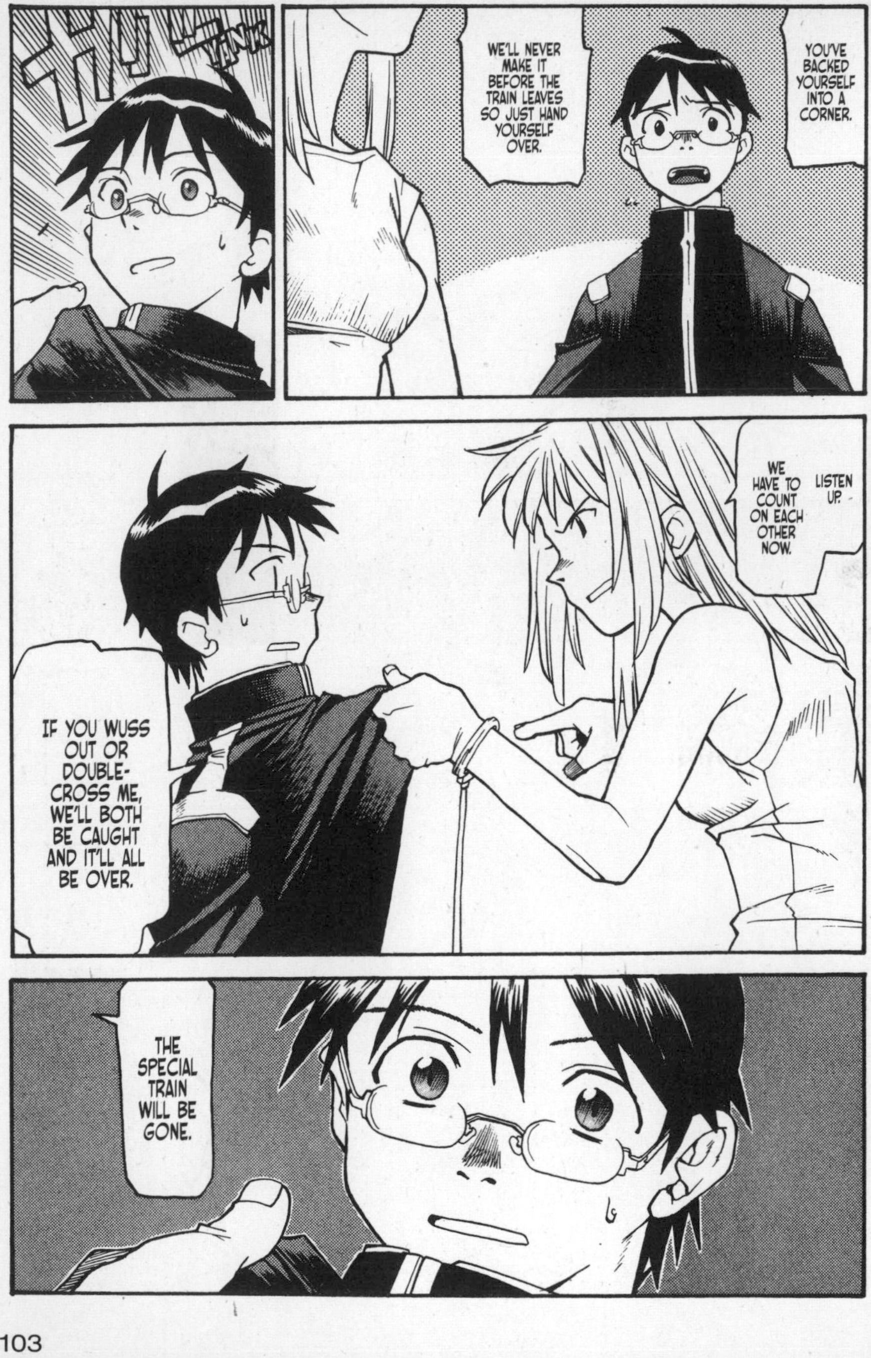
YOU'VE BACKED YOURSELF INTO A CORNER.
WE'LL NEVER MAKE IT BEFORE THE TRAIN LEAVES SO JUST HAND YOURSELF OVER.
YENK
LISTEN UP.
WE HAVE TO COUNT ON EACH OTHER NOW.
IF YOU WUSS OUT OR DOUBLE-CROSS ME, WE'LL BOTH BE CAUGHT AND IT'LL ALL BE OVER.
THE SPECIAL TRAIN WILL BE GONE.

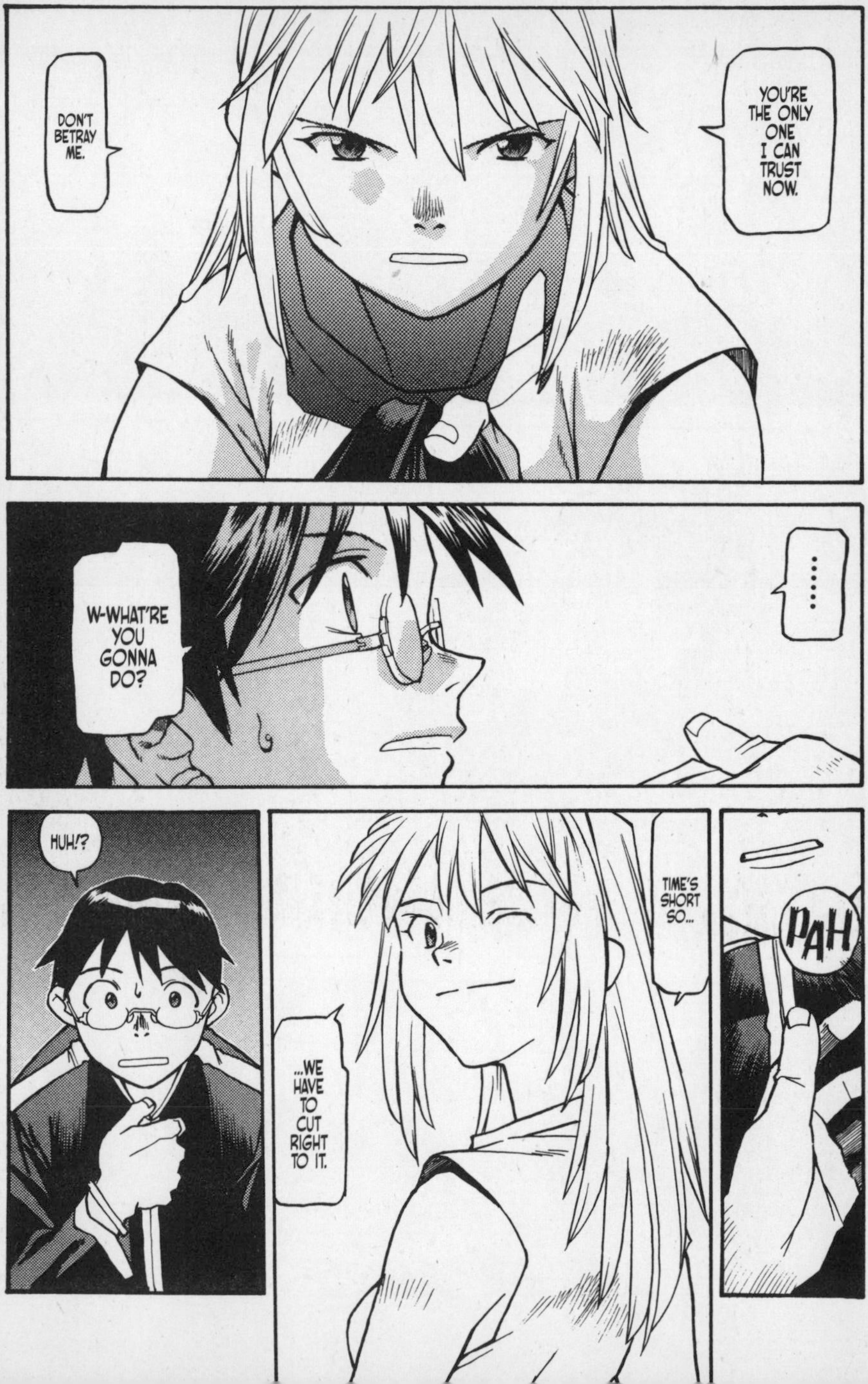
YOU'RE THE ONLY ONE I CAN TRUST NOW.
DON'T BETRAY ME.
......
W-WHAT'RE YOU GONNA DO?
PAH
TIME'S SHORT SO...
...WE HAVE TO CUT RIGHT TO IT.
HUH!?

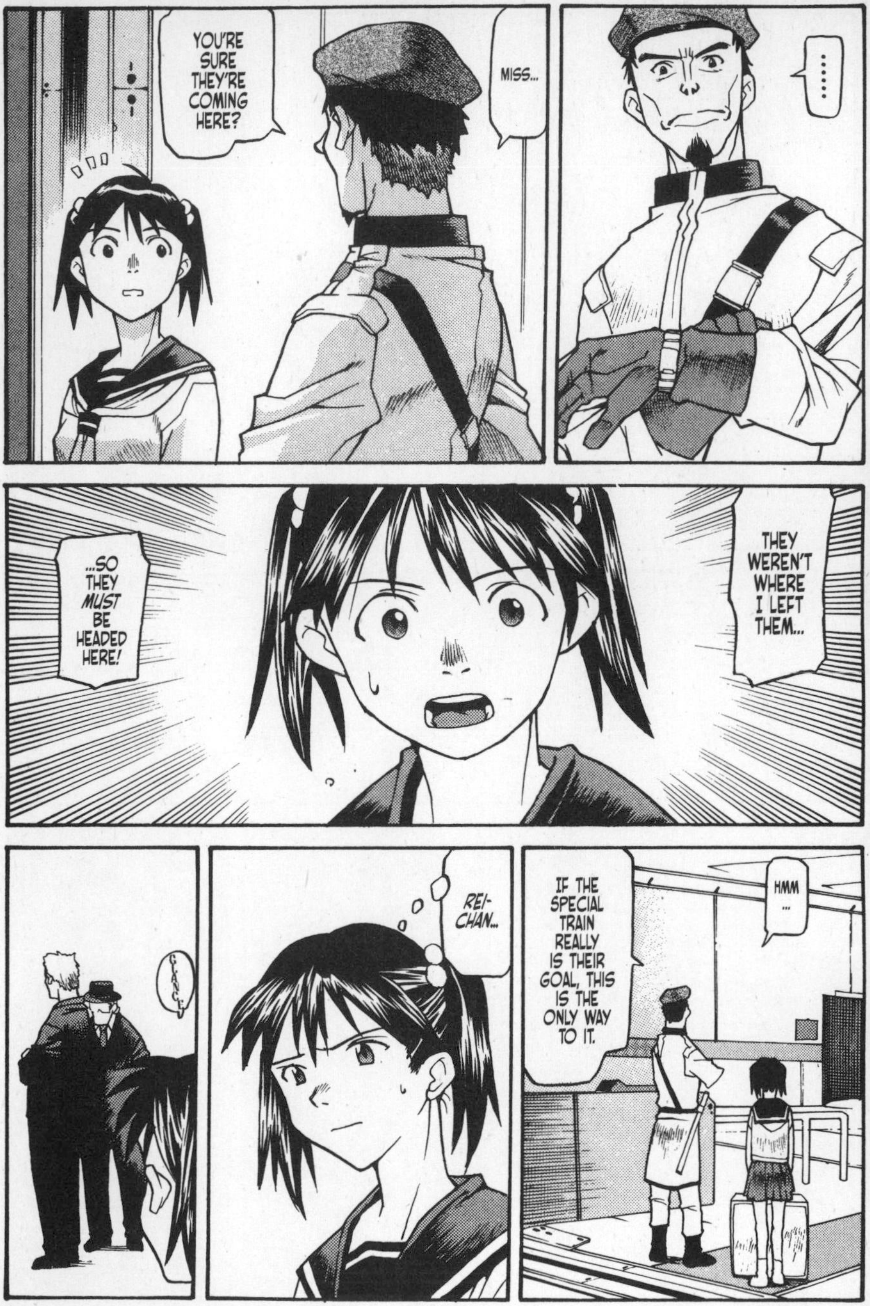
……
MISS...
YOU'RE SURE THEY'RE COMING HERE?
THEY WEREN'T WHERE I LEFT THEM...
...SO THEY *MUST* BE HEADED HERE!
HMM ...
IF THE SPECIAL TRAIN REALLY IS THEIR GOAL, THIS IS THE ONLY WAY TO IT.
REI-CHAN...
GLANCE

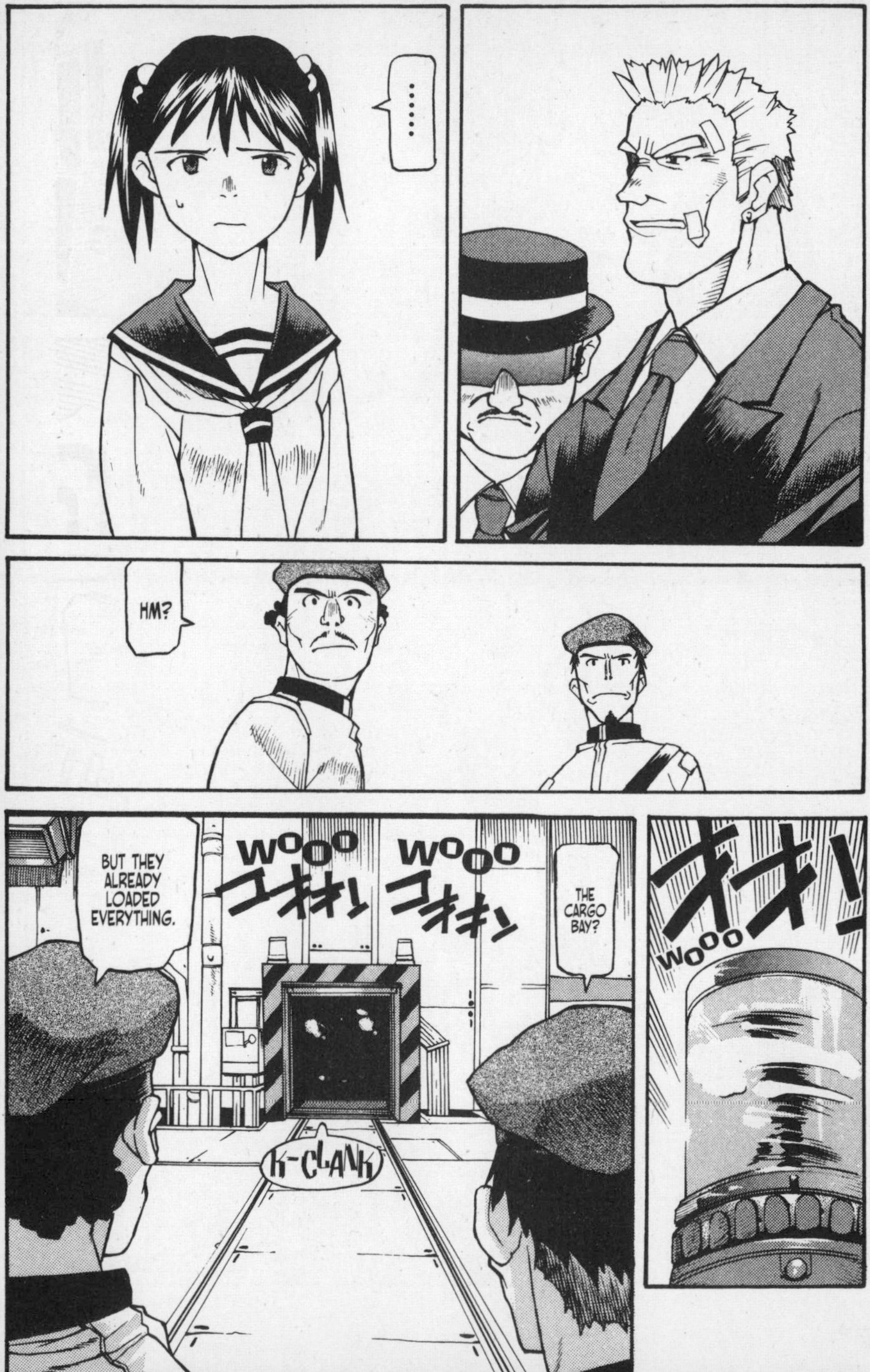
……
HM?
オオ!
WOOO
THE CARGO BAY?
WOOO
コオオン
WOOO
コオオン
BUT THEY ALREADY LOADED EVERYTHING.
K-CLANK

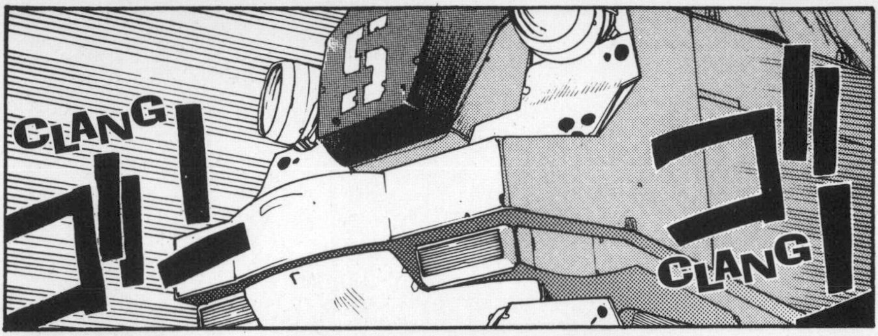
CLANG
CLANG

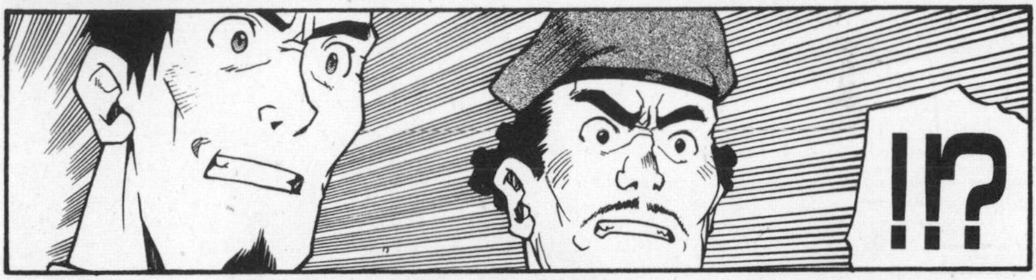
!!?

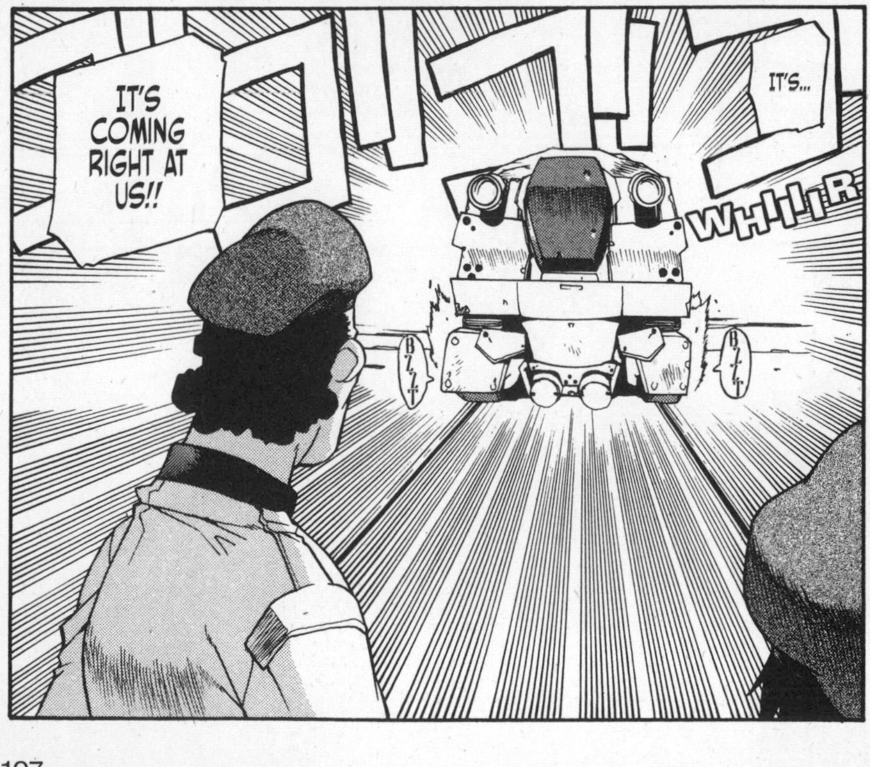
IT'S...
IT'S COMING RIGHT AT US!!
WHIIIR
BZZT
BZZT

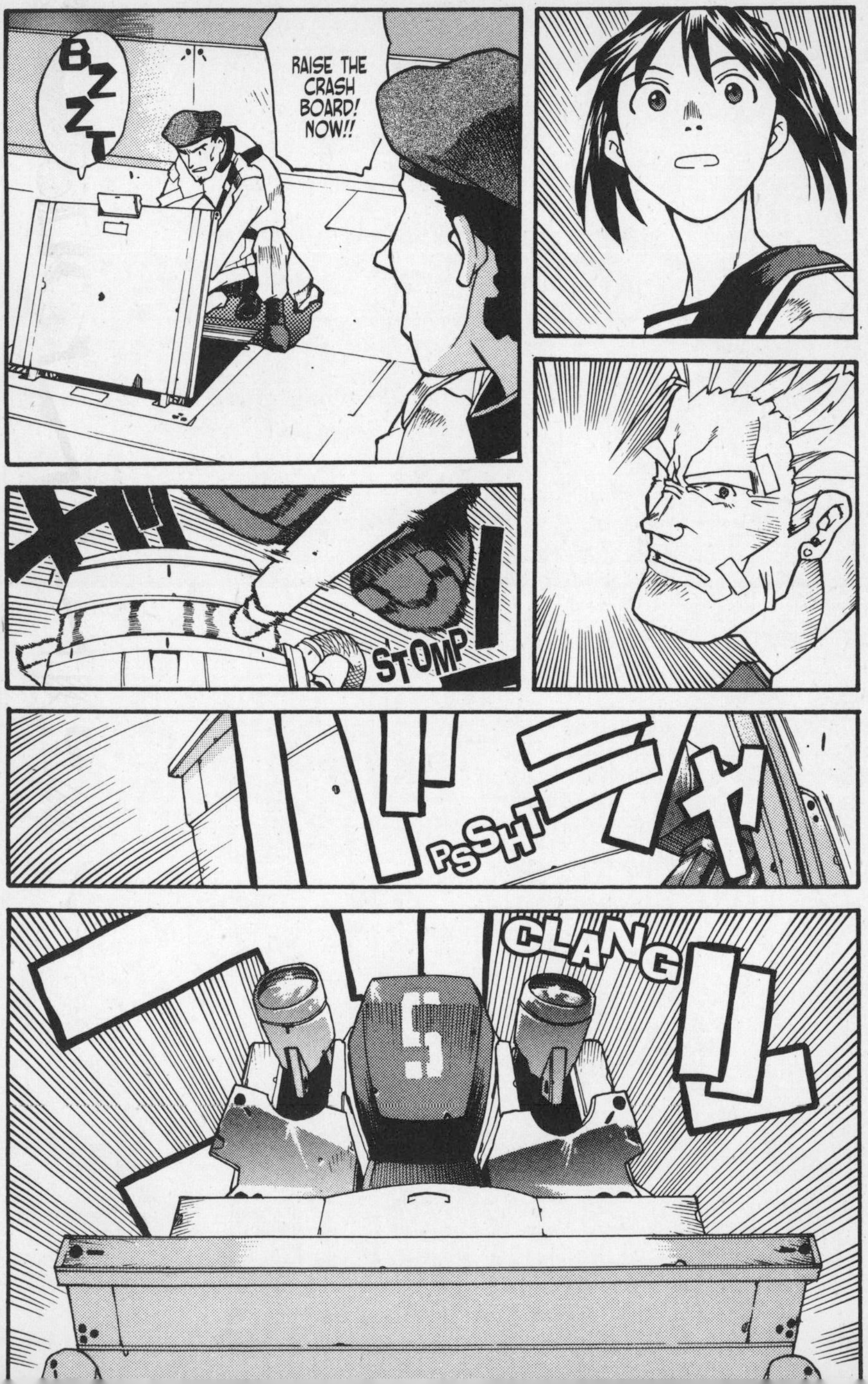
RAISE THE CRASH BOARD! NOW!!
BZZZT
STOMP
PSSHT
CLANG

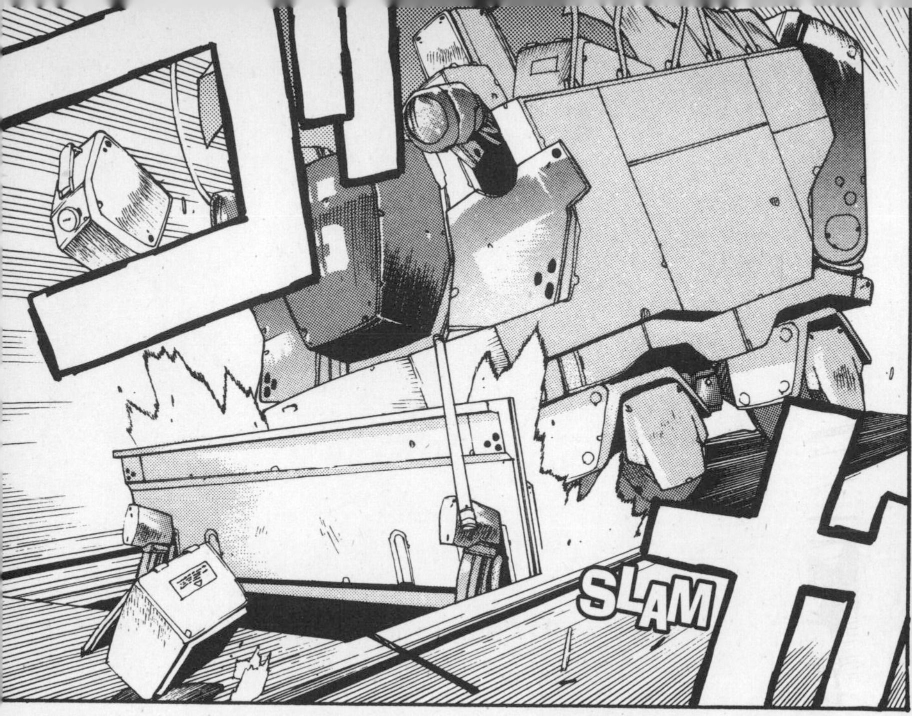
SLAM
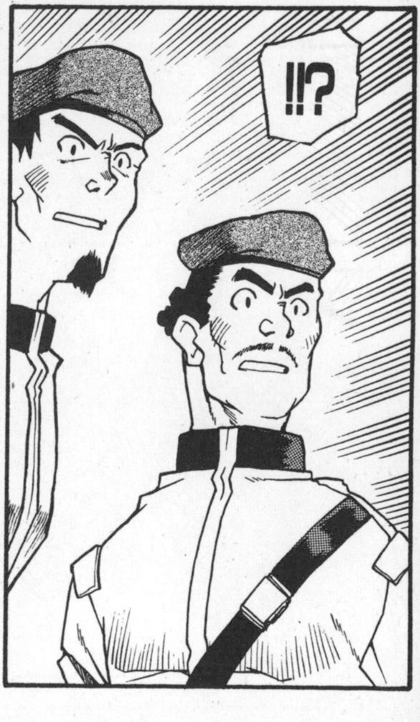
!!?
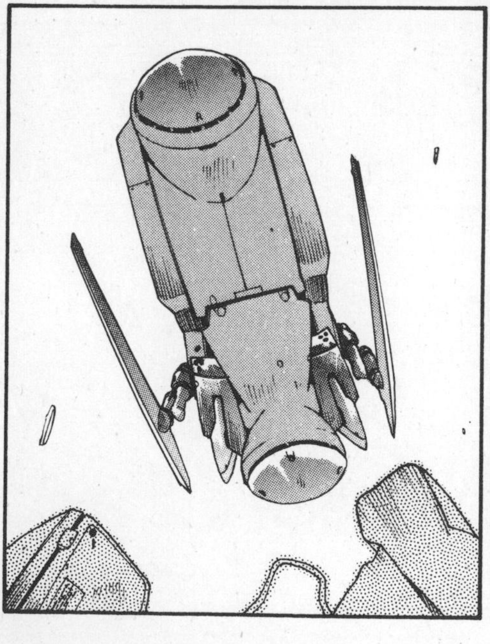

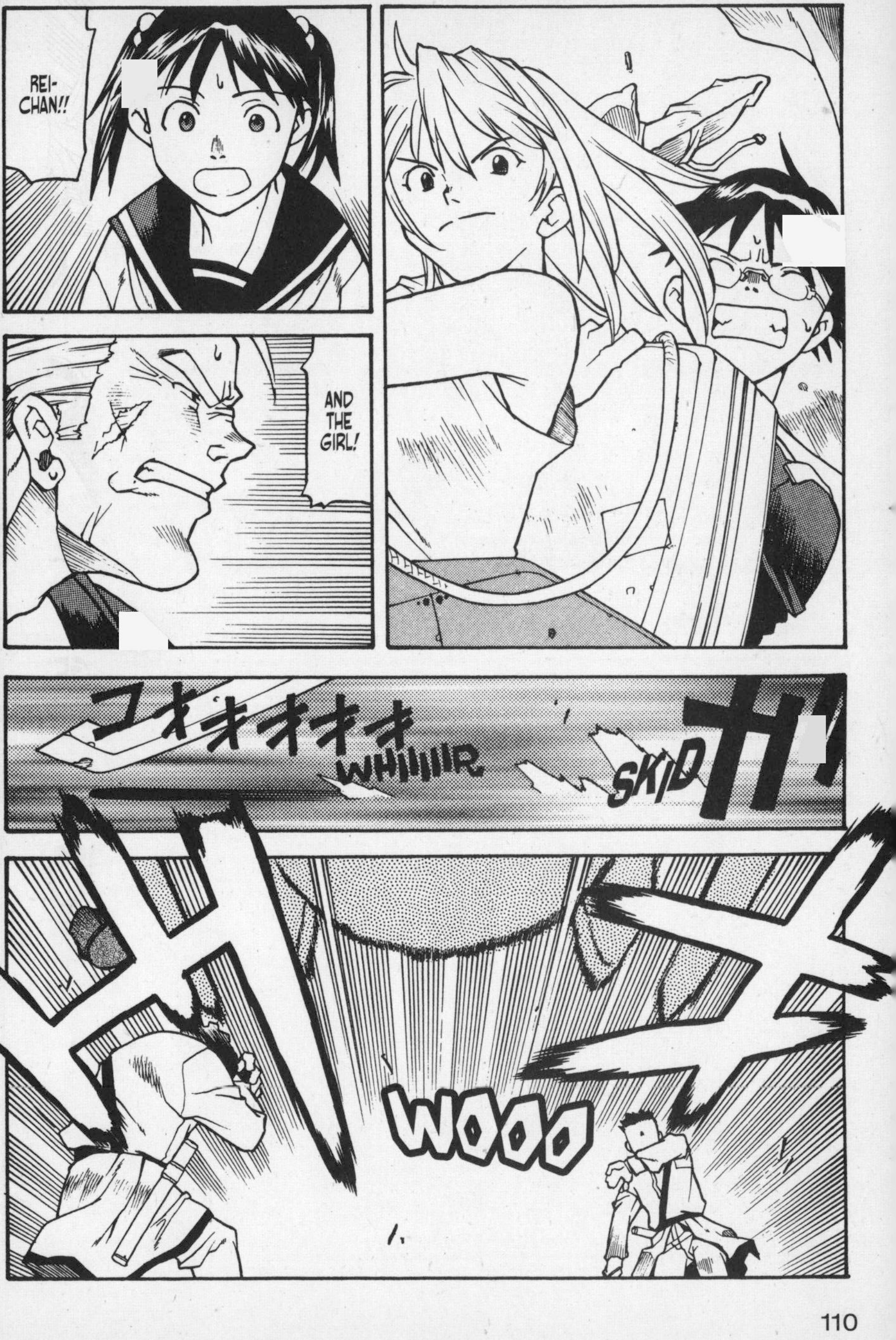
REI-CHAN!!
AND THE GIRL!
WHIIIIR
SKID
WOOO

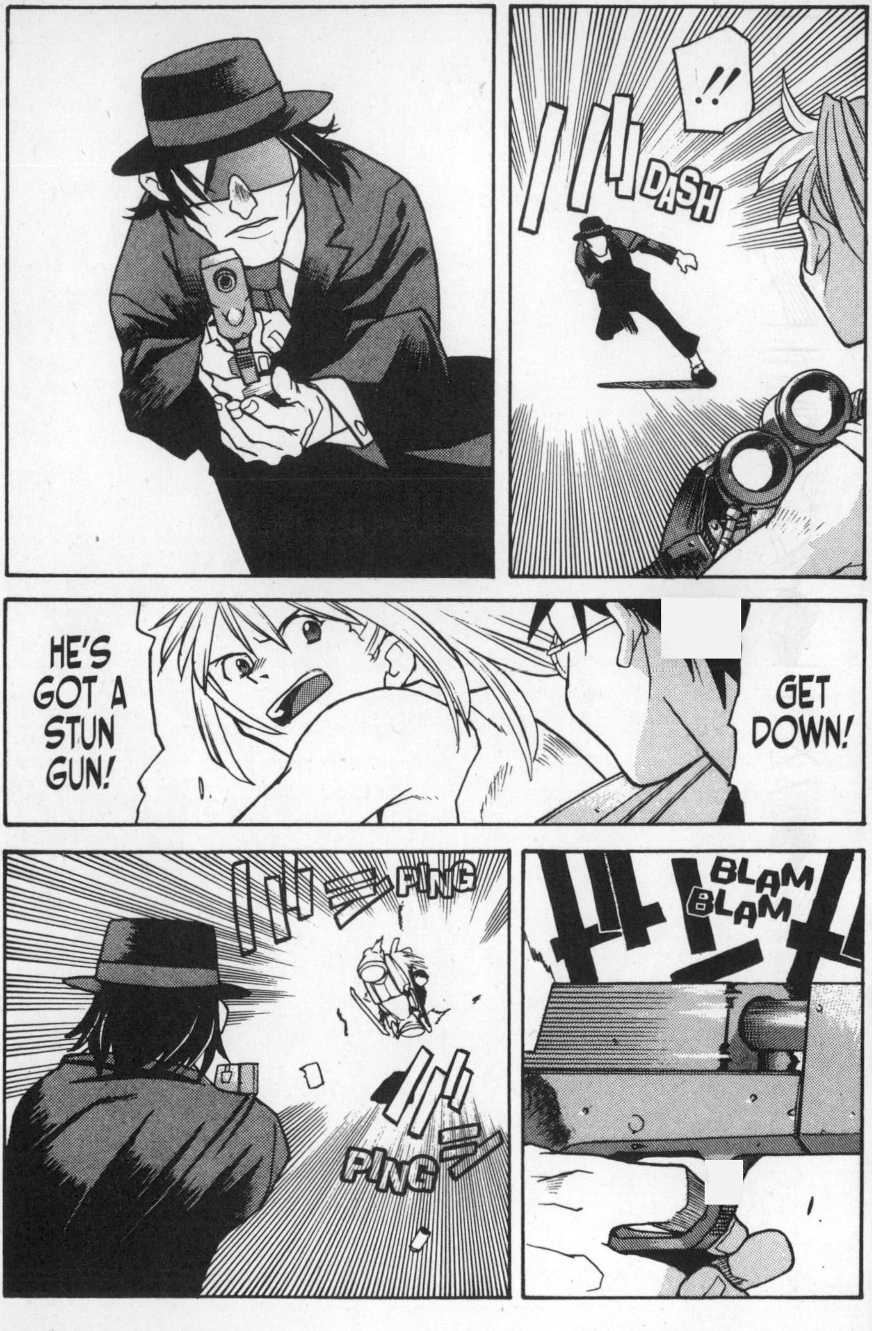
!!
DASH
GET DOWN!
HE'S GOT A STUN GUN!
BLAM BLAM
PING
PING

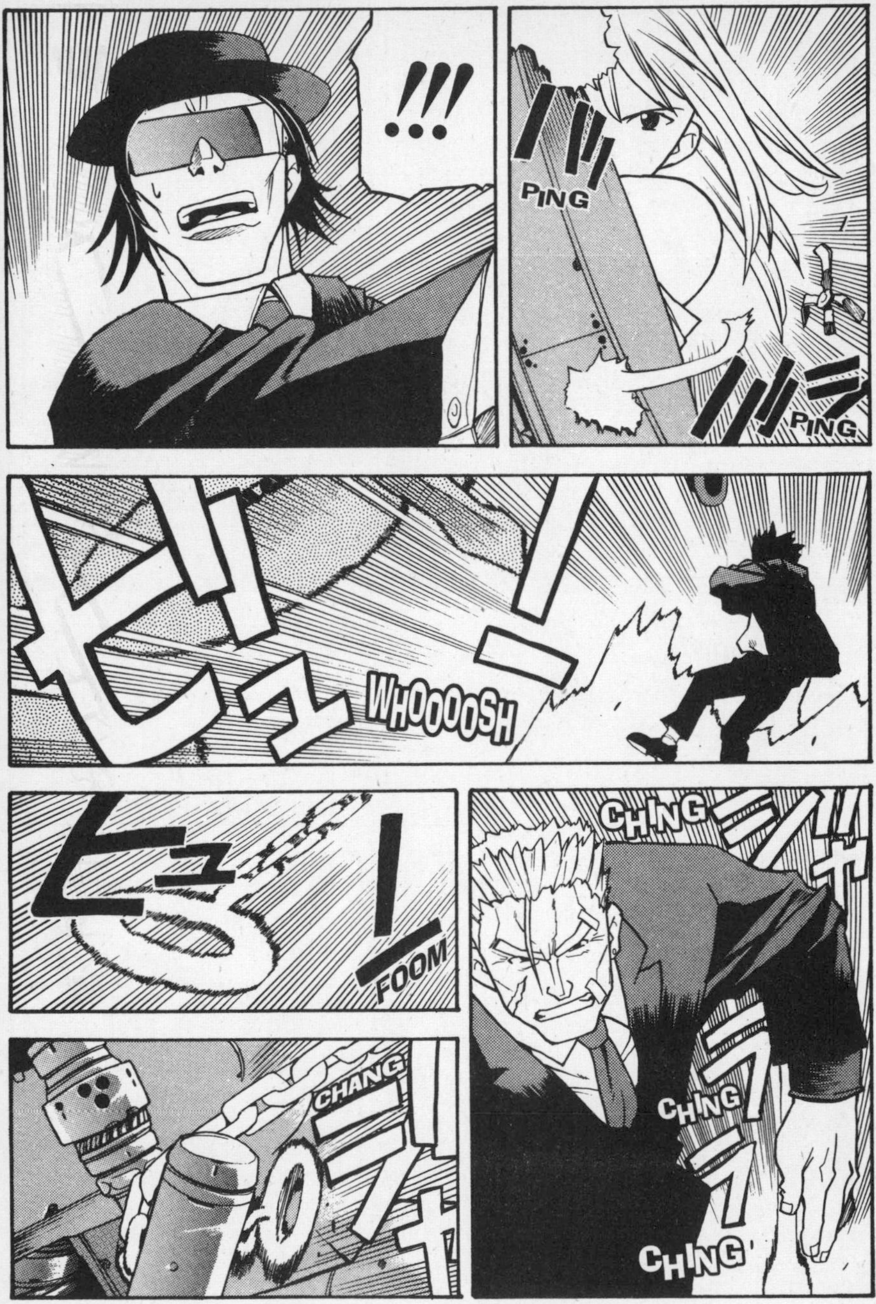
PING
PING
!!!
WHOOOOSH
CHING
CHING
CHING
FOOM
CHANG

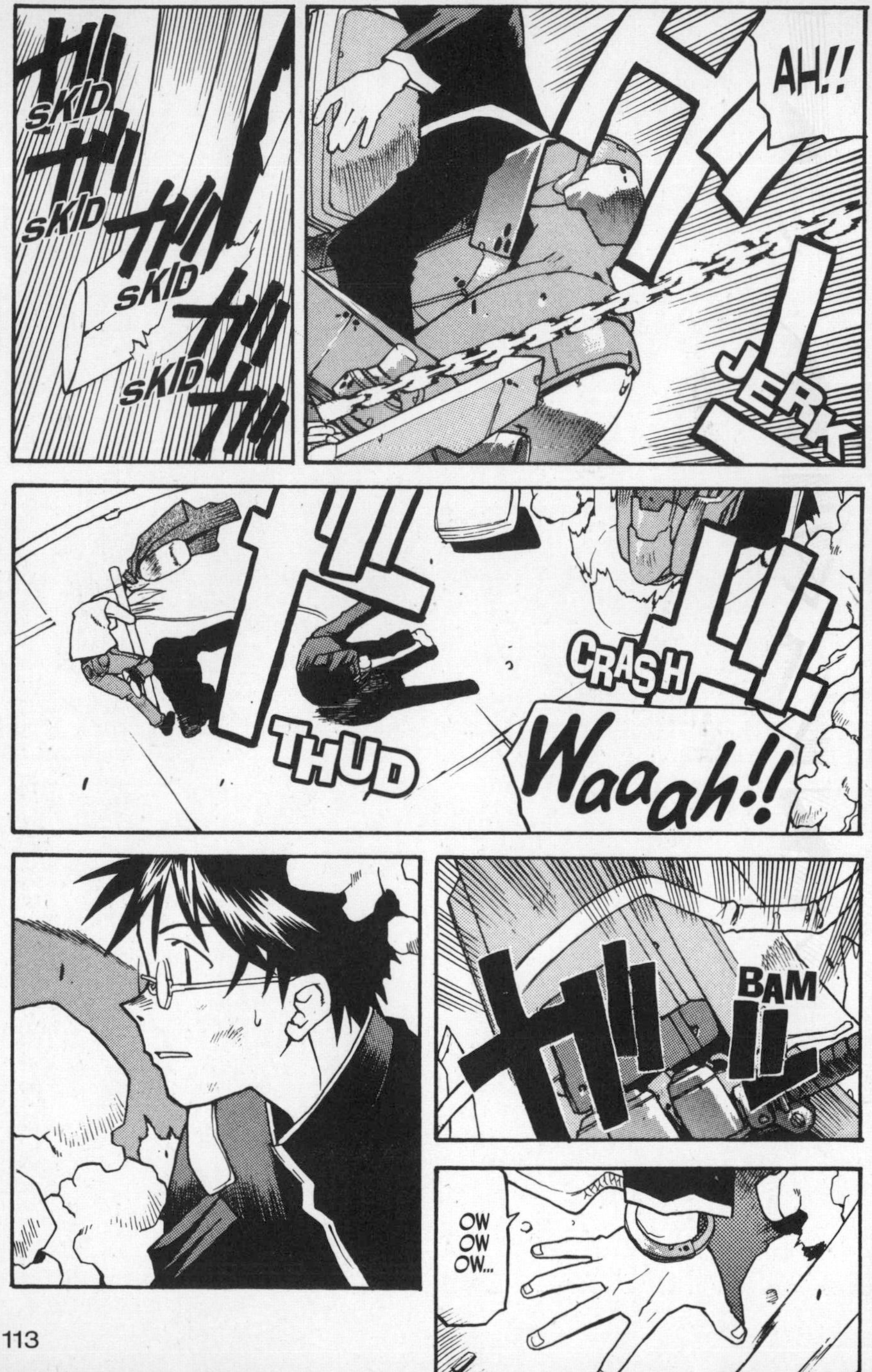
AH!!
JERK
SKID
SKID
SKID
SKID
CRASH
Waaah!!
THUD
BAM
OW
OW
OW...

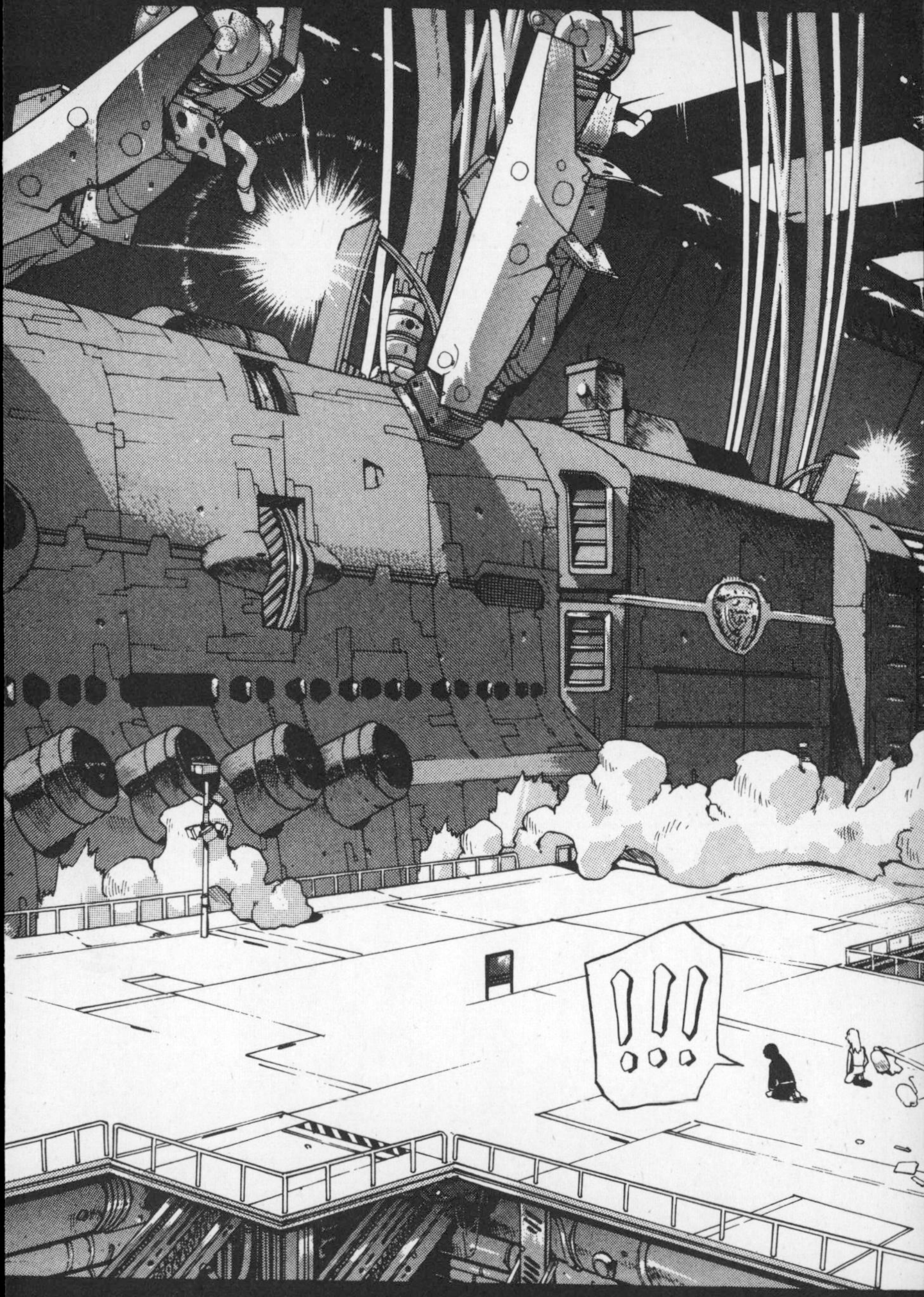
!!!

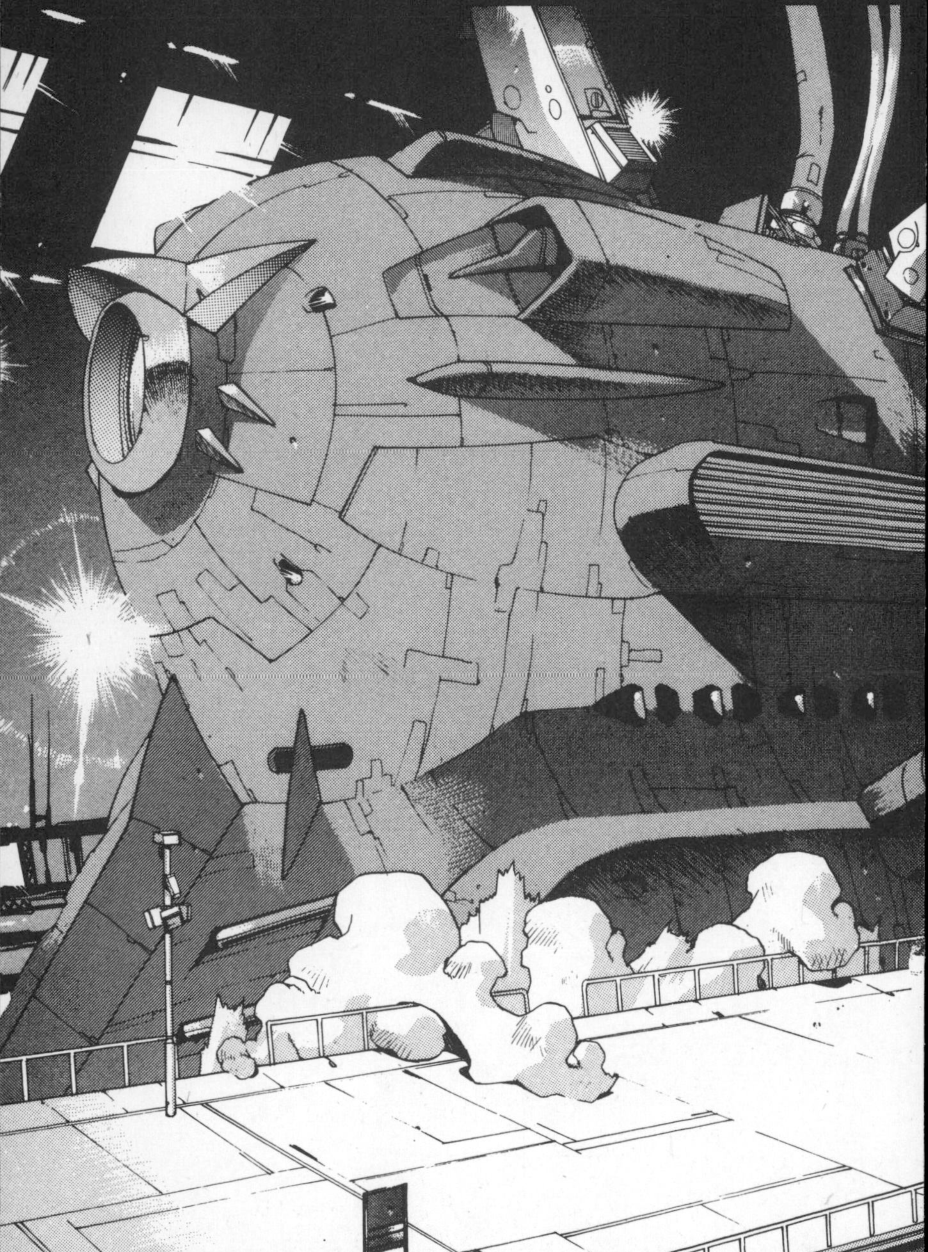

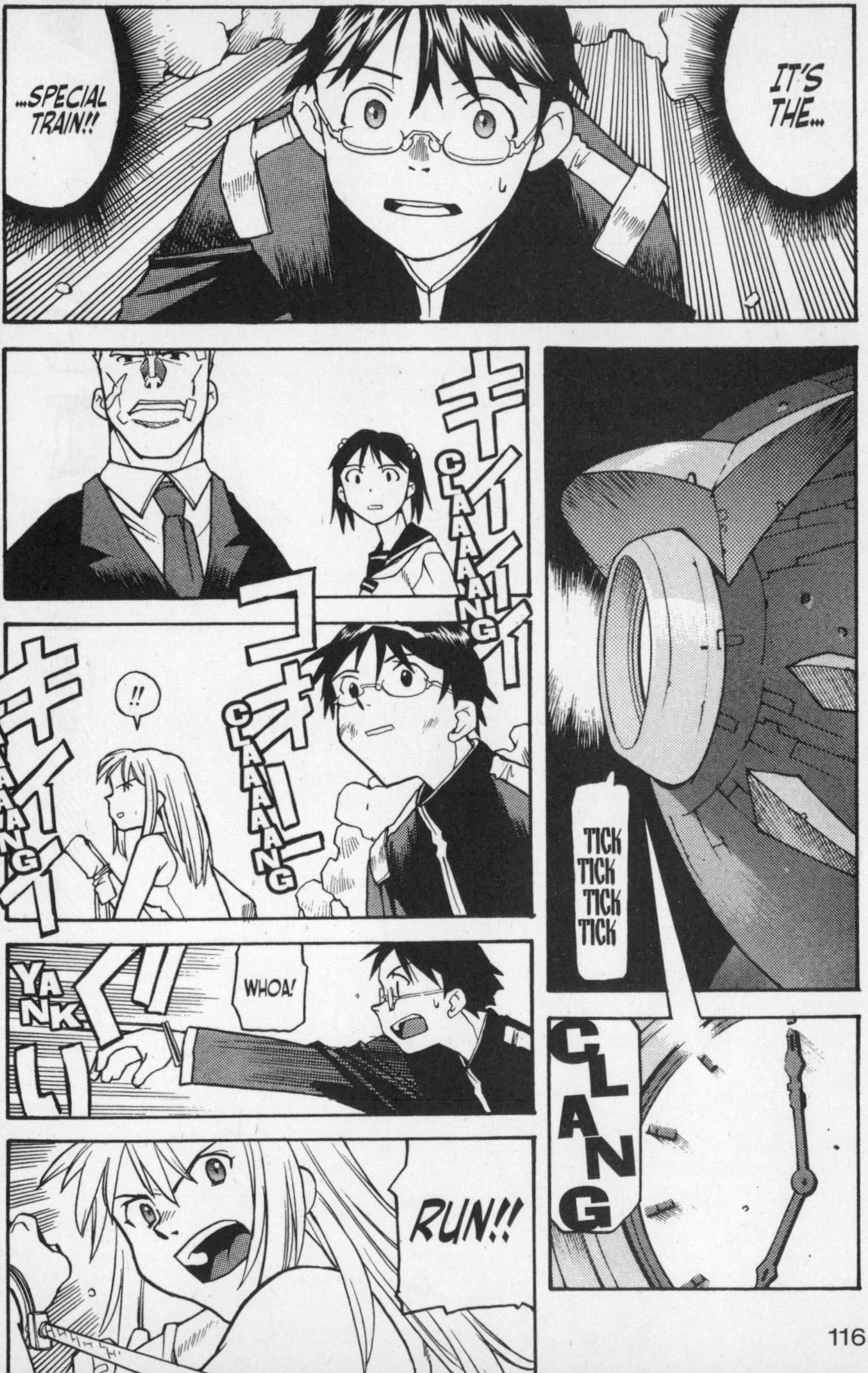
IT'S THE...
...SPECIAL TRAIN!!
TICK TICK TICK TICK
CLANG
CLAAAAAANG
CLAAAAAANG
!!
CLAAAAAANG
WHOA!
YANK
RUN!!

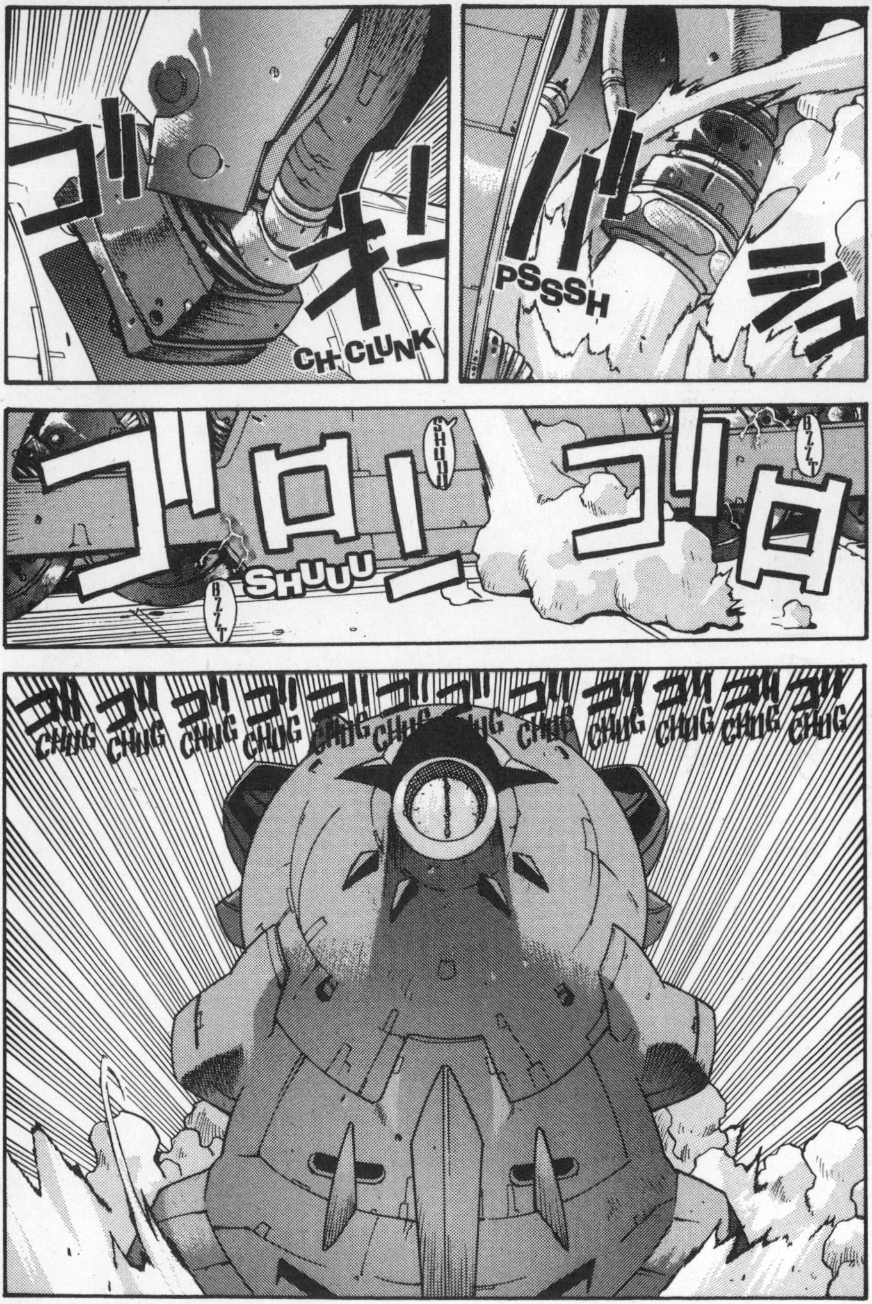
PSSSH
CH-CLUNK
BZZT
SHUUU
SHUUU
BZZT
CHUG CHUG CHUG CHUG CHUG CHUG CHUG CHUG CHUG CHUG CHUG CHUG

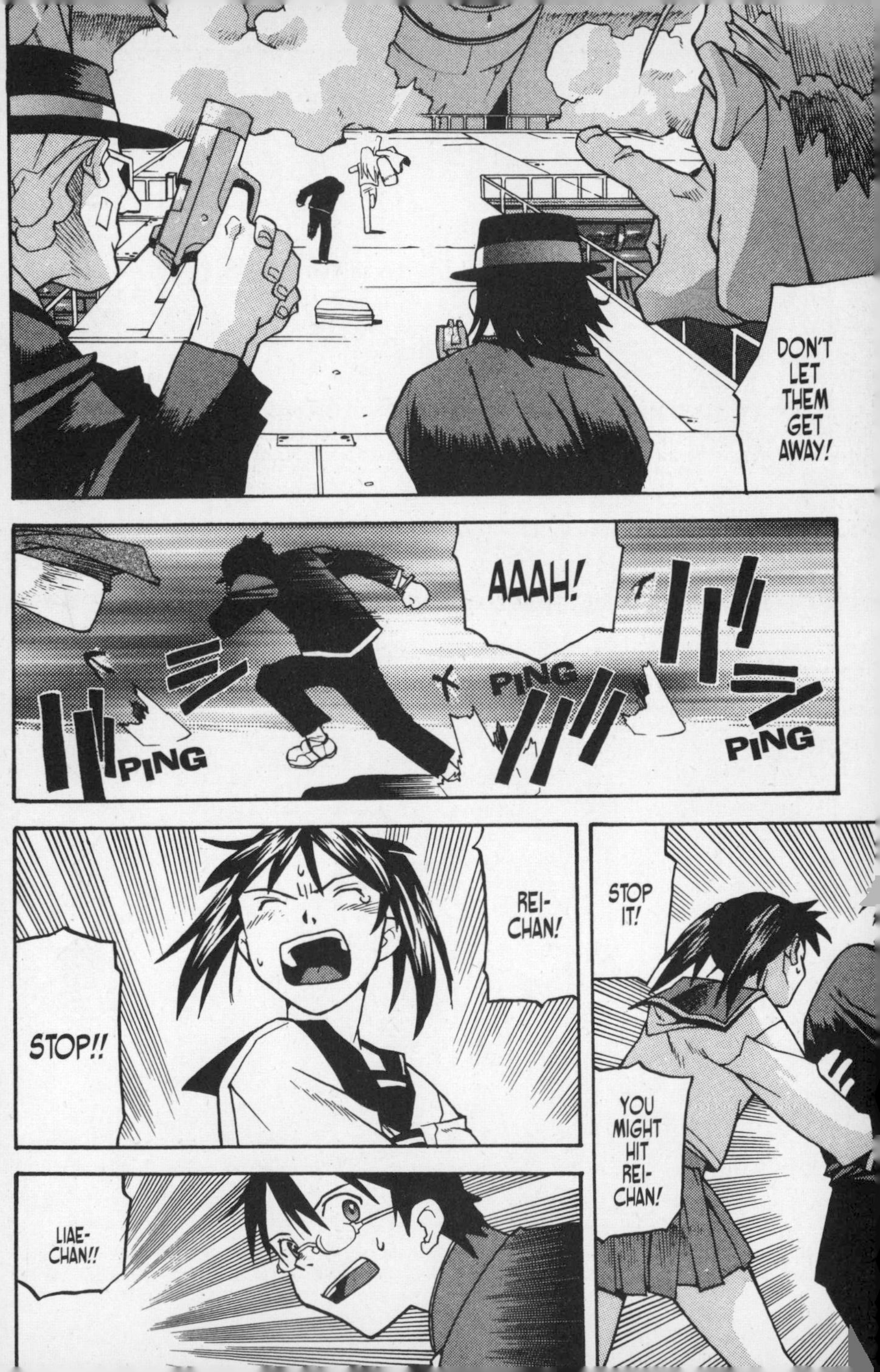
DON'T LET THEM GET AWAY!
AAAH!
PING
PING
PING
STOP IT!
YOU MIGHT HIT REI-CHAN!
REI-CHAN!
STOP!!
LIAE-CHAN!!

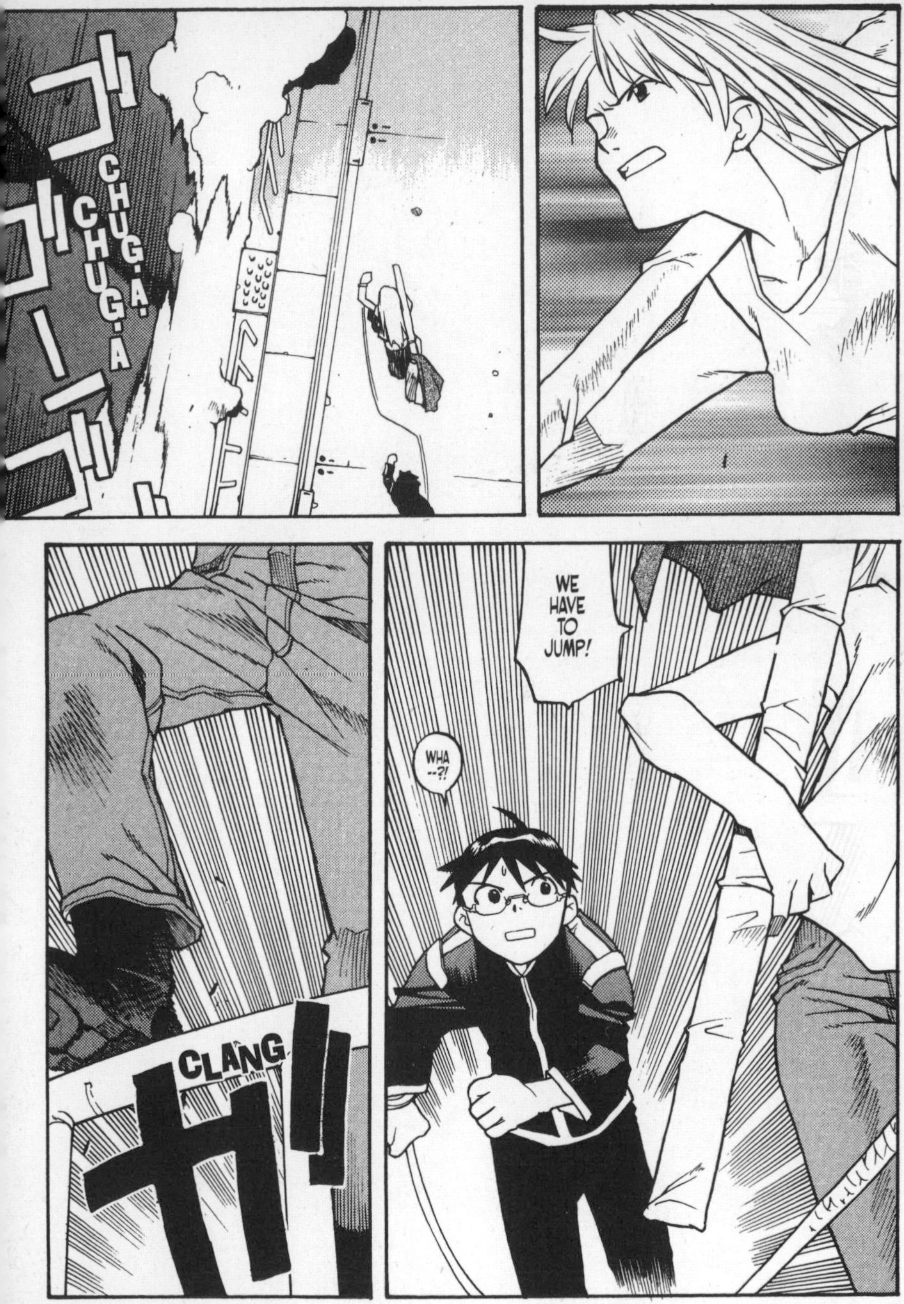
CHUG-A CHUG-A
WE HAVE TO JUMP!
WHA--?!
CLANG

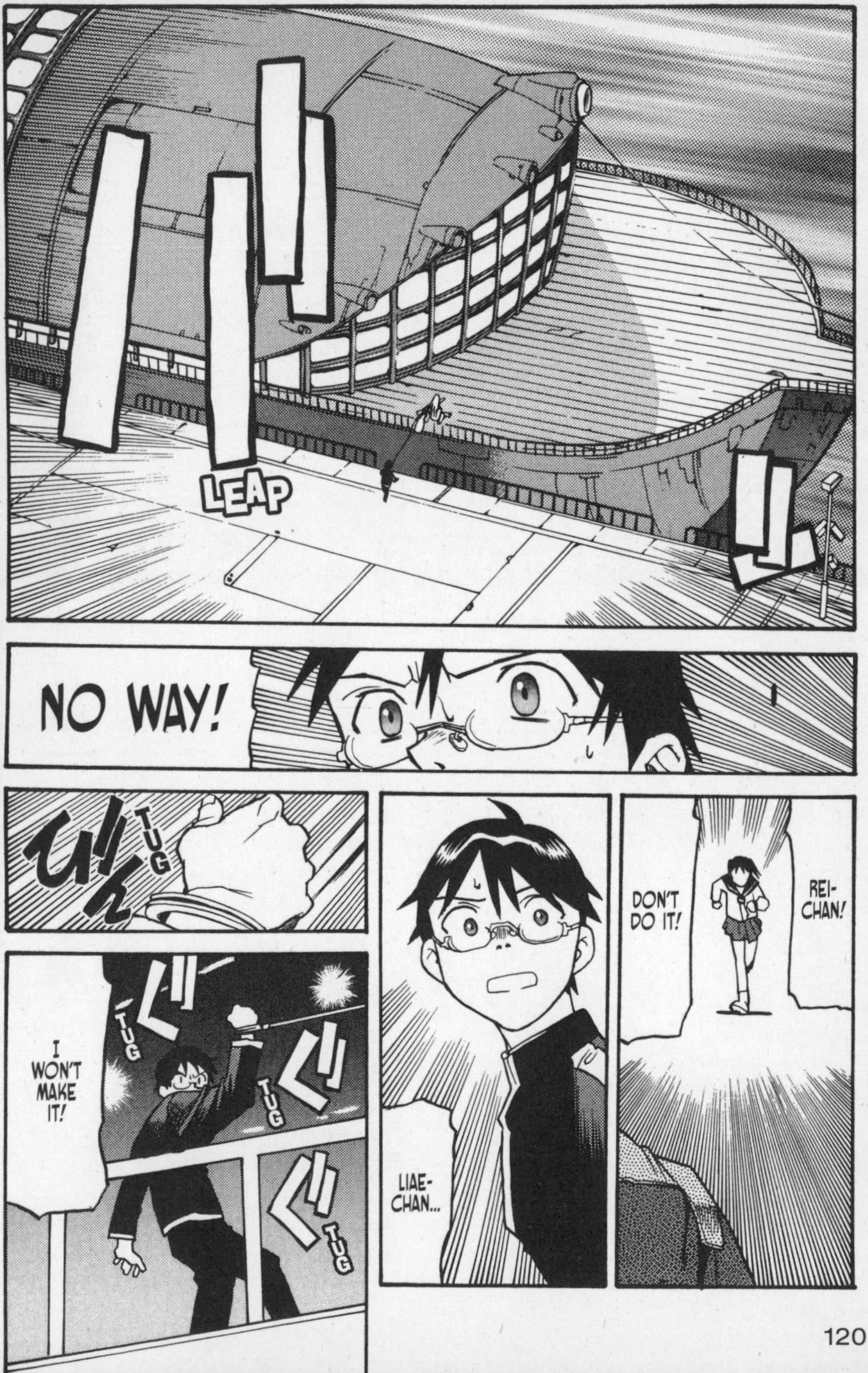
LEAP
NO WAY!
REI-CHAN!
DON'T DO IT!
LIAE-CHAN...
TUG
I WON'T MAKE IT!
TUG
TUG
TUG

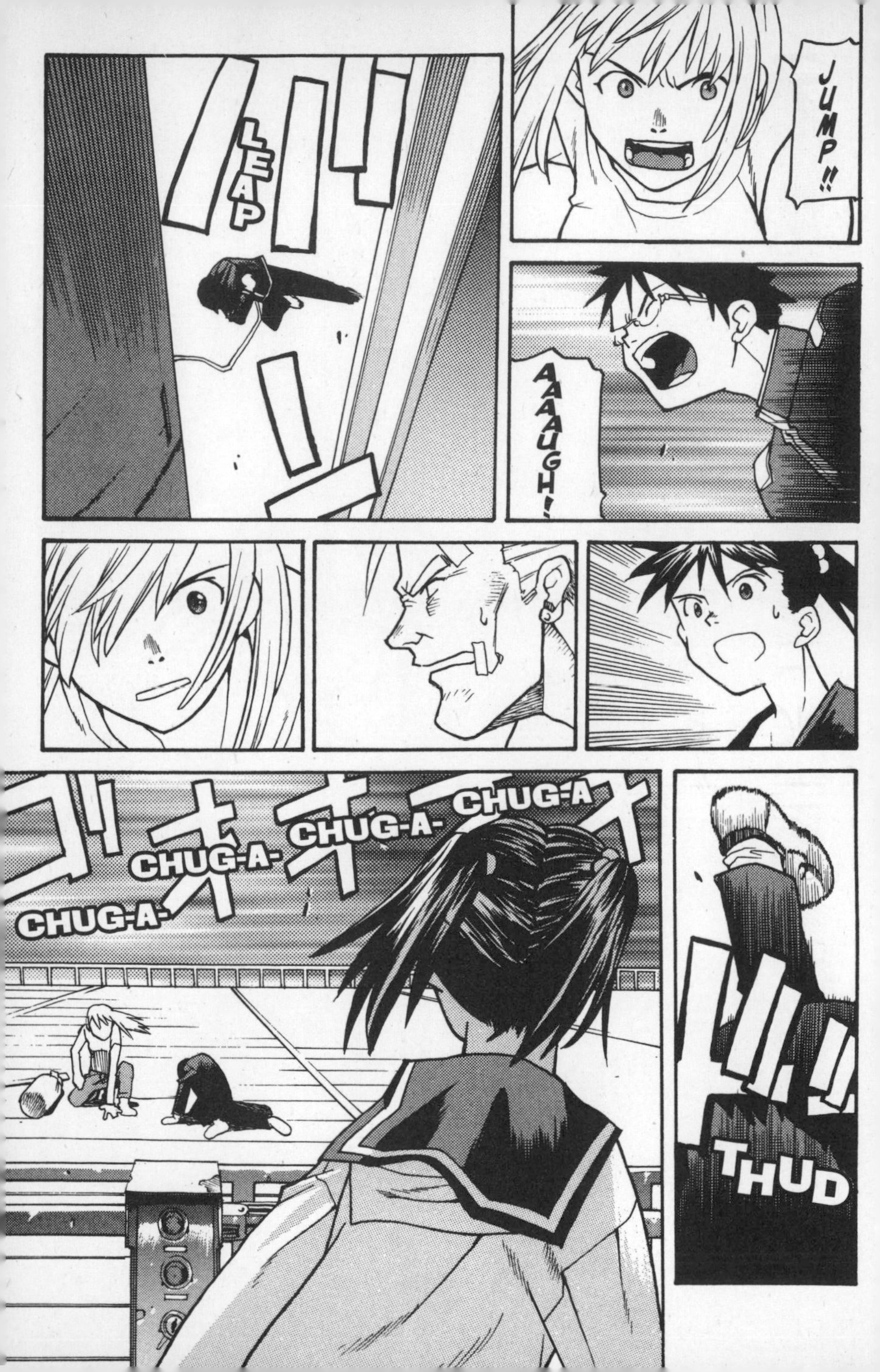
JUMP!!
AAAAUGH!!
LEAP
THUD
CHUG-A
CHUG-A-
CHUG-A-
CHUG-A-

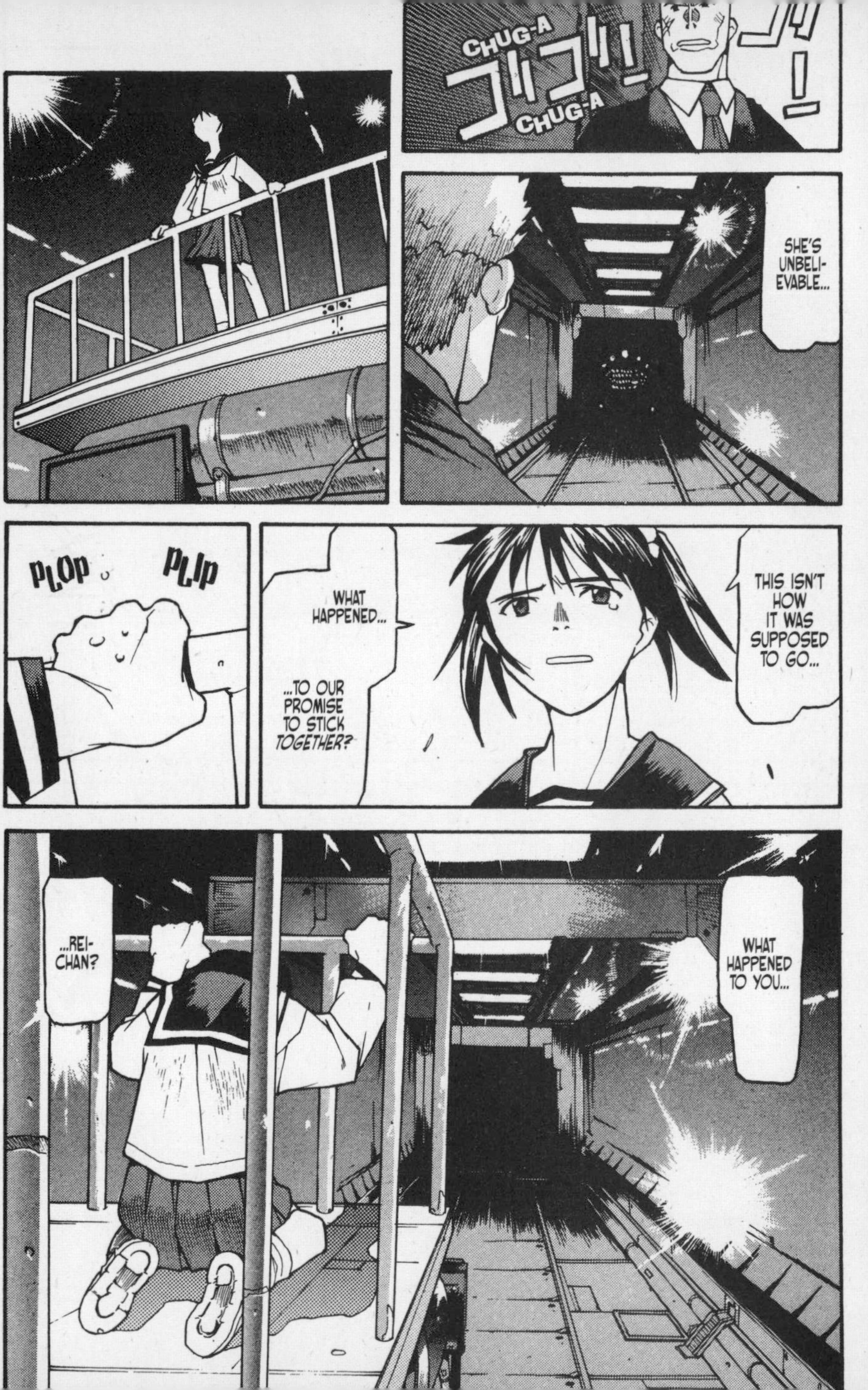
CHUG-A
CHUG-A
SHE'S UNBELI-EVABLE...
THIS ISN'T HOW IT WAS SUPPOSED TO GO...
WHAT HAPPENED...
...TO OUR PROMISE TO STICK *TOGETHER?*
PLIP
PLOP
WHAT HAPPENED TO YOU...
...REI-CHAN?

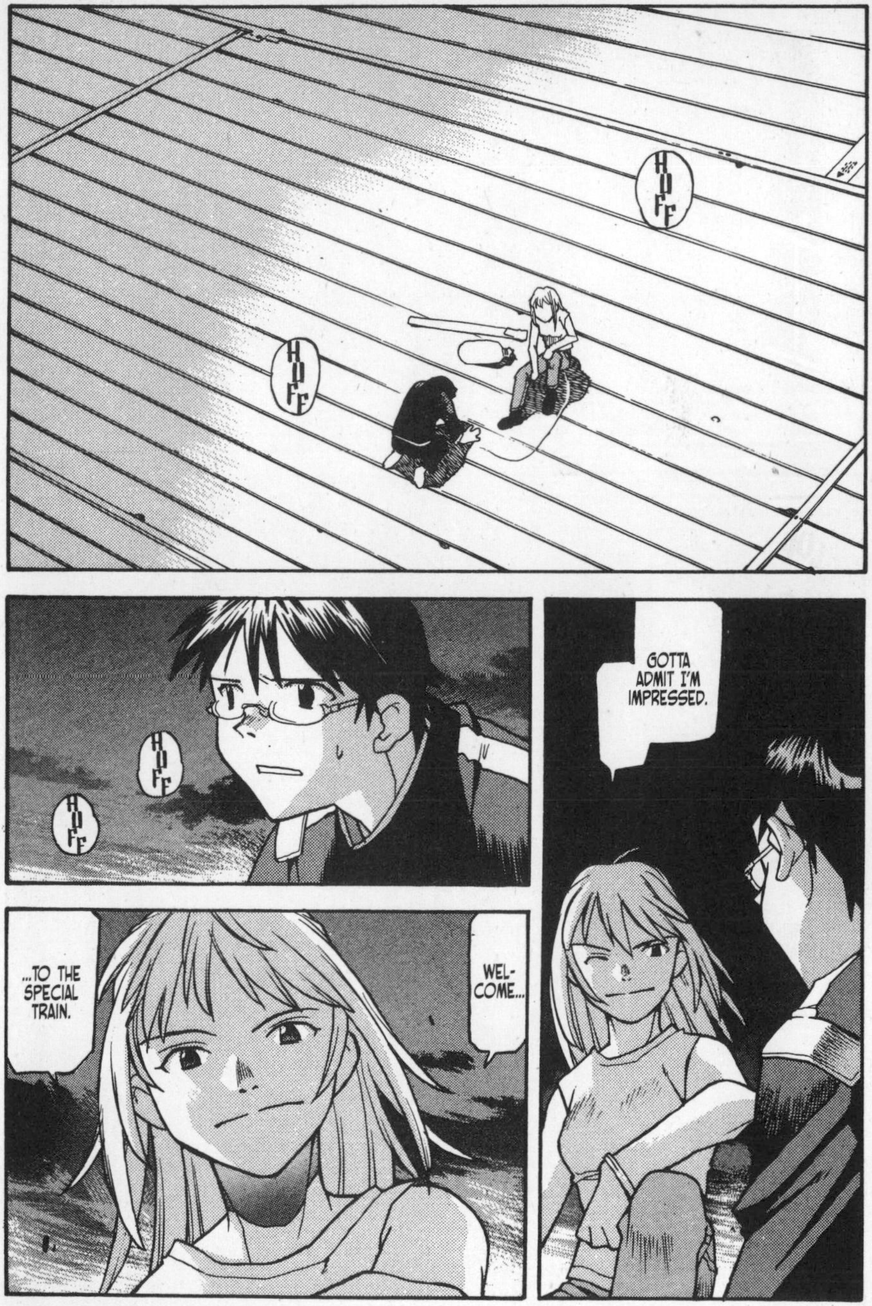
HUFF
HUFF
GOTTA ADMIT I'M IMPRESSED.
HUFF
HUFF
WEL-COME...
...TO THE SPECIAL TRAIN.

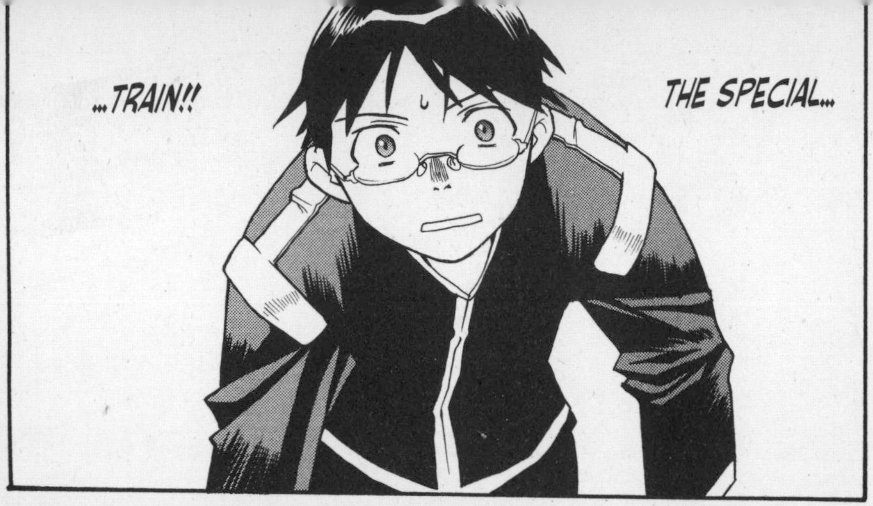
THE SPECIAL...
...TRAIN!!

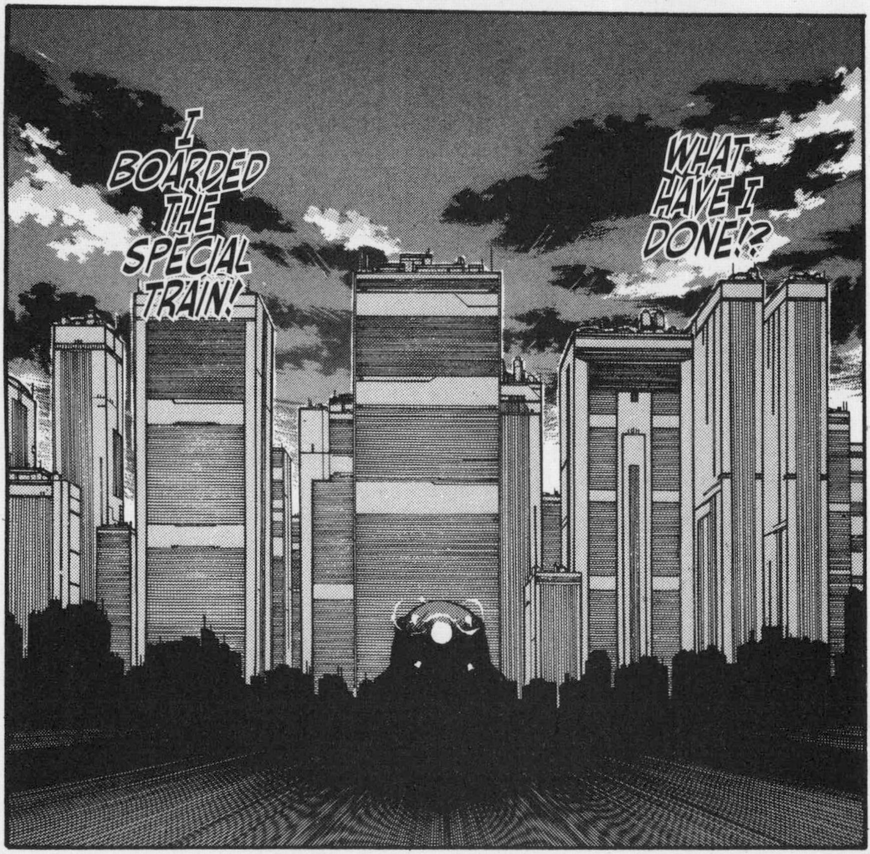
WHAT HAVE I DONE!?
I BOARDED THE SPECIAL TRAIN!

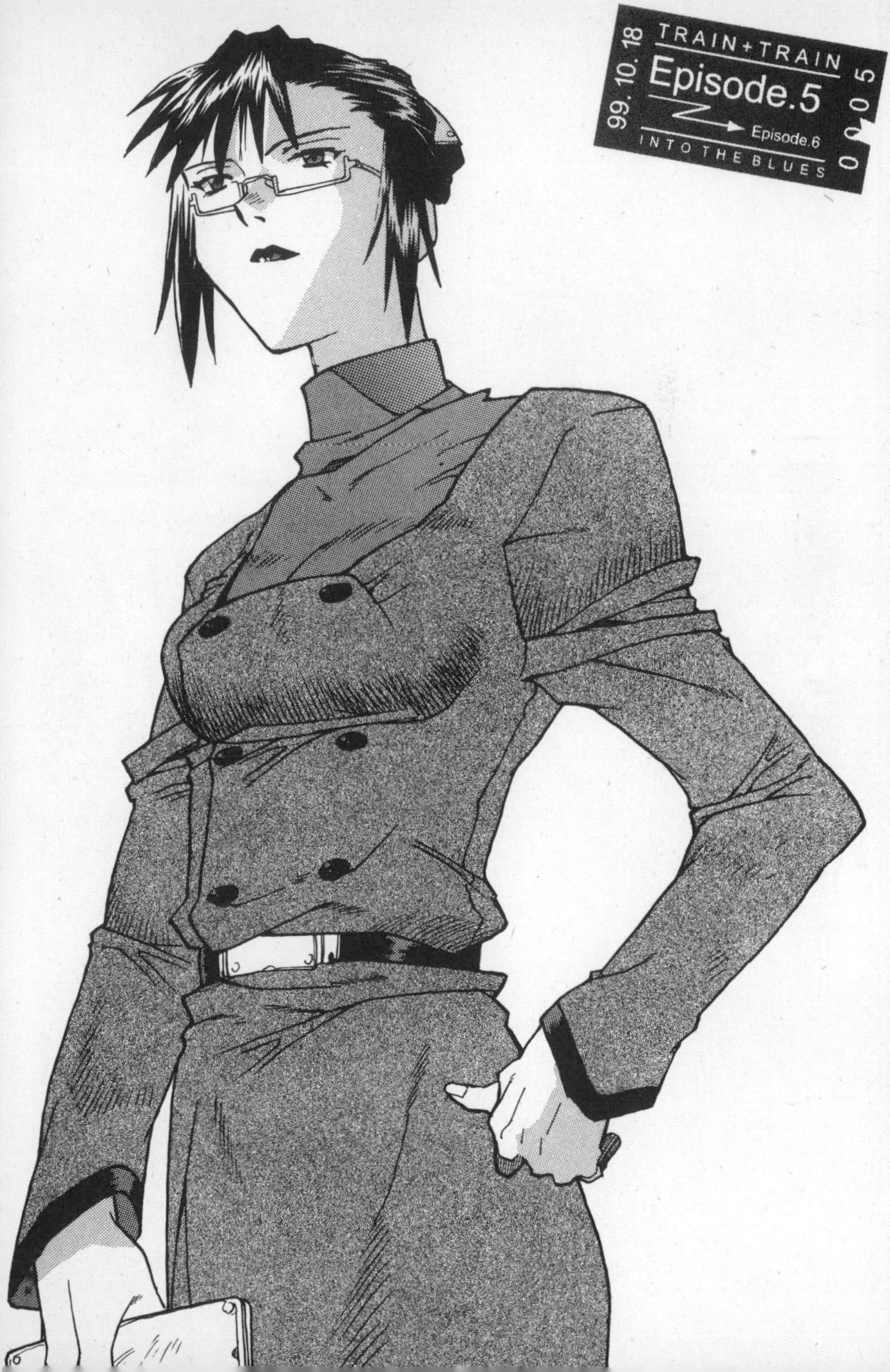
99. 10. 18
TRAIN+TRAIN
Episode.5
Episode.6
INTO THE BLUES
0005

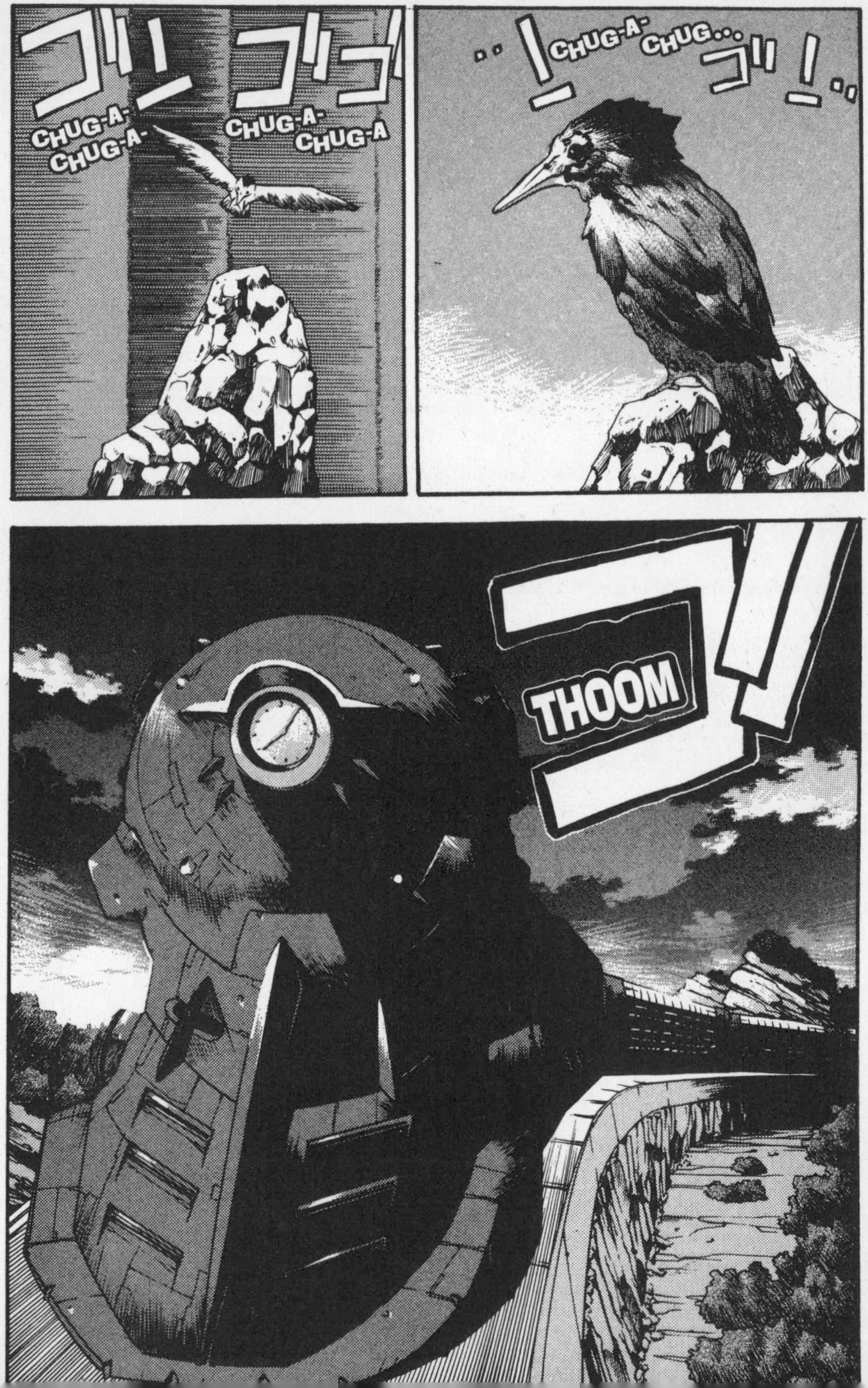
CHUG-A-CHUG...
CHUG-A-CHUG-A-
CHUG-A-CHUG-A
THOOM

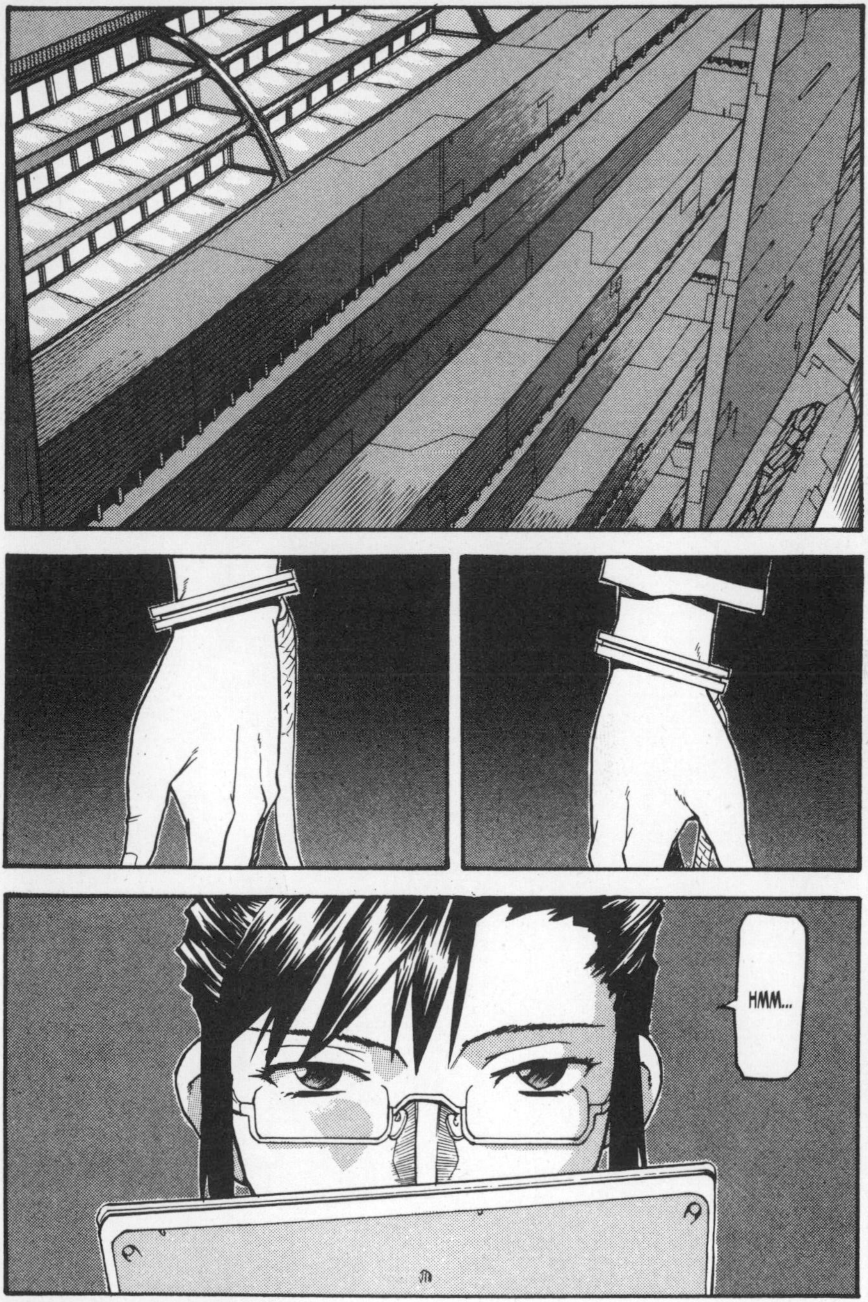
HMM...

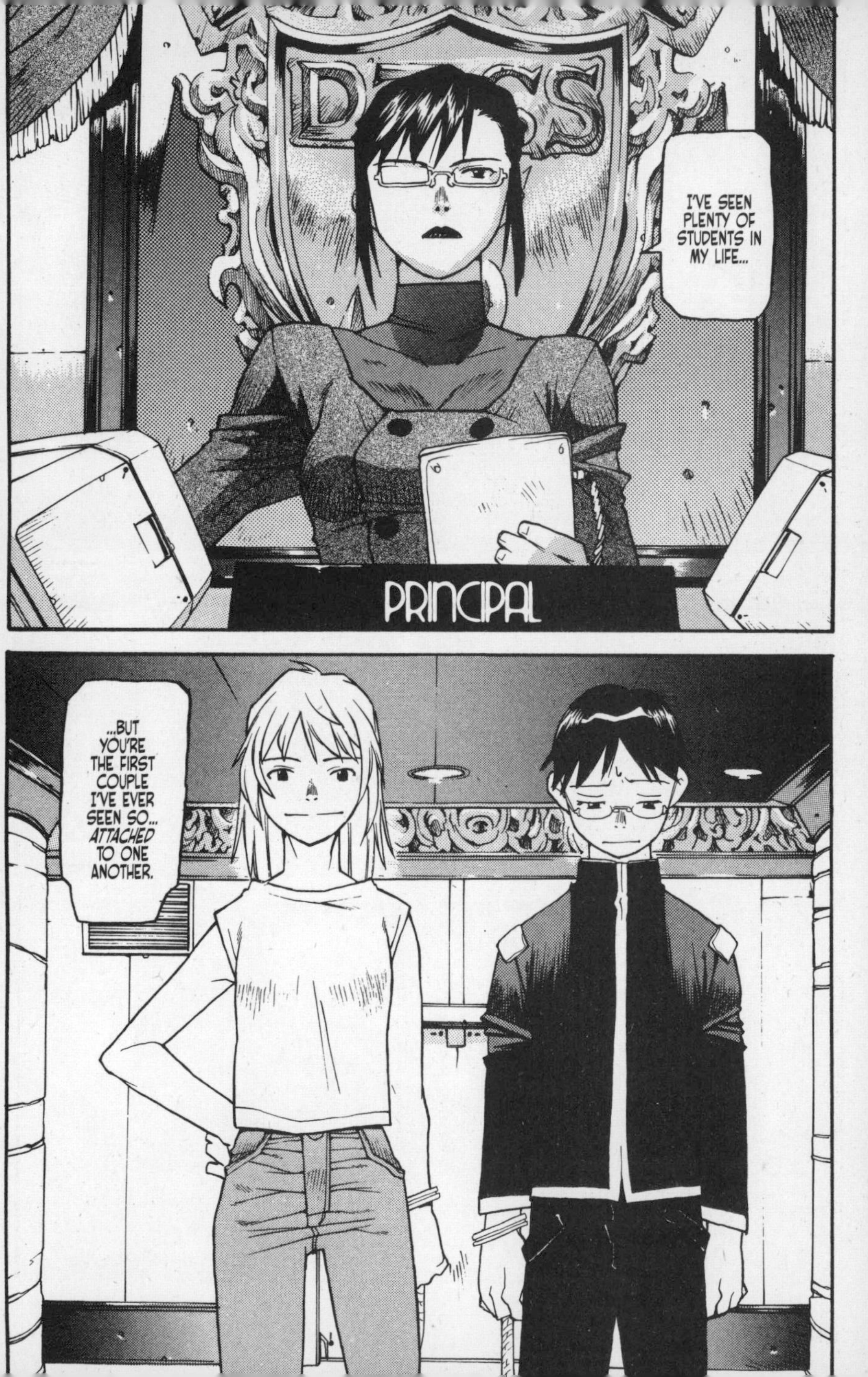
I'VE SEEN PLENTY OF STUDENTS IN MY LIFE...
PRINCIPAL
...BUT YOU'RE THE FIRST COUPLE I'VE EVER SEEN SO... *ATTACHED* TO ONE ANOTHER.

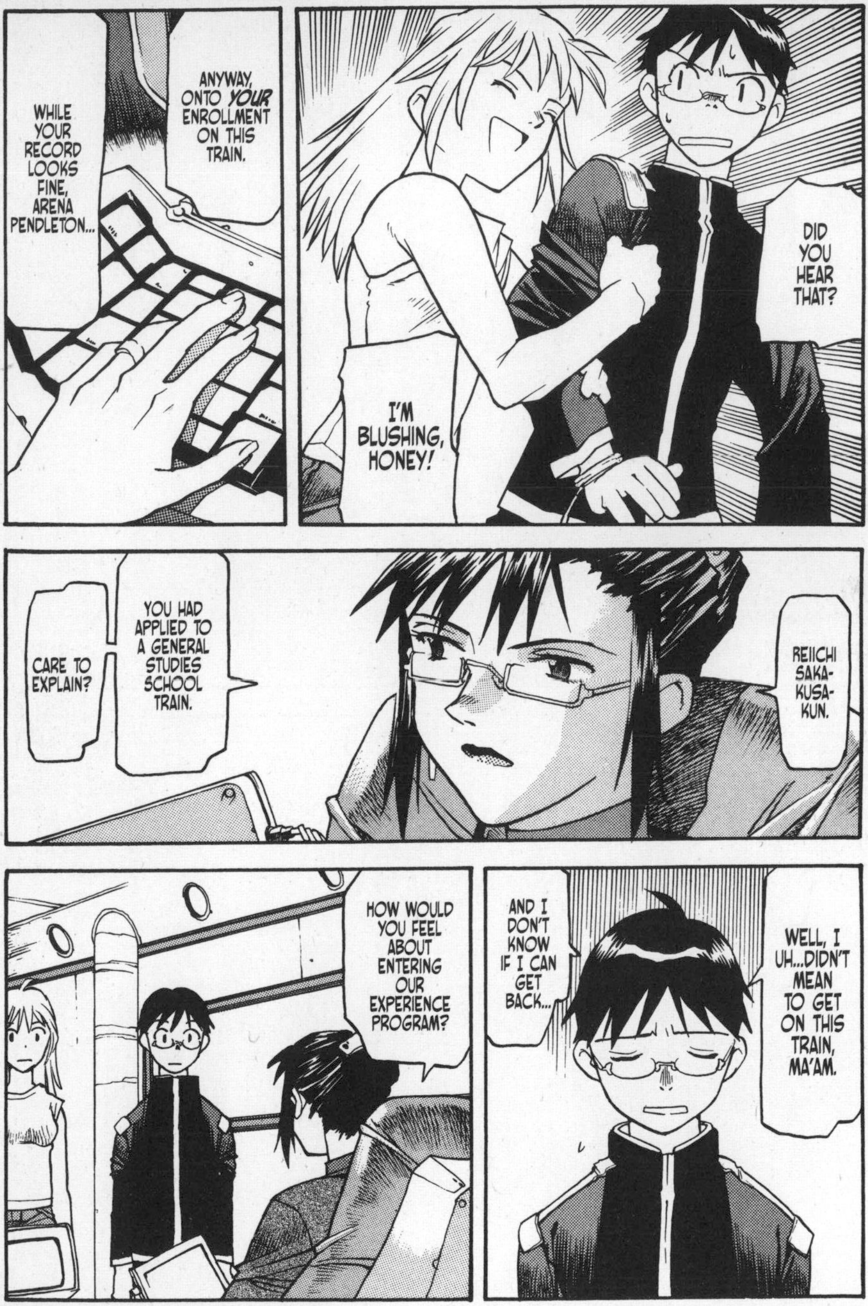
DID YOU HEAR THAT?
I'M BLUSHING, HONEY!
ANYWAY, ONTO *YOUR* ENROLLMENT ON THIS TRAIN.
WHILE YOUR RECORD LOOKS FINE, ARENA PENDLETON...
REIICHI SAKA-KUSA-KUN.
YOU HAD APPLIED TO A GENERAL STUDIES SCHOOL TRAIN.
CARE TO EXPLAIN?
WELL, I UH...DIDN'T MEAN TO GET ON THIS TRAIN, MA'AM.
AND I DON'T KNOW IF I CAN GET BACK...
HOW WOULD YOU FEEL ABOUT ENTERING OUR EXPERIENCE PROGRAM?

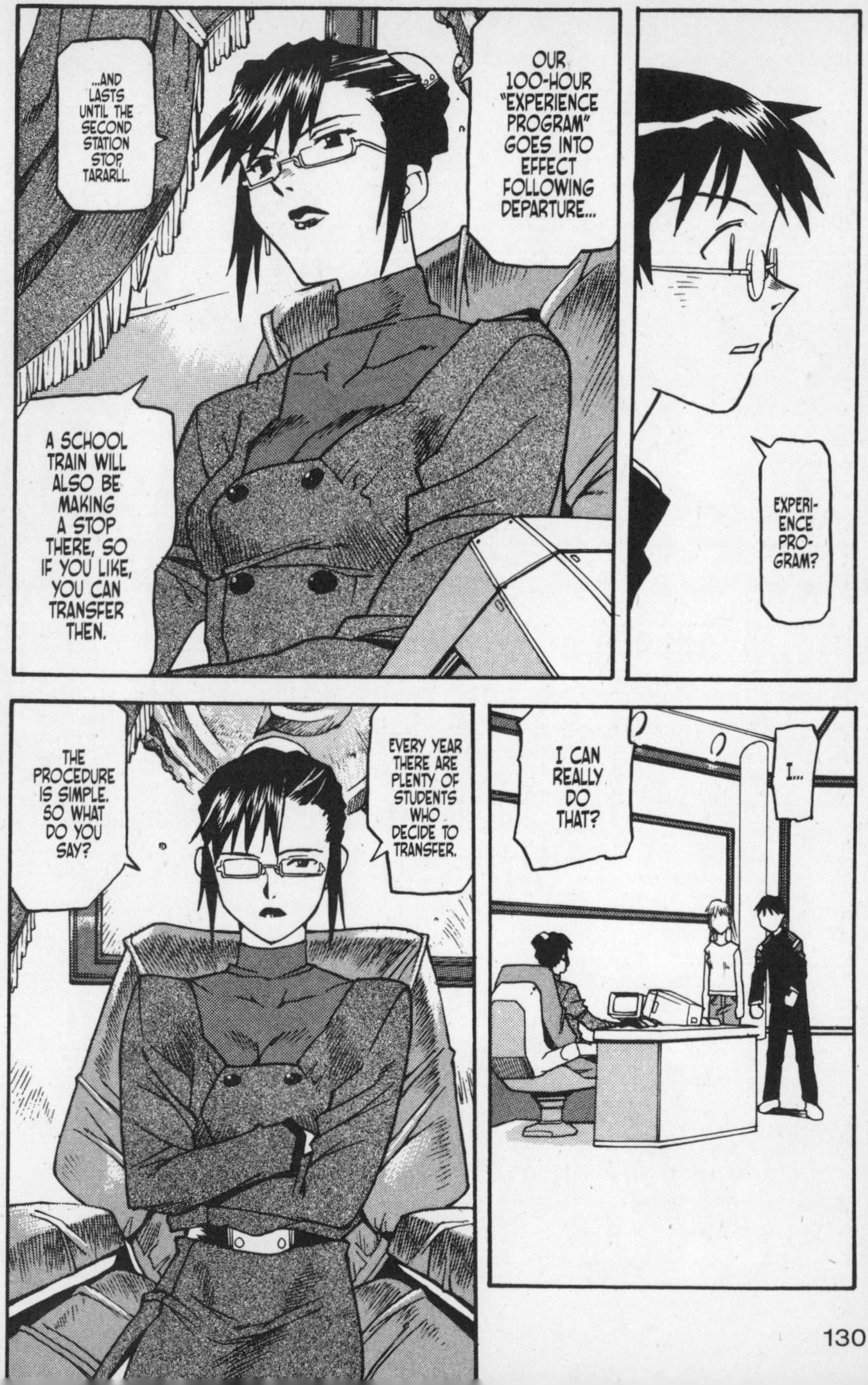
EXPERIENCE PROGRAM?
OUR 100-HOUR "EXPERIENCE PROGRAM" GOES INTO EFFECT FOLLOWING DEPARTURE...
...AND LASTS UNTIL THE SECOND STATION STOP, TARARLL.
A SCHOOL TRAIN WILL ALSO BE MAKING A STOP THERE, SO IF YOU LIKE, YOU CAN TRANSFER THEN.
I...
I CAN REALLY DO THAT?
EVERY YEAR THERE ARE PLENTY OF STUDENTS WHO DECIDE TO TRANSFER.
THE PROCEDURE IS SIMPLE. SO WHAT DO YOU SAY?

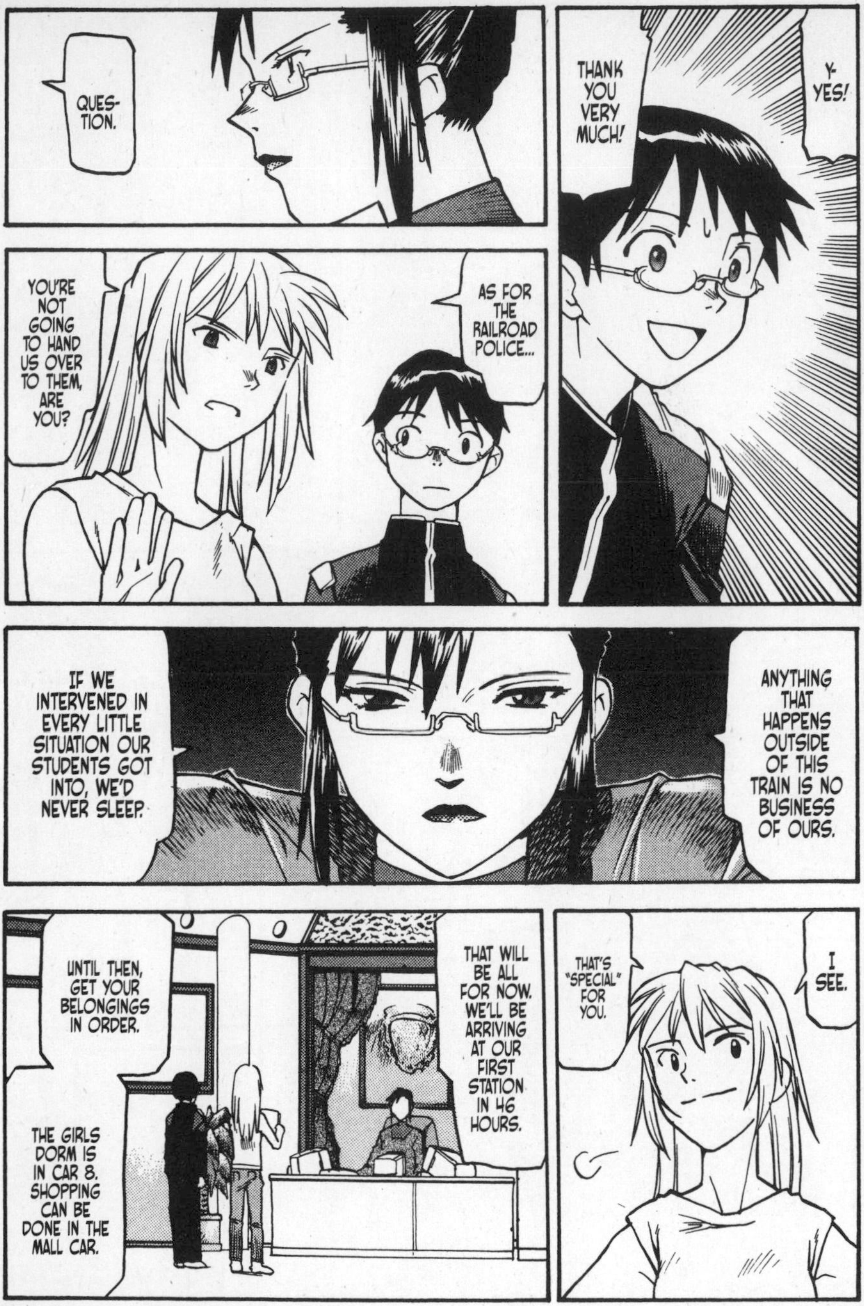
Y-YES!
THANK YOU VERY MUCH!
QUES-TION.
AS FOR THE RAILROAD POLICE...
YOU'RE NOT GOING TO HAND US OVER TO THEM, ARE YOU?
ANYTHING THAT HAPPENS OUTSIDE OF THIS TRAIN IS NO BUSINESS OF OURS.
IF WE INTERVENED IN EVERY LITTLE SITUATION OUR STUDENTS GOT INTO, WE'D NEVER SLEEP.
I SEE.
THAT'S "SPECIAL" FOR YOU.
THAT WILL BE ALL FOR NOW. WE'LL BE ARRIVING AT OUR FIRST STATION IN 46 HOURS.
UNTIL THEN, GET YOUR BELONGINGS IN ORDER.
THE GIRLS DORM IS IN CAR 8. SHOPPING CAN BE DONE IN THE MALL CAR.

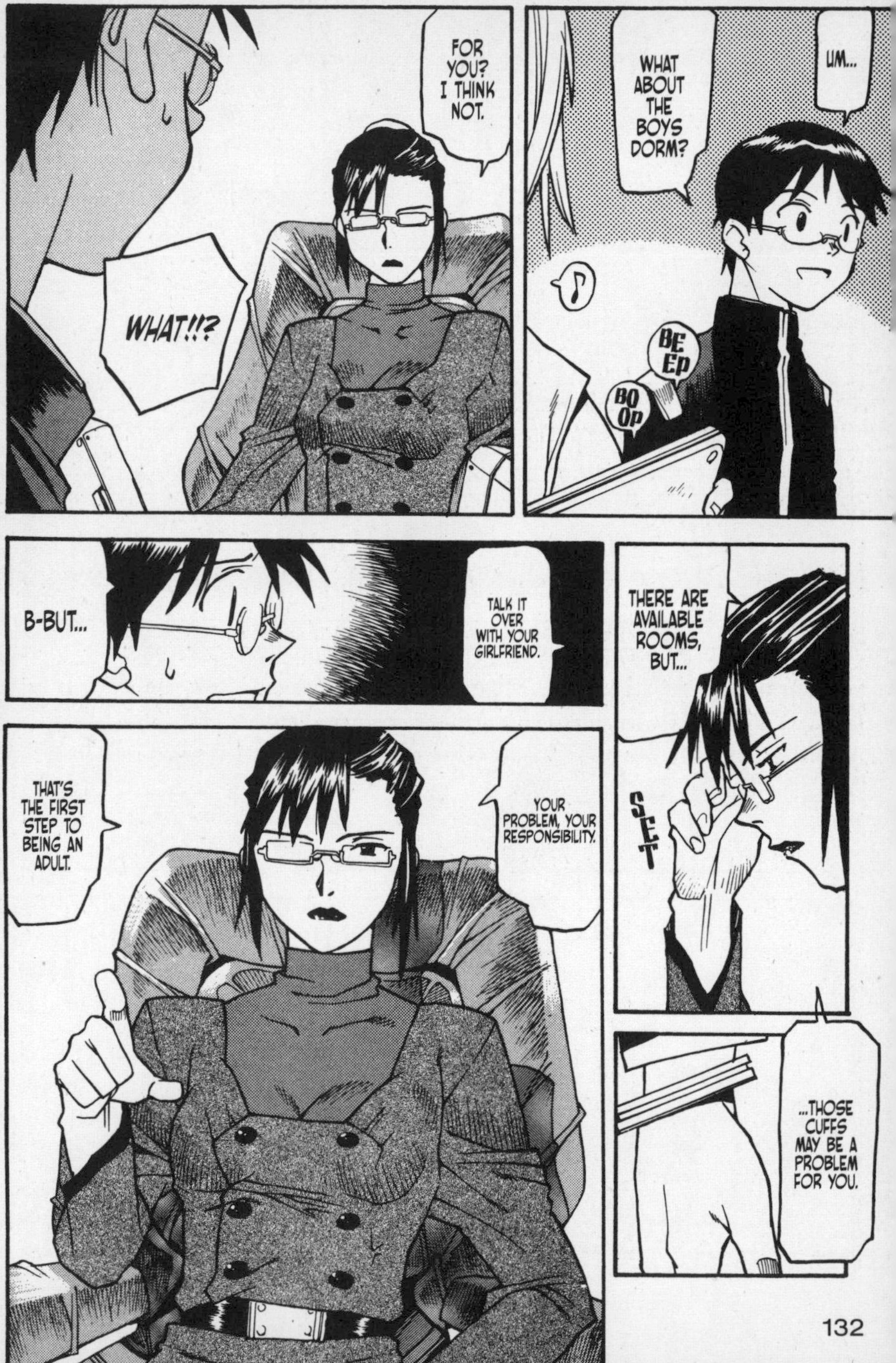
UM...
WHAT ABOUT THE BOYS DORM?
♪
BEEP
BOOP
FOR YOU? I THINK NOT.
WHAT!!?
THERE ARE AVAILABLE ROOMS, BUT...
SET
...THOSE CUFFS MAY BE A PROBLEM FOR YOU.
TALK IT OVER WITH YOUR GIRLFRIEND.
B-BUT...
YOUR PROBLEM, YOUR RESPONSIBILITY.
THAT'S THE FIRST STEP TO BEING AN ADULT.

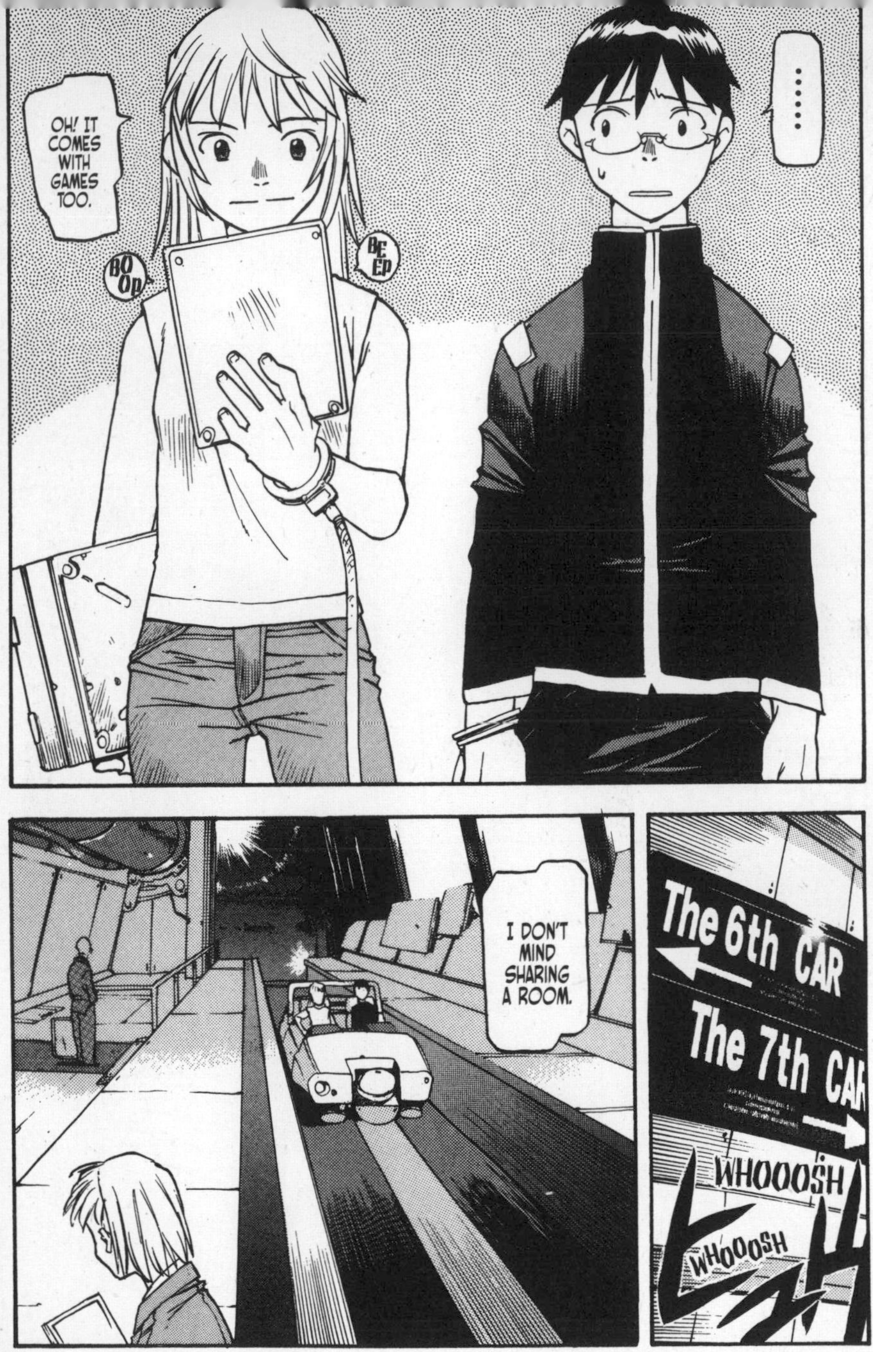
......
BEEP
OH! IT COMES WITH GAMES TOO.
BOOP
The 6th CAR
The 7th CAR
WHOOOSH
WHOOOSH
I DON'T MIND SHARING A ROOM.

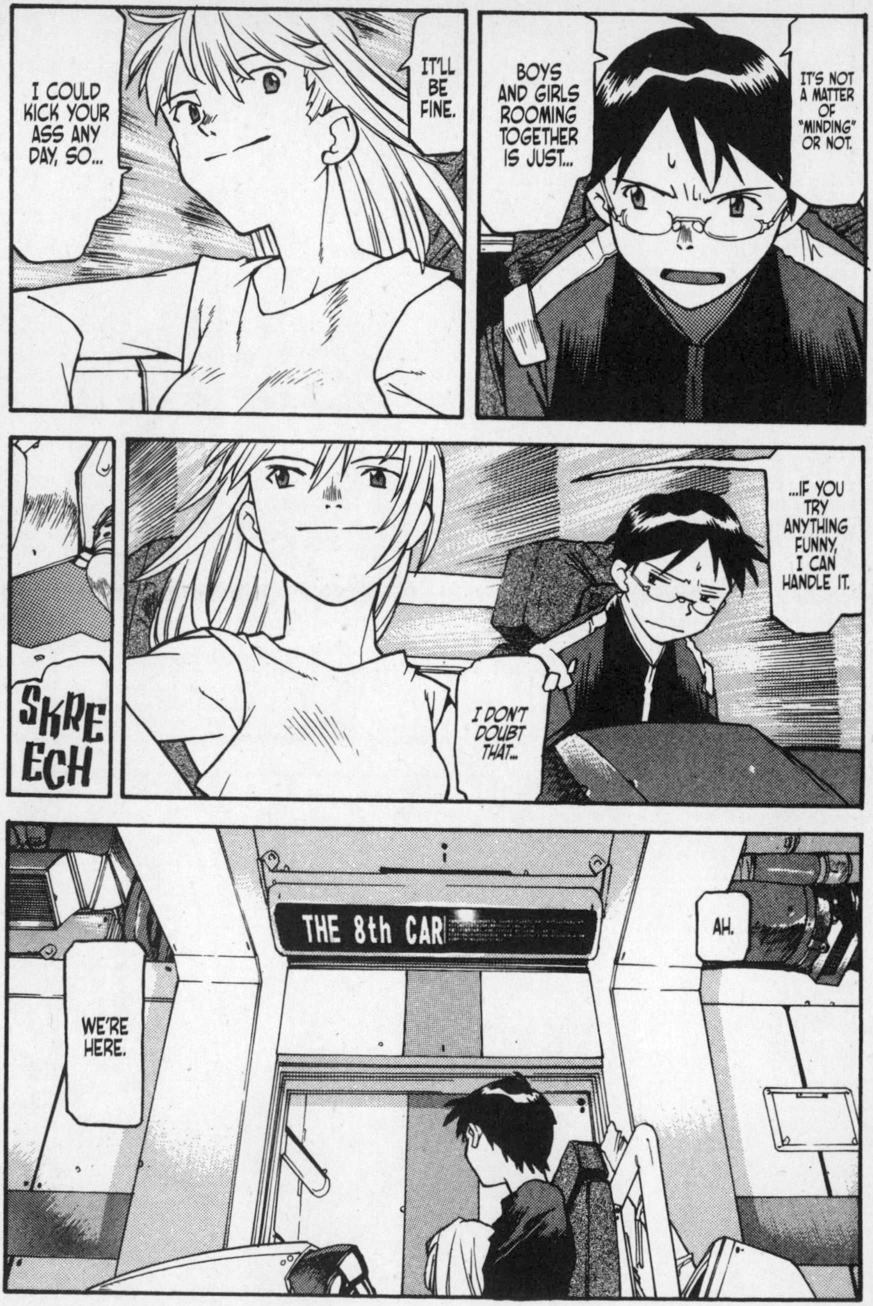
IT'S NOT A MATTER OF "MINDING" OR NOT.
BOYS AND GIRLS ROOMING TOGETHER IS JUST...
IT'LL BE FINE.
I COULD KICK YOUR ASS ANY DAY, SO...
...IF YOU TRY ANYTHING FUNNY, I CAN HANDLE IT.
I DON'T DOUBT THAT...
SKREECH
AH.
THE 8th CAR
WE'RE HERE.

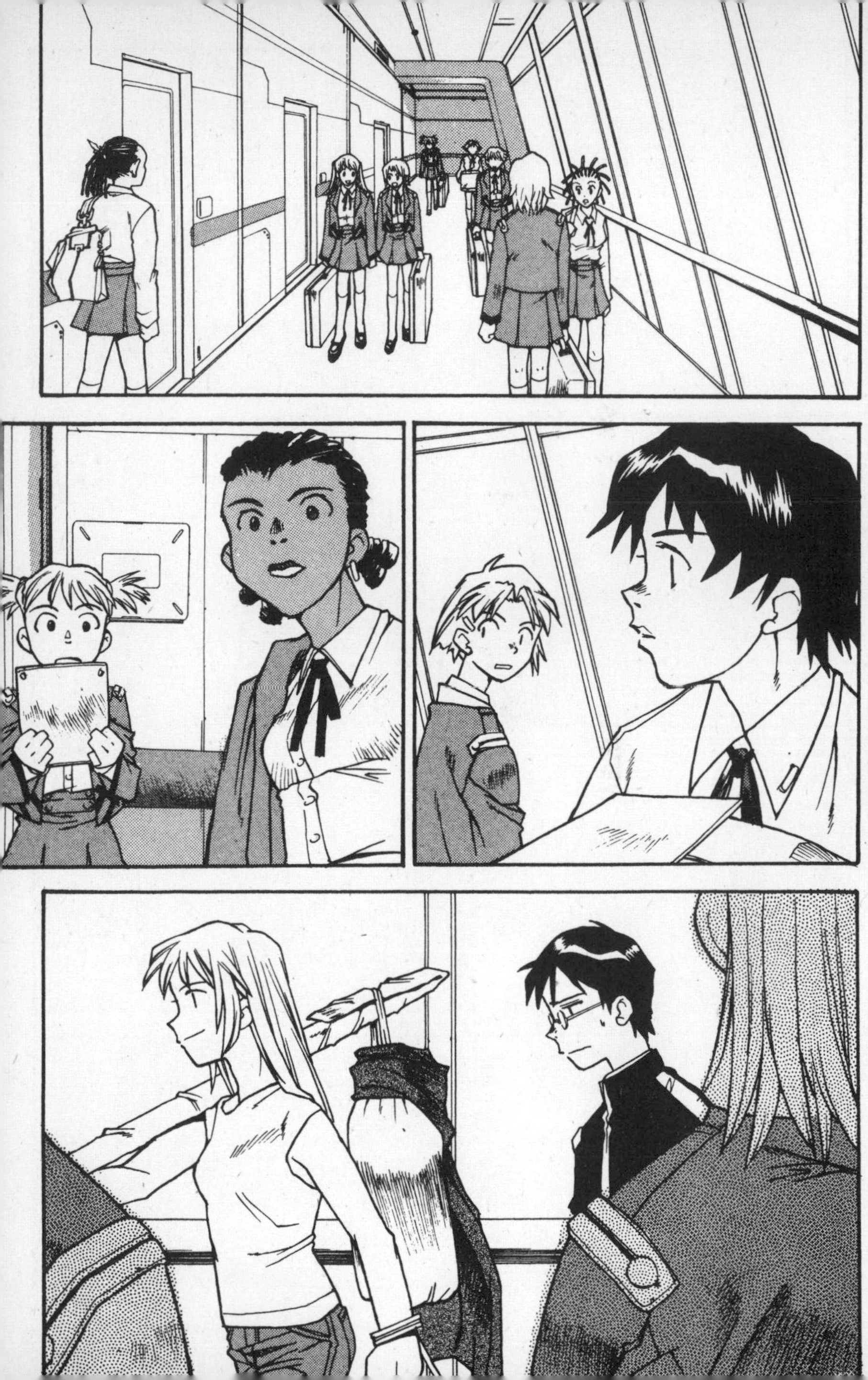

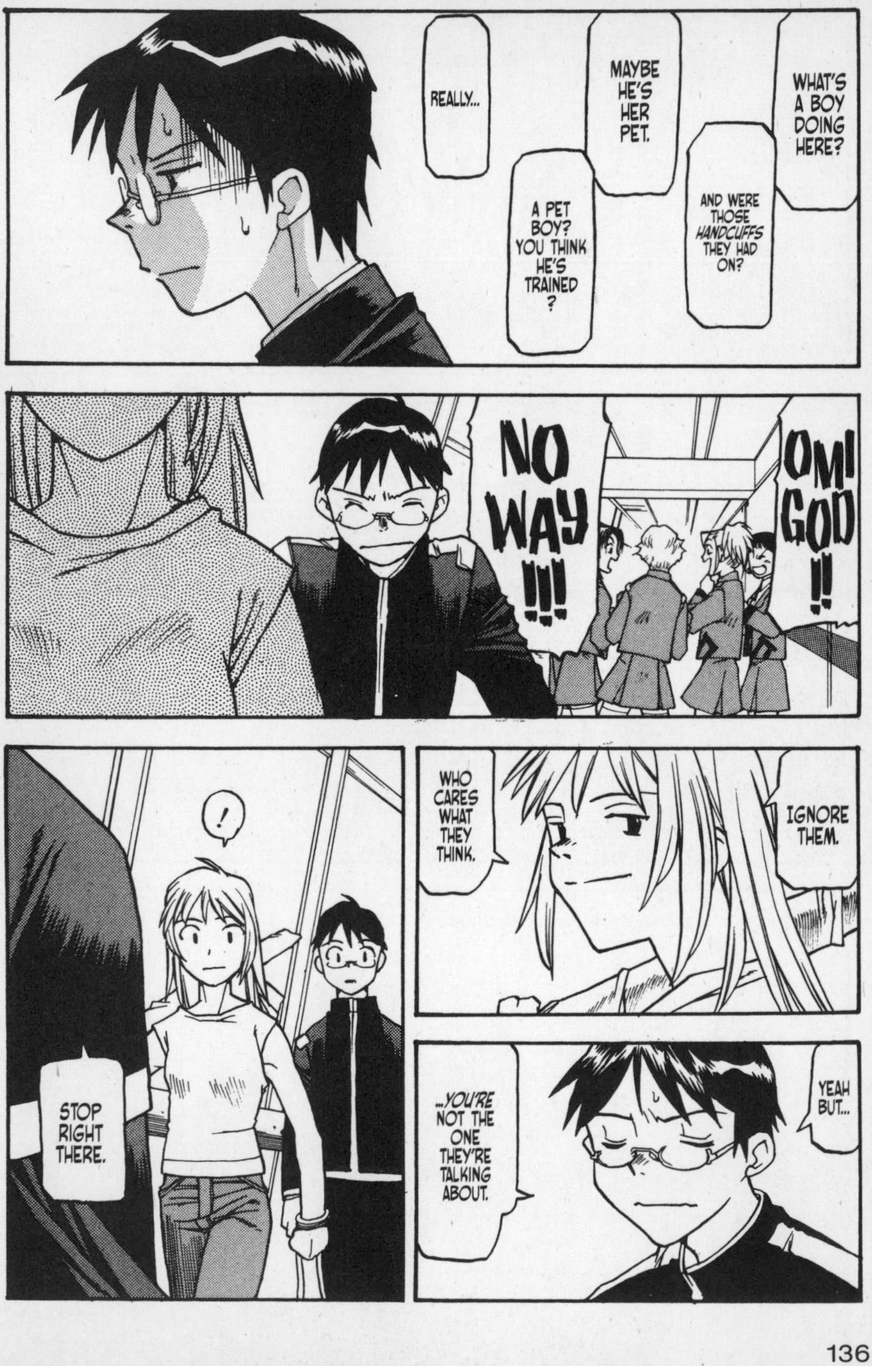
WHAT'S A BOY DOING HERE?
AND WERE THOSE *HANDCUFFS* THEY HAD ON?
MAYBE HE'S HER PET.
A PET BOY? YOU THINK HE'S TRAINED ?
REALLY...
OMI GOD !!
NO WAY !!!
IGNORE THEM.
WHO CARES WHAT THEY THINK.
YEAH BUT...
...*YOU'RE* NOT THE ONE THEY'RE TALKING ABOUT.
!
STOP RIGHT THERE.

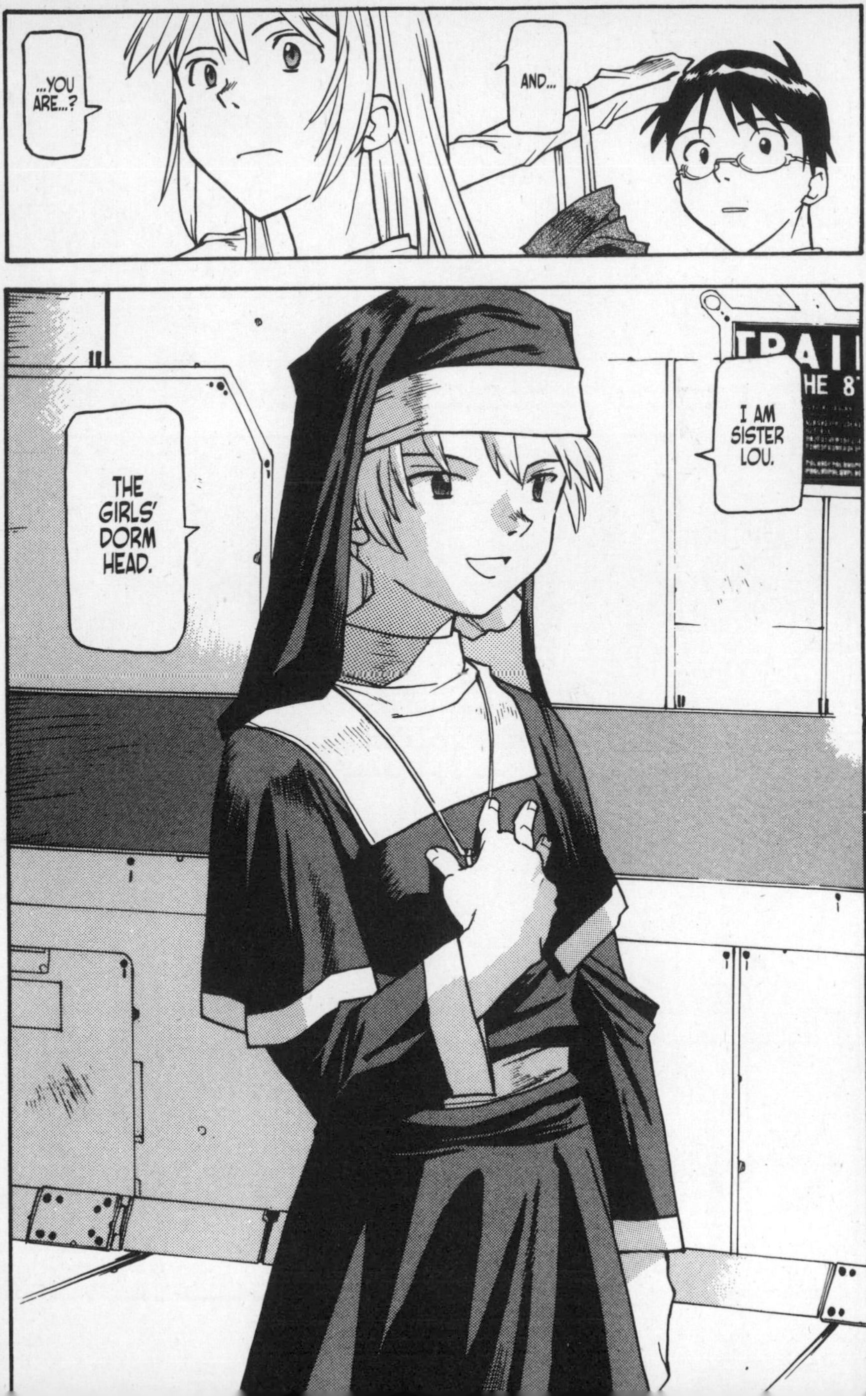
AND...
...YOU ARE...?
I AM SISTER LOU.
THE GIRLS' DORM HEAD.

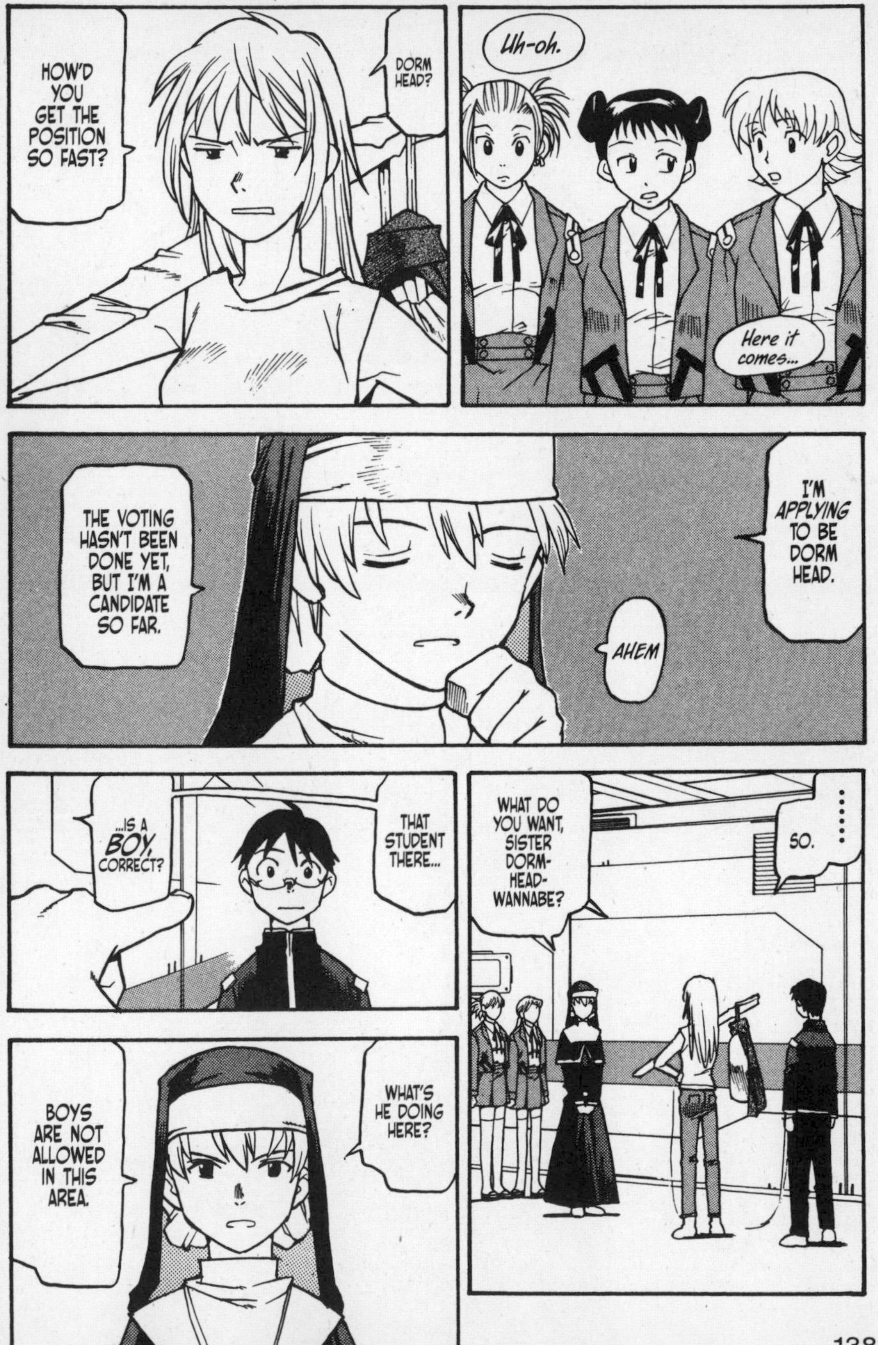
Uh-oh.
Here it comes...
DORM HEAD?
HOW'D YOU GET THE POSITION SO FAST?
I'M *APPLYING* TO BE DORM HEAD.
AHEM
THE VOTING HASN'T BEEN DONE YET, BUT I'M A CANDIDATE SO FAR.
......
SO.
WHAT DO YOU WANT, SISTER DORM-HEAD-WANNABE?
THAT STUDENT THERE...
...IS A *BOY*, CORRECT?
WHAT'S HE DOING HERE?
BOYS ARE NOT ALLOWED IN THIS AREA.

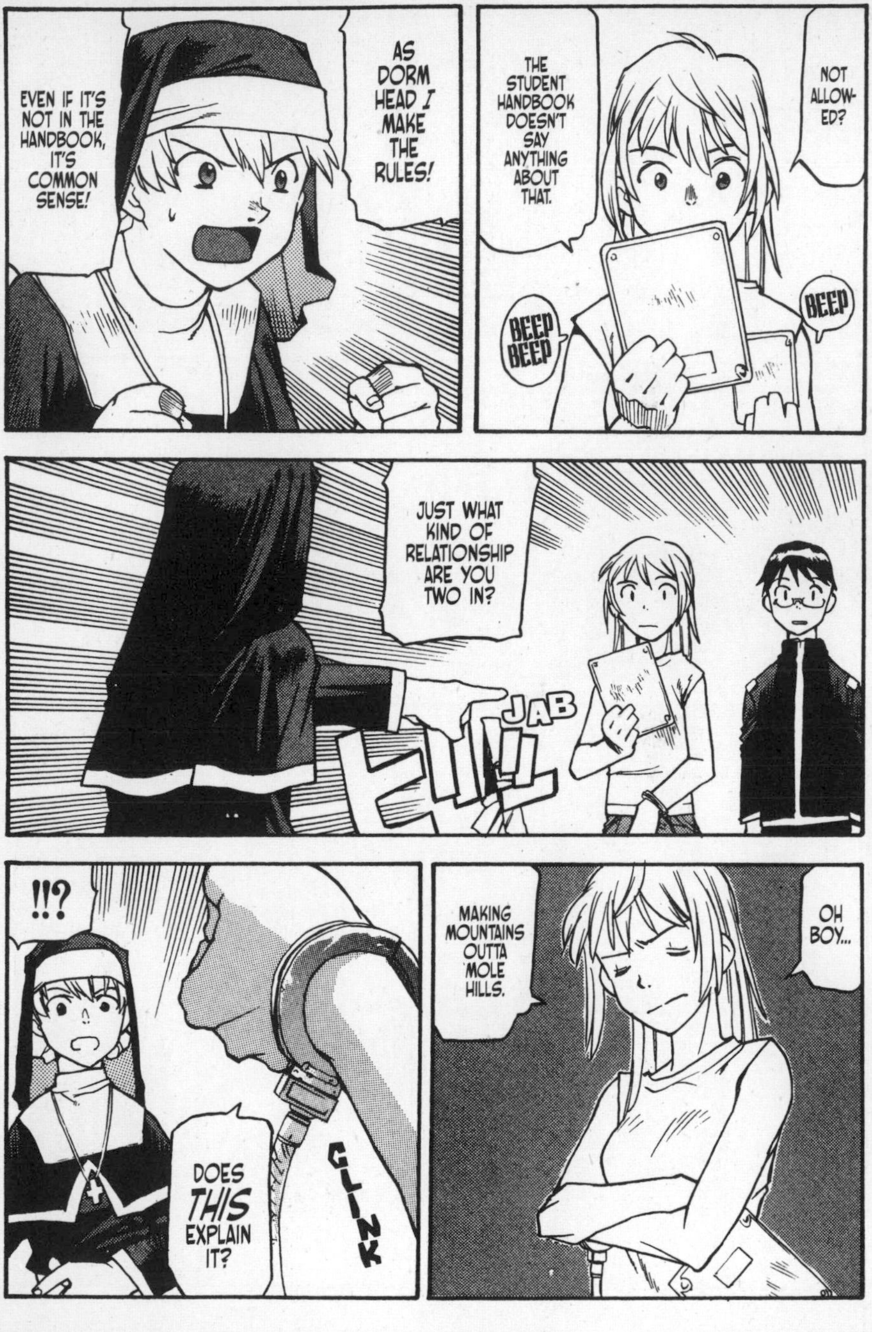
NOT ALLOWED?
THE STUDENT HANDBOOK DOESN'T SAY ANYTHING ABOUT THAT.
BEEP
BEEP BEEP
AS DORM HEAD *I* MAKE THE RULES!
EVEN IF IT'S NOT IN THE HANDBOOK, IT'S COMMON SENSE!
JUST WHAT KIND OF RELATIONSHIP ARE YOU TWO IN?
JAB
OH BOY...
MAKING MOUNTAINS OUTTA 'MOLE HILLS.
!!?
DOES *THIS* EXPLAIN IT?
CLINK

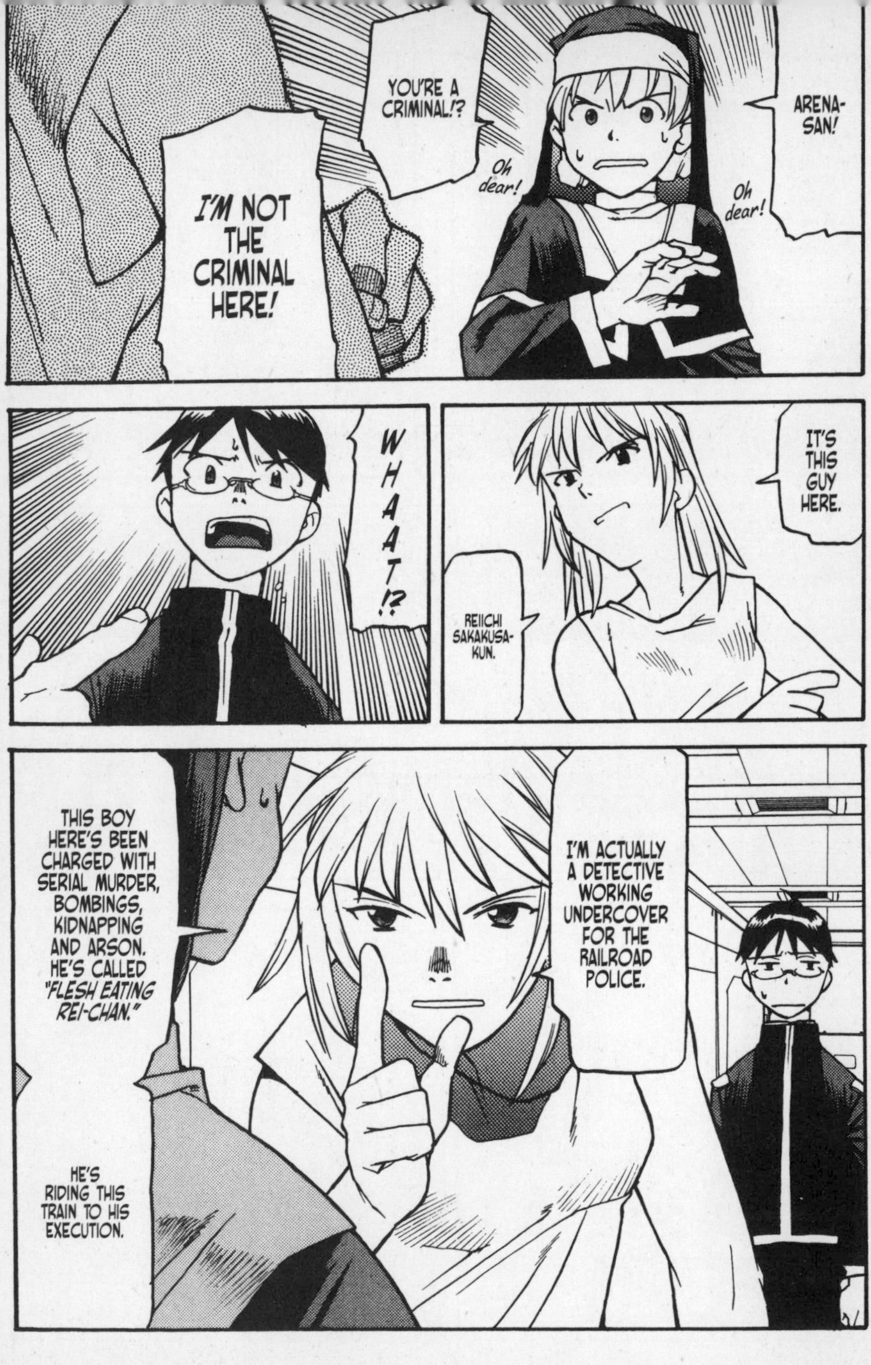
ARENA-SAN!
Oh dear!
Oh dear!
YOU'RE A CRIMINAL!?
I'M NOT THE CRIMINAL HERE!
IT'S THIS GUY HERE.
REIICHI SAKAKUSA-KUN.
WHAAT!?
I'M ACTUALLY A DETECTIVE WORKING UNDERCOVER FOR THE RAILROAD POLICE.
THIS BOY HERE'S BEEN CHARGED WITH SERIAL MURDER, BOMBINGS, KIDNAPPING AND ARSON. HE'S CALLED "FLESH EATING REI-CHAN."
HE'S RIDING THIS TRAIN TO HIS EXECUTION.

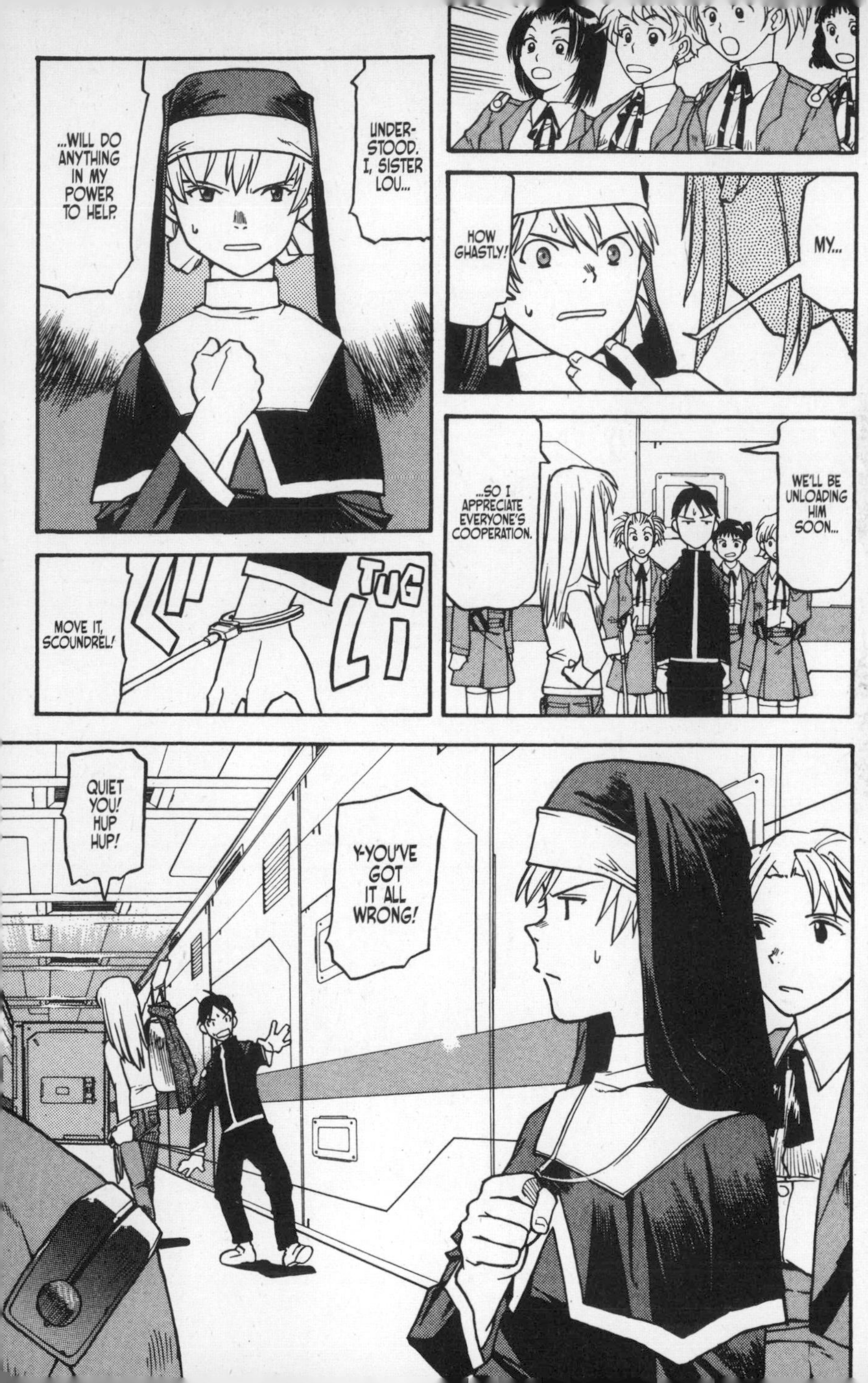
MY...
HOW GHASTLY!
WE'LL BE UNLOADING HIM SOON...
...SO I APPRECIATE EVERYONE'S COOPERATION.
UNDERSTOOD. I, SISTER LOU...
...WILL DO ANYTHING IN MY POWER TO HELP.
TUG
MOVE IT, SCOUNDREL!
Y-YOU'VE GOT IT ALL WRONG!
QUIET YOU! HUP HUP!

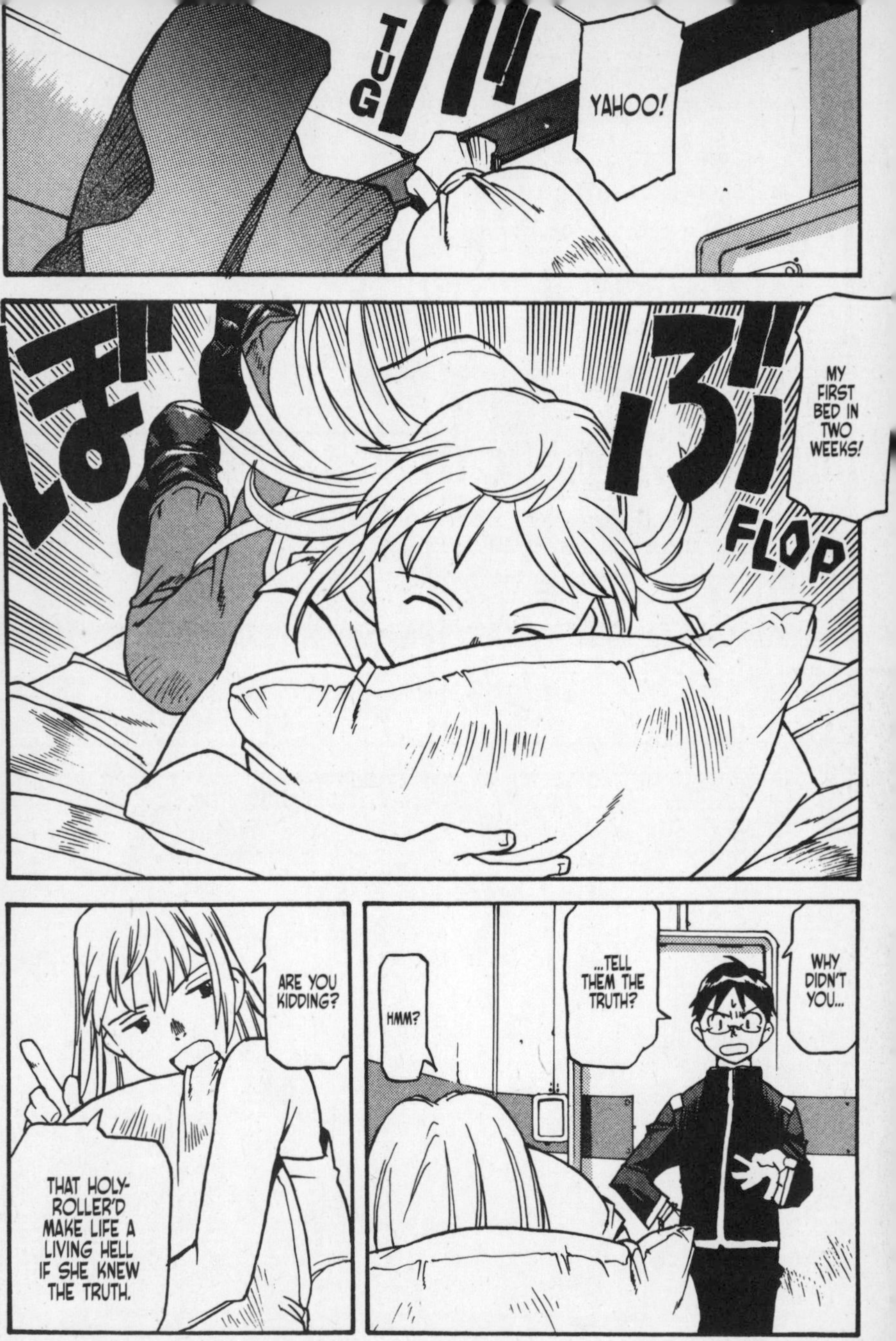
TUG
YAHOO!
MY FIRST BED IN TWO WEEKS!
FLOP
WHY DIDN'T YOU...
...TELL THEM THE TRUTH?
HMM?
ARE YOU KIDDING?
THAT HOLY-ROLLER'D MAKE LIFE A LIVING HELL IF SHE KNEW THE TRUTH.

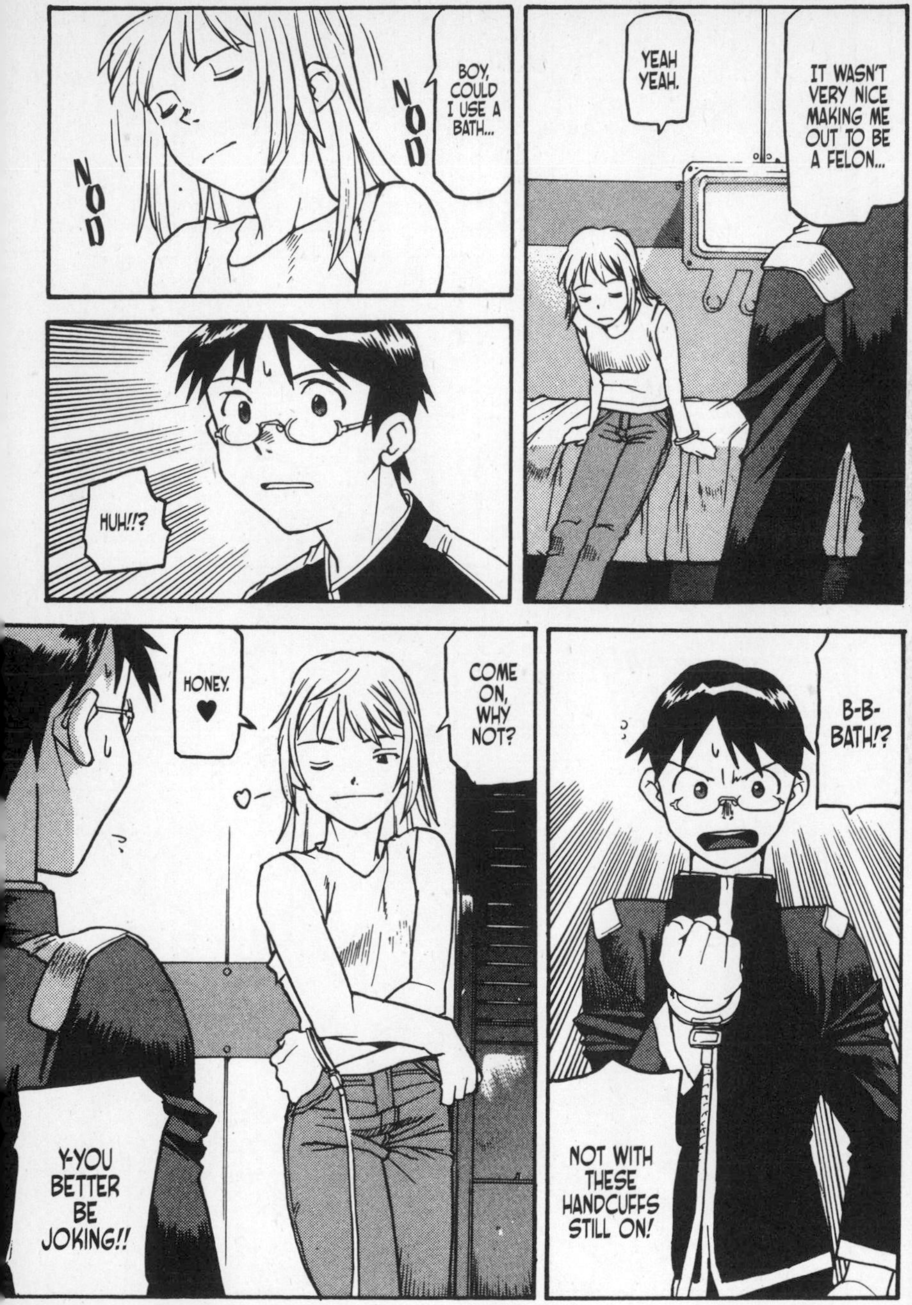
IT WASN'T VERY NICE MAKING ME OUT TO BE A FELON...
YEAH YEAH.
BOY, COULD I USE A BATH...
NOD
NOD
HUH!!?
B-B-BATH!?
NOT WITH THESE HANDCUFFS STILL ON!
COME ON, WHY NOT?
HONEY. ♥
Y-YOU BETTER BE JOKING!!

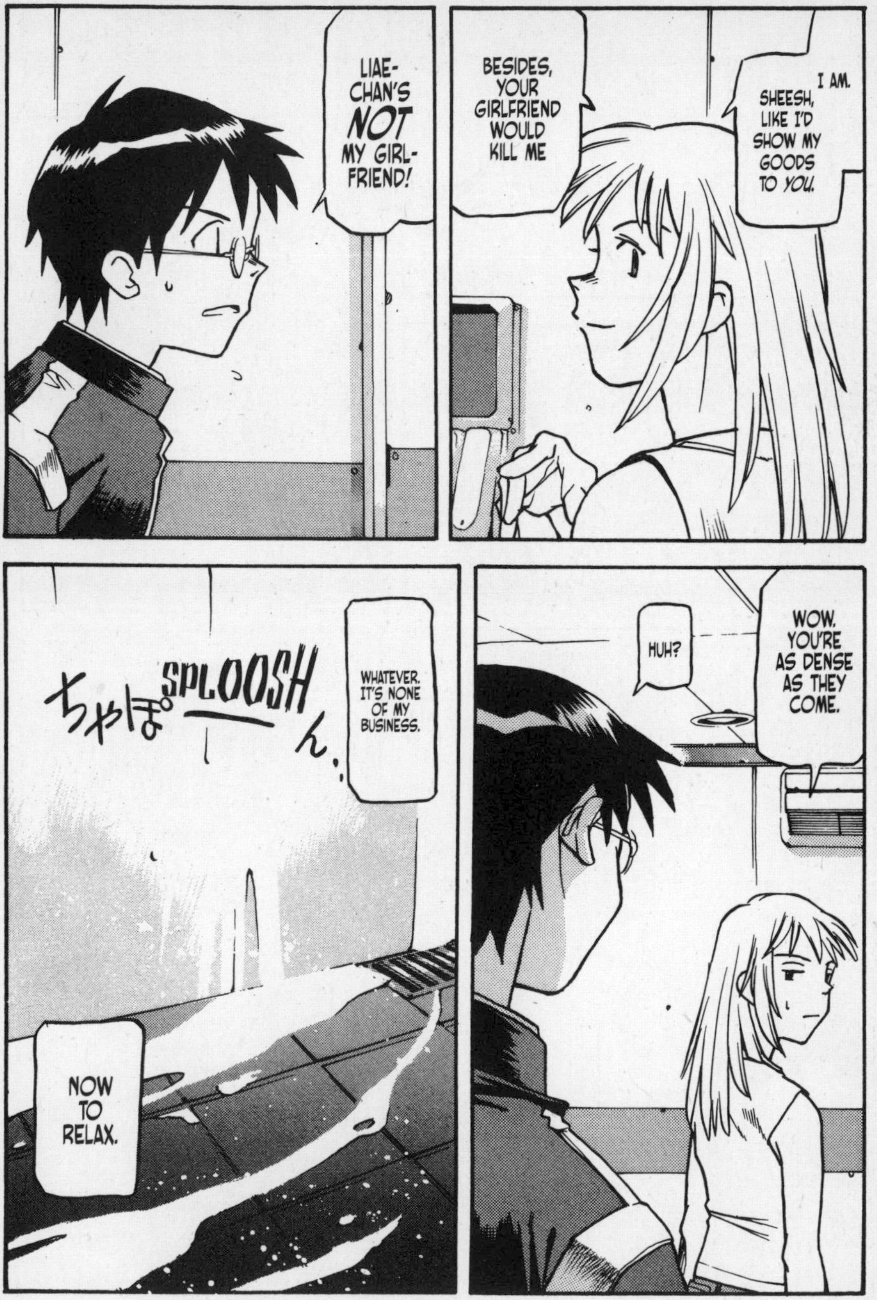
I AM.
SHEESH, LIKE I'D SHOW MY GOODS TO YOU.
BESIDES, YOUR GIRLFRIEND WOULD KILL ME
LIAE-CHAN'S NOT MY GIRL-FRIEND!
WOW. YOU'RE AS DENSE AS THEY COME.
HUH?
WHATEVER. IT'S NONE OF MY BUSINESS.
ちゃぽーん…
SPLOOSH
NOW TO RELAX.

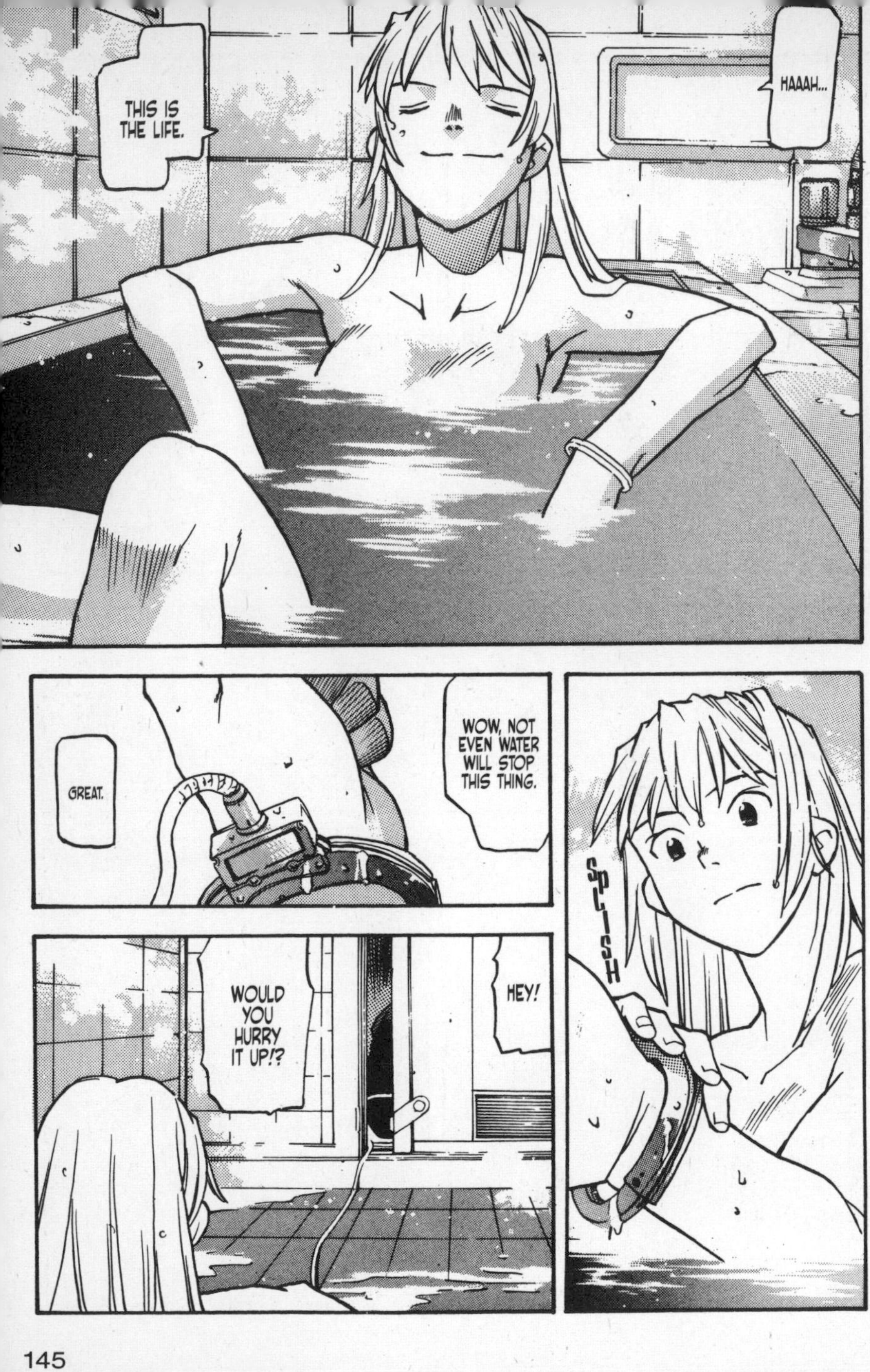
HAAAH...
THIS IS THE LIFE.
SPLISH
WOW, NOT EVEN WATER WILL STOP THIS THING.
GREAT.
HEY!
WOULD YOU HURRY IT UP!?

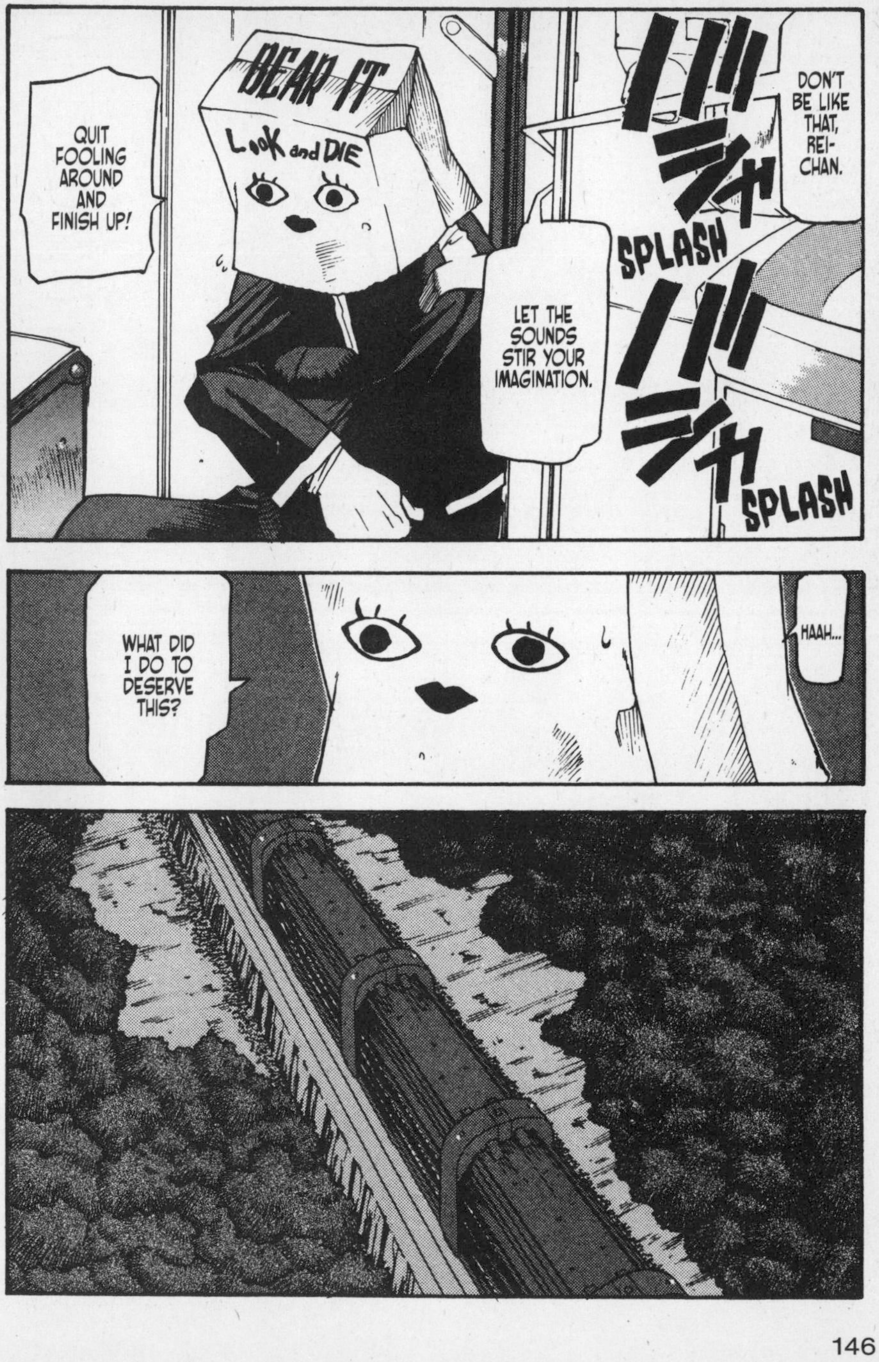
DON'T BE LIKE THAT, REI-CHAN.
バシャ
SPLASH
バシャ
SPLASH
LET THE SOUNDS STIR YOUR IMAGINATION.
BEAR IT
Look and DIE
QUIT FOOLING AROUND AND FINISH UP!
HAAH...
WHAT DID I DO TO DESERVE THIS?

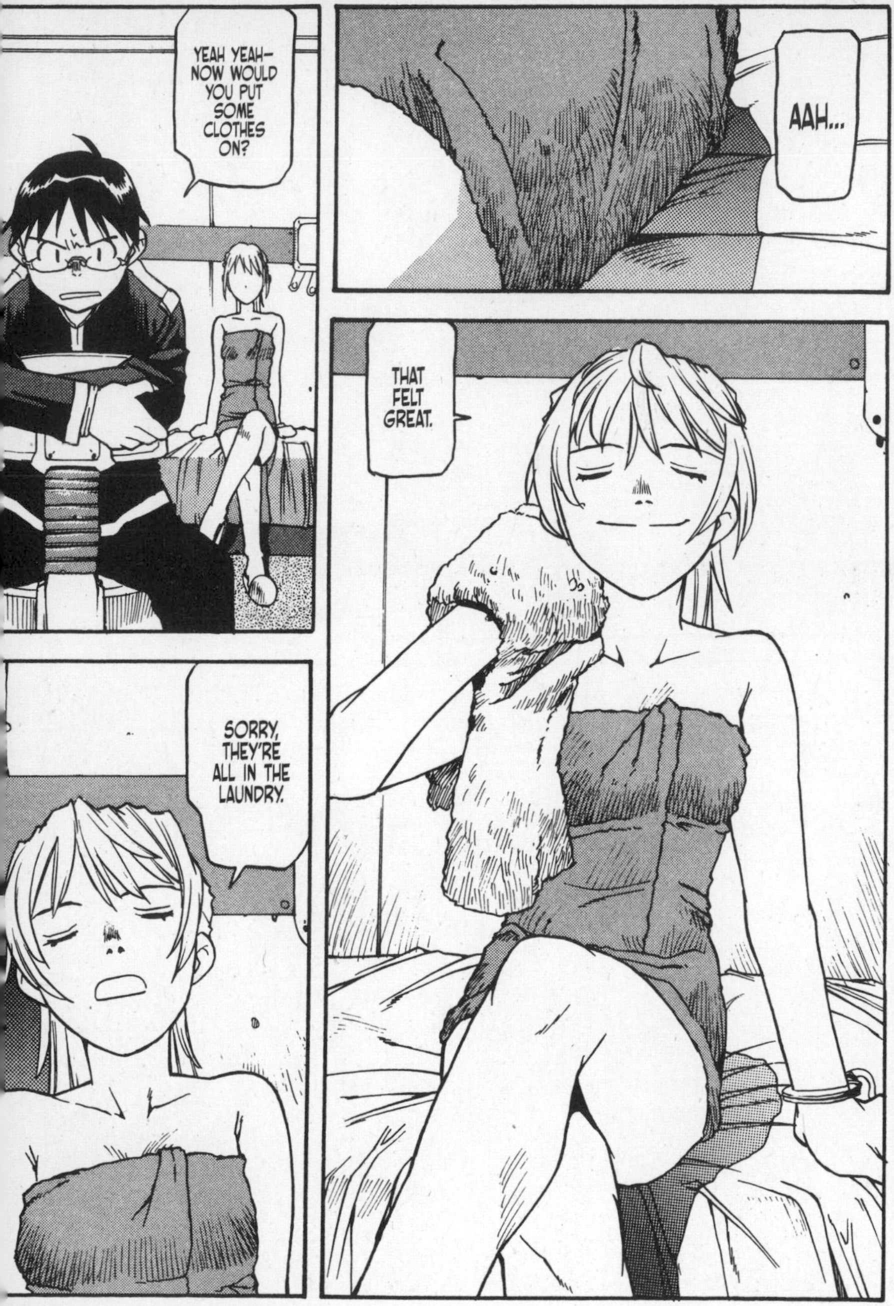
AAH...
YEAH YEAH—NOW WOULD YOU PUT SOME CLOTHES ON?
THAT FELT GREAT.
SORRY, THEY'RE ALL IN THE LAUNDRY.

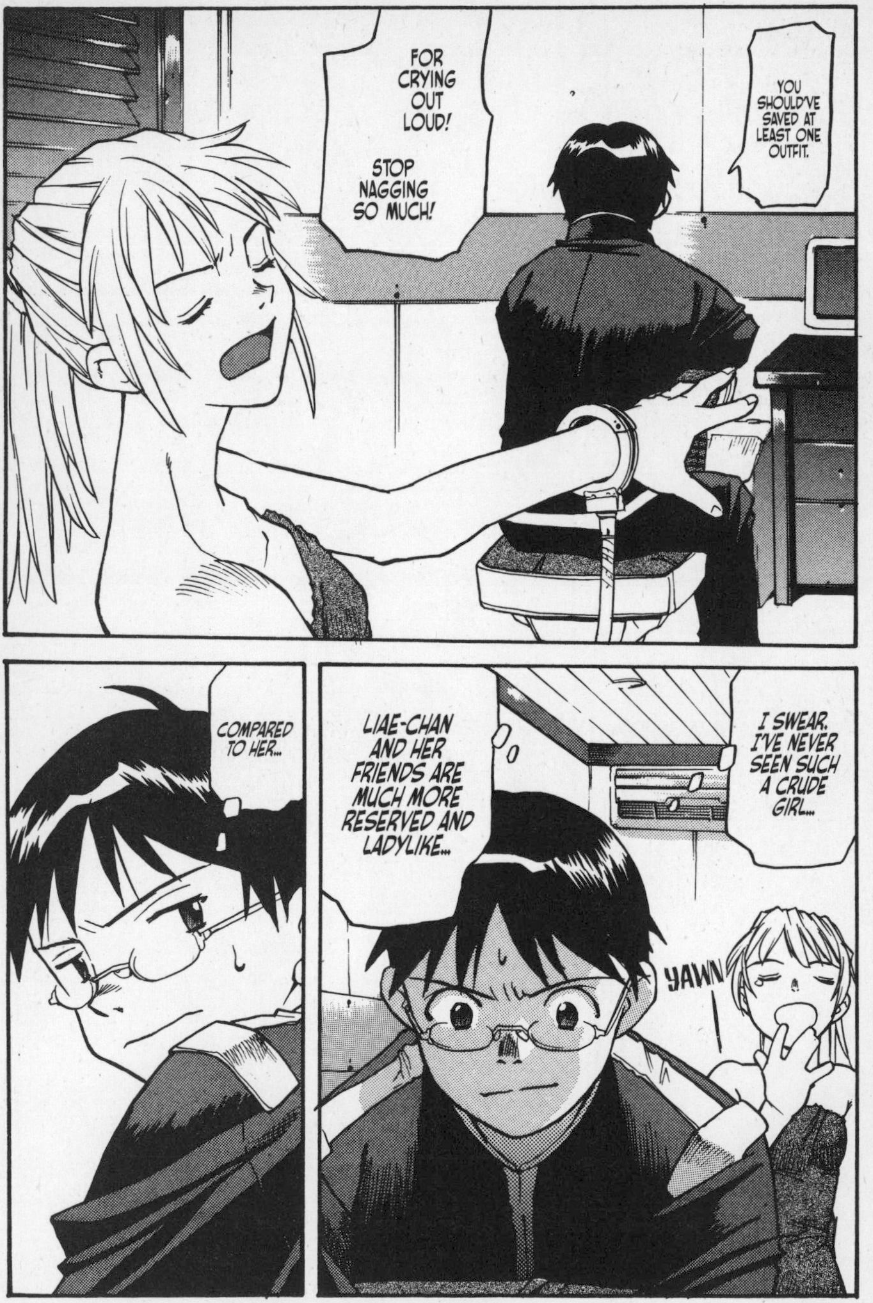
YOU SHOULD'VE SAVED AT LEAST ONE OUTFIT.
FOR CRYING OUT LOUD!
STOP NAGGING SO MUCH!
I SWEAR. I'VE NEVER SEEN SUCH A CRUDE GIRL...
LIAE-CHAN AND HER FRIENDS ARE MUCH MORE RESERVED AND LADYLIKE...
YAWN
COMPARED TO HER...

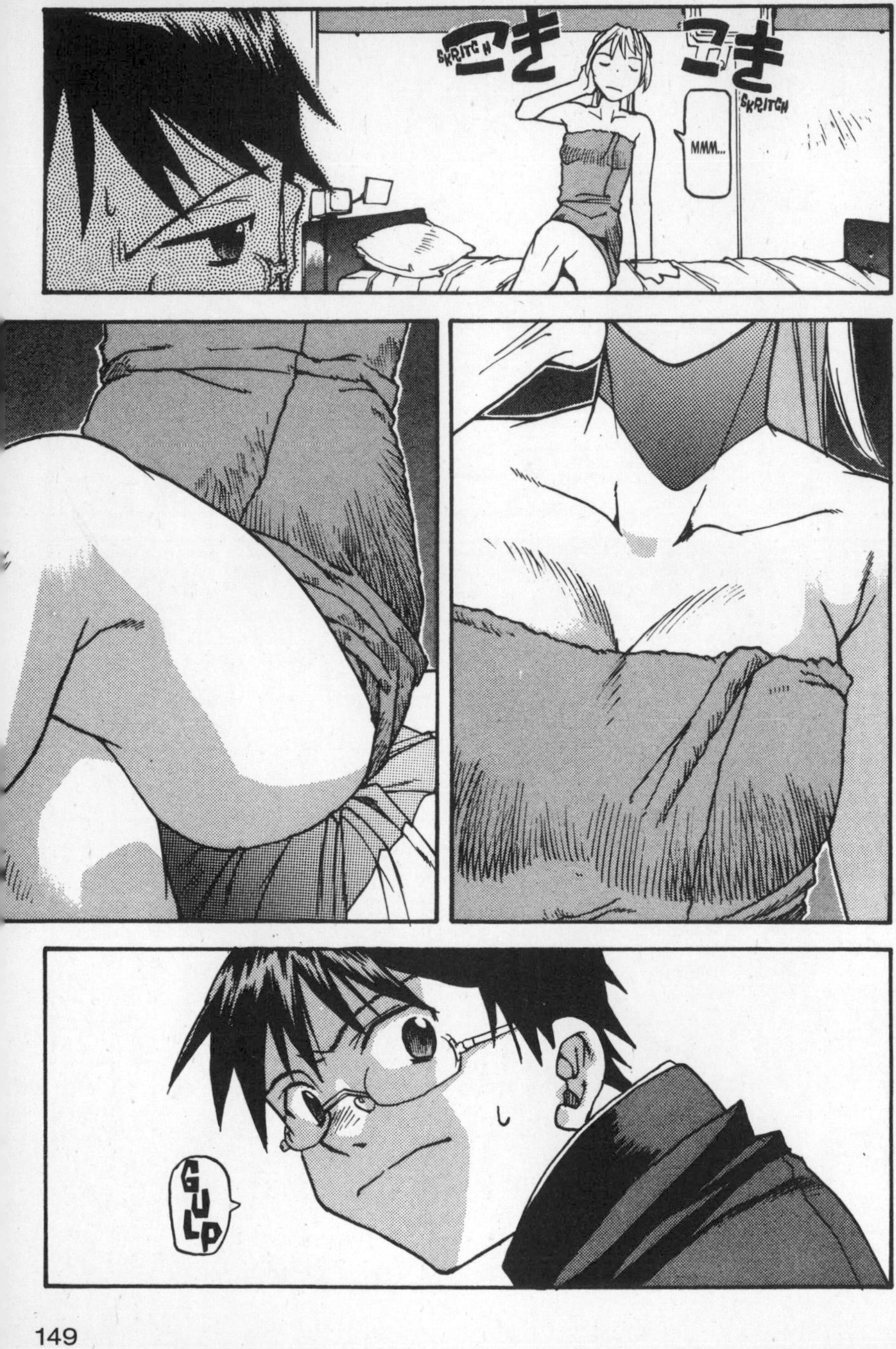
こき
SKRITCH
MMM...
こき
SKRITCH
GULP

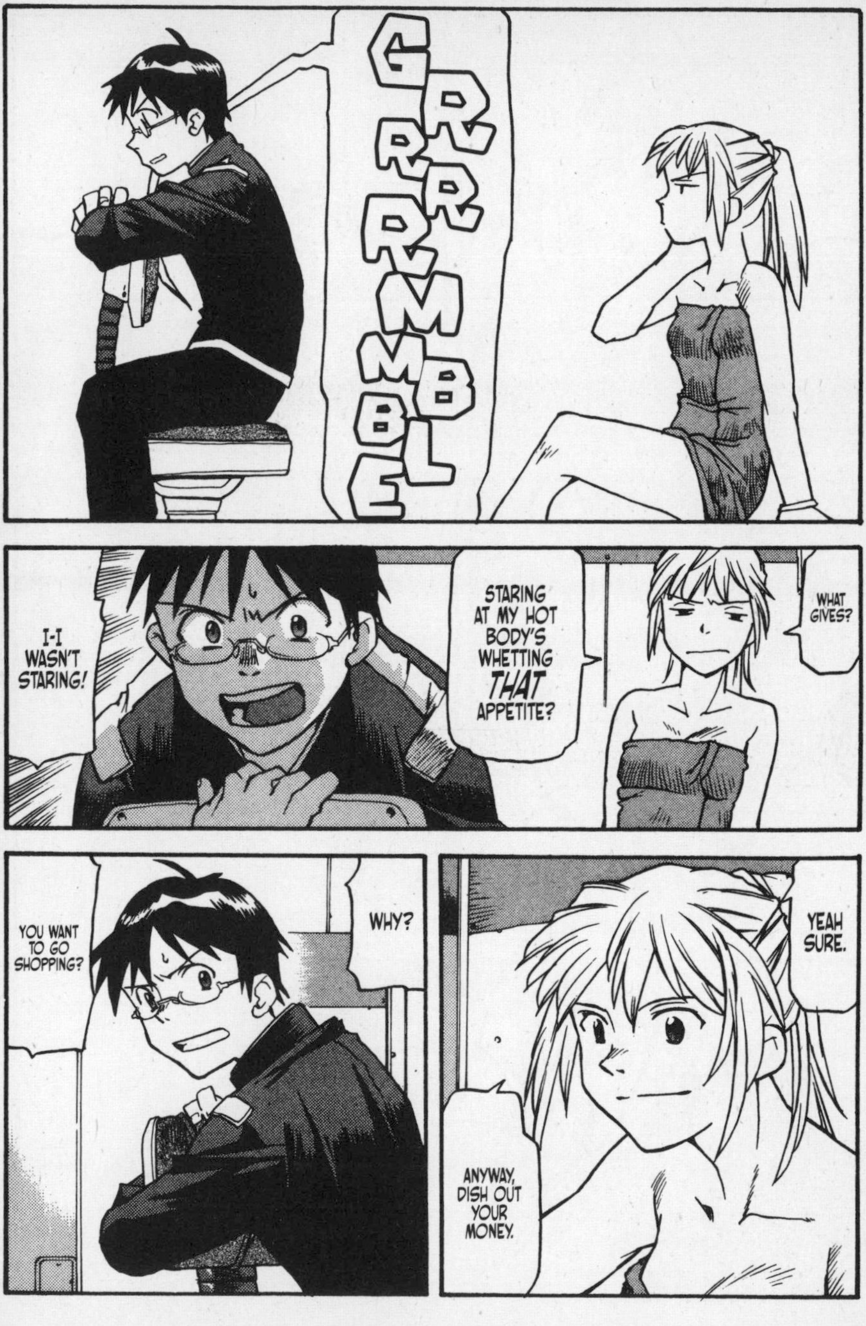
GRRRRMMBBLE
WHAT GIVES?
STARING AT MY HOT BODY'S WHETTING *THAT* APPETITE?
I-I WASN'T STARING!
YEAH SURE.
ANYWAY, DISH OUT YOUR MONEY.
WHY?
YOU WANT TO GO SHOPPING?

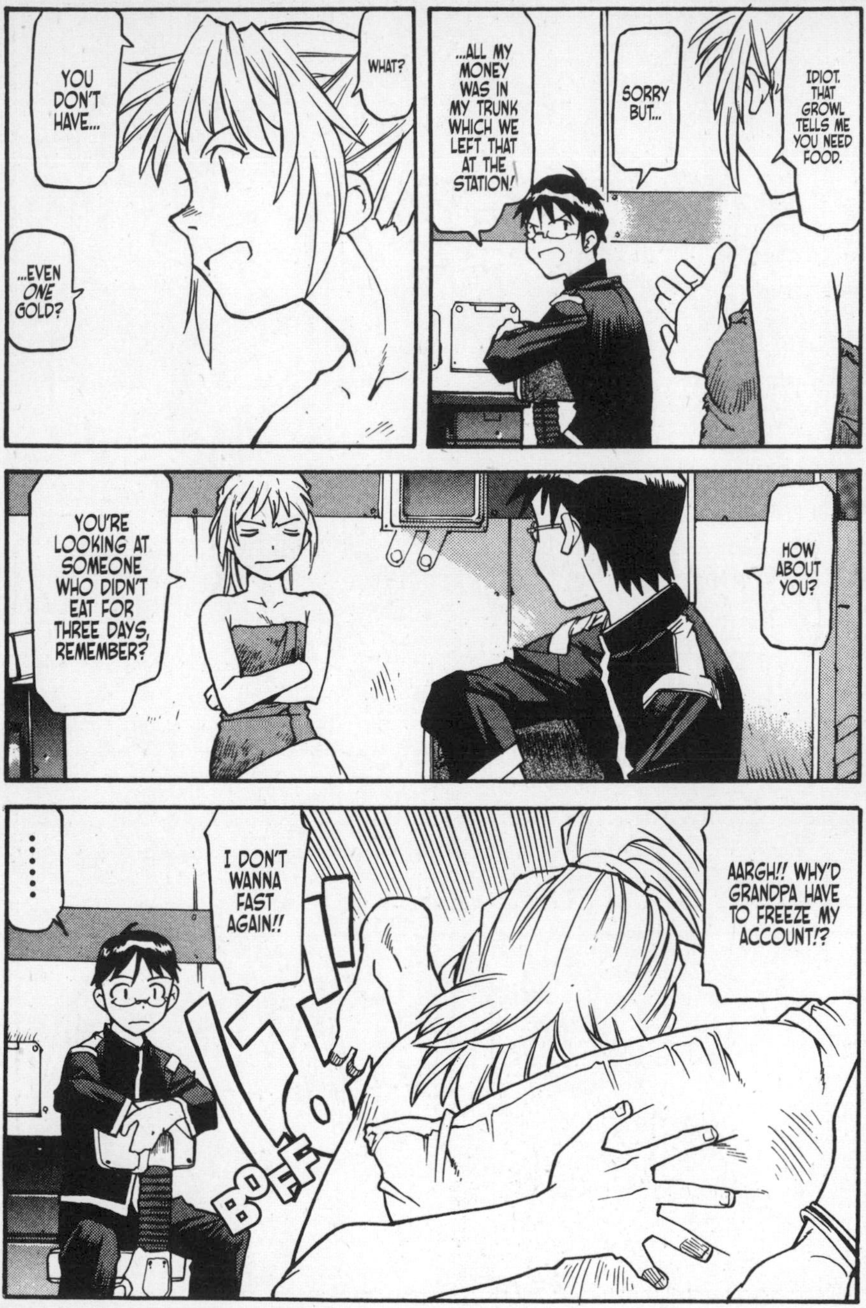
IDIOT. THAT GROWL TELLS ME YOU NEED FOOD.
SORRY BUT...
...ALL MY MONEY WAS IN MY TRUNK WHICH WE LEFT THAT AT THE STATION!
WHAT?
YOU DON'T HAVE...
...EVEN *ONE* GOLD?
HOW ABOUT YOU?
YOU'RE LOOKING AT SOMEONE WHO DIDN'T EAT FOR THREE DAYS, REMEMBER?
AARGH!! WHY'D GRANDPA HAVE TO FREEZE MY ACCOUNT!?
I DON'T WANNA FAST AGAIN!!
BOFF
......

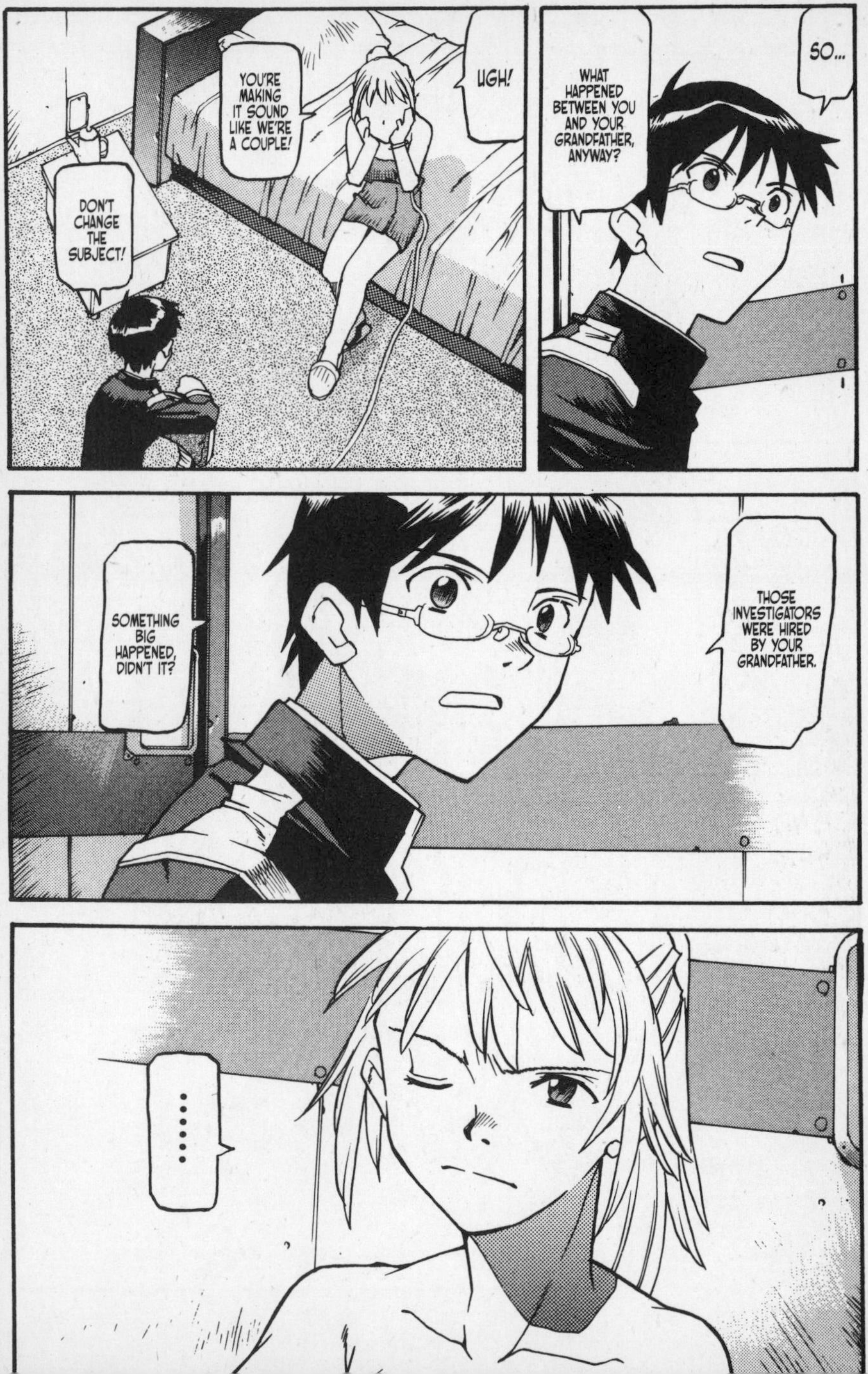
SO...
WHAT HAPPENED BETWEEN YOU AND YOUR GRANDFATHER, ANYWAY?
UGH!
YOU'RE MAKING IT SOUND LIKE WE'RE A COUPLE!
DON'T CHANGE THE SUBJECT!
THOSE INVESTIGATORS WERE HIRED BY YOUR GRANDFATHER.
SOMETHING BIG HAPPENED, DIDN'T IT?
......

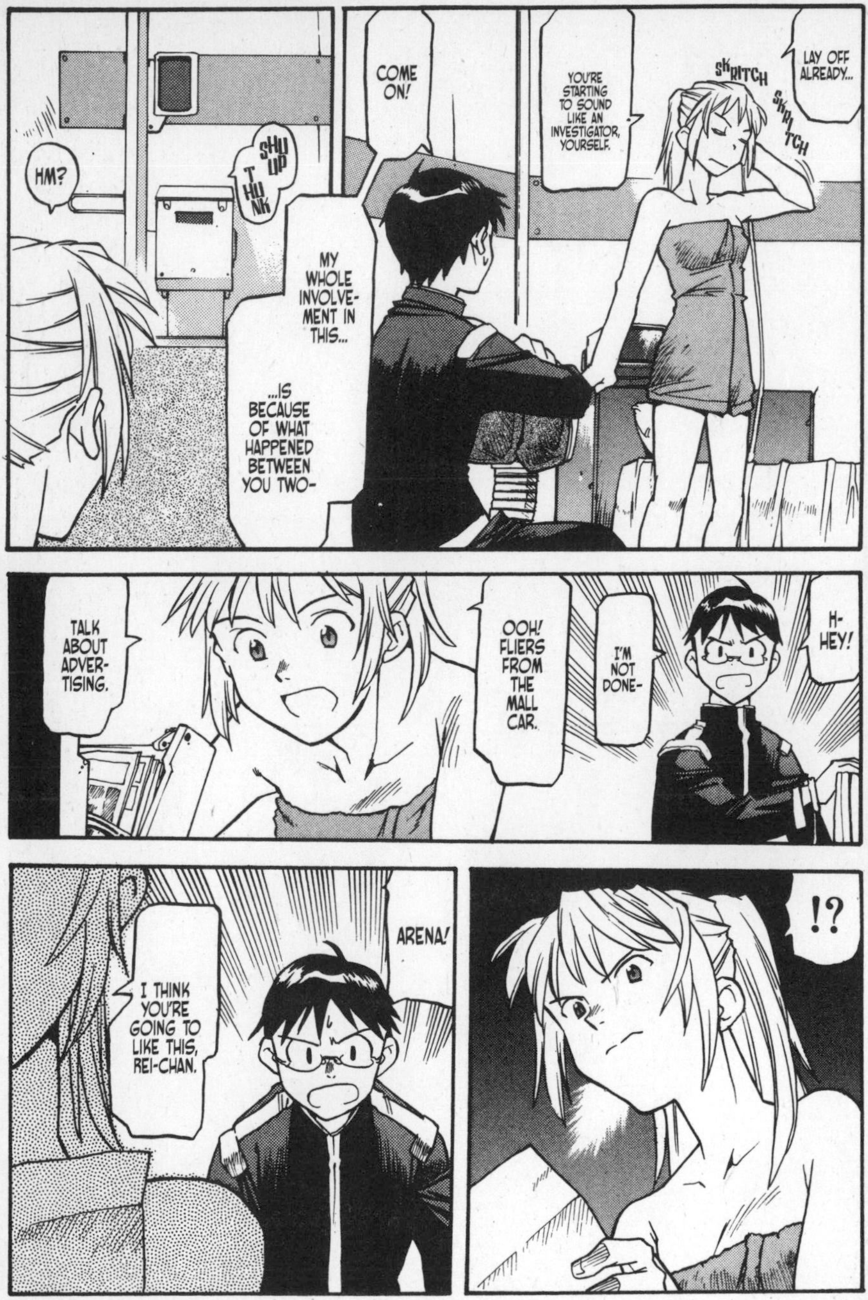
LAY OFF ALREADY...
SKRITCH
SKRITCH
YOU'RE STARTING TO SOUND LIKE AN INVESTIGATOR, YOURSELF.
COME ON!
MY WHOLE INVOLVEMENT IN THIS...
...IS BECAUSE OF WHAT HAPPENED BETWEEN YOU TWO-
SHU UP
THUNK
HM?
H-HEY!
I'M NOT DONE-
OOH! FLIERS FROM THE MALL CAR.
TALK ABOUT ADVERTISING.
!?
ARENA!
I THINK YOU'RE GOING TO LIKE THIS, REI-CHAN.

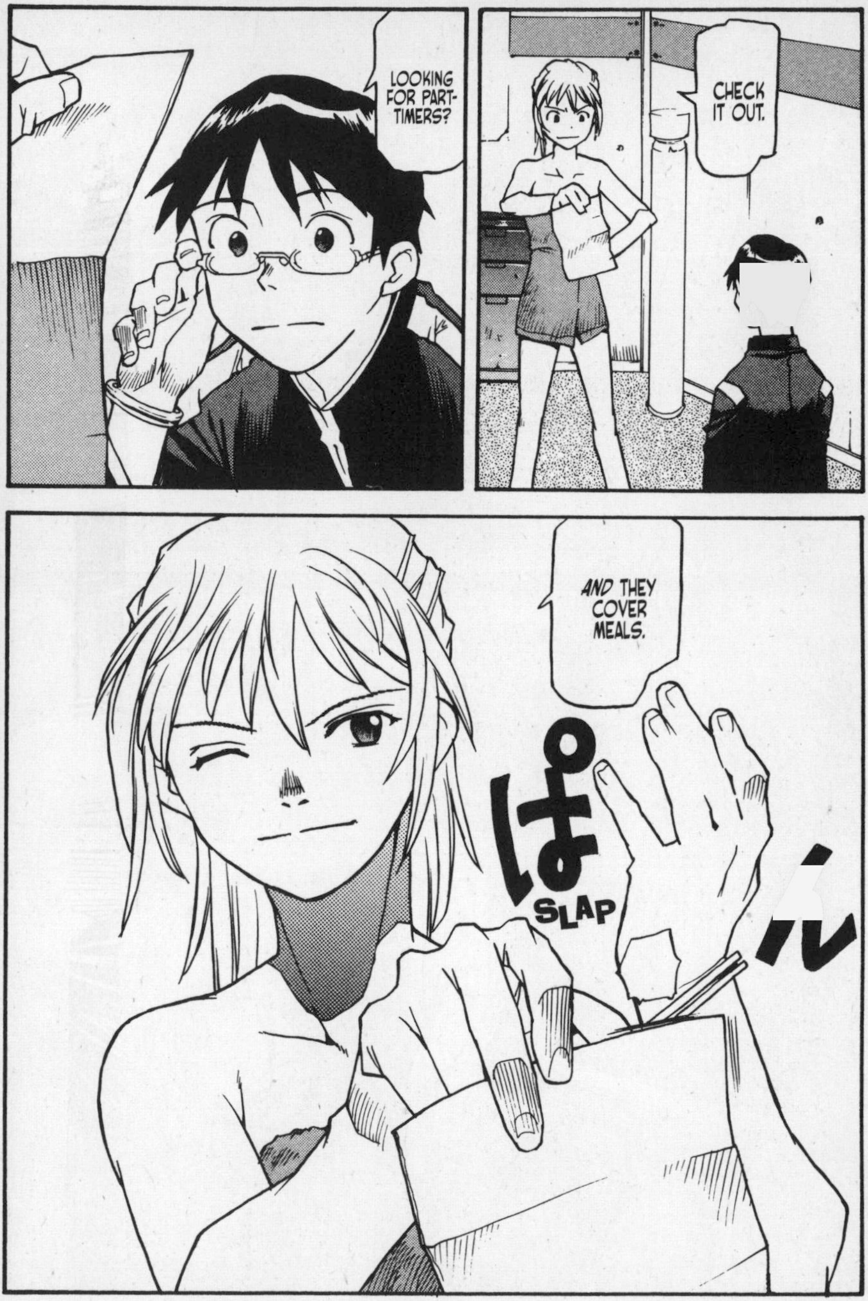
CHECK IT OUT.
LOOKING FOR PART-TIMERS?
AND THEY COVER MEALS.
ぱん
SLAP

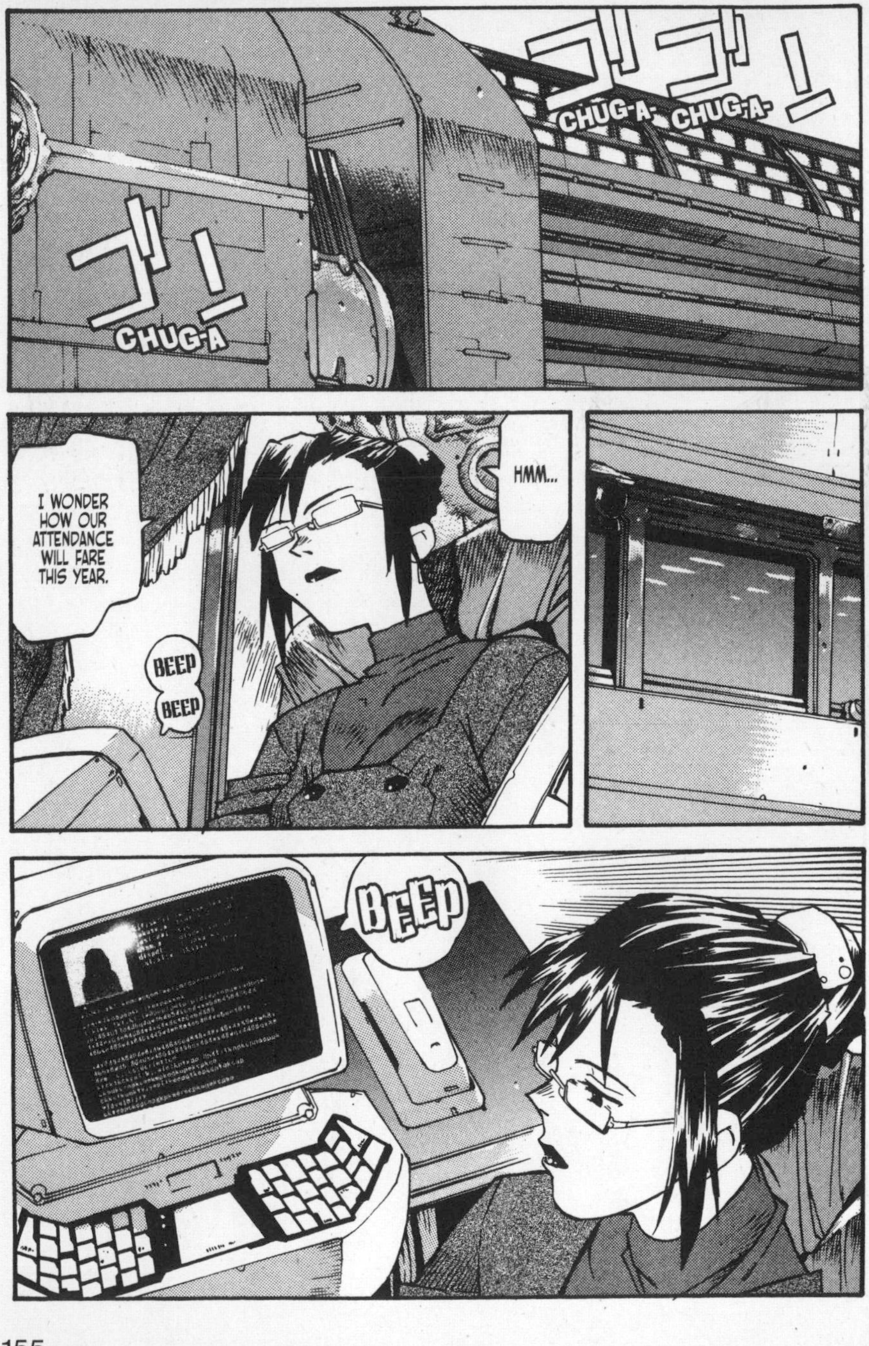
CHUG-A- CHUG-A-
CHUG-A
HMM...
I WONDER HOW OUR ATTENDANCE WILL FARE THIS YEAR.
BEEP
BEEP
BEEP

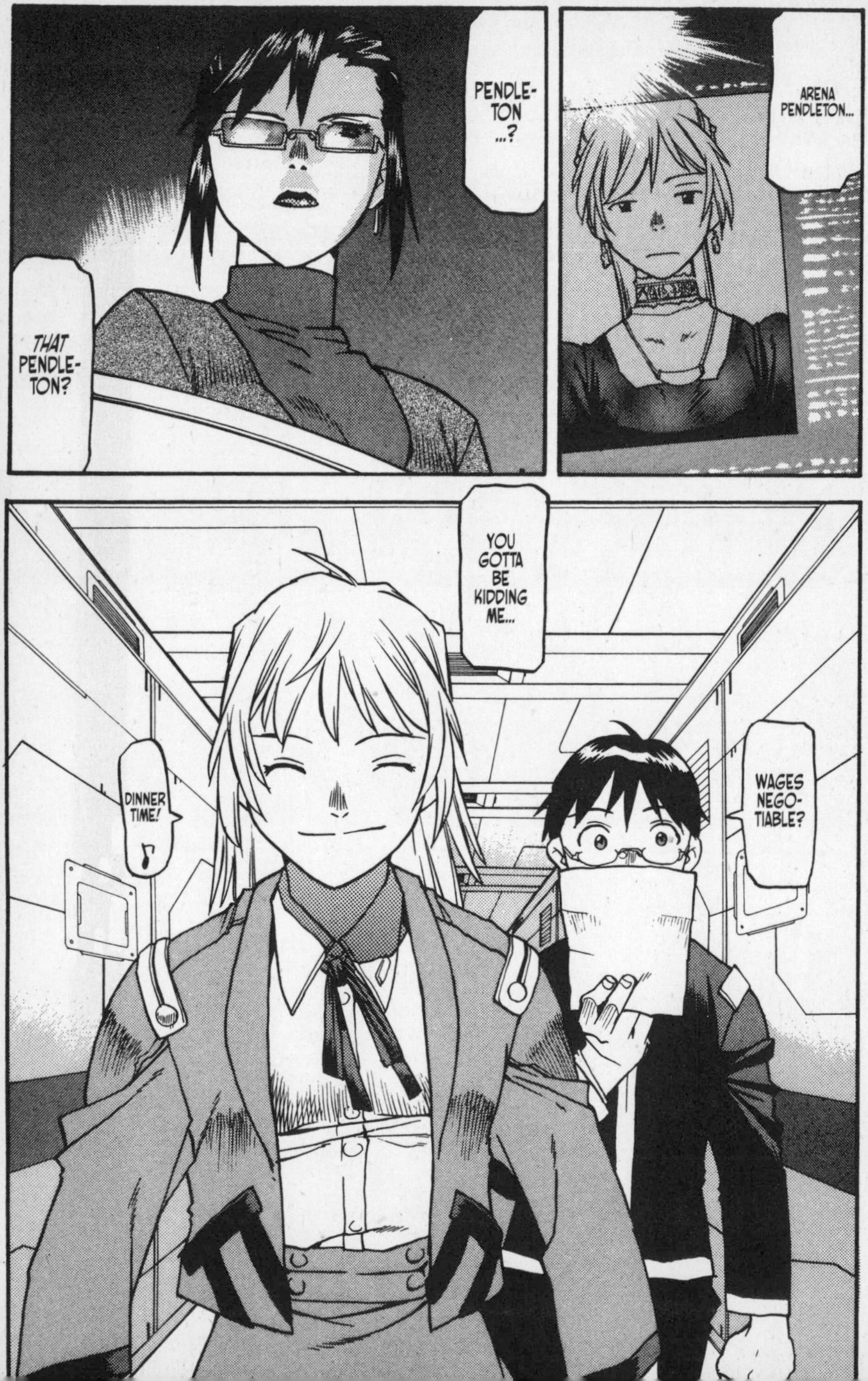
ARENA PENDLETON...
PENDLE-TON ...?
THAT PENDLE-TON?
YOU GOTTA BE KIDDING ME...
WAGES NEGO-TIABLE?
DINNER TIME! ♪

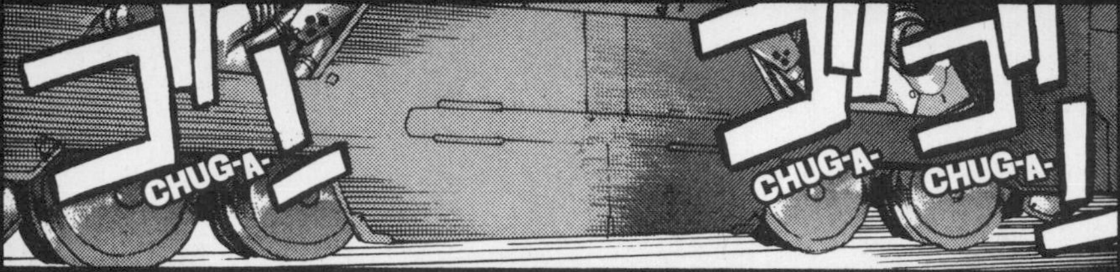
CHUG-A-
CHUG-A-
CHUG-A-

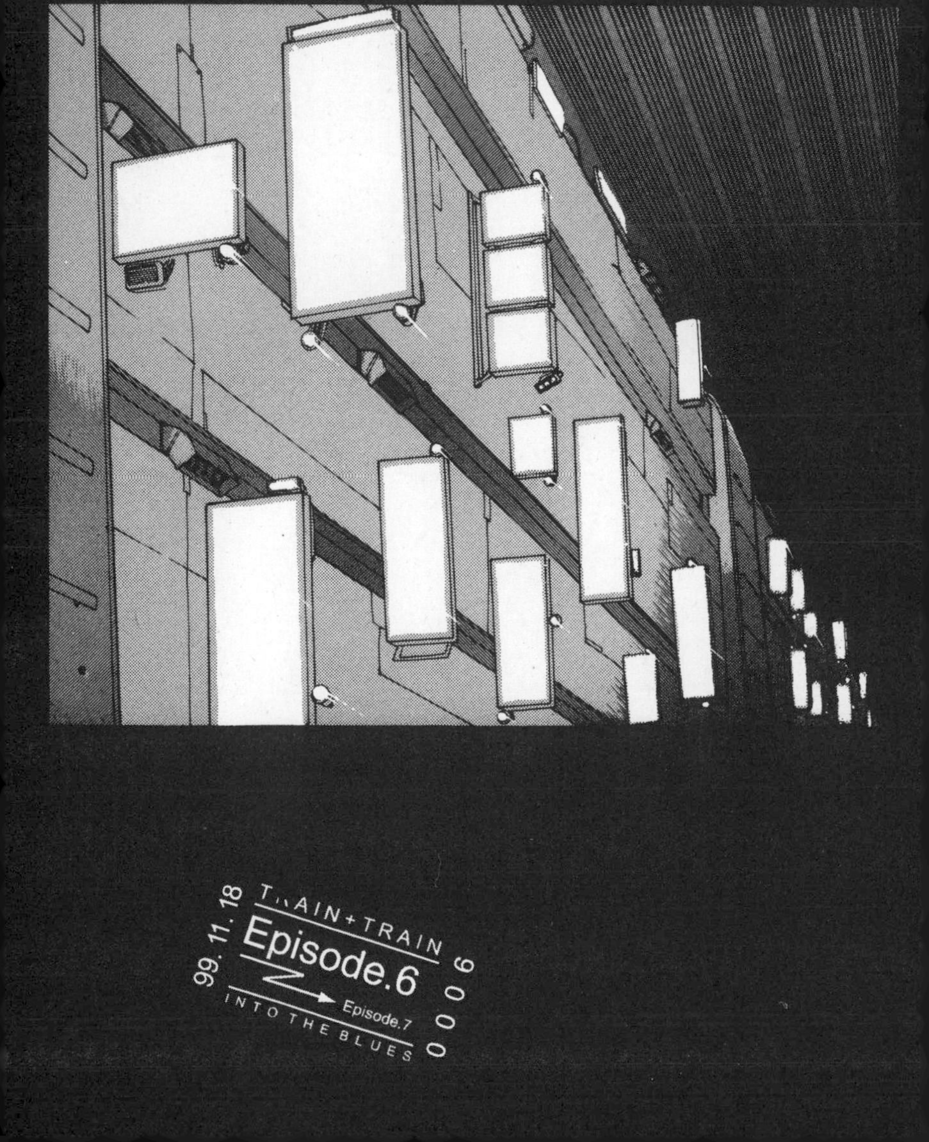

99. 11. 18

TRAIN+TRAIN

Episode.6

→ Episode.7

INTO THE BLUES

0006

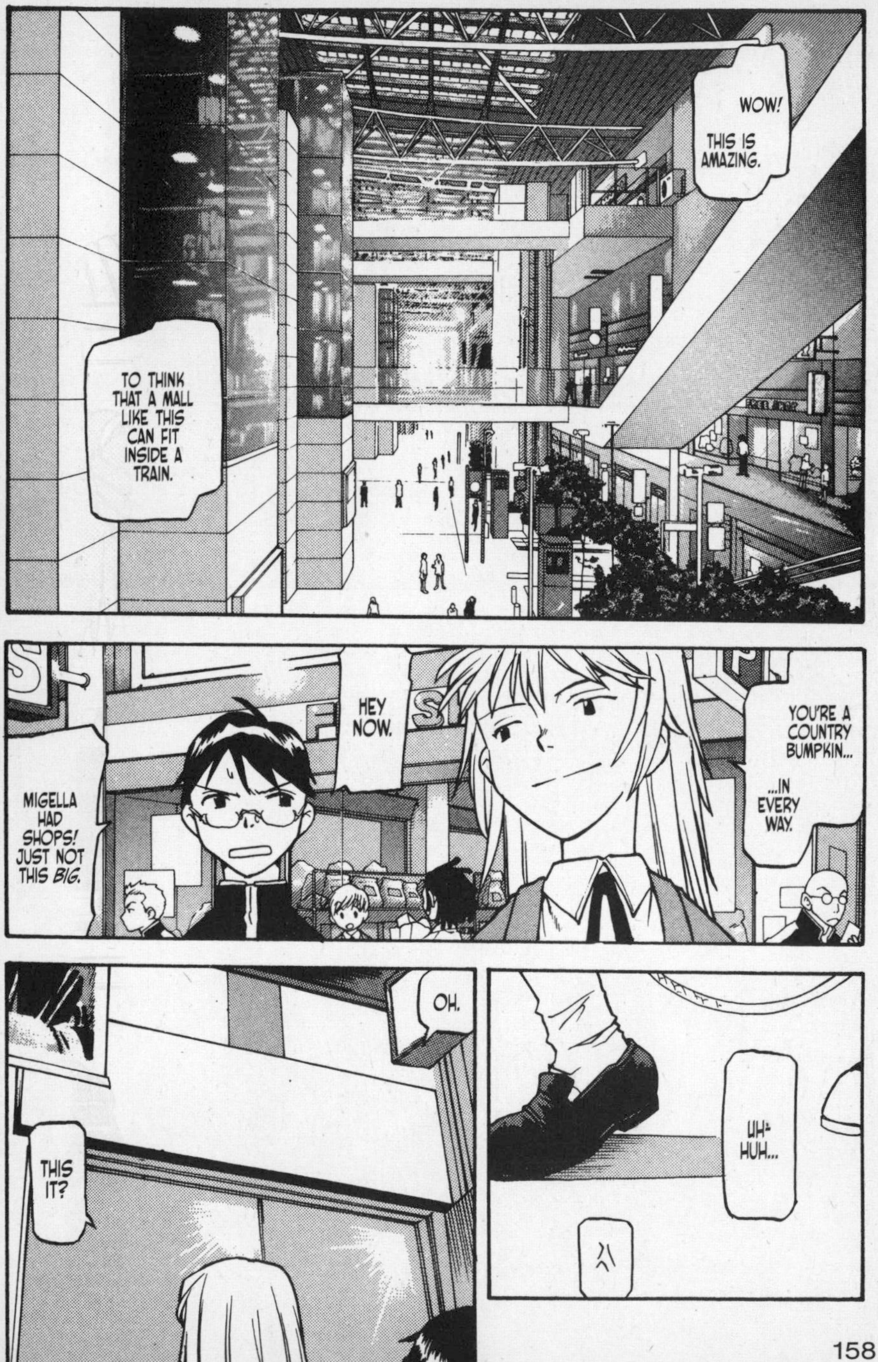
WOW!
THIS IS AMAZING.
TO THINK THAT A MALL LIKE THIS CAN FIT INSIDE A TRAIN.
YOU'RE A COUNTRY BUMPKIN...
...IN EVERY WAY.
HEY NOW.
MIGELLA HAD SHOPS! JUST NOT THIS *BIG*.
UH-HUH...
OH.
THIS IT?

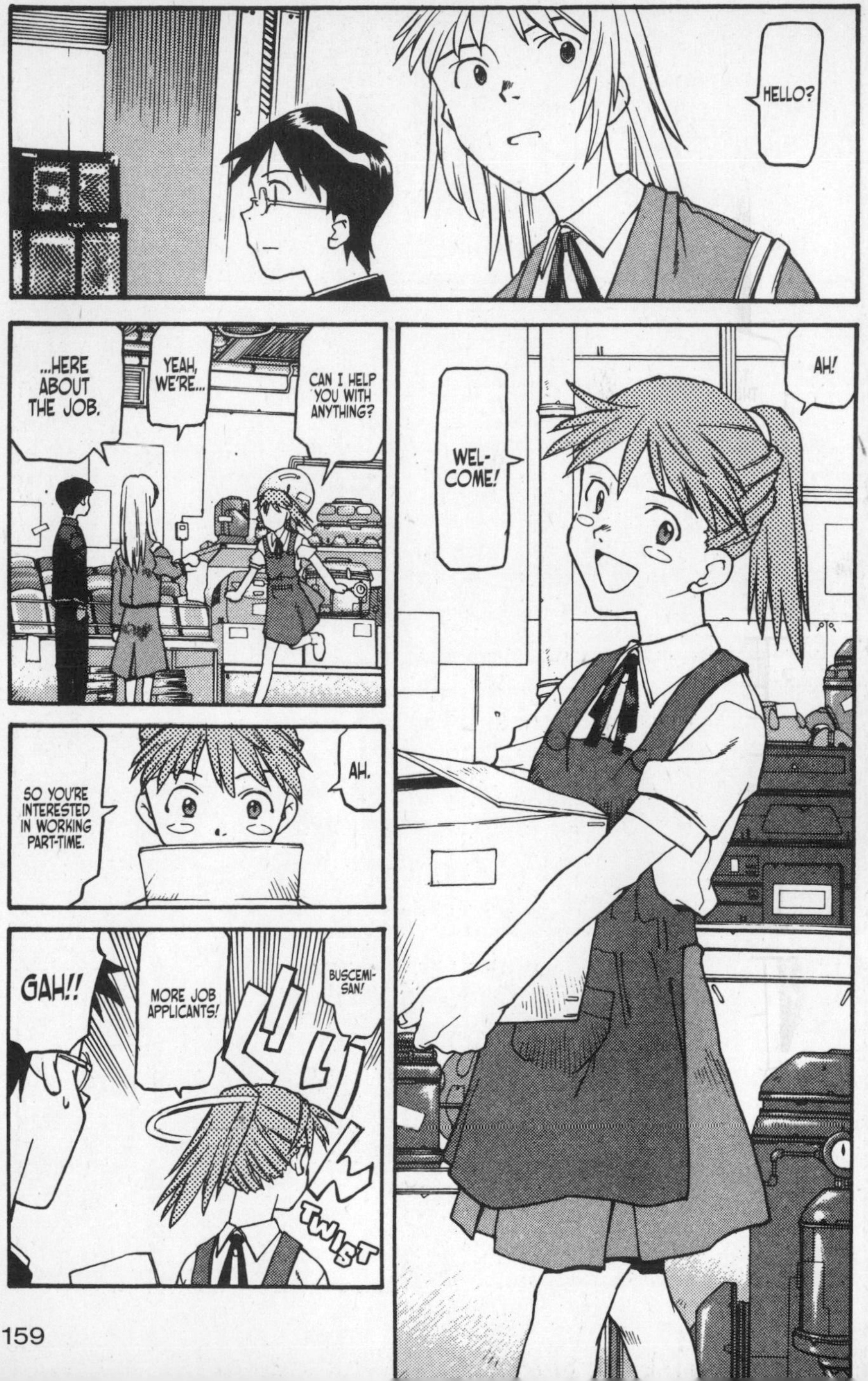
HELLO?
AH!
WEL-COME!
CAN I HELP YOU WITH ANYTHING?
YEAH, WE'RE...
...HERE ABOUT THE JOB.
AH.
SO YOU'RE INTERESTED IN WORKING PART-TIME.
BUSCEMI-SAN!
MORE JOB APPLICANTS!
GAH!!
TWIST

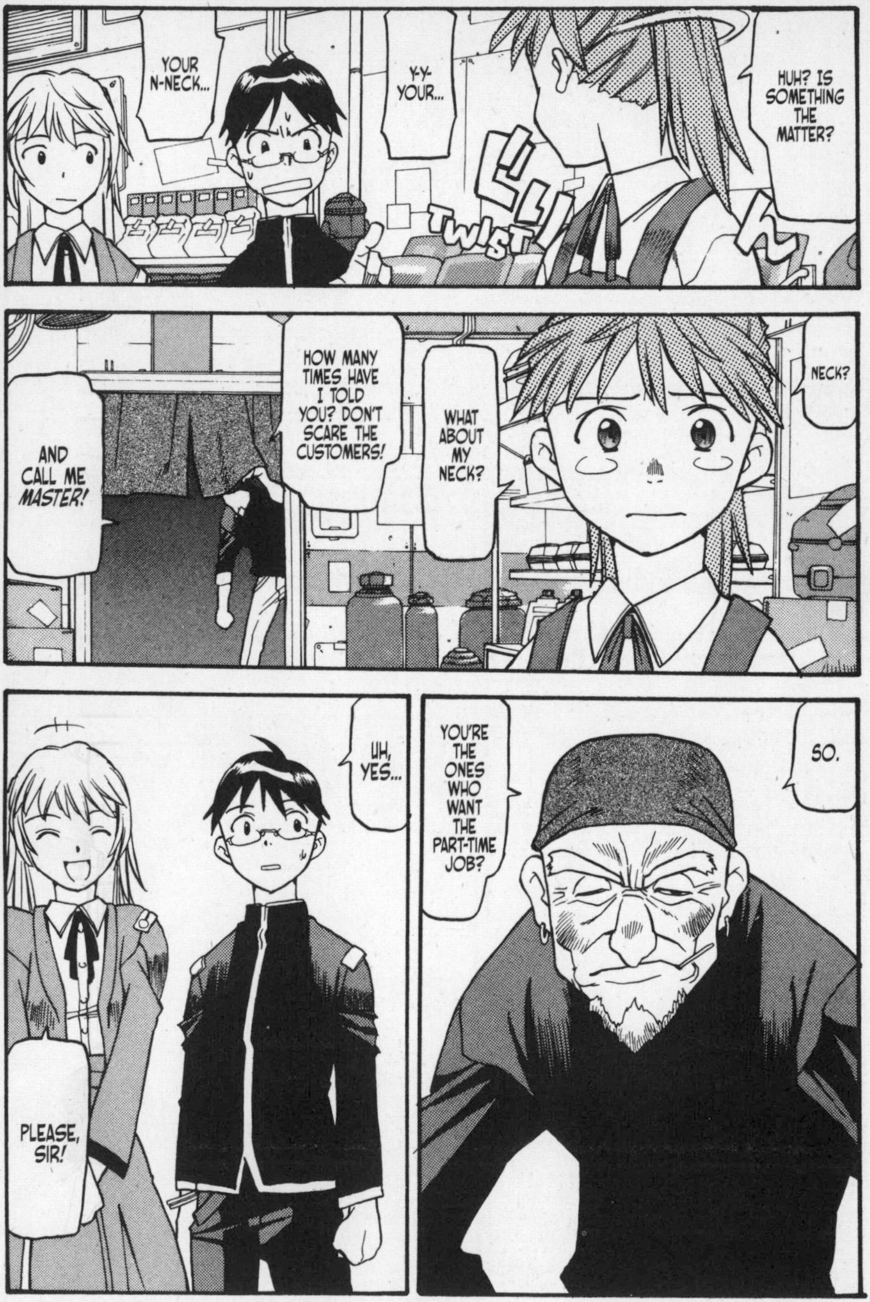
HUH? IS SOMETHING THE MATTER?
TWIST
Y-Y-YOUR...
YOUR N-NECK...
NECK?
WHAT ABOUT MY NECK?
HOW MANY TIMES HAVE I TOLD YOU? DON'T SCARE THE CUSTOMERS!
AND CALL ME *MASTER!*
SO.
YOU'RE THE ONES WHO WANT THE PART-TIME JOB?
UH, YES...
PLEASE, SIR!

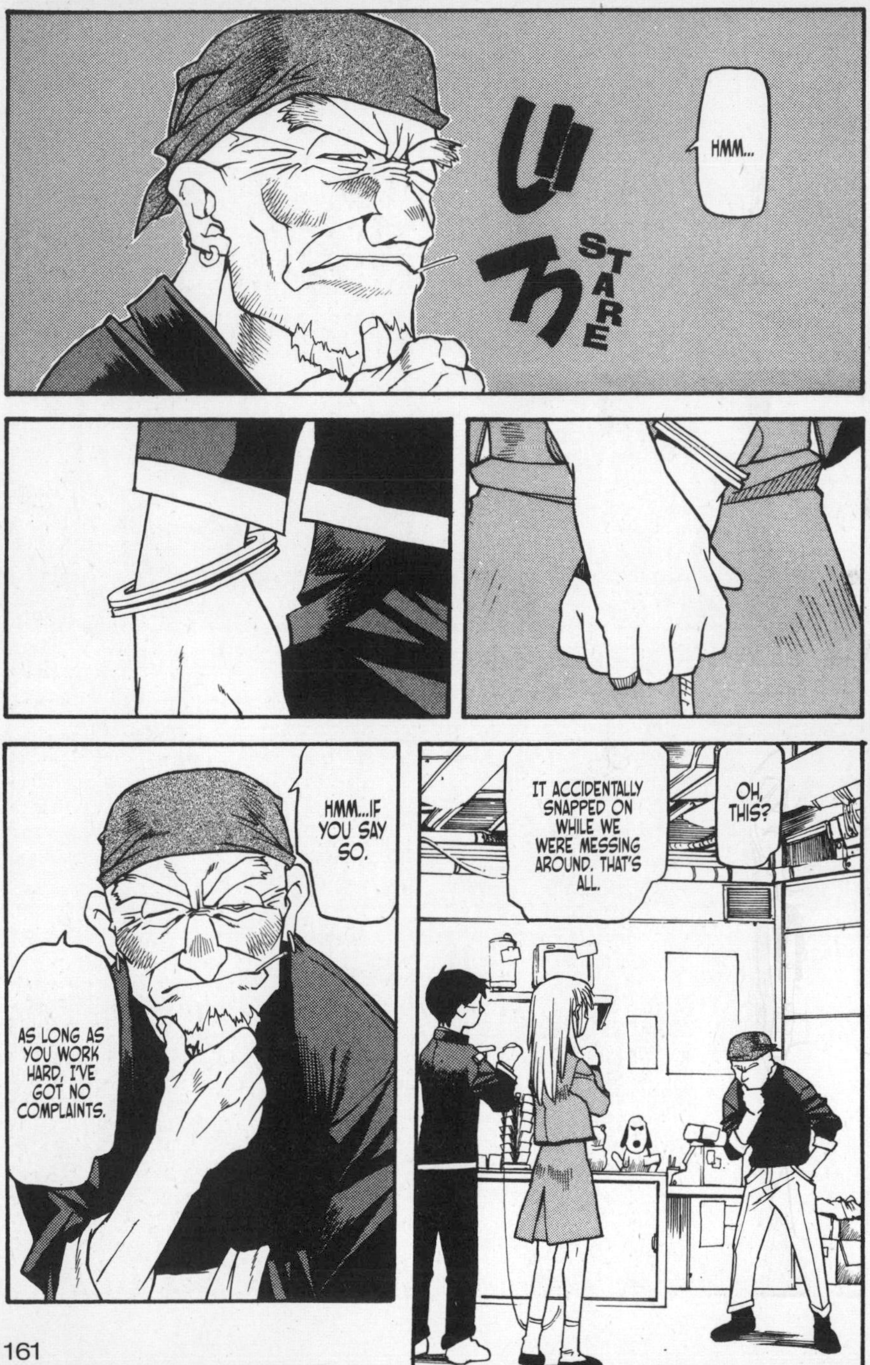
HMM...
じろ
STARE
OH, THIS?
IT ACCIDENTALLY SNAPPED ON WHILE WE WERE MESSING AROUND. THAT'S ALL.
HMM...IF YOU SAY SO.
AS LONG AS YOU WORK HARD, I'VE GOT NO COMPLAINTS.

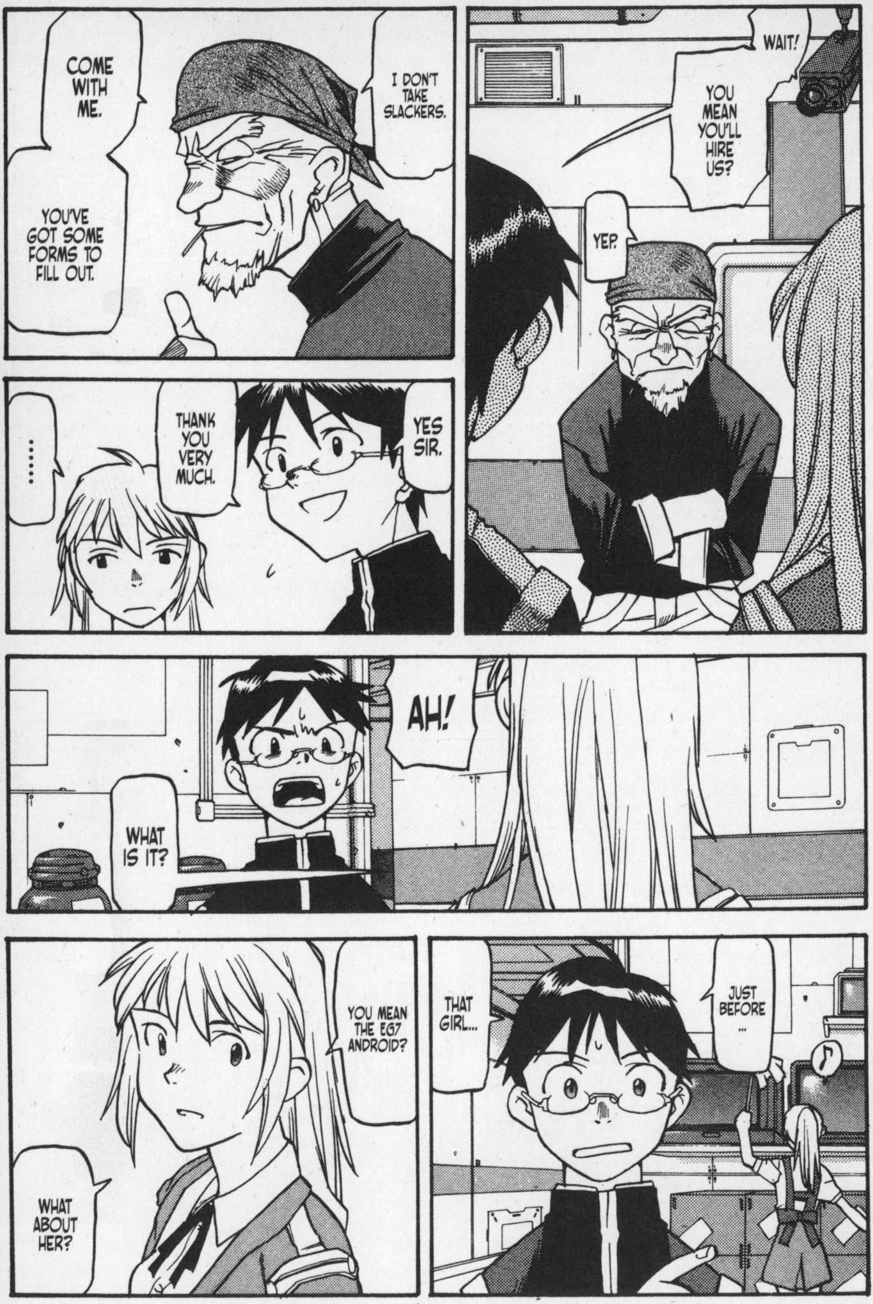
WAIT!
YOU MEAN YOU'LL HIRE US?
YEP.
I DON'T TAKE SLACKERS.
COME WITH ME.
YOU'VE GOT SOME FORMS TO FILL OUT.
YES SIR.
THANK YOU VERY MUCH.
......
AH!
WHAT IS IT?
JUST BEFORE ...
THAT GIRL...
YOU MEAN THE EG7 ANDROID?
WHAT ABOUT HER?

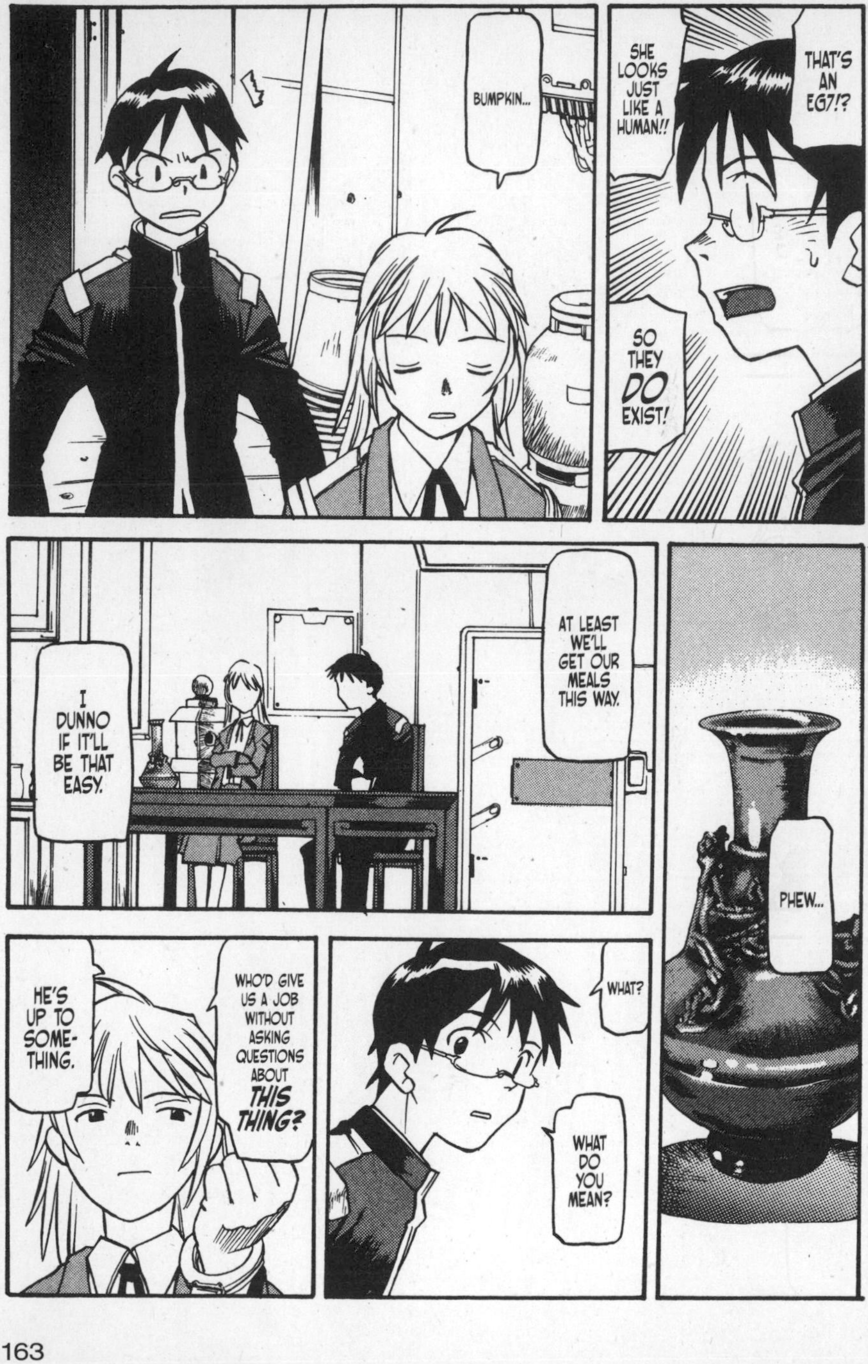
THAT'S AN EG7!?
SHE LOOKS JUST LIKE A HUMAN!!
SO THEY DO EXIST!
BUMPKIN...
PHEW...
AT LEAST WE'LL GET OUR MEALS THIS WAY.
I DUNNO IF IT'LL BE THAT EASY.
WHAT?
WHAT DO YOU MEAN?
WHO'D GIVE US A JOB WITHOUT ASKING QUESTIONS ABOUT THIS THING?
HE'S UP TO SOME-THING.

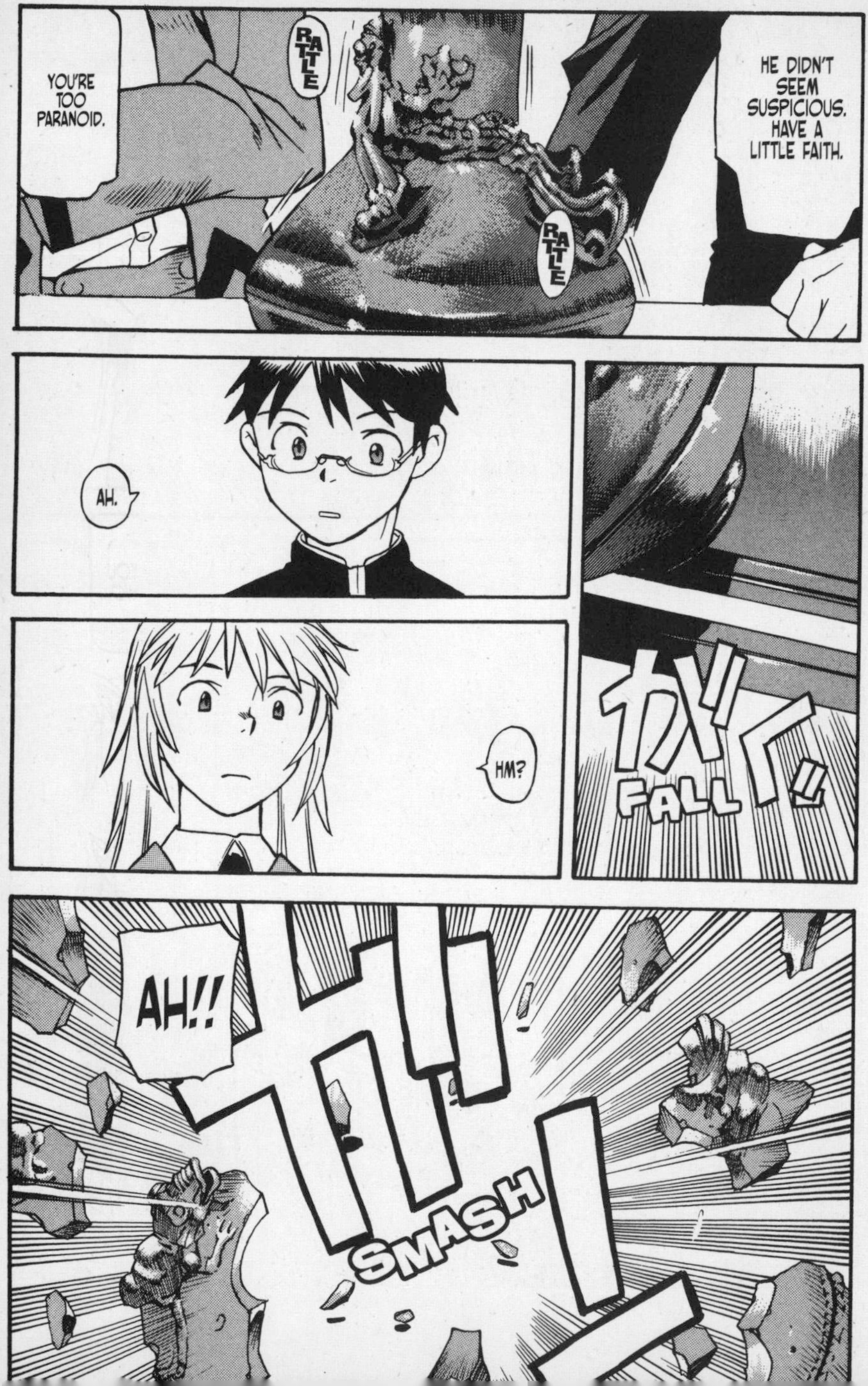
HE DIDN'T SEEM SUSPICIOUS. HAVE A LITTLE FAITH.
RATTLE
YOU'RE TOO PARANOID.
RATTLE
FALL
AH.
HM?
AH!!
SMASH

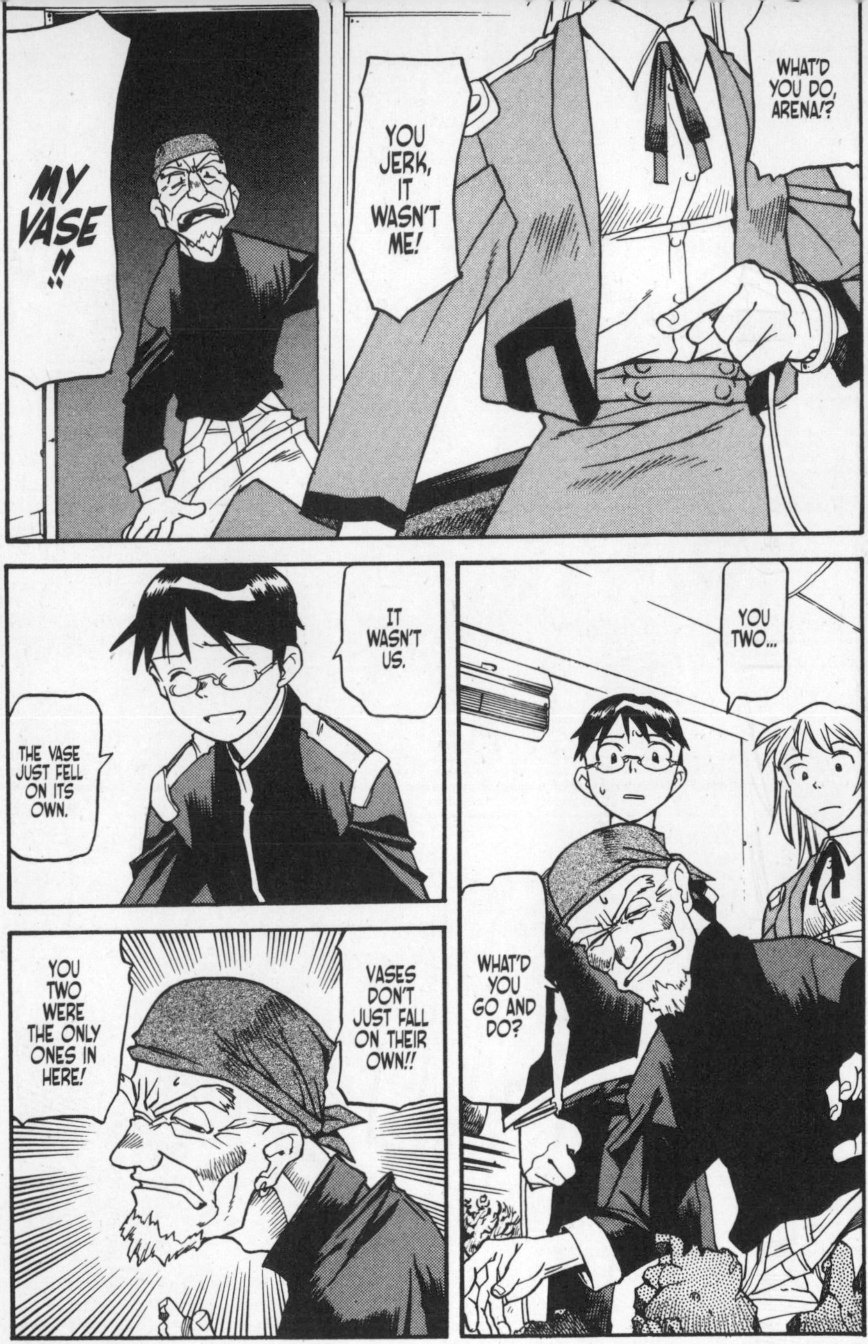
WHAT'D YOU DO, ARENA!?
YOU JERK, IT WASN'T ME!
MY VASE!!
YOU TWO...
WHAT'D YOU GO AND DO?
IT WASN'T US.
THE VASE JUST FELL ON ITS OWN.
VASES DON'T JUST FALL ON THEIR OWN!!
YOU TWO WERE THE ONLY ONES IN HERE!

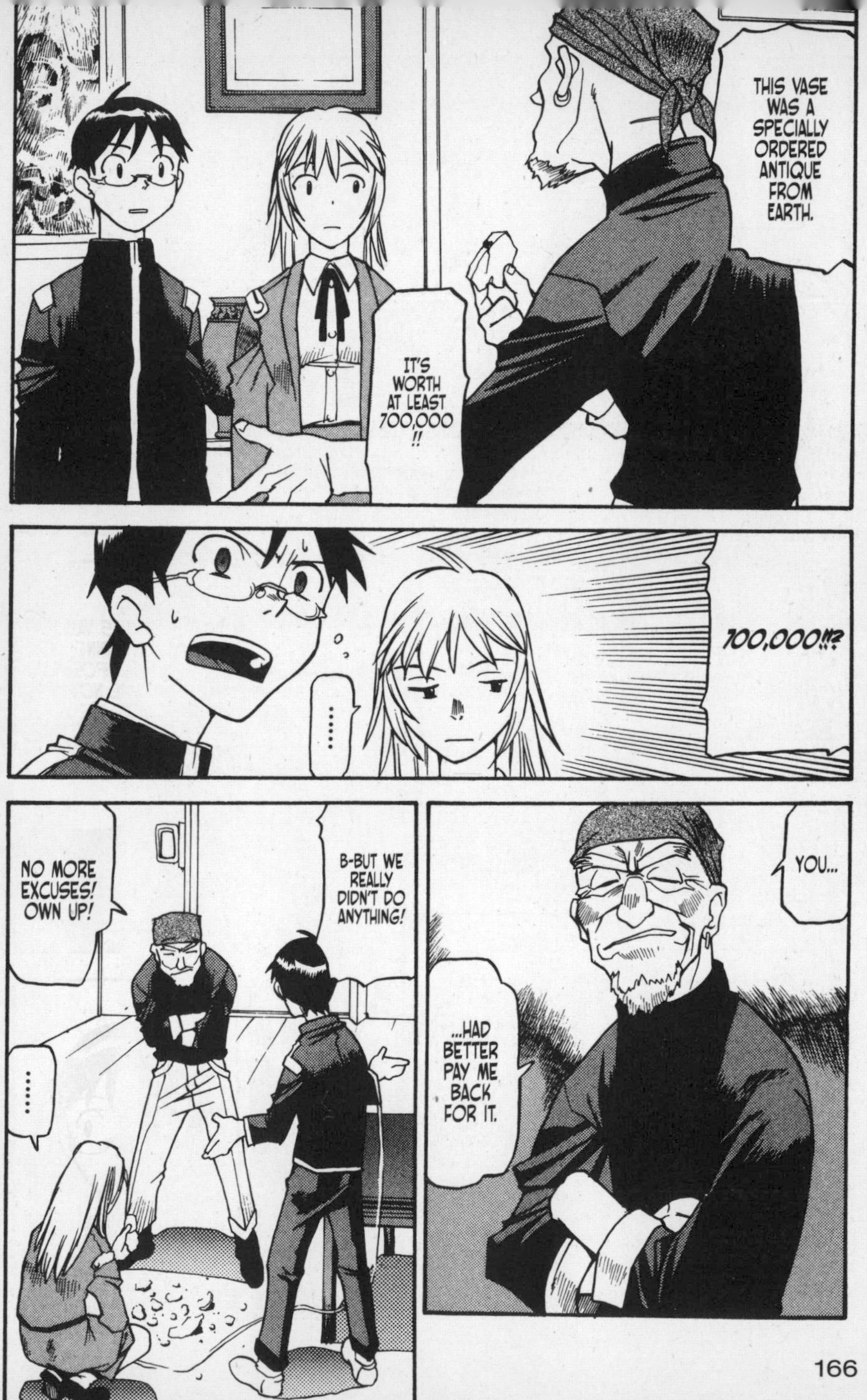
THIS VASE WAS A SPECIALLY ORDERED ANTIQUE FROM EARTH.
IT'S WORTH AT LEAST 700,000 !!
700,000!!?
......
YOU...
...HAD BETTER PAY ME BACK FOR IT.
B-BUT WE REALLY DIDN'T DO ANYTHING!
NO MORE EXCUSES! OWN UP!
......

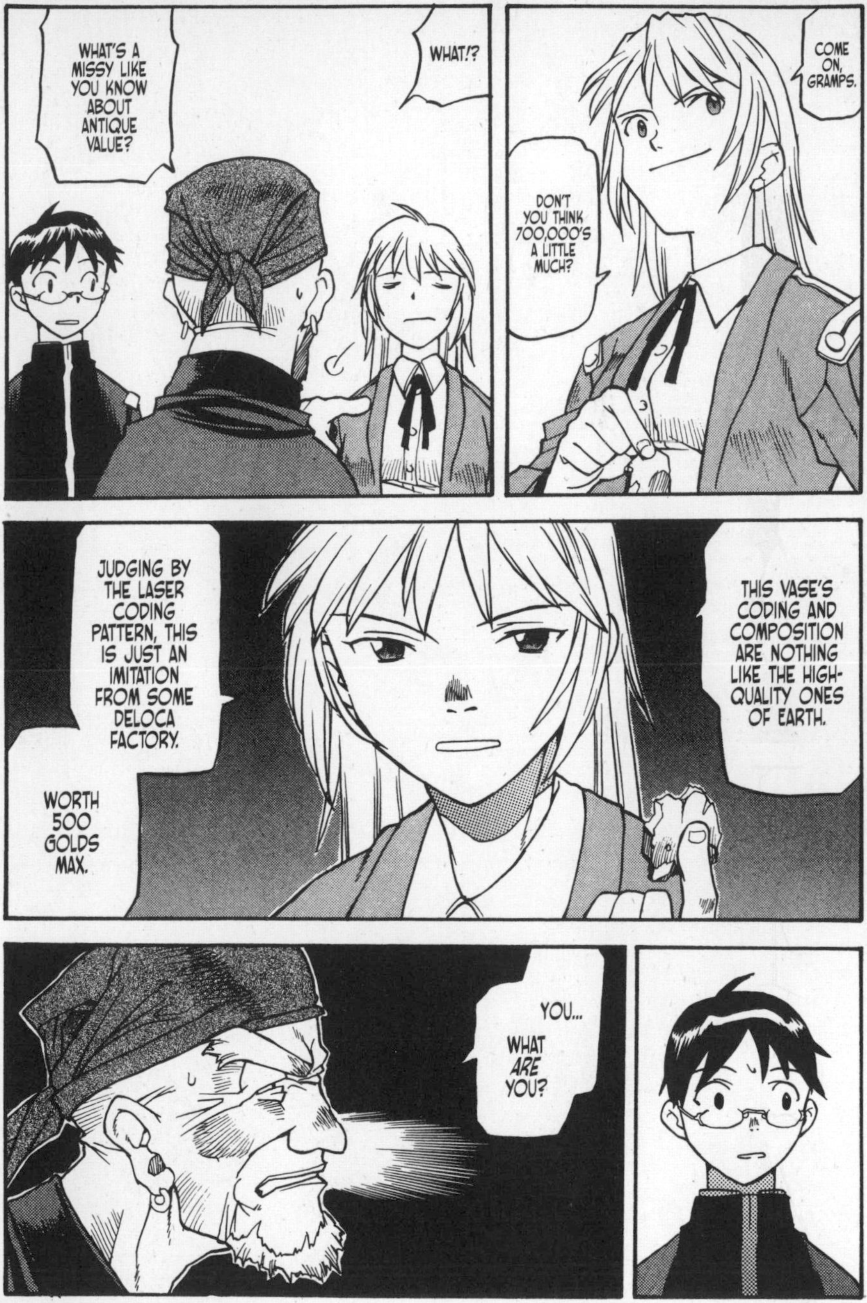
COME ON, GRAMPS.
DON'T YOU THINK 700,000'S A LITTLE MUCH?
WHAT!?
WHAT'S A MISSY LIKE YOU KNOW ABOUT ANTIQUE VALUE?
THIS VASE'S CODING AND COMPOSITION ARE NOTHING LIKE THE HIGH-QUALITY ONES OF EARTH.
JUDGING BY THE LASER CODING PATTERN, THIS IS JUST AN IMITATION FROM SOME DELOCA FACTORY.
WORTH 500 GOLDS MAX.
YOU...
WHAT *ARE* YOU?

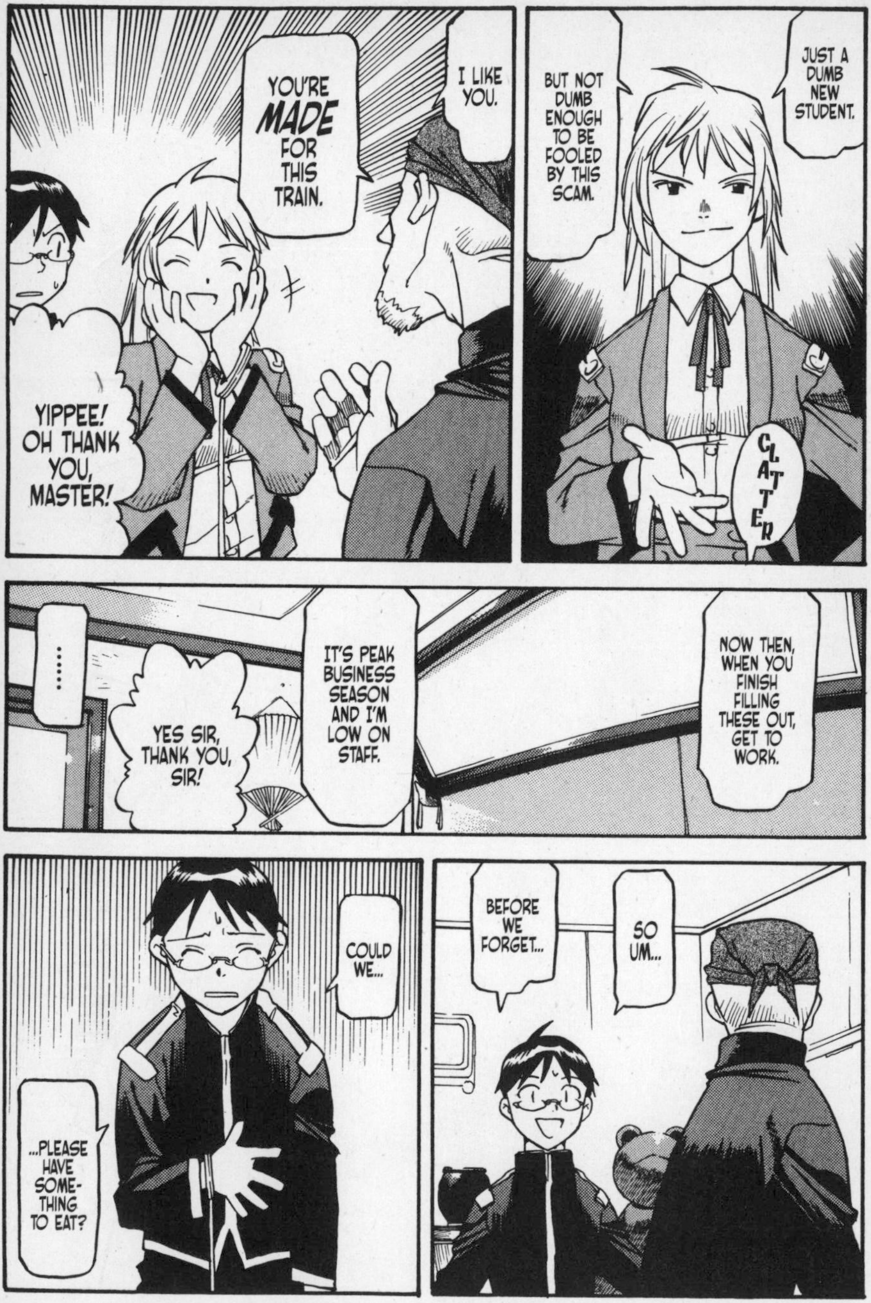
JUST A DUMB NEW STUDENT.
BUT NOT DUMB ENOUGH TO BE FOOLED BY THIS SCAM.
CLATTER
I LIKE YOU.
YOU'RE MADE FOR THIS TRAIN.
YIPPEE! OH THANK YOU, MASTER!
NOW THEN, WHEN YOU FINISH FILLING THESE OUT, GET TO WORK.
IT'S PEAK BUSINESS SEASON AND I'M LOW ON STAFF.
YES SIR, THANK YOU, SIR!
......
SO UM...
BEFORE WE FORGET...
COULD WE...
...PLEASE HAVE SOME-THING TO EAT?

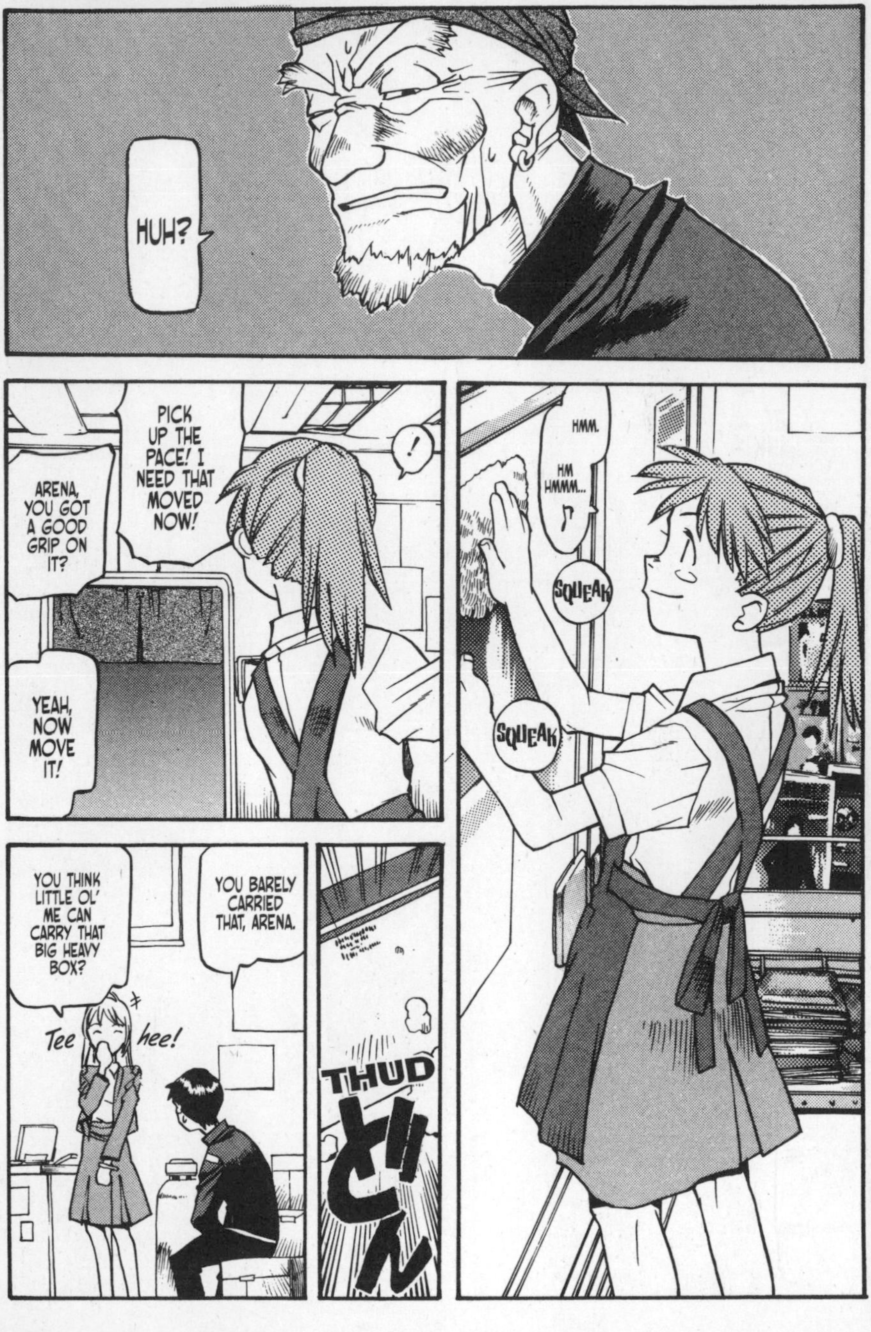
HUH?
HMM.
HM HMMM... ♪
SQUEAK
SQUEAK
!
PICK UP THE PACE! I NEED THAT MOVED NOW!
ARENA, YOU GOT A GOOD GRIP ON IT?
YEAH, NOW MOVE IT!
THUD
どん
YOU BARELY CARRIED THAT, ARENA.
YOU THINK LITTLE OL' ME CAN CARRY THAT BIG HEAVY BOX?
Tee hee!

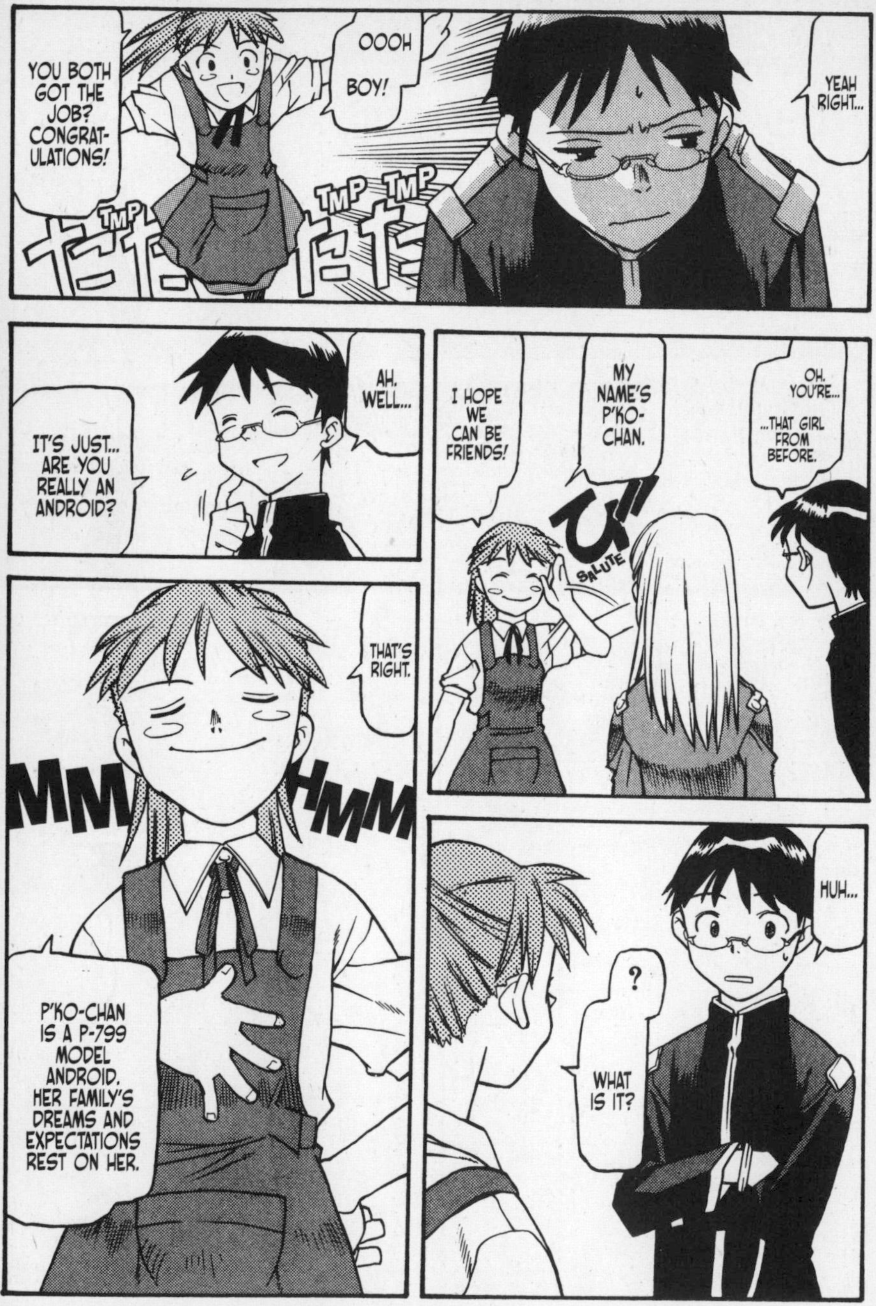
YEAH RIGHT...
OOOH
BOY!
YOU BOTH GOT THE JOB? CONGRAT-ULATIONS!
TMP TMP TMP
たた たた
OH. YOU'RE...
...THAT GIRL FROM BEFORE.
MY NAME'S P'KO-CHAN.
I HOPE WE CAN BE FRIENDS!
び
SALUTE
AH. WELL...
IT'S JUST... ARE YOU REALLY AN ANDROID?
THAT'S RIGHT.
MMHMM
P'KO-CHAN IS A P-799 MODEL ANDROID. HER FAMILY'S DREAMS AND EXPECTATIONS REST ON HER.
HUH...
?
WHAT IS IT?

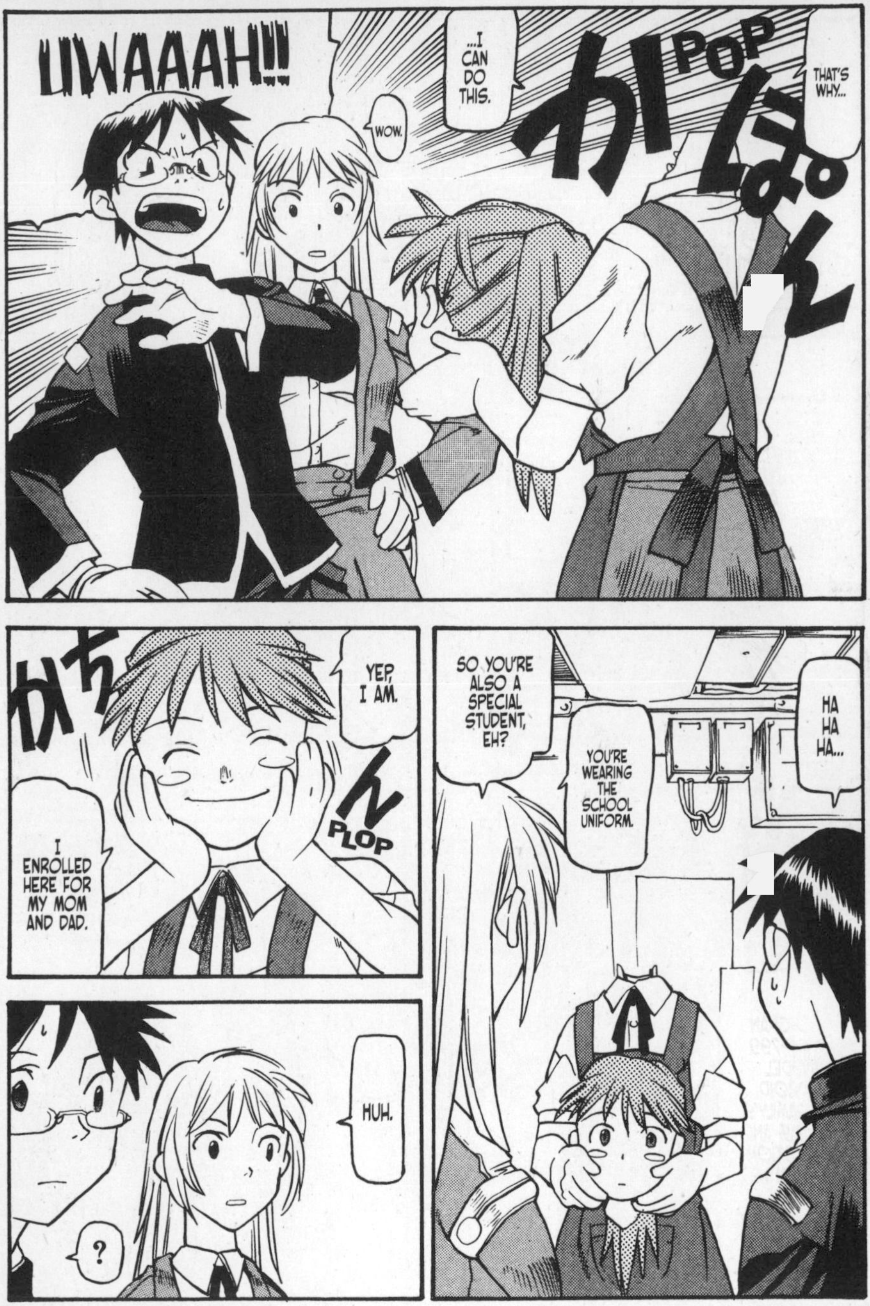
THAT'S WHY...
POP
...I CAN DO THIS.
WOW.
UWAAAH!!!
HA HA HA...
SO YOU'RE ALSO A SPECIAL STUDENT, EH?
YOU'RE WEARING THE SCHOOL UNIFORM.
YEP, I AM.
PLOP
I ENROLLED HERE FOR MY MOM AND DAD.
HUH.
?

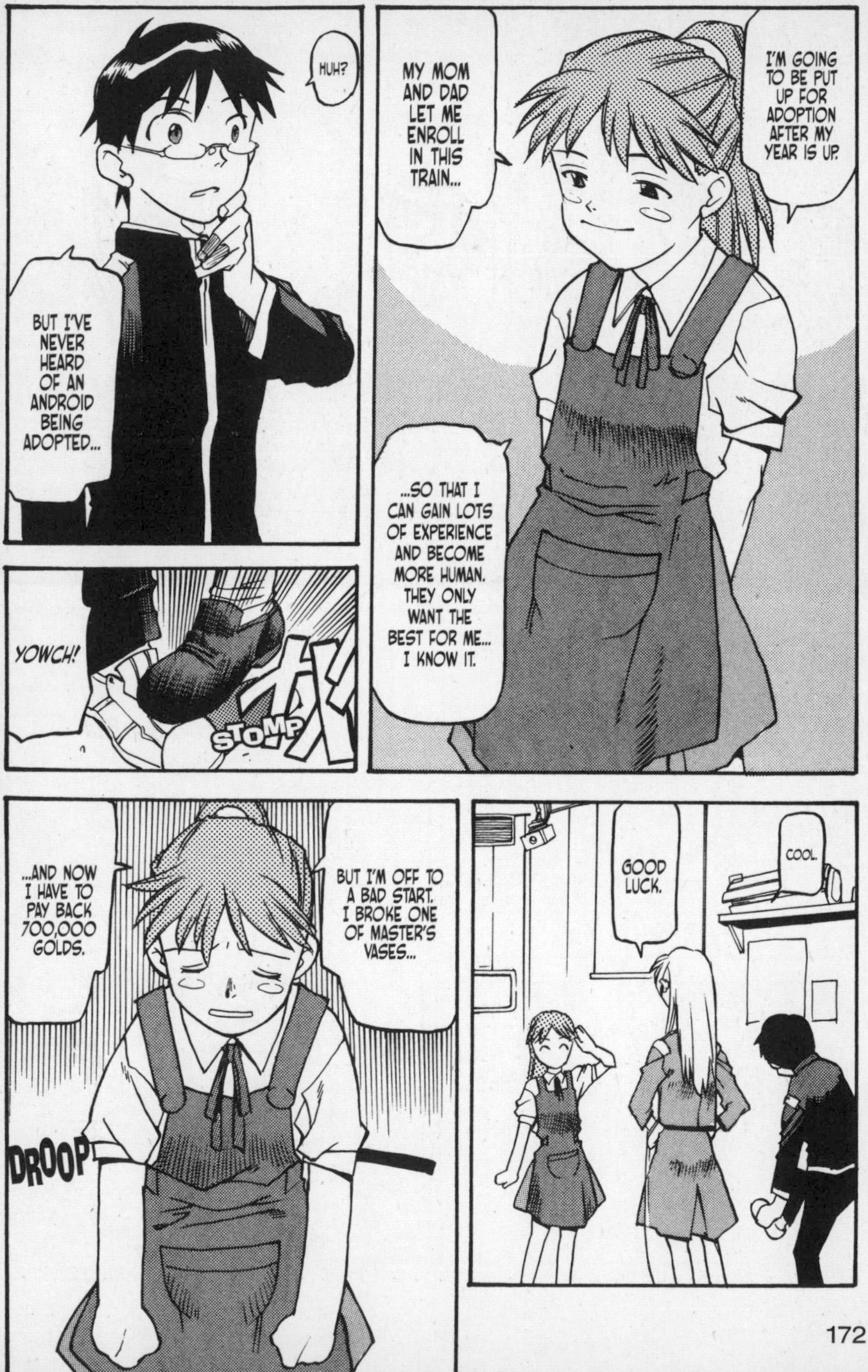
I'M GOING TO BE PUT UP FOR ADOPTION AFTER MY YEAR IS UP.
MY MOM AND DAD LET ME ENROLL IN THIS TRAIN...
...SO THAT I CAN GAIN LOTS OF EXPERIENCE AND BECOME MORE HUMAN. THEY ONLY WANT THE BEST FOR ME... I KNOW IT.
HUH?
BUT I'VE NEVER HEARD OF AN ANDROID BEING ADOPTED...
YOWCH!
STOMP
COOL.
GOOD LUCK.
BUT I'M OFF TO A BAD START. I BROKE ONE OF MASTER'S VASES...
...AND NOW I HAVE TO PAY BACK 700,000 GOLDS.
DROOP

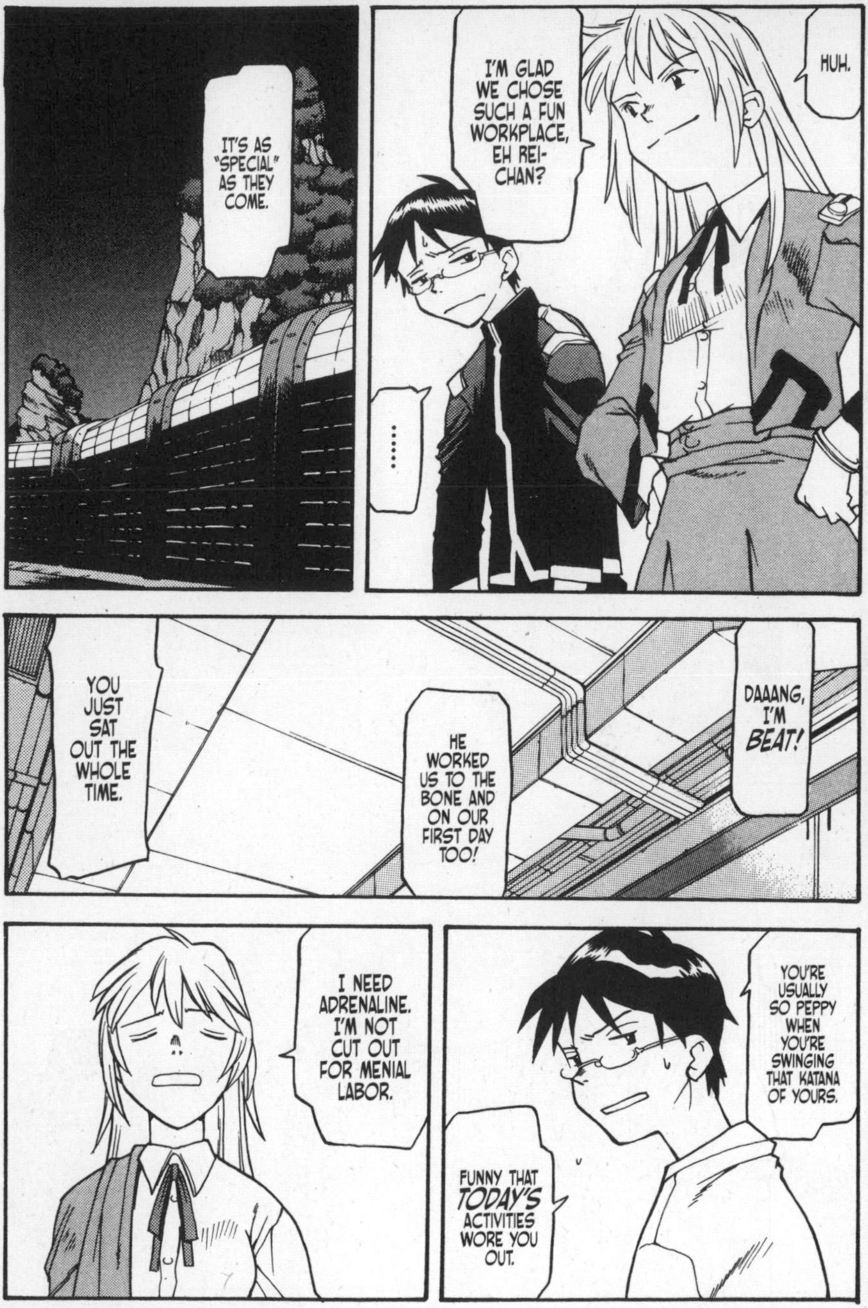
HUH.
I'M GLAD WE CHOSE SUCH A FUN WORKPLACE, EH REI-CHAN?
......
IT'S AS "SPECIAL" AS THEY COME.
DAAANG, I'M *BEAT!*
HE WORKED US TO THE BONE AND ON OUR FIRST DAY TOO!
YOU JUST SAT OUT THE WHOLE TIME.
YOU'RE USUALLY SO PEPPY WHEN YOU'RE SWINGING THAT KATANA OF YOURS.
FUNNY THAT *TODAY'S* ACTIVITIES WORE YOU OUT.
I NEED ADRENALINE. I'M NOT CUT OUT FOR MENIAL LABOR.

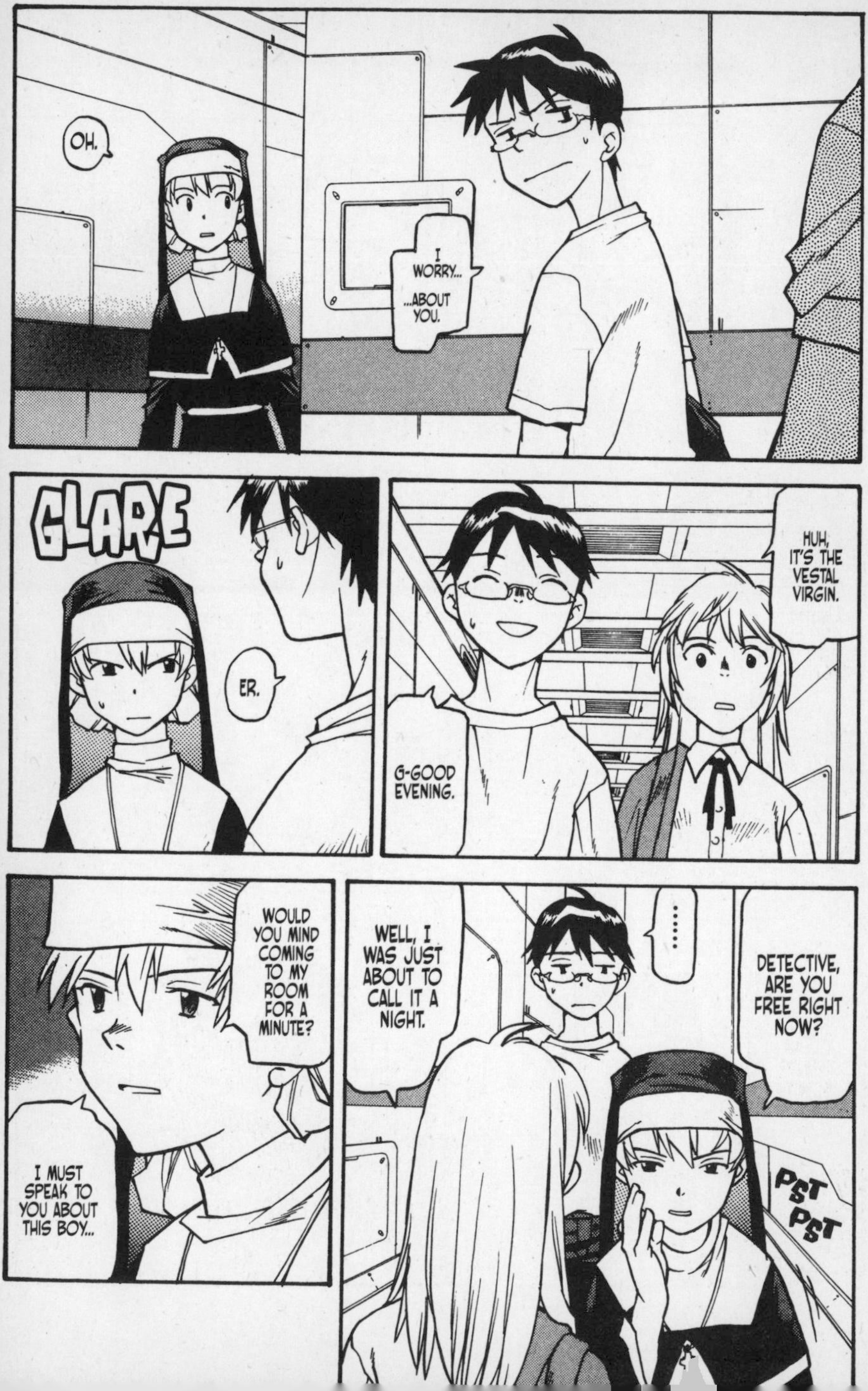
I WORRY... ...ABOUT YOU.
OH.
HUH, IT'S THE VESTAL VIRGIN.
G-GOOD EVENING.
GLARE
ER.
DETECTIVE, ARE YOU FREE RIGHT NOW?
......
WELL, I WAS JUST ABOUT TO CALL IT A NIGHT.
PST PST
WOULD YOU MIND COMING TO MY ROOM FOR A MINUTE?
I MUST SPEAK TO YOU ABOUT THIS BOY...

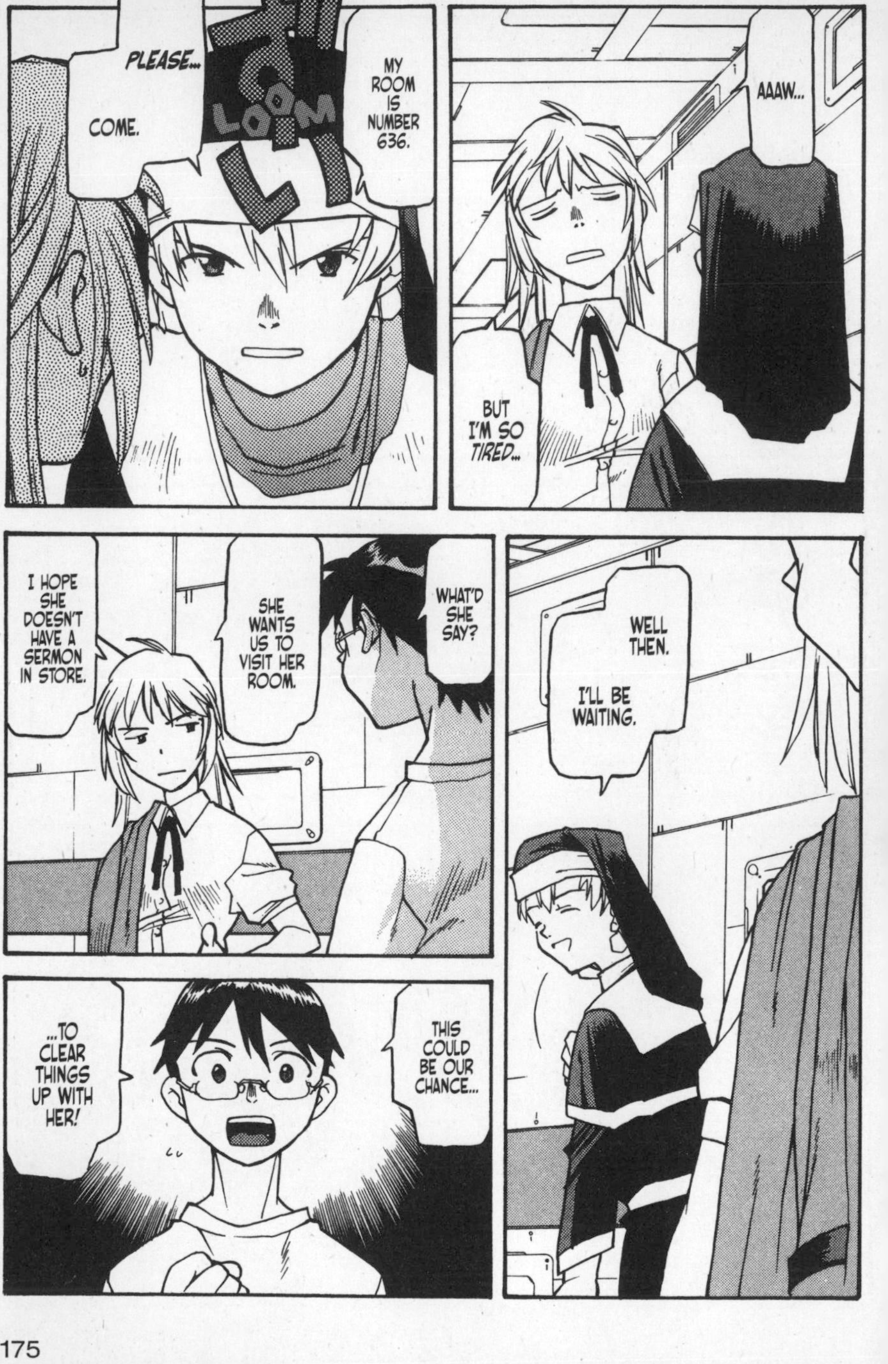
AAAW...
BUT I'M SO *TIRED*...
MY ROOM IS NUMBER 636.
PLEASE...
COME.
WELL THEN.
I'LL BE WAITING.
WHAT'D SHE SAY?
SHE WANTS US TO VISIT HER ROOM.
I HOPE SHE DOESN'T HAVE A SERMON IN STORE.
THIS COULD BE OUR CHANCE...
...TO CLEAR THINGS UP WITH HER!

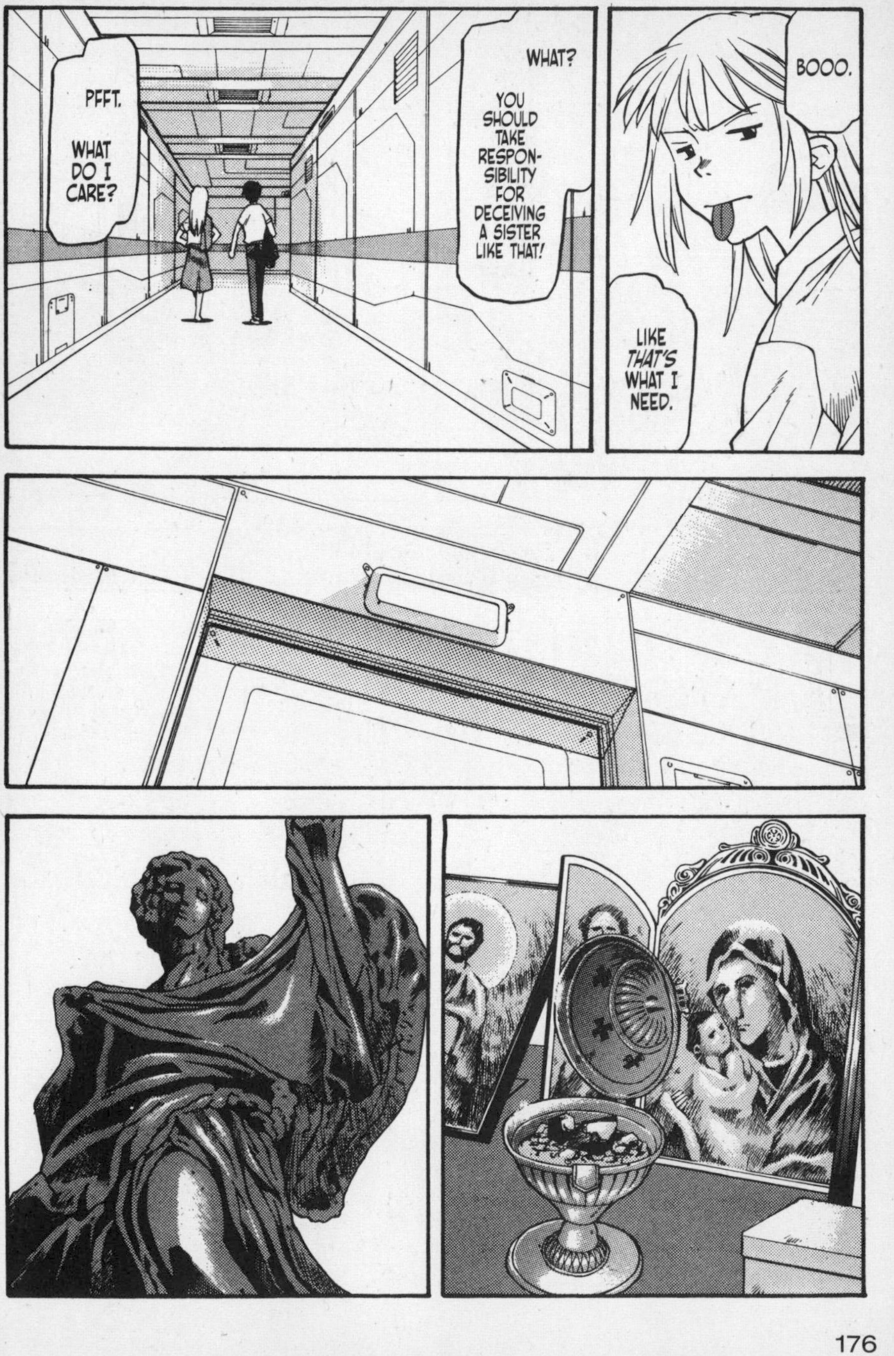
BOOO.
LIKE *THAT'S* WHAT I NEED.
WHAT?
YOU SHOULD TAKE RESPONSIBILITY FOR DECEIVING A SISTER LIKE THAT!
PFFT.
WHAT DO I CARE?

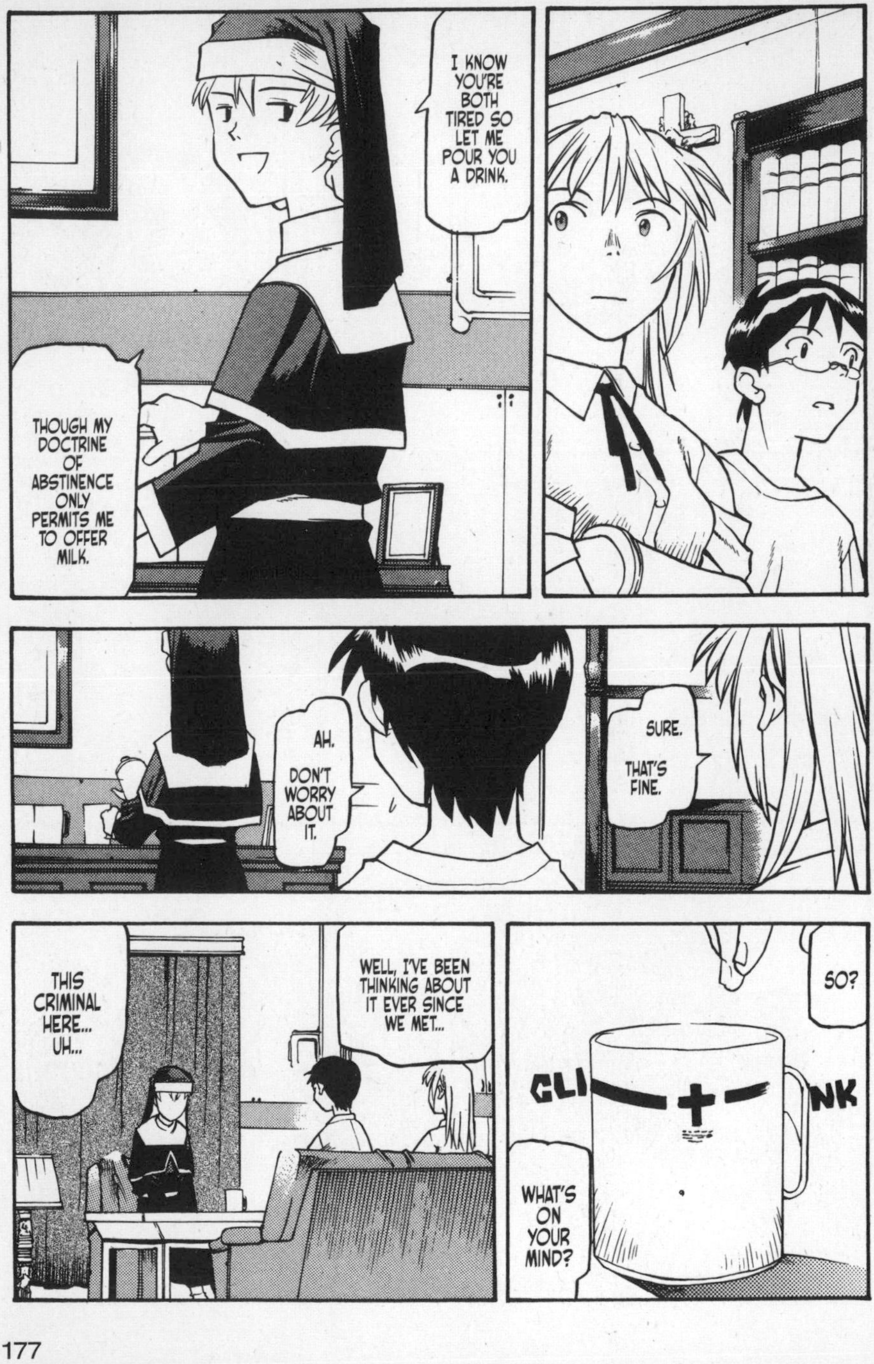
I KNOW YOU'RE BOTH TIRED SO LET ME POUR YOU A DRINK.
THOUGH MY DOCTRINE OF ABSTINENCE ONLY PERMITS ME TO OFFER MILK.
SURE.
THAT'S FINE.
AH.
DON'T WORRY ABOUT IT.
SO?
CLI—+—NK
WHAT'S ON YOUR MIND?
WELL, I'VE BEEN THINKING ABOUT IT EVER SINCE WE MET...
THIS CRIMINAL HERE... UH...

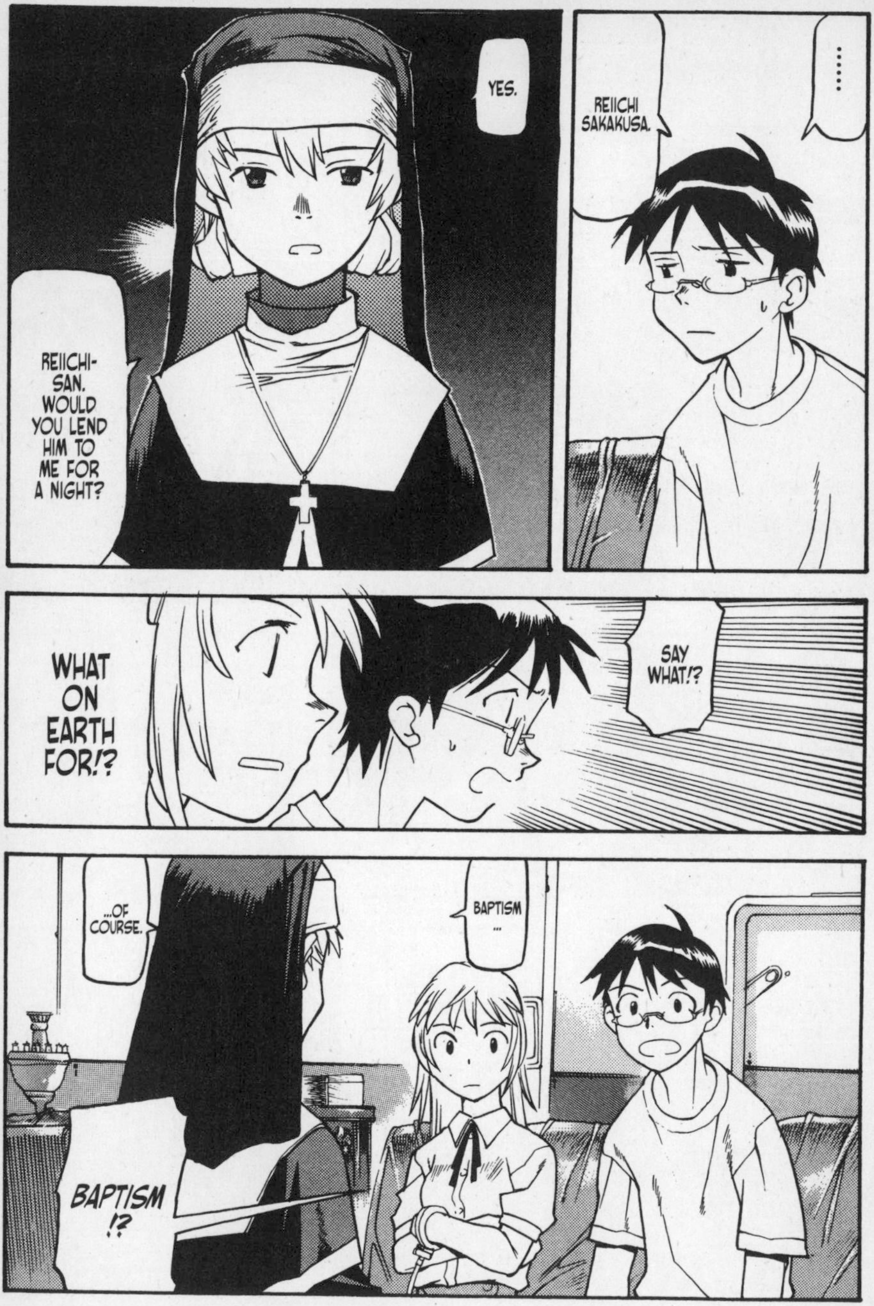
......
REIICHI SAKAKUSA.
YES.
REIICHI-SAN. WOULD YOU LEND HIM TO ME FOR A NIGHT?
SAY WHAT!?
WHAT ON EARTH FOR!?
BAPTISM ...
...OF COURSE.
BAPTISM !?

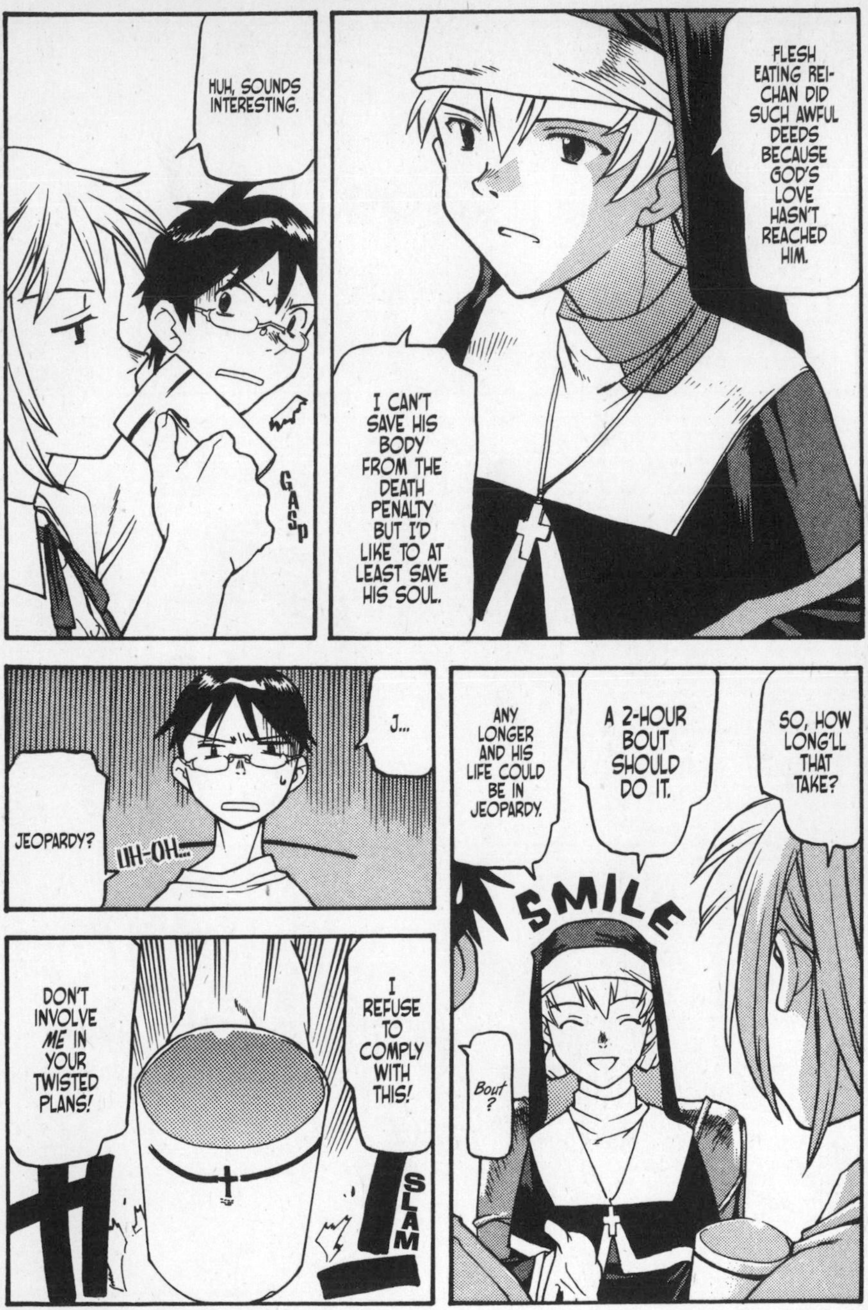
FLESH EATING REI-CHAN DID SUCH AWFUL DEEDS BECAUSE GOD'S LOVE HASN'T REACHED HIM.
I CAN'T SAVE HIS BODY FROM THE DEATH PENALTY BUT I'D LIKE TO AT LEAST SAVE HIS SOUL.
HUH, SOUNDS INTERESTING.
GASP
SO, HOW LONG'LL THAT TAKE?
A 2-HOUR BOUT SHOULD DO IT.
ANY LONGER AND HIS LIFE COULD BE IN JEOPARDY.
SMILE
Bout?
J...
JEOPARDY?
UH-OH...
I REFUSE TO COMPLY WITH THIS!
DON'T INVOLVE *ME* IN YOUR TWISTED PLANS!
SLAM

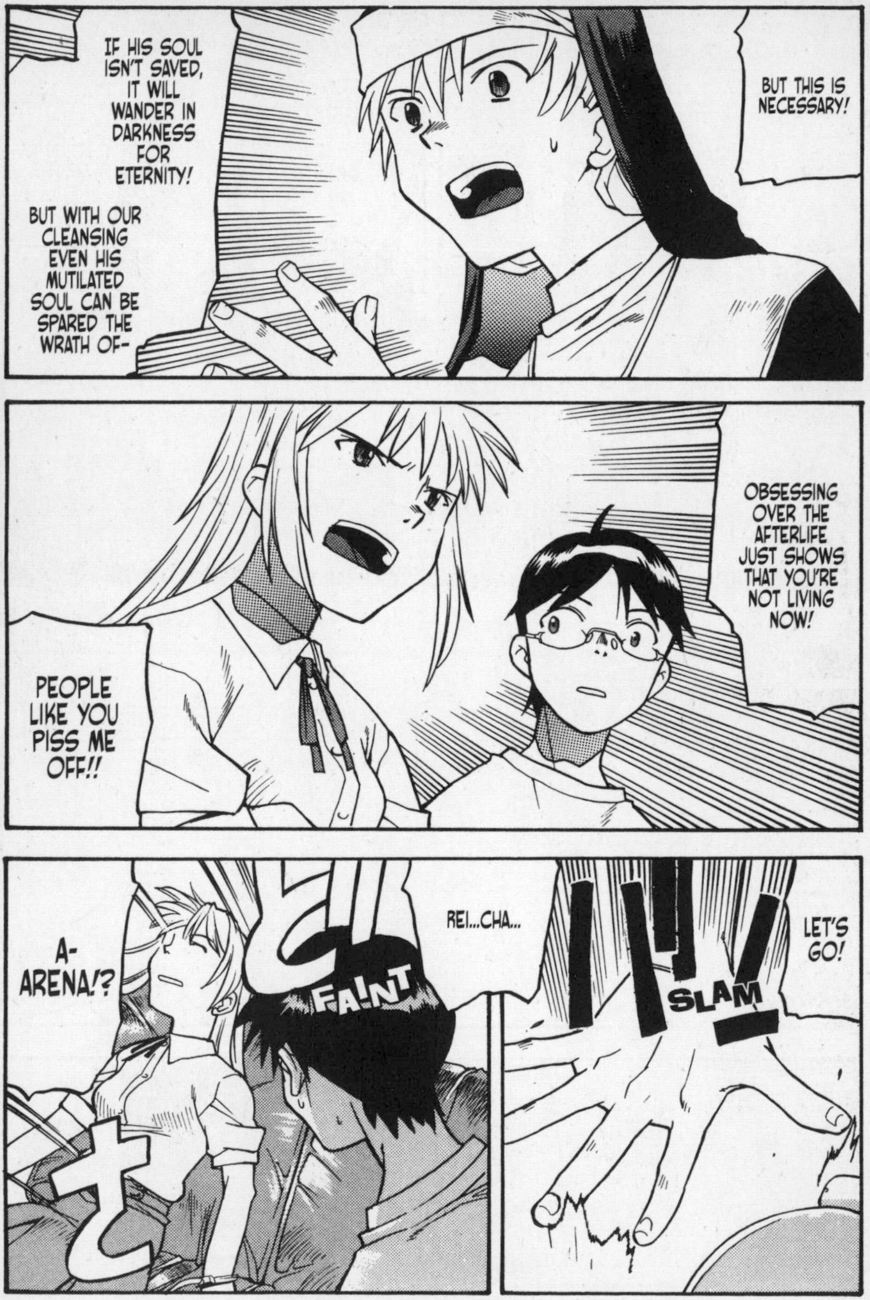
BUT THIS IS NECESSARY!
IF HIS SOUL ISN'T SAVED, IT WILL WANDER IN DARKNESS FOR ETERNITY!
BUT WITH OUR CLEANSING EVEN HIS MUTILATED SOUL CAN BE SPARED THE WRATH OF-
OBSESSING OVER THE AFTERLIFE JUST SHOWS THAT YOU'RE NOT LIVING NOW!
PEOPLE LIKE YOU PISS ME OFF!!
LET'S GO!
SLAM
REI...CHA...
FAINT
A- ARENA!?
と

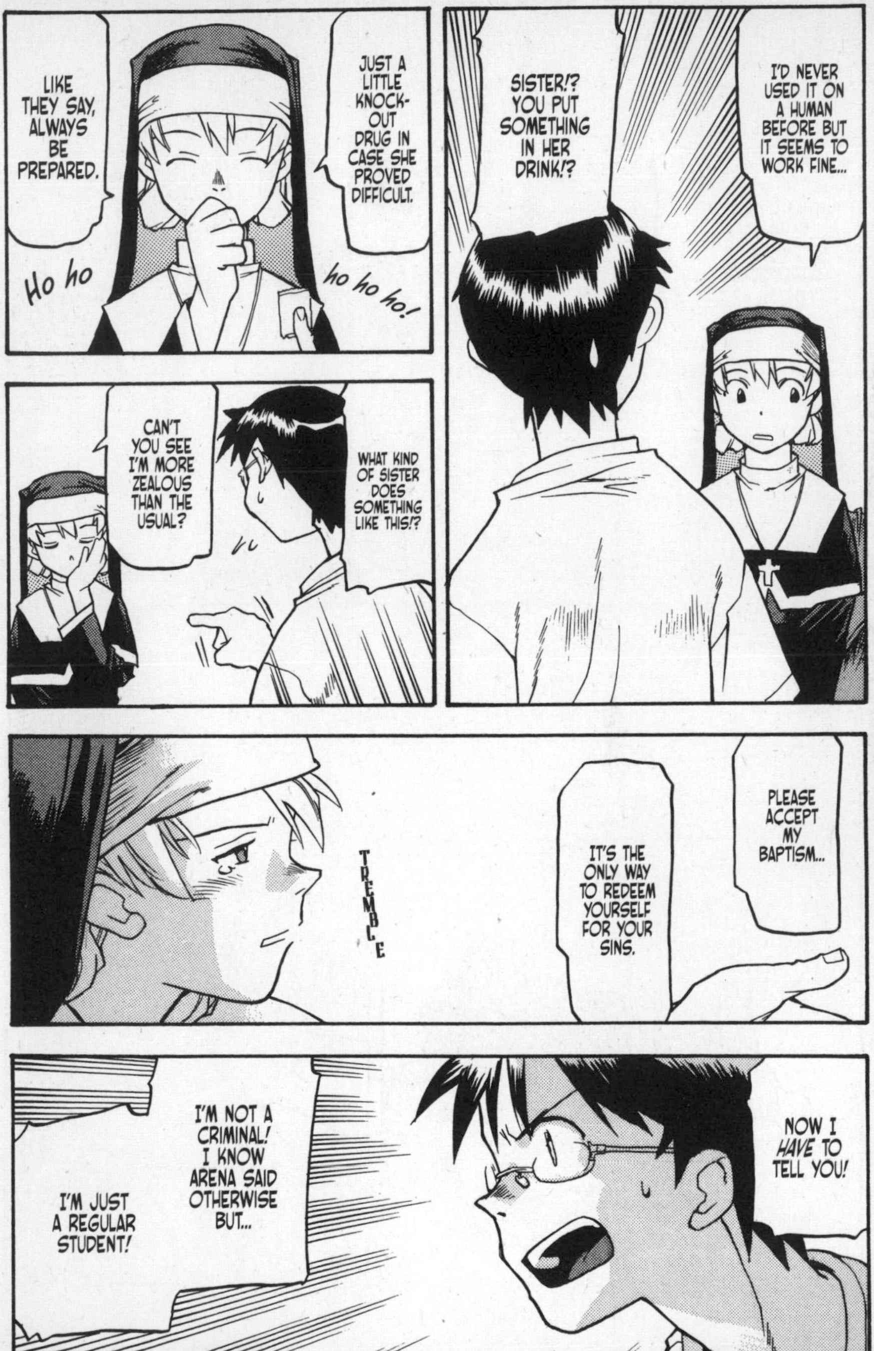
I'D NEVER USED IT ON A HUMAN BEFORE BUT IT SEEMS TO WORK FINE...
SISTER!? YOU PUT SOMETHING IN HER DRINK!?
JUST A LITTLE KNOCK-OUT DRUG IN CASE SHE PROVED DIFFICULT.
LIKE THEY SAY, ALWAYS BE PREPARED.
ho ho ho!
Ho ho
WHAT KIND OF SISTER DOES SOMETHING LIKE THIS!?
CAN'T YOU SEE I'M MORE ZEALOUS THAN THE USUAL?
PLEASE ACCEPT MY BAPTISM...
IT'S THE ONLY WAY TO REDEEM YOURSELF FOR YOUR SINS.
TREMBLE
NOW I *HAVE* TO TELL YOU!
I'M NOT A CRIMINAL! I KNOW ARENA SAID OTHERWISE BUT...
I'M JUST A REGULAR STUDENT!

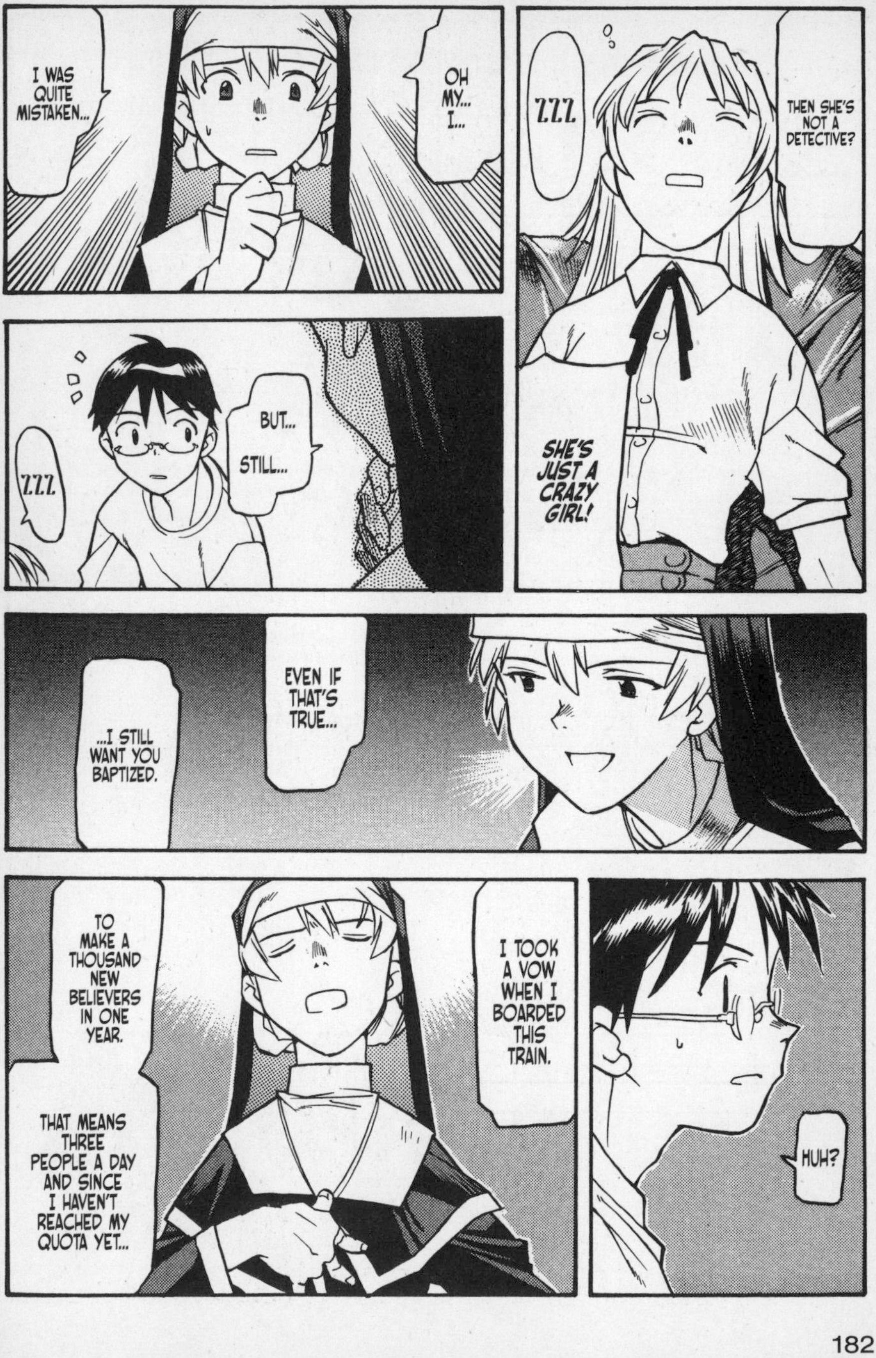
THEN SHE'S NOT A DETECTIVE?
ZZZ
SHE'S JUST A CRAZY GIRL!
OH MY... I...
I WAS QUITE MISTAKEN...
BUT... STILL...
ZZZ
EVEN IF THAT'S TRUE...
...I STILL WANT YOU BAPTIZED.
HUH?
I TOOK A VOW WHEN I BOARDED THIS TRAIN.
TO MAKE A THOUSAND NEW BELIEVERS IN ONE YEAR.
THAT MEANS THREE PEOPLE A DAY AND SINCE I HAVEN'T REACHED MY QUOTA YET...

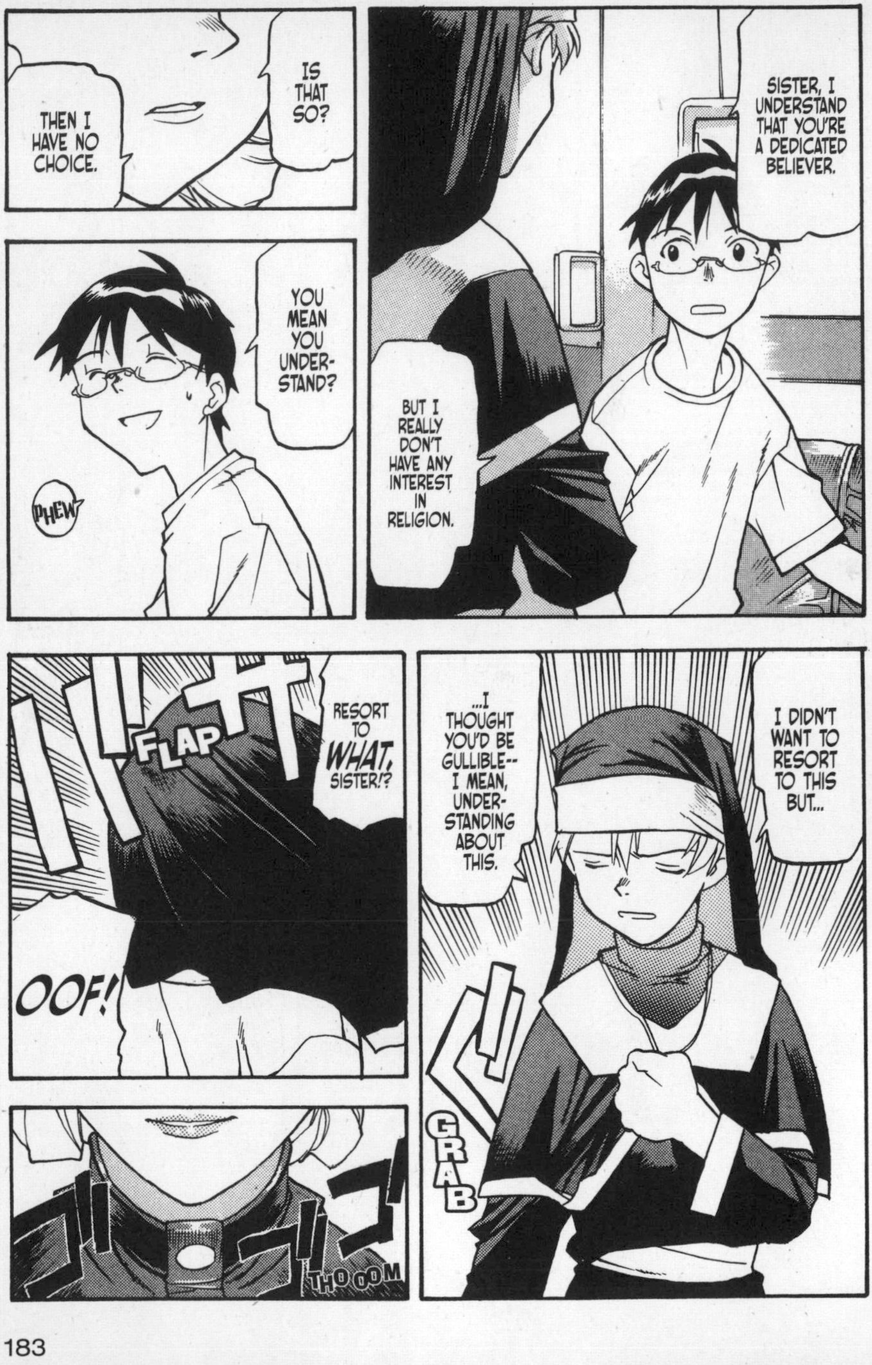
SISTER, I UNDERSTAND THAT YOU'RE A DEDICATED BELIEVER.
BUT I REALLY DON'T HAVE ANY INTEREST IN RELIGION.
IS THAT SO?
THEN I HAVE NO CHOICE.
YOU MEAN YOU UNDER-STAND?
PHEW
I DIDN'T WANT TO RESORT TO THIS BUT...
...I THOUGHT YOU'D BE GULLIBLE-- I MEAN, UNDER-STANDING ABOUT THIS.
GRAB
RESORT TO WHAT, SISTER!?
FLAP
OOF!
THOOOM

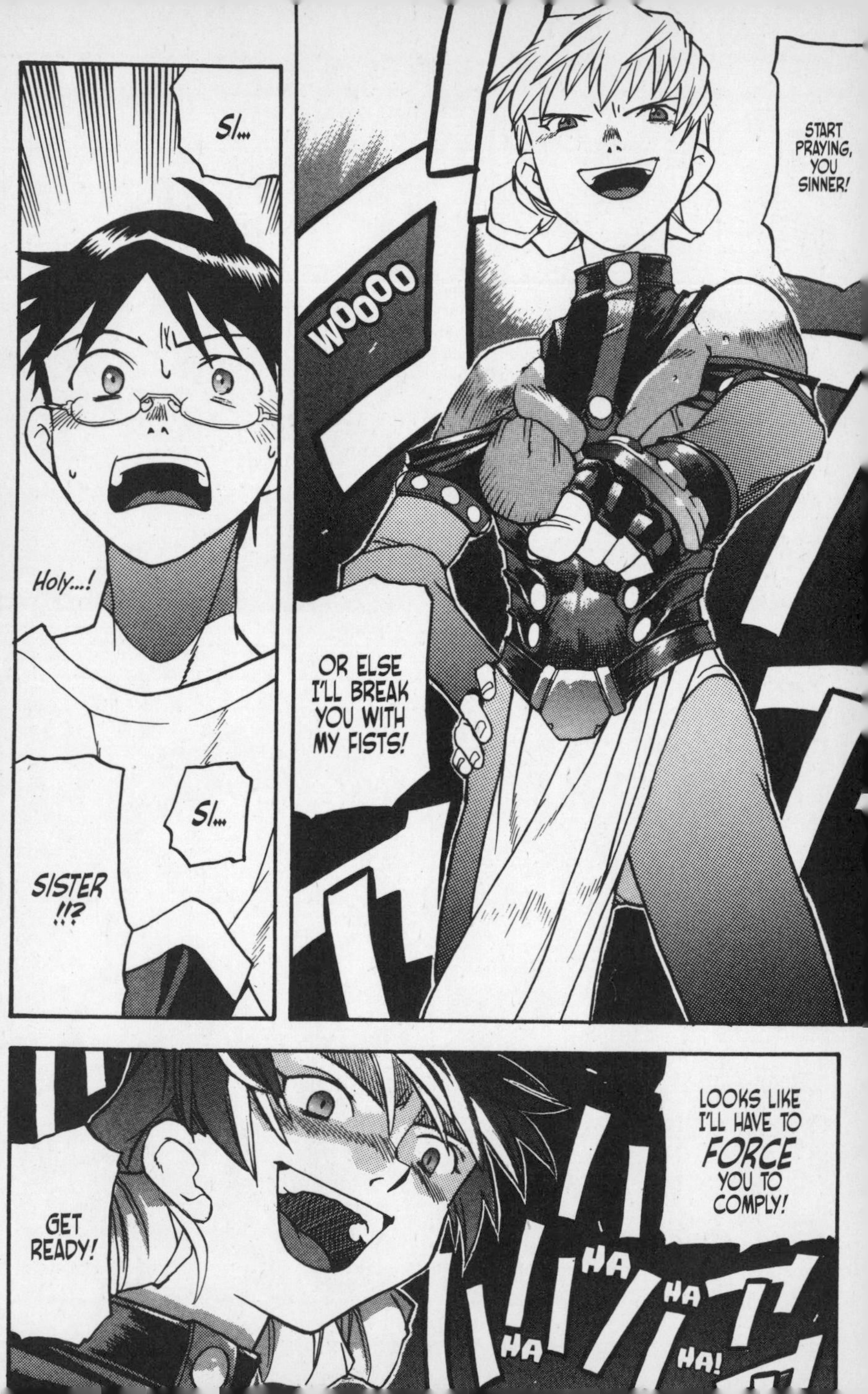
START PRAYING, YOU SINNER!
WOOOO
OR ELSE I'LL BREAK YOU WITH MY FISTS!
SI...
Holy...!
SI...
SISTER !!?
LOOKS LIKE I'LL HAVE TO FORCE YOU TO COMPLY!
HA HA HA HA!
GET READY!

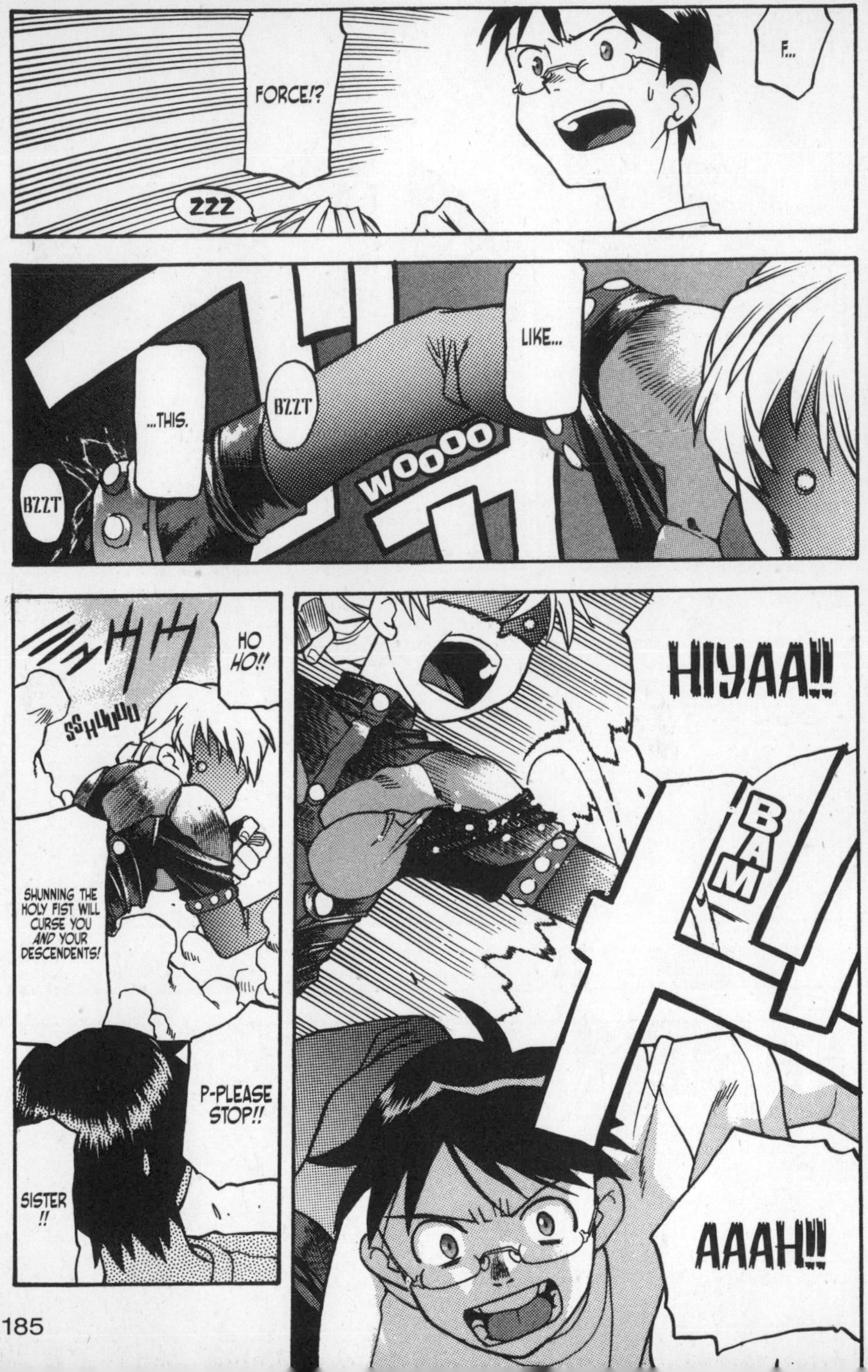
F...
FORCE!?
ZZZ
LIKE...
BZZT
...THIS.
WOOOO
BZZT
HIYAA!!
BAM
AAAH!!
HO HO!!
SHUNNING THE HOLY FIST WILL CURSE YOU *AND* YOUR DESCENDENTS!
P-PLEASE STOP!!
SISTER !!

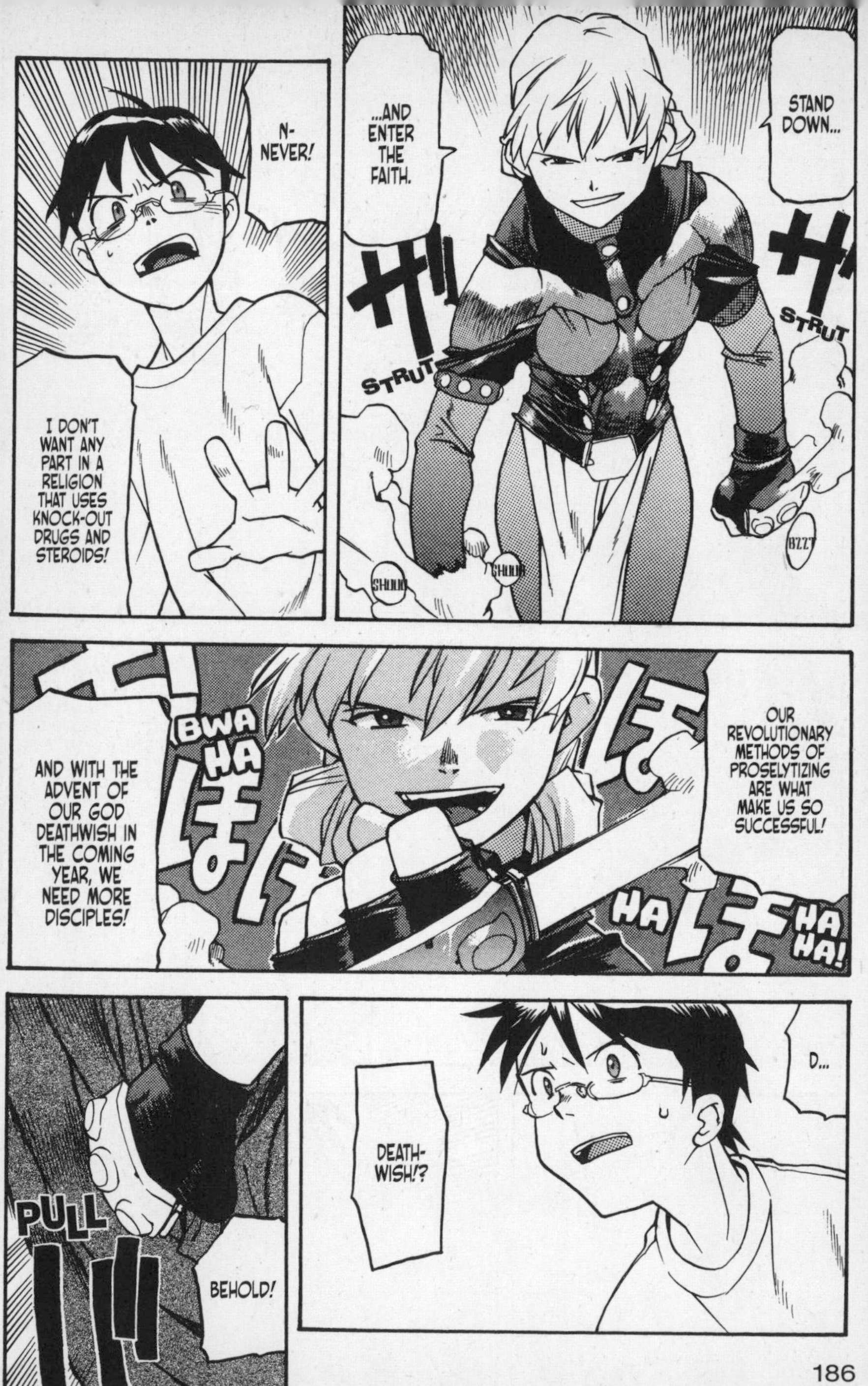
STAND DOWN...
...AND ENTER THE FAITH.
STRUT
STRUT
BZZT
N-NEVER!
I DON'T WANT ANY PART IN A RELIGION THAT USES KNOCK-OUT DRUGS AND STEROIDS!
OUR REVOLUTIONARY METHODS OF PROSELYTIZING ARE WHAT MAKE US SO SUCCESSFUL!
AND WITH THE ADVENT OF OUR GOD DEATHWISH IN THE COMING YEAR, WE NEED MORE DISCIPLES!
BWA HA
HA HA HA!
D...
DEATH-WISH!?
BEHOLD!
PULL

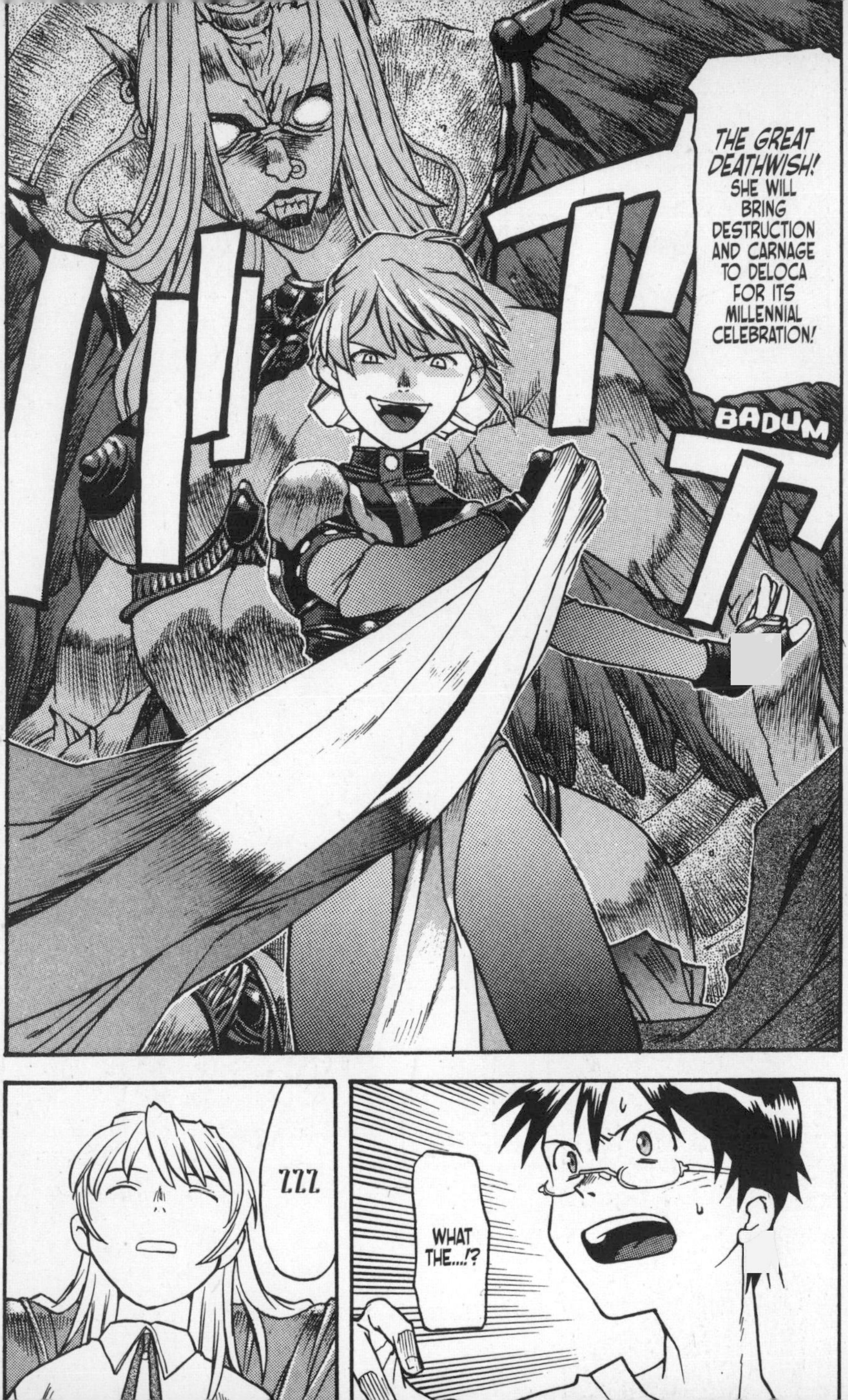
THE GREAT DEATHWISH! SHE WILL BRING DESTRUCTION AND CARNAGE TO DELOCA FOR ITS MILLENNIAL CELEBRATION!
BADUM
WHAT THE...!?
ZZZ

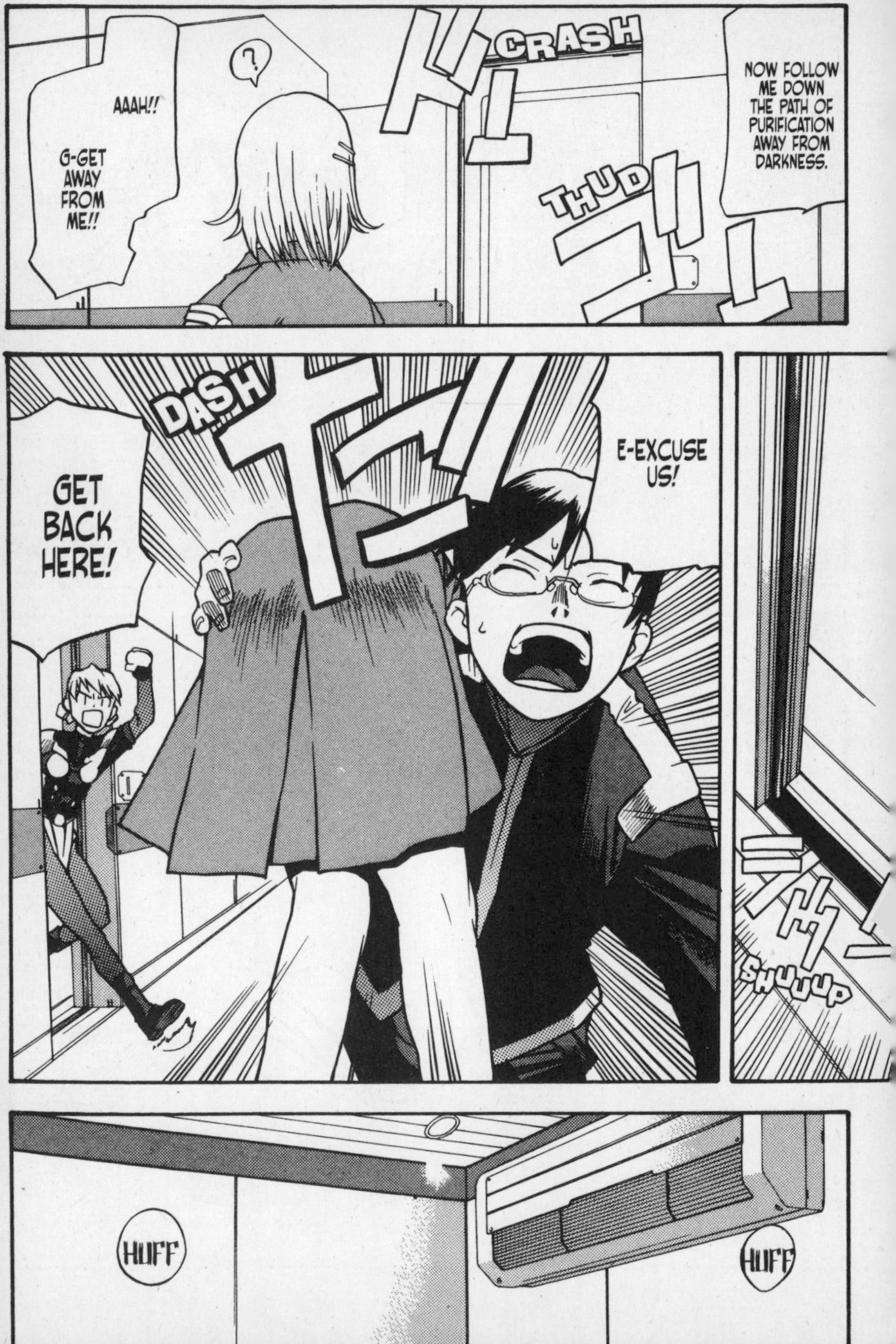
NOW FOLLOW ME DOWN THE PATH OF PURIFICATION AWAY FROM DARKNESS.
CRASH
THUD
?
AAAH!!
G-GET AWAY FROM ME!!
SHUUUP
E-EXCUSE US!
DASH
GET BACK HERE!
HUFF
HUFF

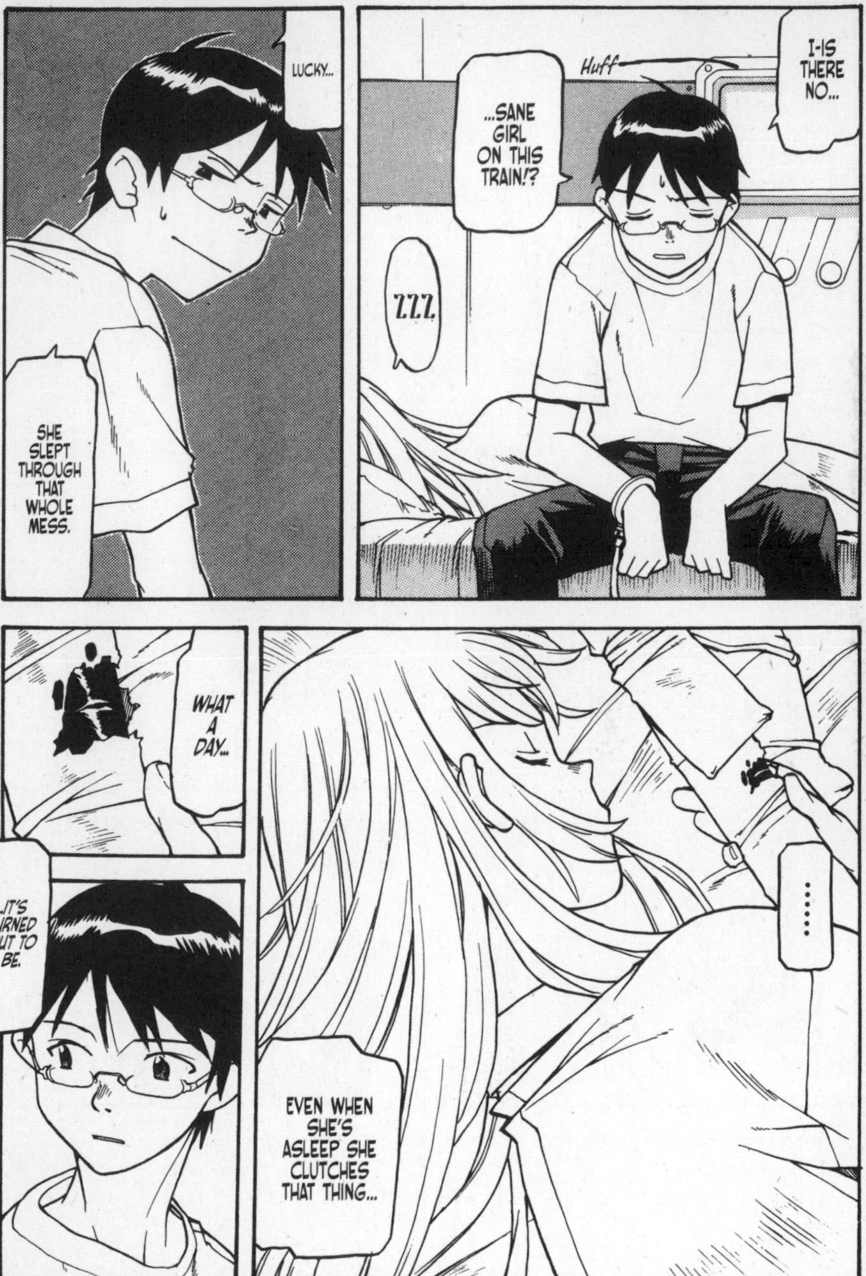
I-IS THERE NO...
Huff
...SANE GIRL ON THIS TRAIN!?
ZZZ
LUCKY...
SHE SLEPT THROUGH THAT WHOLE MESS.
......
EVEN WHEN SHE'S ASLEEP SHE CLUTCHES THAT THING...
WHAT A DAY...
...IT'S TURNED OUT TO BE.

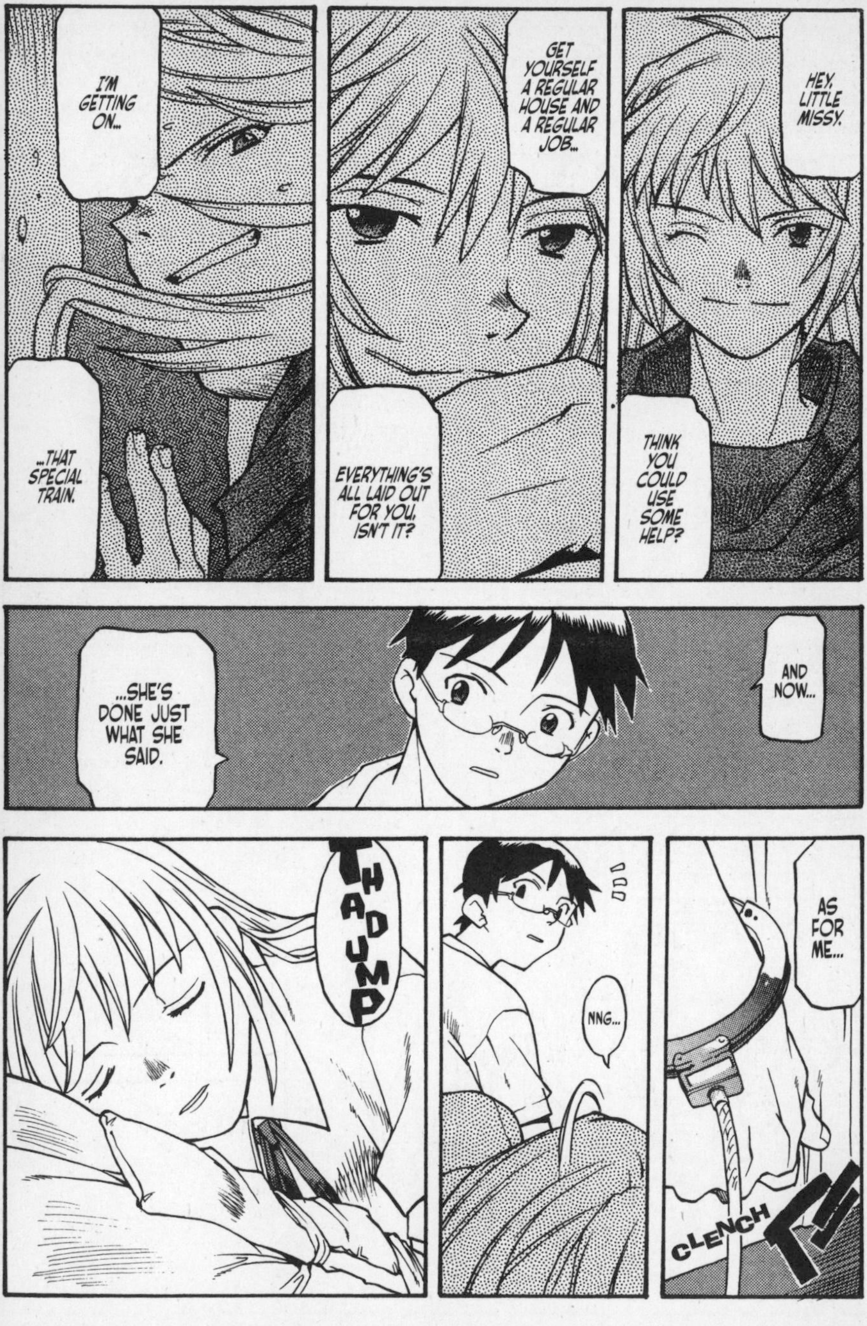
HEY, LITTLE MISSY.
THINK YOU COULD USE SOME HELP?
GET YOURSELF A REGULAR HOUSE AND A REGULAR JOB...
EVERYTHING'S ALL LAID OUT FOR YOU, ISN'T IT?
I'M GETTING ON...
...THAT SPECIAL TRAIN.
AND NOW...
...SHE'S DONE JUST WHAT SHE SAID.
AS FOR ME...
CLENCH
NNG...
THADUMP

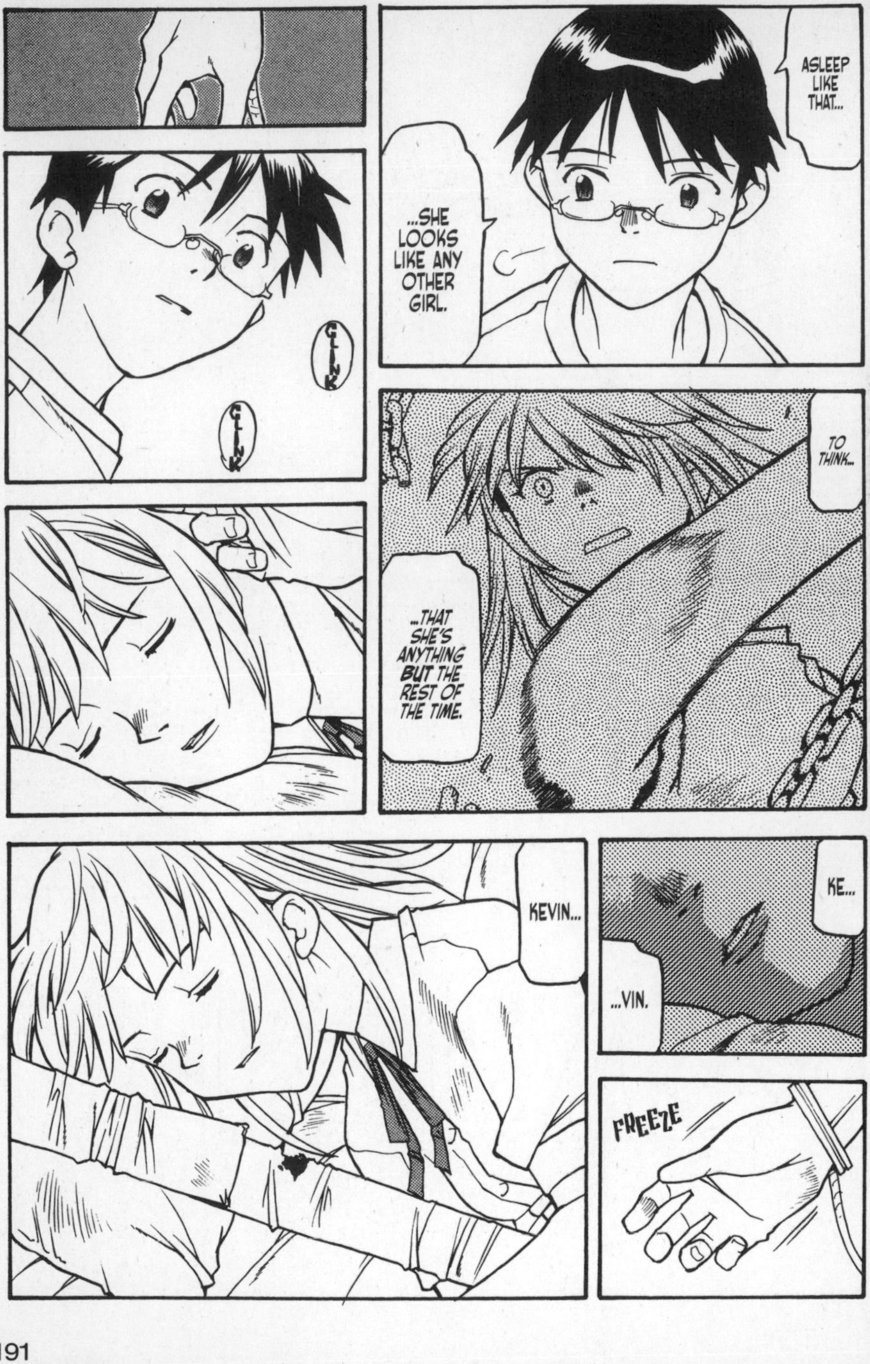
ASLEEP LIKE THAT...
...SHE LOOKS LIKE ANY OTHER GIRL.
GLINK
GLINK
TO THINK...
...THAT SHE'S ANYTHING BUT THE REST OF THE TIME.
KE...
...VIN.
FREEZE
KEVIN...

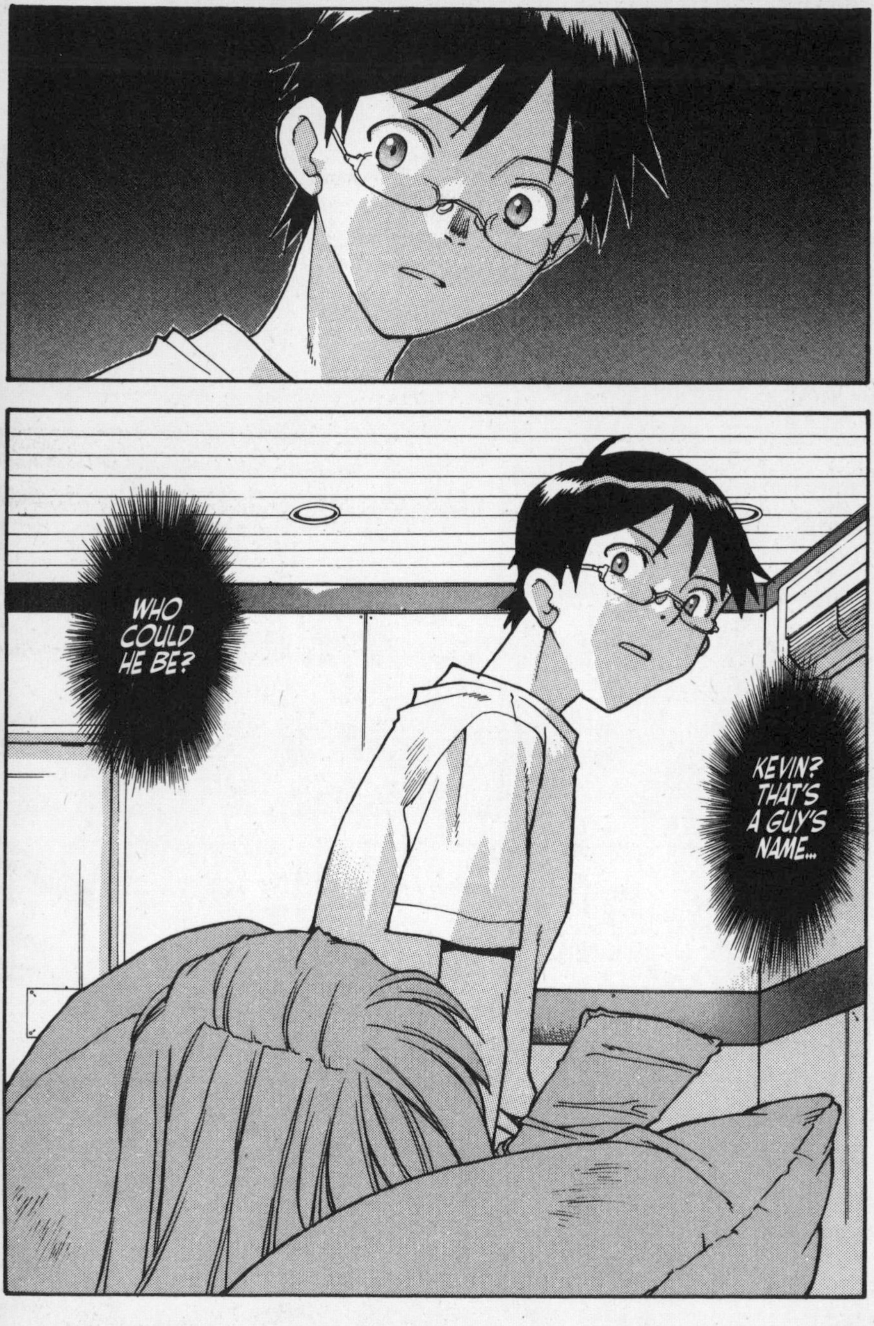
KEVIN? THAT'S A GUY'S NAME...
WHO COULD HE BE?

Beautiful but violent. Selfish and dishonest. Audacious but strong and egotistical. Arena's got the kind of attitude that, if she were a guy, would make you want to steer clear. But you still can't deny her looks. Thanks to a solid build that accompanies a solid mindset, she's more hero than heroine. In fact, I sometimes call her the "Big Brother." I'm sure you can't blame me. I like action movies but my favorite genre has to be when people with polar-opposite personalities have to partner up. It's usually between same-sex characters since male-female couples turn the whole situation into a love story. Are male-female combos really incapable of sustaining a non-romantic partnership? Since I considered that when making Arena, I tried giving her a half-male personality to see if that would help. I myself am interested in seeing what direction her partnership with Reiichi will take her.

ARENA PENDLETON

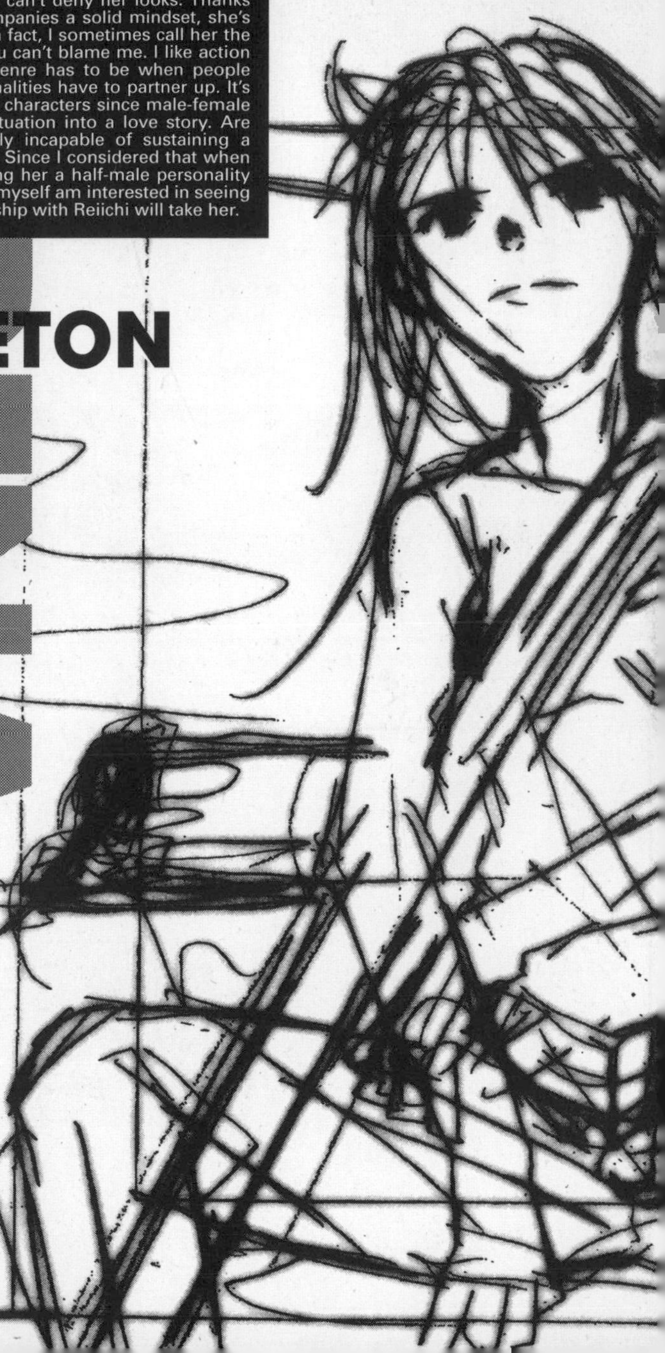
PENDLETON
TRAIN + TRAIN PROT WRITERS NOTE
FILE NO. 002

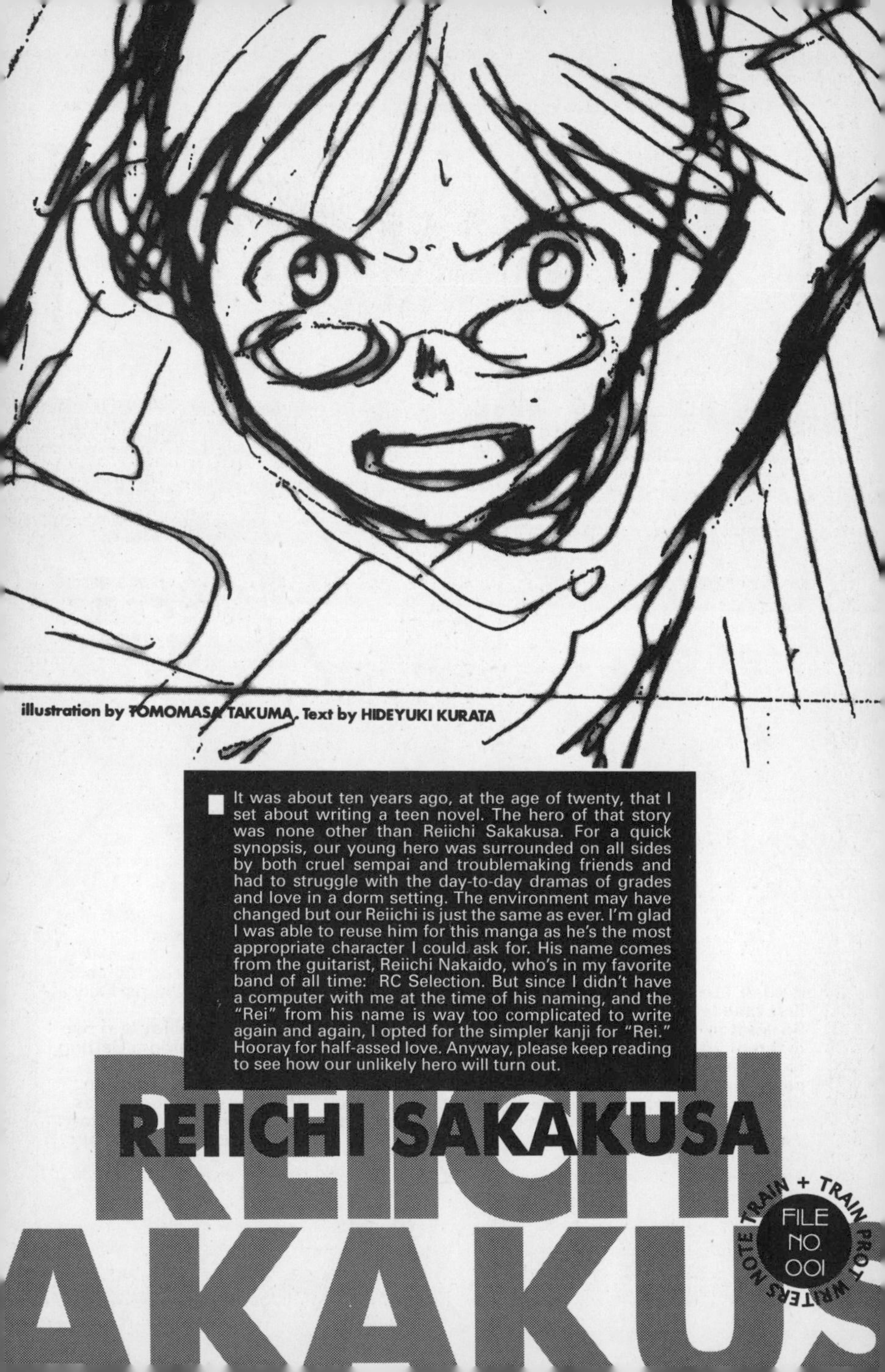

illustration by TOMOMASA TAKUMA, Text by HIDEYUKI KURATA

It was about ten years ago, at the age of twenty, that I set about writing a teen novel. The hero of that story was none other than Reiichi Sakakusa. For a quick synopsis, our young hero was surrounded on all sides by both cruel sempai and troublemaking friends and had to struggle with the day-to-day dramas of grades and love in a dorm setting. The environment may have changed but our Reiichi is just the same as ever. I'm glad I was able to reuse him for this manga as he's the most appropriate character I could ask for. His name comes from the guitarist, Reiichi Nakaido, who's in my favorite band of all time: RC Selection. But since I didn't have a computer with me at the time of his naming, and the "Rei" from his name is way too complicated to write again and again, I opted for the simpler kanji for "Rei." Hooray for half-assed love. Anyway, please keep reading to see how our unlikely hero will turn out.

REIICHI SAKAKUSA

REIICHI SAKAKUSA

TRAIN + TRAIN PROT WRITERS NOTE

FILE NO. 001

TRAIN

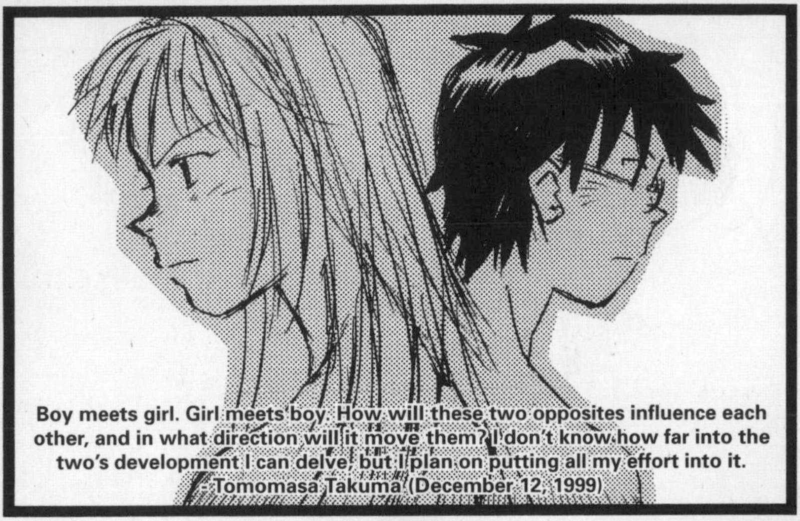

Boy meets girl. Girl meets boy. How will these two opposites influence each other, and in what direction will it move them? I don't know how far into the two's development I can delve, but I plan on putting all my effort into it.
- Tomomasa Takuma (December 12, 1999)

作画 たくま朋正
Tomomasa Takuma

POSTSCRIPT

Hideyuki Kurata
原作 倉田英之

Wow, I am beyond nervous right now.
TRAIN+TRAIN is my first original story and when I was told it was being made into a manga, I felt so nervous, confused and excited that it was no use trying to tell me to calm down.
I mean, can you imagine what it's like to walk into a bookstore and see your name listed on manga sitting on the shelf? I've enjoyed manga my whole life and as someone who enjoys taking on a new project, the offer elated me to no end. Call it my original work all you like, but all I did was write the novel version and then hand it off to Takuma-san, who took care of the manga adaptation of it. So I'm partially a first-time reader of this, too.
So what to say...being both the writer and a reader I've been able to enjoy it in two different ways and I like to think of myself as lucky to be in such a position. Getting to see the characters, train stations and train interiors finally be manifested on paper after they'd only existed in my mind for so long really moved me! I'd often find myself saying, "Oh! So that's what they look like!" This transformation gives me the motivation and inspiration I need to plan the next development in the story. And since I'm the writer, I doubt there's anybody as excited as I am over the comic release of "TRAIN+TRAIN."
Anyway, I hope all you readers out there keep "TRAIN+TRAIN" on your bookshelves at home forever. As for myself, I made room for it next to my "Tomorrow's Joe" collection.

- Hideyuki Kurata (December 15, 1999)

TRAIN

In volume 2 of TRAIN + TRAIN

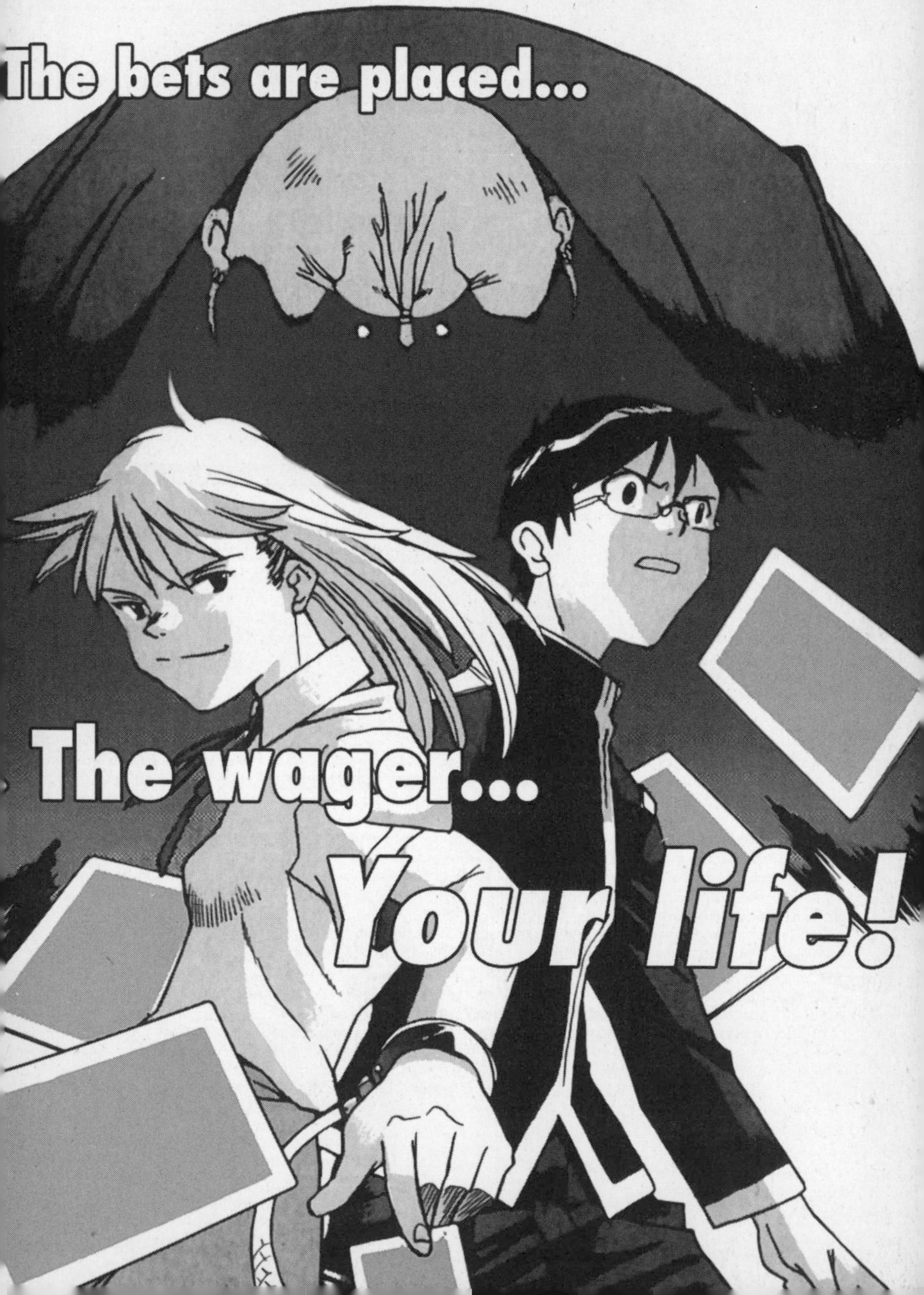
The bets are placed...
The wager...
Your life!

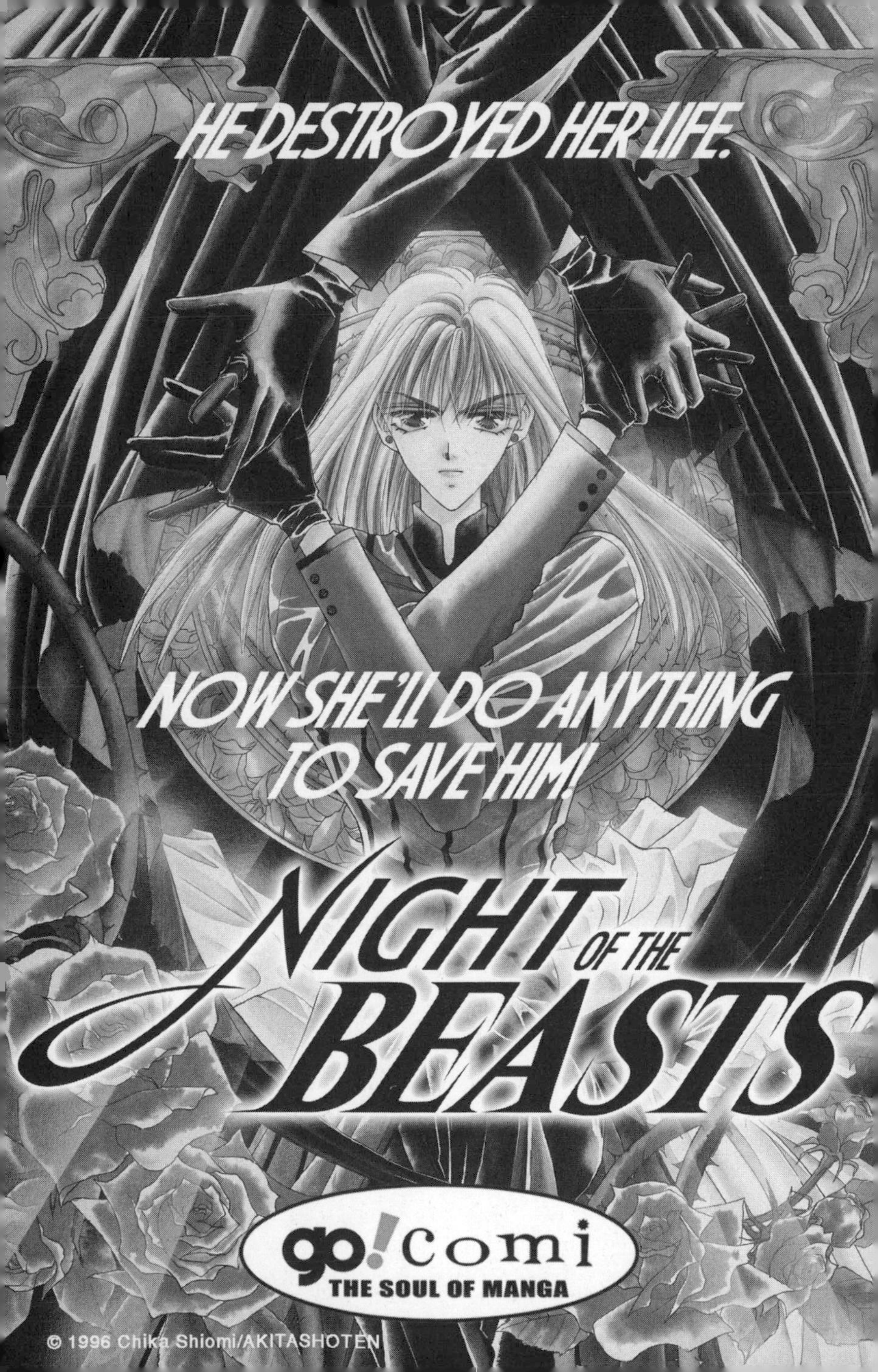
HE DESTROYED HER LIFE.
NOW SHE'LL DO ANYTHING TO SAVE HIM!
NIGHT OF THE BEASTS
go!comi
THE SOUL OF MANGA
© 1996 Chika Shiomi/AKITASHOTEN

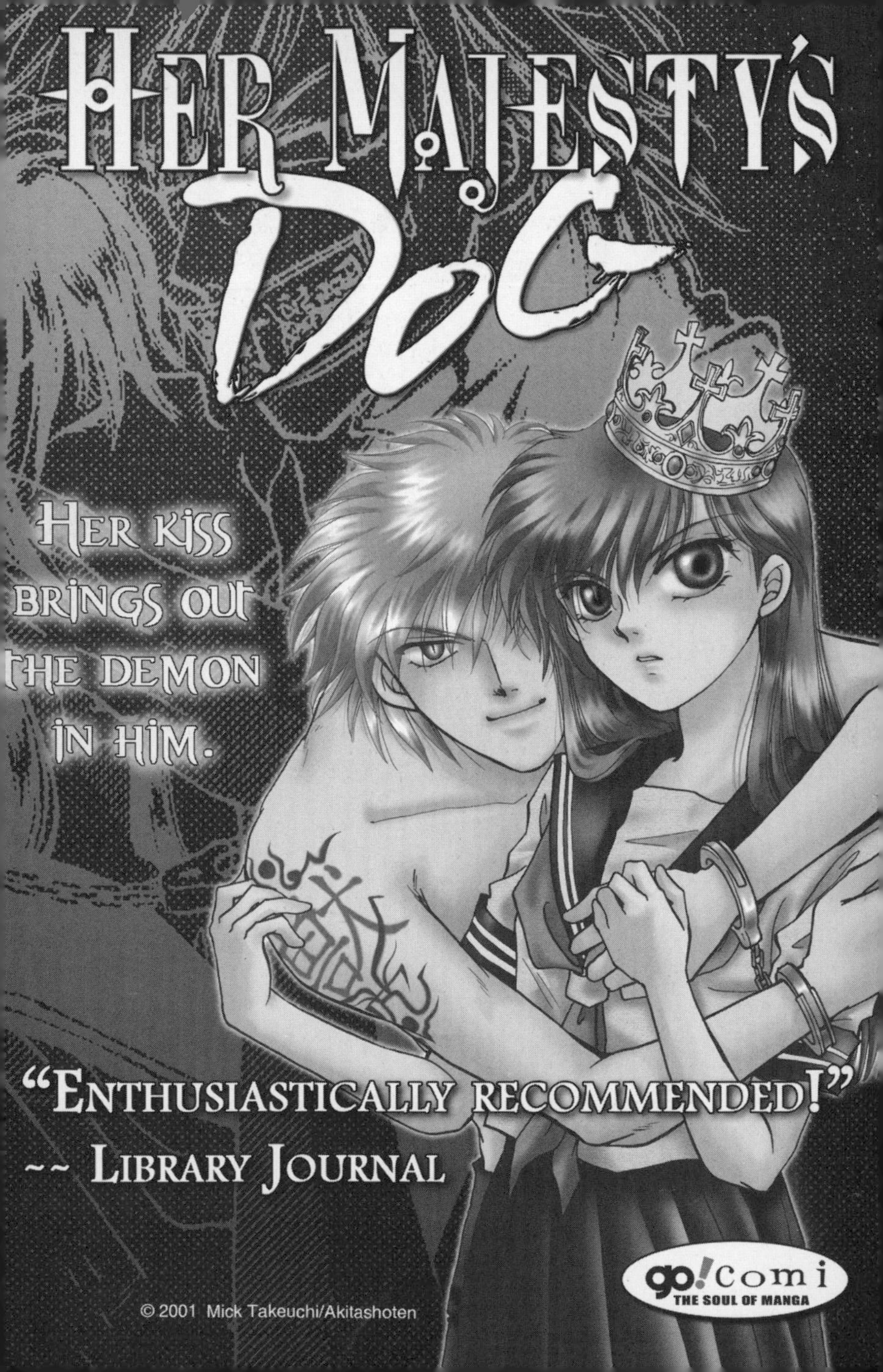
HER MAJESTY'S DOG
HER KISS BRINGS OUT THE DEMON IN HIM.
"ENTHUSIASTICALLY RECOMMENDED!"
~~ LIBRARY JOURNAL
go! comi
THE SOUL OF MANGA
© 2001 Mick Takeuchi/Akitashoten

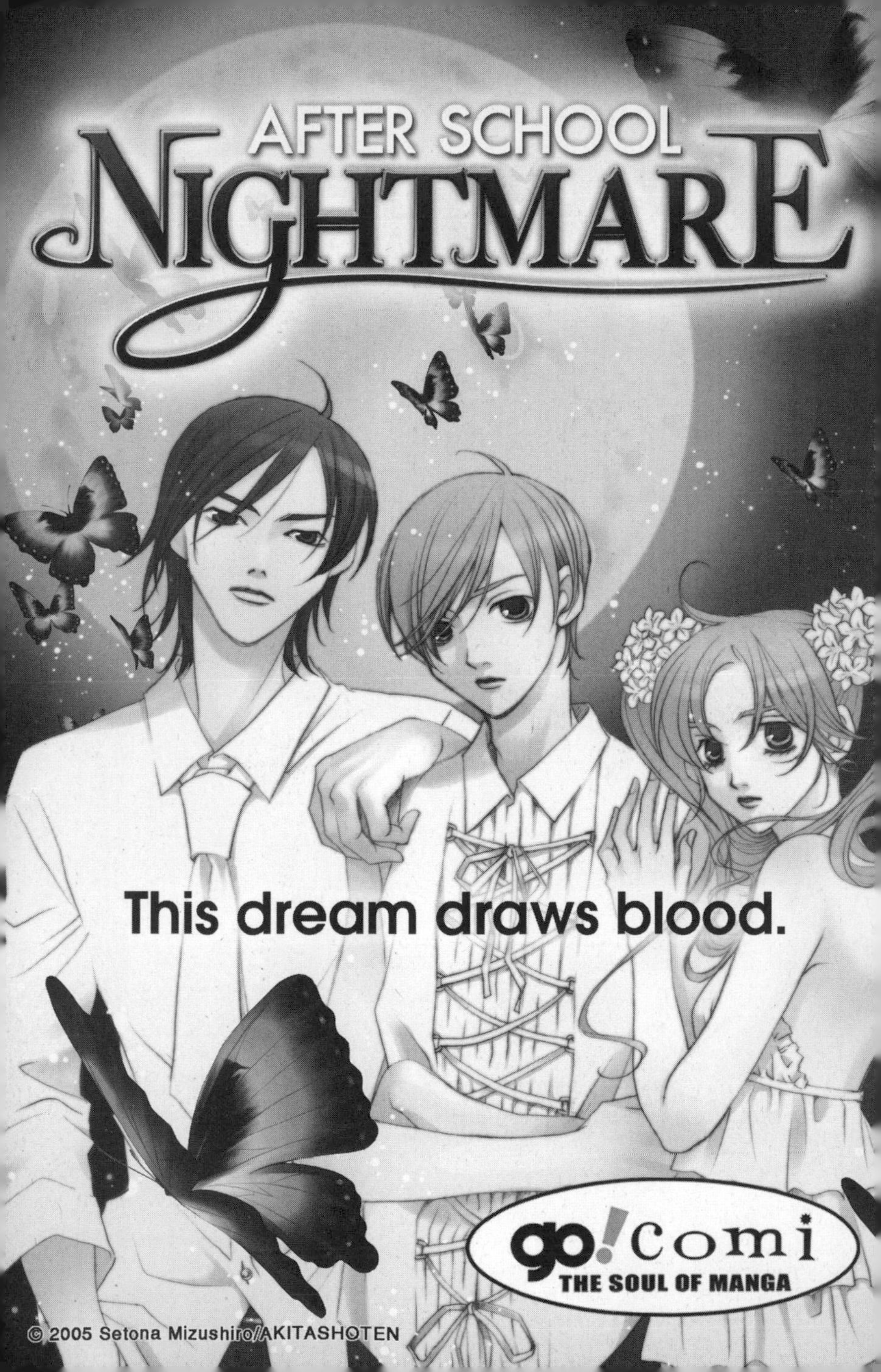

AFTER SCHOOL
NIGHTMARE
This dream draws blood.
go!comi
THE SOUL OF MANGA
© 2005 Setona Mizushiro/AKITASHOTEN

Launched into fame by his incredible design work on the video game "Roommate," **Tomomasa Takuma** went on to produce "Comic House" in 1994. Since 1996 his clean, exciting style has been seen in "Iron Communication", "Gureperi", "Frame Saber", and "TRAIN+TRAIN"; and in 2002 he produced several episodes for the animated series of his popular creation "Iron Communication". Takuma-sensei has a 1 1/2 year old son.

Renowned novelist **Hideyuki Kurata** is the author of *R.O.D., GunXSword, El Hazard and Battle Athletes.* A native of Okayama, Ibaraichi and a member of "Studio Orphee," Kurata-sensei is an accomplished screenwriter: He's written such anime as *Excel Saga*, the *Helsing* OAV, and *Magical Girl Pretty Sammy.*

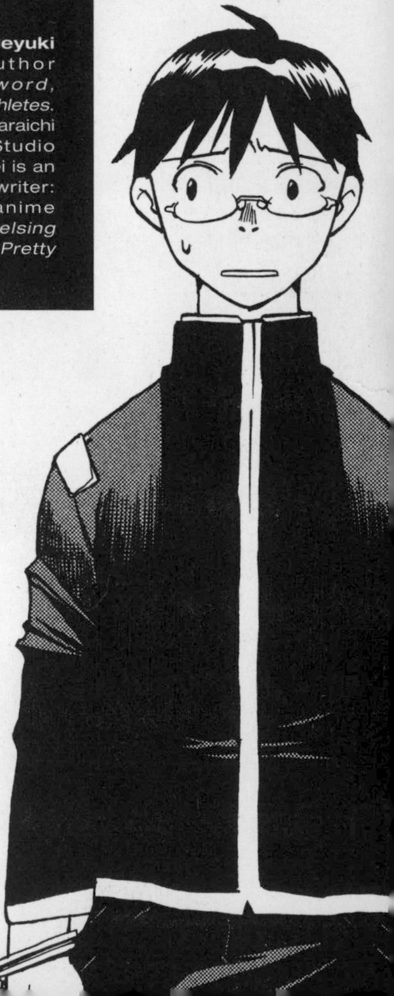

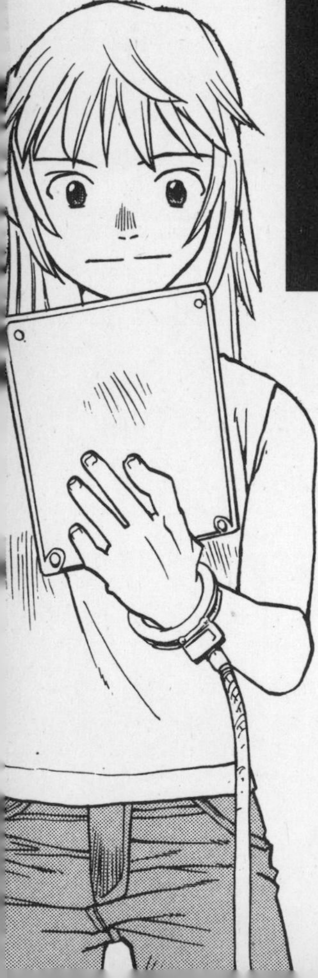